A Concise Handbook of the Indian Economy in the 21st Century

A Concise Handbook of the Indian Economy in the 21st Century

Edited by
ASHIMA GOYAL

OXFORD
UNIVERSITY PRESS

OXFORD
UNIVERSITY PRESS

Oxford University Press is a department of the University of Oxford.
It furthers the University's objective of excellence in research, scholarship,
and education by publishing worldwide. Oxford is a registered trademark of
Oxford University Press in the UK and in certain other countries.

Published in India
by Oxford University Press
22 Workspace, 2nd Floor, 1/22 Asaf Ali Road, New Delhi 110 002, India

© Oxford University Press, 2019

The moral rights of the authors have been asserted.

First Edition published in 2015

Second Edition published in 2019

ISBN-13 (print edition): 978-0-19-949646-4
ISBN-10 (print edition): 0-19-949646-3

ISBN-13 (eBook): 978-0-19909816-3
ISBN-10 (eBook): 0-19-909816-6

Typeset in Minion Pro 10.5/13.2
by Tranistics Data Technologies, New Delhi 110 044
Printed in India by Replika Press Pvt. Ltd

CONTENTS

....

TABLES AND FIGURES

....

FIGURES

THE INDIAN ECONOMY

structure, reform, and change

ASHIMA GOYAL

The Indian economy has shown dynamism but also faced difficulties on its path of transformative growth. After the liberalizing reform in the 1990s, growth rates were higher but also more volatile. The countries that did manage to sustain a high rate of growth followed a pragmatic reform path suited to context rather than a pure market- or government-led approach. Since structure and context affect change, such pragmatic reform requires a deep knowledge of the economy derived from careful fact-based research. The chapters in this volume contribute to the required knowledge on a range of issues, such as drivers of growth, domestic compared to external reforms, macroeconomic policy coordination, macroeconomic policy institutions and practices, the effect of openness and of global economic integration, poverty and the degree of inclusion, bottlenecks in infrastructure, and the performance of major sectors, such as agriculture, industry, and finance. They contribute to a finer understanding of the interaction between domestic strengths, external opportunities, and government interventions.

Interesting paradoxes have arisen on the path, such as the domination of services in a non-standard growth pattern, high rural wage growth combined with persistent inflation for 2007–13 despite a large population that continued to be underemployed, and a rapid turn-around after the global financial crisis but subsequent growth below potential.

Despite difficulties, there are fundamental reasons for India's dynamism. First is the growing strength of participative democracy. Inclusive institutions make the flexible and contextual policies necessary to sustain high catch-up growth more likely. India started out with highly inclusive political institutions since it adopted universal suffrage at the time of Independence. But extractive economic institutions, inherited from the British, were made more so by economic controls. In addition, a heterogeneous electorate allowed politicians to cultivate vote banks with populist schemes instead of providing good governance and public goods.

India's opening out was nuanced and flexible but was sometimes used as a substitute for harder domestic reforms. It, however, added to the growing constituencies that benefit from growth and are pushing for more productivity enabling inclusive institutions. Broader interest groups create better institutions and incentives. A common insight from a number of chapters is that obvious controls have gone, but empowerment through genuine decentralization is still a work in progress. Even so, the 2014 election, which delivered a decisive mandate for good governance, shows the demand for progress to be substantial. It ended 30 years of fragmented politics when governments used doles to appeal to different interest groups.

The second fundamental advantage is the presence of large numbers of skilled youth, together with technological changes that give them the opportunity for entrepreneurship and innovation. An example of this is the active net neutrality debate of 2015. Surprisingly, many young people spoke out, asking for net neutrality rather than accepting the consumption subsidies being offered as an alternative, because they favoured entrepreneurship. They wanted opportunities to create new businesses and even to compete in international markets. In addition, the demographic profile creates a large potential domestic market, which is especially valuable when global conditions are uncertain.

Only a government that nourishes these trends will succeed. But the voter is pushing in the right direction now. Facilitating opportunities requires bettering skills and infrastructure, including Internet-related infrastructure and its penetration; reducing the obstacles in doing business and the transaction costs to make India one market; and improving the delivery of public services. To achieve all this, the composition of public expenditure has to be changed, legal/regulatory/tax structures simplified, institutions modernized, and the administration streamlined to remove overlaps. Bottlenecks in agriculture also need to be attended to. These steps will lead to 'active inclusion' that will allow more and more people to participate in growth, and this is what the majority want today. Jobs will be created for the lower skill segment as well, both in manufacturing and a range of services.

There are useful initiatives in some of these areas. Examples include: the focus on infrastructure, more competitive reforms in and freedoms to states, better financial inclusion, internet connectivity and technology-based innovations, improvement in the ease of doing business, more formalization, generalized sales tax implementation, and widening of the tax base. However, the list of actions required to be taken for sustained growth and development remains long, as our experts (mentioned below) show us.

Laveesh Bhandari and Sumita Kale study the underlying factors behind the acceleration in India's economic growth and its puzzling structure. The services sector has been the engine of growth for the economy, with different sub-sectors taking the lead in different time periods as each responded to a policy change, such as bank nationalization in the 1970s, construction boom in the 2000s, et cetera. However, industrial reforms have not resulted in sustained high growth due to constraints in land, labour, and infrastructure. States have followed diverse trajectories, initial conditions in each leading to differential responses to central reforms. Growth and governance are now crucial for electoral outcomes, making them a focal point for the path ahead.

Pulapre Balakrishnan and Ashima Goyal point to domestic factors rather than global economy as the cause of the growth slowdown in the last decade. It follows that more importance needs to be given to domestic demand and difficult domestic reforms such as improvements in governance. Since macroeconomic policy has impacted growth, attention to the interaction between the two would also yield dividends. To do so, the inflation forecast–targeting regime requires to be flexibly implemented with supportive government action to relieve supply-side restrictions.

Romar Correa continues to use the Godley–Cripps (1983, *Macroeconomics*, Oxford: Oxford University Press) stock-flow consistent (SFC) framework in this update to refine the thesis that the monetary authority is the 'handmaiden' of the fiscal authority. The bank, commercial and central being indistinguishable, is central to the account. A revitalized 'real bills doctrine' is proposed. The deleterious consequences of promoting the alternative—'financialization'—are traced.

K. Kanagasabapathy, Rekha A. Bhangaonkar, and Shruti Pandey address the issue of whether the rate and quantum channels were complementary to each other between April 2001 to December 2017. Reserve Bank of India's (RBI's) monetary policy framework is characterized by the use of multiple instruments combining adjustments in the policy rate, with a complex use of liquidity management operations despite changes in the functioning of the monetary policy. They study easing and tightening phases of the policy cycle and bring out stylized facts on several relationships, highlighting the impact of policy rate changes and liquidity conditions on short- and medium-term market interest rates, and output and prices. An empirical analysis confirmed the linkage between the repo rate and the market-related rates. On the quantum side, a bi-causal relationship is observed between repo and liquidity. Transmission to money and financial markets is established better than that to the real sector. Shruti Pandey and K. Kanagasabapathy have worked on the revised version for the new edition.

Soumyen Sikdar attempts to understand the contribution of external liberalization to post-reform growth performance. Current account openness has reduced the cost of importing intermediate inputs and technical knowledge. The services sector, helped by the telecom revolution, has efficiently exploited the burgeoning global demand for business process services. The demand–pull effect has been much weaker for manufacturing due to persistent domestic inefficiency and serious infrastructural deficiencies, in addition to competition from China. Agriculture also continues to be hamstrung by supply-side constraints, in which decline in public investment has played a crucial role. There is a movement up the value ladder in exports, and import composition too has changed for the better, though much scope for improvement still remains. There is evidence of total factor productivity growth, particularly in services. But foreign direct investment (FDI) has failed to effect any major supply-side change, and foreign portfolio investment (FPI) has failed to bring down the cost of capital significantly or to stimulate stock markets adequately. The need to counter exchange rate volatility, due to global risk-driven volatility in the FPI, forced the RBI to take measures that impacted growth adversely. These risks are continuing as we wait for monetary policy to normalize in the major countries. A fact that greatly redounds to the credit of our regulatory framework is that despite its considerable openness, the Indian economy could escape the global financial crisis of 2008 relatively unscathed due to quick and appropriate policy response on many fronts.

Nagesh Kumar brings out how the reforms pursued since 1991 have deepened the global integration of the Indian economy in terms of a rising share of trade and an even more dramatic transformation of services trade, as well as the emergence of the country as one of the most attractive destinations for and an important source of the FDI flows. Analysis shows, however, that opportunities for product and market diversification remain to be fully exploited to sustain export growth and create more jobs, especially as the anaemic growth of world trade becomes a new normal in the aftermath of the global financial crisis. Despite healthy trade surpluses earned by services as India emerged to be a global hub for the information and communications technology (ICT) outsourcing, the balance of payments situation continues to face occasional pressures related to fluctuations in oil prices. Export competitiveness needs to be strengthened through appropriate exchange rate management, and opportunities for strategic import substitution need to be exploited by leveraging India's large domestic market size using industrial policy measures. The revival of manufacturing under the 'Make in India' initiative will not only make the current account situation more sustainable but will also create jobs for India's youthful population. While far-sighted policies have led India to become a part of the emerging broader regional economic arrangement, Indian industry has yet to learn to exploit the opportunities provided by preferential access to the East Asian markets rather than passively grant market access.

Raghabendra Jha and Anurag Sharma point out that despite 20 years of accelerated growth, the persistence of mass poverty, perceived rising inequality, and their spatial variation cause disquiet. The accuracy of yardsticks that show improvement is questioned. Adequacy of nutrition, the traditional rationale for the poverty line, has not recorded impressive gains. The best means of lowering poverty, which reforms have not achieved, is to create mass-scale jobs for poor and unskilled workers. The chapter advances suggestions for this and for better targeting of anti-poverty interventions. Aadhar-based direct benefit transfers and attempts to expand low-skilled manufacturing in India are therefore hopeful signs.

Ashwini Deshpande argues that the translation and impact of momentous post-reform changes on inter-group disparities has been uneven. Caste inequality shows very strong inter-state variation and some convergence, but no clear relationship between growth and convergence. Gender wage gaps are substantial, despite the reduction in the average gender wage gap for regular wage and salaried employees over the last decade, and these are greater for the lower part of the wage distribution. A decomposition of these gaps between 'explained' and 'residual' indicates that the discriminatory component is greater among the bottom four wage deciles, implying the presence of a 'sticky floor' rather than a 'glass ceiling' for women. While poverty incidence has reduced, class inequality has increased sharply, which has fuelled a protracted armed insurgency in large parts of the country.

S. Sriraman attempts to understand the impact of the governance structure in the Indian context on the provision of transport infrastructure and services. Government-owned railways have taken some initiatives to promote freight movement in a big way through the establishment of dedicated corridors with a different model of investment and operation. Equally significant are the initiatives taken by different transport-related ministries to promote multi-modalism, which involves a change in the governance structure. The issue is whether there can be effective implementation of these policy initiatives given the continuing poor practices and deviation from an ideal institutional governance framework. One other issue discussed critically relates to the effective implementation of the planning and operating of information technology practices in the context of smart cities that are being encouraged against the background of poor urban physical infrastructure.

Aradhna Aggarwal, in examining the formation and evolution of the special economic zone (SEZ) policy and its contribution to Indian industrialization over different phases, draws lessons for new policies. Contextual solutions require experimentation, but continuity of government support over the political cycles is also essential.

Commercial sustainability with some legal backing may be the way for policy consistency, making special initiatives independent of the government. To the extent special concessions are given, some sun-set clause, or else use of competition and appropriate regulation to prevent rent-seeking, would be required. Tax concessions could be reduced as other constraints ease. A report by the Comptroller and Auditor General of India (CAG) that highlighted the large tax losses and the large percentage of unutilized land in SEZs points to the necessity of both proper design and implementation. But a blind anti-industry position is counterproductive when employment generation is the way to reduce poverty. Strategic vision and dynamic learning must combine with a political will to implement.

S. Mahendra Dev, Srijit Mishra, and Vijay Laxmi Pandey contextualize Indian agriculture by an evaluation of its performance, with a focus on the roles, challenges and opportunities for smallholders. They observe a turn-around over 2004/5–2010/11 compared to the immediate post-reforms period, which had witnessed stagnation in comparison to the pre-reforms period. Public policy initiatives on investment, research, extension and credit, and a set of good monsoons were among the reasons for improvement. But livelihood sustainability of smallholder farmers is a matter of concern. Even so, there are opportunities to reduce costs and risks, and use low external input sustainable agriculture without compromising on production. There were sharp peaks in agricultural prices that contributed to inflation. But after these prices moderated with the export prices, there was a severe small-farmer distress. The supply response has to keep up with the demand growth without excessive inflation, even as the population dependent on agriculture shrinks.

Bandi Ram Prasad places the canvas of Indian industry in relation to the financial sector. Reforms gave the much needed impetus to industries with opportunities to pursue growth, diversification, and global expansion even as policy support, changing dynamics of global manufacturing, and financial reforms emerged as new sources of dynamism. The rapid expansion of India's financial sector in terms of the reach of institutions, products, and domestic and foreign financial flows have had a significant impact on the financing of the Indian industry—from the corporate sector in the conventional economy to the new infrastructure projects to start-ups—though concerns continue to exist in terms of inadequate financial flows to small businesses and small and medium-sized enterprises (SMEs) that have greater potential for employment generation in the context of bank non-performing assets (NPAs). The focus on finance raises interesting issues, such as risks from volatilities arising from global geopolitics and the scope for domestic policy to evolve alternatives to ensure sustained financial flows to the industry.

Rajesh Chakrabarti gives an overview of the financial sector in India. For him, a financial system is akin to the circulatory system in the human body, tapping and transporting savings throughout the economy, with markets and banks being the two competing and complementary arteries. The Indian financial system ranks slightly below the median in the World Economic Forum rankings, but has virtually re-booted since the still-ongoing liberalization that started in 1991. The four pillars of a financial system—laws, technology, creditors' rights, and corporate governance—have all undergone and are still undergoing major transformations. Financial access and inclusion remain key challenges despite serious efforts and experimentation. The banking system is stable, public-sector dominated, fragmented, and heavily regulated. Financial markets have witnessed a sea-change but still have limited liquidity. The corporate bond market—key for the much-needed infrastructure financing—remains seriously underdeveloped. The regulatory system is fragmented, rule-based, and—generally speaking—quite conservative. Globalization of the financial system has been steadily increasing with time and while not the most innovation-friendly in the world, it has succeeded in providing stability and averting crises in an increasingly turbulent global financial environment. Aadhaar and big data–based fintech has the potential for inclusive innovations. The chapter's focus on the institutional and legal base brings out the deep-seated transformational changes taking place, which perhaps need more time to be fruitful in increasing domestic savings, allocating them better while reducing the cost of credit, improving its availability, and encouraging entrepreneurship.

CHAPTER 1

·····································

SOURCES OF
GROWTH IN INDIA

·····································

LAVEESH BHANDARI AND SUMITA KALE

Economic growth in India has been accelerating steadily since the 1970s; yet, most agree that the reforms in 1991 and after have taken the growth path to another level. India has since left far behind the 'Hindu rate of growth', and with growth spread across all parts of the country, laggard states are well on their way to discard the other highly demotivating term *'bimaru'* (or sickly states in north India). Growth has been sustained, has not been limited to urban India, and some argue that economic growth in rural India continues to lead economic growth, even though agriculture now accounts for a small share of the economy. Sectorally as well, growth has been quite well-spread; take, for instance, agriculture—while the overall agricultural growth has been far lower than that in other sectors and centered around 2.8 to 3 per cent in the 1990s and 2000s, there are states such as Gujarat and Nagaland that have shown double-digit growth in agriculture for close to a decade. Further, sectors such as transportation, communications, and logistics were not the only ones that saw double-digit growth in the last decade, and were accompanied by strong and sustained growth in other sectors as well, such as construction and finance.

Since the 1980s, India has seen two significant changes, which are arguably closely connected. The first is what has been generally termed as economic policy reforms that have led to a significant change in the way the state deals with economic activity. The second is a significant change in technologies being used both inside and outside the country. High growth, therefore, has spread far and wide (though by no means smoothly). Where did this high growth come from? Which sectors led the changed trajectory?

The answer is not easy to decipher, as the reforms have themselves been quite staggered and uncoordinated.[1] Implementation of announced policy changes has many a times been delayed and has sometimes been quite ineffective. On top of that, the underlying data collection mechanisms have remained poor. The net result is that it is very difficult to adequately decipher how reforms impacted India at a microeconomic level. This is not to say that studies have not been attempted. In other words, while the evidence on aggregate economic growth having improved is unambiguous, the data to pinpoint the *sources of that growth* and acceleration are not as unambiguous as is shown in this chapter. To confound matters, the latest gross domestic product (GDP) series with base year 2011–12 has significant methodological differences with the previous series, making trend analysis inappropriate across time. This has, arguably, also severely impacted studies on growth and productivity changes and how they are evolving. Consequently, the data analysis in this monograph also suffers from that weakness.

This chapter proceeds as follows. 'Economic growth since Independence' provides a base for later sections by first looking into the aggregate growth figures in the post-Independence period, with special emphasis on the period since 1991. 'Economic Reforms and Economic Growth' reviews studies that have attempted to link the reforms with growth. 'Productivity and Growth' delves into issues of productivity growth and the total factor productivity growth (TFPG). 'Inter-State Differences' looks at inter-state differences and whether states are converging and why. 'Reforms towards

---

[1] The process of reforms has not been smooth, rather it has been stop and go, thanks to inter-departmental and inter-ministerial differences and differences between states, between states and the Centre, as well as between successive political denominations that have ruled at the Centre and the state.

Formalization and Digitization' looks at the economy post 2011, while the last section gives a conclusion.

Economic Growth
since Independence

The Central Statistical Office (CSO) of the Ministry of Statistics and Programme Implementation has been releasing annual National Accounts Statistics, which contain key economic variables, such as the GDP. The bulk of the studies on growth uses these GDP figures from the CSO. The base year changes every few years, though recent practices have been to change them every five years. In other words, the GDP figures are estimated in detail every five years, in line with the large sample quinquennial employment and expenditure survey of the NSSO; and the intervening years involve an updation to the GDP, which requires lesser data inputs. Every time the base year changes, the CSO publishes a document on the latest methods of estimating and updating the GDP.[2] A detailed examination of this document reveals—(a) the government is very well aware of the possible limitations of the underlying data sources and aims to circumvent most pitfalls; and (b) the GDP in India is probably underestimated, and this downward error is arising out of the government's inability to capture the value added in the informal sector. Since the methods of data collection have, so far, been more or less standard and consistent over time, the underlying data, though somewhat flawed, are good enough for most studies on growth, especially in the absence of alternatives. The situation has, however, changed with the latest national accounts series with 2011–12 base-growth estimates; they are now not strictly comparable with the previous datasets.[3] Further, as the CSO

[2] The methodology for the 2004–5 base year series is available in CSO (2010).
[3] For full details on the changes in methodology, see CSO, June 2015, 'Changes in Methodology and Data Sources in the New Series of National Accounts, Base Year 2011–12'. Available at: http://www.epwrfits.in/Changes_in_Methodology_NS_2011_12_percent2oJune_2015.pdf. Last accessed on 18 January 2018.

has not yet released a back series for years prior to 2011–12, the current estimates are too few and still under revision. This constrains the possibility of trend analysis for the most recent years. Consequently, in this updated study, while the growth estimates post 2011–12 are presented, they must be seen with appropriate caveats in place.

Looking at the years before 2011–12, while growth rates have shown an increasing trend, the volatility in the annual growth rates has reduced significantly as well, as Figure 1.1 shows. Arguably, this is a result of the diversification in the economic activity caused by the reforms. Figure 1.1 reveals a simple story. Growth has varied tremendously year to year since the 1970s. Depending upon how one estimates growth and determines the periods and sub-periods, it is possible to get somewhat different results. And some of the differences in interpretation we find in the literature are indeed due to differences in the time periods being covered. Figure 1.1 shows: (*a*) growth has been on an increasing path over the last few decades, (*b*) the improvements in growth not only precede the 1990s but also

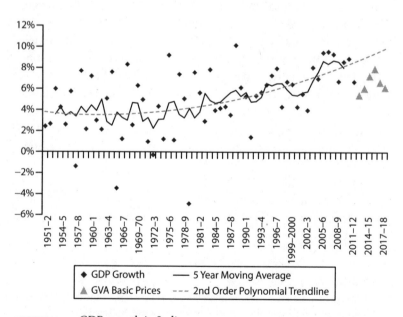

FIGURE 1.1   GDP growth in India

Source: Author's estimations from the CSO data.

the 1980s, and arguably go back to the latter half of the 1970s, and (c) the current slowdown may very well be a temporary component of a long term political economic cycle. Each of these elements is taken up in later sections. As explained previously, while the growth rates for the gross value added (GVA) at basic prices for the latest 2011–12 series have been marked in Figure 1.1, it is not appropriate to compare these growth estimates for 2011–12 to 2017–18 with the earlier trend, as the new series differs significantly from the earlier series.

The Sectoral Picture: Pre-1991

Following the low growth phase in the 1960s and first half of the 1970s, the high growth phase of the 1980s was not limited to a single sector, but all three—agriculture, industry, and services—achieved a higher growth plane.

Consider first agriculture and allied activities, which registered an average growth of 3.1 per cent in the 1980s, following the low 1.8 per cent annual average seen in the 1970s. This, it is well known, occurred as the Green Revolution took hold in Punjab and spread across Haryana and western Uttar Pradesh. Other states also started to benefit from the increased availability of fertilizers and better seeds, though maybe not to the same extent as north-western India. (See, for instance, Swaminathan 2010.)

Registered manufacturing and electricity were the focus of the early years in planning, but the dividends soon ran out as controls stifled growth. Industry, therefore, suffered a sharp decline through two decades after seeing high growth in the 1950s. The Janata Party in the latter part of the 1970s, the first non-Congress government at the Centre, did not do much apart from extending some support to the small-scale sector.[4] Devaluation in the late 1960s was followed by a steady depreciation in the first half of the 1970s (the latter not by design but because the rupee was tied to the depreciating sterling). Though it is not clear whether it was

---

[4] It accorded greater protection to small industry by increasing the list of reserved items to 504 in April 1978; it also increased the small-scale industries (SSI) limit from INR 10 lakh to INR 30 lakh capital investment.

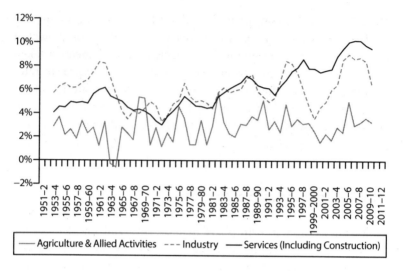

FIGURE 1.2   Sector-wise growth rates: 5-year moving average
Source: Author's estimates from the CSO data.

support to the small-scale industries (SSI) and other interventions or the reducing relative value of the rupee, but manufacturing did grow, backed by a steady increase in exports (see Mohan (2006) and Panagriya (2008), for instance).

The services sector has, for a long time, led the Indian economy in terms of size. But it was by no means the growth engine of the Indian economy as it grew roughly at the same rate as manufacturing. The major change occurred in the 1970s with the nationalization of banks. Command and controls did contribute to the spread of the banking system and the consequent growth in the financial sector. On the other hand, other sectors such as construction, trade, telecom, business services, Information Technology (IT), and others did not benefit significantly from any of the technology changes that were occurring in their domains at the time, as the sectors remained protected. The 1980s saw, for the first time, government recognition and limited support to the IT and communications sectors. But this delay in the entry of new communications and the IT technologies would also have been partly responsible for the delay in the commencement of the high growth phase in the post-reforms period.

Post-1991 Growth

Over 1991–2011, the economy grew at an annual average rate of 6.8 per cent. Though significantly higher than the period before, the aggregate figure hides some important aspects. The GDP grew at a little over 6 per cent in the 1990s, but accelerated to slightly over 7 per cent in the first half of the 2000s and then further to a little over 8 per cent for 2006–12. The post reform churn very quickly corrected itself and the economy appeared to be on a high-growth path by the middle of 1990s, but the acceleration in growth was hit in the second half of the 1990s. There were a number of factors contributing to this: Asian crisis, post-nuclear test sanctions, stalling of reforms after 1995, and rising fiscal deficits from 1996 (see Acharya 2002 for a detailed exposition of these factors). The NDA (National Democratic Alliance) years saw an improvement in growth despite some of the worst agricultural years and a tightening of the fisc. The major sectors that were leading India's march towards a high growth economy in the early 2000s were (a) construction, (b) transport, storage and communications, and (c) financial and business services which also include the IT. Each of these was preceded by some important institutional development. The communications sector gained from the more open policies of the government and the actions of an independent regulator in the form of the Telecom Regulatory Authority of India (TRAI). Together, they succeeded in creating an environment that enabled free and fair competition, consumer interest was considered foremost, and both entry and exit were allowed while keeping government intervention to a minimum. The construction sector growth was boosted by housing and highway construction, an outcome of lower interest rates, income tax incentives, more disposable income, and government investment in roads under Pradhan Mantri Gram Sadak Yojana (PMGSY) and the Golden Quadrilateral Programme, among others.

Developments in financial markets in the mid- and later-1990s included the entry and strengthening of two major institutions. First, an independent regulator in the form of Securities and Exchange Board of India (SEBI) had overcome its teething troubles. Second, perhaps as importantly, new trading technologies introduced by the National Stock Exchange (NSE) created a transparent system of trade; moreover, the spread of the electronic communications technologies also had its secondary impact on the financial sector (ATMs and offsite trading terminals being just two examples).

The 1990s finally saw the IT sector come into its own, both as an exporter[5] and as an employment generator.[6] If there is one institutional element that can be identified as synchronous with growth in the IT sector, it would be the efforts of the NASSCOM. The association is a textbook example of how cooperative lobbying by a highly competitive sector can help in creating and sustaining a far more enabling environment than unilateral action. Some important government decisions pertinent to the IT sector included low tariff on imports of the IT hardware, greater depreciation of hardware and software and ensured, at the same time, that the industry built for itself a set of quality standards that were in sync with those operating internationally.[7]

A comparison of the overall growth rate and that in manufacturing shows that apart from the first post-1991 period, the manufacturing sector has not been able to significantly pull up aggregate growth in India. This has remained one of the most curious aspects of the reforms and their impact. The first and the deepest set of reforms—industrial delicensing and relaxation in bottlenecks to international and domestic investment, as well as in international and domestic trade occurred specifically for releasing the manufacturing sector from the stranglehold of government intervention. But the manufacturing sector growth could not take off. Popular discourse has

---

[5] Total export revenues earned by this sector have grown from INR 6,723 crore (USD 1.8 billion) in 1997–8 to INR 104,500 crore (USD 23.6 billion) in 2005–6, according to the Eleventh Plan Working Group on Information Technology, Planning Commission.

[6] Number of IT professionals in India increased from barely 50,000 in 1990–1 to about 1.045 million in 2004–5. See Singh (2006).

[7] For more details, refer to Ministry of Information and Technology, http://www.mit.gov.in/content/schemes-and-policies-electronic-hardware and http://www.mit.gov.in/content/export-promotion-schemes-dpl-elec. Last accessed on 12 June 2019.

Table 1.1 Sectoral growth since 1990s (percentage)

Sectors	1991–6	1996–2001	2001–6	2006–11	Sectors 2011–12 Series	2011–18
Agriculture, forestry, and fishing	3.6	2.1	2.3	2.9	Agriculture, forestry, and fishing	2.4
Mining and quarrying	4.5	4.5	5.1	4.3	Mining and quarrying	6.3
Manufacturing	9.5	4.0	7.5	7.7	Manufacturing	7.6
Electricity, gas, and water supply	7.8	5.7	6.1	5.5	Electricity, gas, water supply, and other utility	5.8
Construction	3.7	7.7	12.8	7.5	Construction	3.1
Trade, hotels, and restaurants	9.3	7.1	9.1	7.8	Trade, hotels, transport, communications, and services related to broadcasting	8.7
Transport, storage, and communication	7.7	11.5	12.9	13.1		
Financing, insurance, real estate, and business services	7.2	8.2	8.4	10.9	Financial, real estate, and professional services	9.5
Public administration, community, social, and personal services	4.7	9.6	5.3	9.6	Public administration, defence, and other services	7.3
GDP	6.2	6.0	7.2	8.1	GVA at basic price	6.8

Source: Authors' estimates using data from CSO, Ministry of Statistics and Programme Implementation, GOI. Data for 2011–18 is based on GVA at basic prices (2011–12 series) and is not strictly comparable with the previous periods; data for 2014–15 are Third Revised Estimates, for 2015–16 are Second Revised Estimates, for 2016–17 are First Revised Estimates, and for 2017–18 are First Advance Estimates.

identified labour laws, inspector *raj*,[8] or lack of foreign direct investment (FDI),[9] among others, as the institutional constraints that have
added to the costs and, therefore, inhibited manufacturing growth.
At the same time, we find that none of these have been able to stifle
growth in selected sectors—the automobile manufacturing sector
being one example. Over the entire period, the lagging sectors were
predictably forestry and logging, agriculture including livestock, and
mining and quarrying. Since the Green Revolution, the agriculture
sector has not received significant investment or policy focus; this
shows up in the declining agricultural productivity, which is discussed later in this chapter.

This section has briefly sketched out the shifting trajectory in
growth and also alluded to some institutional developments that
preceded high growth phases. The next few sections delve into the
determinants behind this growth to understand the impact of reforms,
productivity, and political economy on overall growth and, by extension, to the sectors that have registered stellar performances. But that
is best achieved by first looking into the received wisdom on reforms
and how they impacted growth.

ECONOMIC REFORMS
AND GROWTH

Reforms—in short, the changes that work towards amending and
improving a system—are an ongoing process in any economy. There
are various facets of reforms and this section reviews studies that have
attempted to link the *process* of reforms to growth in the Indian economy.

---

[8] 'World Economic Forum's Global Competitiveness Report 2003–4 ranked
India at the fifth place out of the 102 countries on the parameter of burden of
regulatory inspection. The World Bank's 'Investment Climate Survey' in 2004
estimated that on an average, 11.9 per cent of senior management's time in India
was spent in dealing with government agencies. See GOI (2005).

[9] For a review of the FDI policy path in India and the changing definitions and
lack of FDI in the infrastructure sector, see Singh K. (2006).

When did the growth turnaround begin? We have shown in the previous section that an argument could be made for the latter half of the 1970s. But that is an argument that is rarely made in literature. Deepak Nayyar (2006) makes the point that during the past century, 1951 was the turning point for India's growth performance and since Independence, it was 1980 that framed the break point with a growth surge. While the 1980s saw a definite surge in the growth trajectory, studies have not been able to pin the shift down to a particular year.[10] Virmani (2005), for instance, documents the growth phases and contentious debates over the break points in these phases and notes that most studies have pinned the change in growth trajectory to the 1990s, while his earlier papers in 1989 and 1997 showed that growth acceleration predated the new economic policy launched in 1991. Further, his analysis for 1950–2002 shows no break point other than 1980–1, showing that the turnaround effectively happened in the 1980s.[11]

What part did reforms play in the higher growth in the 1980s? Even a cursory look at Figure 1.1 shows that it is possible to create many different stories depending upon the periods where growth rates are aggregated.[12] Each of those stories need not be incorrect, but are rarely indicative of the larger picture. For instance, it would be difficult to disagree with Panagariya (2004) that the high growth in 1988–91 pushed the average growth for the 1980s upwards and the variance of growth in the 1980s was much higher than that in the 1990s. While relaxation of controls was ongoing since the 1970s, the pace of reforms actually picked up in 1985, especially over 1985–8. These were important reforms and covered exports, industrial licensing and production (Monopolistic and Restrictive Trade Practices [MRTP], cement and aluminium), tax (modified value added tax

[10] See Wallack (2003) for the shift in cut-off year, depending on which series of national income was taken.

[11] See also J. Bradford DeLong (2004).

[12] A recent paper by Dholakia and Sapre (2011) finds that the detection of break dates is sensitive to base year changes, marginal extension of time series, and alteration of the length of the partition. The paper concludes that due to empirical limitations, there is no conclusive evidence of break dates and hence cannot help settle the debates over different growth and policy regimes of the Indian economy.

[MODVAT]), and management of the real exchange rate.[13] These 'dipstick reforms' of the 1980s were indeed the precursor for the far deeper changes of the 1990s, as they yielded important insights on growth outcomes.

The consequent impact on trade and manufacturing showed immediately in the second half of the 1980s. Apart from the usual greater business orientation type of arguments, Virmani (2005) points to the importance of credibility. He argues that the credibility of intent of policy change was firm. This was critical in achieving a high rate of growth of private investment. This observation is substantiated through the rise in the annual growth rate of the gross fixed capital formation (GFCF) in the 1980s to 6.9 per cent as compared to 4.8 per cent in the previous two decades and higher growth for manufacturing. There is also a view that the key reason behind this increase in growth and reduction in volatility was a shift in the political economy towards a more pro-business policy stance (see, for instance, Rodrik and Subramanian 2004).

We, however, find it difficult to classify reforms as pro- or anti-business. On the one hand, the overall economic freedom has increased and entry and exit is easier. Independent regulatory entities have been set up and are functioning relatively well. On the other, as many reforms have arguably created greater discretion in the hands of a few, there is some cause to believe that corrupt practices have increased, and there is little evidence of increase in small business activity.

What went wrong in the reforms–growth equation of the 1980s? Despite the growth surge, the very nature of the reforms of the 1980s has in fact been attributed as the determinant of the 1991 crisis faced by the Indian economy. As argued by Joshi and Little (1994), the expansion of government expenditures was considerable, with the bulk of this expenditure being on defence, interest payments, and subsidies. Growth in the 1980s was primarily due to unsustainable increases in public expenditures and excessive foreign borrowing that finally ended in the balance of payments crisis of 1991, when the

---

[13] Joshi and Little (1994) note that the exchange rate policy became more active from 1985, 'though the fiction of a fixed basket peg was maintained'.

international environment soured. It was because of this that though Bhagwati (1998) accepted the higher rate of growth in the 1980s, he did not consider it a new phase in India's development. Therefore, though the higher rate of growth is accepted by all studies, this was not considered healthy growth, as the reforms were lopsided and created more problems than they set out to resolve.

What went right in the reforms–growth equation of the 1980s? Ahluwalia (1994) identifies the changes in the 1980s as 'the result of a process of evolutionary reform'. More importantly, he correctly identifies the changes as 'marginal rather than fundamental'. This was why we term these as 'dipstick reforms' for there was no 'comprehensive shift away from a regime of controls', but they went a long way to make further reforms palatable to a democracy that had grown up with socialism as the dominant paradigm. But there is another argument—Panagriya(2004) argues that it is difficult to perceive any such change in attitude within the government or bureaucrats and quotes some personal instances and communications to underscore the arguments. We believe that this was all a part of the same picture—massive reforms of the 1990s required political support and the dipstick reforms were an important element in achieving that political consensus.

What changed in the 1990s and later in the reforms–growth equation? The key difference from the previous decade was that now the reforms were systemic, coordinated across ministries, and received strong political support. The first and most important set of reforms unarguably occurred in the Ministry of Industry—delicensing and removal of controls on investment being the two most critical changes. Though, as shown earlier, these reforms did not translate into stronger manufacturing growth immediately, they signalled a major change in the policy mindset from the previous decades, as they were accompanied by sustained changes in the Ministry of Commerce with an easing of import barriers and the rupee was also devalued in tandem by the Ministry of Finance.

Whatever the reasoning and analysis, it is indisputable that reforms had set in by the 1990s. The next section explores the mechanism through which the reforms impacted growth—by raising productivity.

PRODUCTIVITY AND GROWTH

Growth in output can stem in a natural way through increase in factor inputs of labour and capital, or through improvements in the efficiency of these inputs; for example, a unit of labour produces more output than before. Reforms would work on growth in output by raising efficiency, by raising the total factor productivity (TFP); Dholakia (2001) shows that the post-1985 growth acceleration is, to a very large extent, due to improvements in the efficiency of factor use, or the TFP: over 1960–85, the growth of total factor productivity contributed less than 22 per cent of the overall growth rate, while the TFP growth accounted for 48 per cent of the overall GDP growth during 1985–2000.

Bosworth et al. (2007) worked on deciphering the link between growth acceleration and the TFPG in finer detail. The analysis was conducted over a four-decade period divided into smaller sub-periods:[14] 1960–73, 1973–83, 1983–93, 1993–9, and 1999–04. They found that over 1960–73, nearly all the output growth can be attributed to growth in factor inputs, with nearly two-thirds accounted for by increased employment, and a third by increases in capital per worker. A little over half the small acceleration in growth seen over 1973–83 is attributed to the TFPG and the remainder is associated with increased labour inputs or employment. During this period, the determinants of the TFPG are the Green Revolution increasing the agricultural TFP and sectoral reallocation of employment towards other sectors. A marginal rise in output growth in 1983–93 over the previous decade's performance can be completely attributed to the increased TFP, but this time the gains are concentrated in services and industry (especially manufacturing). Therefore, with growth associated with the TFPG, reforms are linked directly to the TFPG in this period.

The period 1993–9 saw annual growth at 7 per cent levels. This was a short period where the impact of reforms of 1991 and thereafter

---

[14] The breakpoints have been chosen in line with data availability from various NSSO survey rounds.

had not fully played out. There was a decline in employment, along with a particularly large jump in labour productivity, mainly in the services sector but which was also evident in other sectors.[15] The most recent period in their analysis, 1999–2004, saw slower growth in all sectors, with the TFP and capital deepening slowing in both services and industry.

Both popular discourse and the authors have identified the slow-down in the early years of the NDA regime due to (*a*) international conditions and (*b*) poor monsoons during the period. Bosworth et al. (2007) further investigate the strong rise in the service sector's TFP and provide another more mundane explanation that output growth in services has been overstated due to an underestimate of services price inflation. However, other studies have delved deeper into the services sector to investigate the high productivity growth, which is discussed next.

Goldar and Mitra (2008) examined the services sector in depth as their analysis showed that the rise in the TFP growth at the economy level in the post-1980 period is mainly traceable to the increase that took place in the growth rate of the TFP in the services sector. Of the 2.4 percentage point increase in growth in the post-1980 period, they attribute about 40 per cent to a faster growth in the TFP in services. Going into the sub-sectoral performance within services, Goldar and Mitra found that on labour productivity, it was the financial services that saw the highest growth across the years, but when it came to capital productivity, trade, hotels, and restaurants stood out with a very sharp decline in the pre-1980 period being reversed dramatically after 1980. Overall, while the TFP rose fastest in financial and business services from the 1970s; the crucial determinants for the post-1980 turnaround were trade, hotels and restaurants, and public administration and other community services[16] (see Table 1.2). There are severe data caveats and too much should not be read into the

[15] Bosworth et al. (2007) note that this decline in employment is 'puzzling' as they have no explanation for it. It could be stemming from the data limitations in their study.

[16] In public administration, the downsizing of the public sector as well as pay scale hikes for government employees has raised the output per worker. This could account for a part of the growth in productivity in this sub-sector.

Table 1.2 Growth rates in the total factor productivity, sub-sectors, and services

Sub-sectors of services	Growth in the TFP (per cent per annum)		
	Pre–1980	Post–1980	1960–1 to 2006–7
Trade, hotels, and restaurants	–3.4	2.9	0.2
Transport, storage, and communications	2	3	2.2
Financing, insurance, real estate, and business services	2	3.9	3.5
Public administration and other community, social, and personal services.	1.1	3.5	2
Services sector (total)	1.3	3	2.1
Memo: Estimates of Bosworth, Collins, and Virmani (2006) for aggregate services sector	0.4	2.9	1.7

Source: Goldar and Mitra (2008, 14).

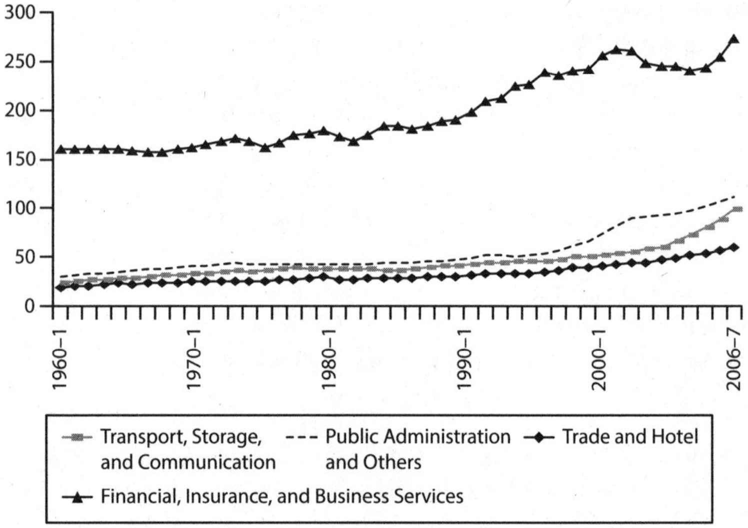

FIGURE 1.3   Total factor productivity index (1960–1 = 100)

Source: Goldar and Mitra (2008, 14).

rise in productivity of these sectors, since the higher TFPG in public administration could stem from the rise in the pay scales of public sector employees. Moreover, it is not clear whether the measurement of capital stock and definitions of the sectors have remained consistent over the large time periods being analysed.[17]

Despite these problems, Goldar and Mitra's results clearly indicate the turning points of financial sector productivity improvements to be as early- to mid-1980s, that of trade and hotels to be the mid-1990s, and that of transport, storage, and communications to be the 2000s. The lack of event studies, however, prevents us from identifying whether the infusion of technology in the mid-1980s in the banking sector or the greater international orientation of post-1991 India impacted the trade sector; whether infrastructure improvements in the road sector that commenced in the early 2000s or, for that matter, mobile telephony that was finally spreading in the 2000s can be held responsible for these patterns.

It must be noted that the high growth in productivity in the services sector had a beneficial impact on the other sectors. For instance, industrial productivity growth is related to financial, physical, and social infrastructure (Mitra et al. 2002), and the new skill-intensive activities, particularly in the IT sector, that are a part of services provide significant support to the manufacturing productivity growth. Similarly, trade and transport have high linkages, supporting both agricultural and manufacturing growth and productivity. In short, the high productivity growth in the services sector was also crucial for other sectors.

The impact of reforms in the services sector on manufacturing productivity was analysed by Arnold et al. (2012). They found expectedly that the rise in service sector productivity contributed significantly to manufacturing productivity, but they also found an ordering—banking, telecom, insurance, and transport, all of which led to significant productivity rises in manufacturing firms. Using the panel data for 4000 firms over 1993–2005, they showed that a one-standard-deviation increase in the aggregate index of services liberalization

---

[17] There are severe issues of definitions across the years that have caused different researchers to come out with different results.

resulted in a productivity increase of 11.7 per cent for domestic firms and 13.2 per cent for foreign enterprises.

What about productivity in agriculture? Some studies find that there has been a moderation in the agricultural productivity growth in recent years. Bosworth et al. find the TFPG in agriculture increasing till 1999, but moderating thereafter. The reasons behind the rise were of course the Green Revolution, improvements in inputs, and labour reallocation away from agriculture, while moderation has been explained by lower returns to government research and development (R&D) and extension services. On similar lines, Saikia (2009) found that the TFPG for agriculture declined in the 1970s, grew in the 1980s, and declined again in the 1990s, showing a possible connect with public sector investments. Goldar et al. (2016) obtain a similar result. Das (2016), however, finds an increase in the agriculture TFPG in 2000–2008 (1.7 per cent) vis-à-vis 1981–2000 (1 per cent). However, these studies are based on pre-2011 data and little is understood of the improved agri-growth rates of the 2010s.

When it comes to manufacturing, Bosworth et al. find the TFPG for industry slowing and not accelerating in the post-reform period that they analyse till 2004. However, this has been accepted as a natural phenomenon in economies that are starting from a protected environment that adapting to new technology in a liberalized world has a time lag. On the other hand, employment growth has not been commensurate with growth overall, leading to improved labour productivity. However, a note of caution by all researchers investigating the industry TFPG, results are not conclusive: as Kathuria et al. (2010) report, 'Krishna and Mitra (1998), Pattnayak and Thangavelu (2005), Unel (2003), among others, find an acceleration in total factor productivity growth (TFPG) in the reform period, whereas studies by Trivedi *et al.* (2000), Srivastava (2000), Balakrishnan *et al.* (2000), and Das (2004) find a deceleration in the TFPG in the 1990s.'

A comprehensive study on the TFPG in manufacturing in India by Trivedi et al. (2011) systematically lays out all the issues in the estimation of the TFPG in India, and one of their results is that for 1980–1 to 2003–4, the contribution of the TFPG to output growth for the organized manufacturing sector ranges between 13 and 25 per cent, *depending* on which methodology is used. Before analysing the reform impact per se on growth, they put forth two issues: it is difficult to isolate the impact of reforms from the other factors which affect the TFPG, and there could be time lags, only after which the impact of the reforms could be felt on the TFPG. Despite the caveats they give, their results across various industries and states do indicate an increase in the TFPG post-1990s.

Interestingly, Rodrik and Subramanian (2004) analyse the surge in aggregate factor productivity after 1979 and reject all commonly postulated causes behind this rise in productivity—external and internal liberalization, aggregate demand, public investment, fiscal expansion, Green Revolution, etc. They make the point that the pro-business stance of the government post-1980 led to a higher productive utilization of resources. They base their reasoning on regional analysis to show that states whose governments were allied with the Centre grew faster than the others post 1980, thereby benefitting only those states that already had large formal manufacturing, the focus of the pro-business attitude.

On similar lines, Aghion et al. (2008) argue that there is a differential impact across states when it comes to manufacturing productivity, their main result being that the response to delicensing varies significantly depending on the labour market conditions prevailing in different Indian states. The fact that there would be strong state-level factors that are playing a role is quite obvious and needs to be looked at in greater detail; the next section looks precisely into this aspect of regional differences in growth.

Despite all the studies done so far, there is still a lot we do not know. For instance, how has infrastructure impacted growth? While many point to how poor infrastructure is harming growth in India, few studies pointed to how successes in the sector had a positive impact on growth rates. Since the latter part of the 1990s, India has built an impressive network of rural roads, constructed a massive telecom network which is accessed by all including the very poor, and has been able to make almost all children who are at the primary school-going age literate. Few studies are able to tie-in the productivity impact of these social and physical infrastructure developments of the 2000s.

Under the World KLEMS Initiative, the project 'Disaggregate Industry Level Productivity Analysis for India: The KLEMS' (RBI, 2016) has been ongoing since 2009, with the support of the

Table 1.3 Key results on the total factor productivity growth in
           India

Author	Time Period	Main Results
Dholakia (2001)	1960–1 to 2000–1	1960–85, the TFPG contributed less than 22 per cent of the overall growth rate. 1985–2000 TFPG accounted for 48 per cent of the overall growth.
Bosworth et al. (2007)	1960 till 2004	Effect of the TFPG in growth shows post-1983.
Saikia (2009)	1960–2000	The TFPG for agriculture declined in the 1970s, grew in the 1980s and declined in the 1990s, showing a possible connect with public sector investments.
Goldar and Mitra (2008)	1960–80 and 1980–2004	40 per cent of the 2.4 percentage point increase in growth post-1980 is due to faster Services TFPG. Overall, the TFP rose the fastest in financial and business services from the 1970s. Trade, hotels and restaurants, and public administration and other community services were crucial for the post-1980 turnaround.
Arnold et al. (2012)	1993–2005	Rising service sector productivity contributed significantly to manufacturing productivity. Banking, telecom, insurance, and transport all led to significant productivity rises in manufacturing firms.
Kathuria et al. (2010)		Review of studies giving conflicting results for manufacturing sector productivity depending on the period analysed and methodology used.
Trivedi et al. (2011)	1980–1 to 2003–4	Contribution of the TFPG to output growth for organized manufacturing sector ranges between 13 and 25 per cent, *depending* on which methodology is used.
Rodrik and Subramanian (2004)	1970s to 2000	Surge in aggregate factor productivity after 1979 due to the pro-business stance of the government post-1980, leading to higher productive utilization of resources.

Aghion et al. (2008)	1980–97	Differential impact of delicensing across states on manufacturing productivity, depending on the state's prevailing labour markets conditions.
Goldar et al. (2016)	1980–2011	The average TFP growth for informal manufacturing lower than that of formal manufacturing over 1980–2011; both segments showed a decline in the rate of TFP growth during 1994–2002 as compared to 1980–93, with marked acceleration over 2003–11. For 2003–11, the rate of TFP growth achieved by the formal segment of Indian manufacturing was higher than that of Korean manufacturing, even as labour productivity in Indian industrial enterprises was lower than that in Korean manufacturing enterprises in most industries.
Das (2016)	1981–2008	The agricultural TFP growth in India ranged around 1 per cent during 1981–90 to about 1.7 per cent during 2000–8.

Source: Authors' compilation.

Reserve Bank of India. The KLEMS methodology, with gross output as a measure of output and capital (K), labour (L), energy (E), material (M), and services (S) as inputs, is being applied in many countries and the India study examines the productivity performance for 1980–2011 using both value added as well as gross output specifications of the production function. The main results indicate wide industry variations in productivity growth for the 27 industries under study; majority of industries show a faster TFP growth since 2000. However, in three broad sectors—agriculture, construction, and mining and quarrying—productivity performance was poorer in the post-2000 period.

Goldar et al. (2016) use the KLEMS dataset to analyse the productivity performance in the formal and informal segments of Indian manufacturing industries. The average growth rate in the TFP in informal manufacturing over 1980–2011 was found to be significantly lower at 0.4 per cent per annum, compared to 4.2 per cent per annum for formal manufacturing. Both segments showed a decline in the rate of TFP growth during 1994–2002 as compared to 1980–93, with marked acceleration again over 2003–11. The improvement in the TFP growth in the aggregate formal manufacturing segment since 2003 is mainly due to the improvement in the TFP growth performance of the petroleum refining industry, with some contribution made by chemicals and chemical products industry. Within informal manufacturing, the improved performance after 2003 is mainly due to three sectors—Textiles and Leather Products, Wood and Wood Products, and Chemicals and Chemical Products. Interestingly, the paper found that for 2003–11, the rate of the TFP growth achieved by the formal segment of Indian manufacturing was higher than that of Korean manufacturing, even as it found that labour productivity in the Indian industrial enterprises was lower than that in the Korean manufacturing enterprises in most industries. The authors noted that this 'puzzle' calls for a deeper investigation.

INTERSTATE DIFFERENCES

India's 35 states and Union Territories (UTs) have diverse socio-economic profiles and despite planning and controls aimed at a balanced regional growth, the states were quite far apart even till the 1980s. Did liberalization accentuate these differences or did it provide an environment for convergence? There is a caveat at the beginning of any regional study in India that analysis over a long period, as done for national income, is not possible for all states, especially since the data for the newly formed states is not available pre-1993.

Further, studies looking at convergence of states over time have had diverse results depending on the time period analysed, the number of states in the sample, the benchmarks used for comparison, etc.[18] Focusing purely on the impact of reforms, there are again a number of studies that show that states adopted disparate growth paths

[18] For more details on these studies, see Singh et al. (2003).

post-reforms, for example, Bhattacharya and Sakthivel (2004) found increasing inequality in the per capita regional output after 1991, Kar and Sakthivel (2007) used the 'new geography' framework to analyse the impact of reforms on the per capita regional output to validate the theory of post-reform divergence across states, Sachs et al. (2002) worked on 1980–98 for 14 states and found that there was an overall increasing divergence over the period, with greater divergence during 1992–8. Interestingly, the richer states showed convergence over 1992–8, while the poorer states in the sample did not. The reason postulated by the authors for the divergence was the regional differences in the marginal productivity of investments by the sub-sector. This stemmed from the general business environment and also the specific geographical factors. Therefore, the Green Revolution benefitted the states of Punjab and Haryana, while the service sector reforms benefitted Maharashtra, Tamil Nadu, Karnataka, and Delhi where the initial conditions were favourable for these activities.

Singh et al. (2003) noted that the results on regional inequality were sensitive to the measures of attainment used; hence, while the analysis using state income showed divergence over the post-reform period, human development indices did not show the same increase in regional inequality. Liberalization had led to a more efficient allocation of private capital, foreign as well as domestic, and while this would lead to a more uneven balance, depending on the state policies, they found that governments in poorer states such as Madhya Pradesh and Rajasthan had improved, on average, the relative standard of living of their constituents. Their conclusion, therefore, was that liberalization does not necessarily leave certain states behind.

A more recent study using club convergence and polarization as the methodology, by Kar et al. (2010), shows that there is an increasing inequality and polarization into two clubs, that is, over the period analysed (1993–2005), some of the middle-income states have moved up (relatively) and other middle-income states have fallen back, creating two separate groups. According to their analysis, the middle-income states that have fallen back are either inland, as opposed to coastal states, or have political unrest in the form of insurgencies. The reasons given, therefore, show that reforms have been favourable to those states that have conducive geographies or social structures.

It is difficult to robustly decipher whether states are converging or diverging. Table 1.4 shows state growth divided by the all-India growth rate for each of the sub-periods for the 21 larger states in the country. A ratio of 1 indicates that the state growth rate was the same as national growth, states with lower growth rates have ratios less than 1, while states whose growth rate exceeded the national growth have ratios greater than 1. The analysis in Table 1.4 shows that there is some correlation with growth from the previous period, but this figure will differ depending on the period considered. At the same time, historically poor states have sometimes grown at a rate that is significantly higher than India, but then fallen back; while there are other states that have fallen for a while, to pick up again. Despite all this, it is evident that states such as Delhi, Maharashtra, Tamil Nadu, Gujarat and, to a lesser extent, Karnataka have been performing consistently better than the average since the 1960s. States such as Kerala, Uttarakhand, Chhattisgarh, Tamil Nadu and, to a lesser extent, Bihar are among the accelerating states, whereas those such as Punjab and Rajasthan appear to be falling behind in terms of growth rates.

A sectoral analysis of state growth reveals an interesting picture in Table 1.5. Taking five-year periods from 1991 to 2010, we find the highest growth sector in these sub-periods changing across time, even as the services sector dominates. In the early 1990s, banking and insurance was the fastest growing sector in eight states, reflecting the financial sector reforms that benefited states such as Maharashtra, Karnataka, and West Bengal. In the late 1990s, it was transport, storage, and communications that had the highest growth in nine states, again reflecting the telecom reforms benefiting states such as Andhra Pradesh, and Haryana. The most striking result comes from the early 2000s, which reveal the massive thrust on construction through public investment in roads coming through, with this sector being the fastest growing one in 15 states. The late 2000s again show diversity as the states moved on different paths. Three sectors—banking and insurance (built upon the boom in household savings), public administration (the pay commissions) and transport, storage, and communications (predominantly telecom and greater road network) had the highest growth across six states each, with construction now being

Table 1.4 Growth of states relative to India's growth

State	1961–2 to 1970–1	1971–2 to 1980–1	1981–2 to 1990–1	1991–2 to 2000–1	2001–2 to 2010–11	2011–12 to 2015–16
Andhra Pradesh	0.4	1.0	1.1	0.9	1.1	0.96
Assam	1.1	0.8	0.5	0.3	0.6	0.82
Bihar	0.3	0.9	0.9	0.6	1.1	0.61
Chhattisgarh				1.5	2.5	1.13
Gujarat	0.9	1.6	0.9	1.1	1.3	1.47
Haryana	1.8	1.5	1.0	0.8	1.1	1.04
Himachal Pradesh	1.0	0.9	1.0	1.1	0.9	1.21
Jammu and Kashmir	1.1	1.3	0.4	0.7	0.7	0.54
Jharkhand				1.6	0.7	0.99
Karnataka	1.0	1.2	1.0	1.1	1.0	1.07
Kerala	1.2	0.5	0.7	0.9	1.0	0.76
Madhya Pradesh	0.6	0.5	0.8	0.8	0.9	0.87
Maharashtra	0.9	1.6	1.2	1.0	1.3	0.97
Orissa		0.8	0.8	0.6	1.1	0.86
Punjab	1.6	1.5	1.0	0.7	0.8	0.67
Rajasthan	0.8	1.0	1.2	1.0	0.9	0.78
Tamil Nadu	0.7	0.8	1.0	1.0	1.2	0.81
Uttar Pradesh	0.6	1.0	1.0	0.6	0.8	0.65
Uttaranchal				1.7	1.5	1.11
West Bengal	0.6	0.9	0.9	1.1	0.8	–
Delhi	1.5	1.9	1.5	2.4	1.3	1.03
Telangana						0.74
India GDP Growth (percentage)	3.60	3.50	5.30	6.20	8.10	6.5
Correlation of State growth with previous decade (percentage)		*54.19*	*45.80*	*68.37*	*45.51*	–

Source: Authors' calculations from the CSO, the GOI, and the data of national accounts. Data for 2011–12 to 2015–16 uses net value added at basic prices and is not strictly comparable with the previous periods; data for West Bengal under the 2011–12 series is not available.

the fastest growing sector in just five states. In the beginning of the next decade, over 2011–12 to 2015–16, mining and quarrying was the fastest growing sector in eight states, while two service sectors—real estate, ownership of dwellings and business services, and trade, repair, and hotels and restaurants—were the fastest growing in five states each.

To conclude, at the state level, manufacturing has been among the leading sectors in very few states, despite the early reforms centering around that sector. Services have led growth in India for a long time and continue to do so even at state level. Though again, which services have been leading differs across states depending upon the idiosyncratic conditions of the state.

As mentioned earlier, researchers have given varied explanations for the disparate growth paths of states. Whatever the rationale, what is apparent is that the initial response to liberalization varied across states due to local institutions and economic structures.

An additional question that is of particular importance at a regional level arises. In a vibrant democracy such as India where there are so many political calculations, what do aspirations, growth, and therefore reforms have to do with being in power? Studies have linked growth performance to voting behavior and election outcomes. Virmani (2004) argues that the benchmark for growth performance has been rising over the years and voters can discern the gap between what is professed and the actual outcomes on the ground. Gupta and Panagriya's (2011) analysis of the 2009 elections also shows the importance of growth performance for an incumbent party to win. Their results include the following: Personal characteristics of candidates are significant only in states that have shown slow growth, while the incumbency factor is much larger in high-growth states. In fact, when alternative-defining issues are absent, growth is likely to be increasingly central to determining election outcomes. In effect, growth and governance matter much more now than they did before, a point that political parties are beginning to grasp. With a multitude of political parties and split votes, the various forces that pull the state in different directions will dictate the pace of change in the future and, therefore, the growth trajectory.

Table 1.5 High growth sectors at the state level

2001–2 to 2005–6 (1999–2000 GSDP series)		2006–7 to 2010–11 (2004–5 GSDP series)		Highest growth sectors net state value added (NSVA) at basic prices for 2011–12 till 2015–16	
Highest growth sector	No. of States/UTs	Highest growth sector	No. of States/UTs	Highest growth sector	No. of States/UTs
Construction	15	Banking and insurance	6	Mining and quarrying	8
Transport, storage, and communications	6	Public administration	6	Real estate, ownership of dwelling, and professional services	5
Manufacturing	4	Transport, storage, and communications	6	Trade, repair, and hotels and restaurants	5
Mining and quarrying	3	Construction	5	Electricity, gas, water supply, other utility services	3
Electricity, gas, and water supply	2	Electricity, gas, and water supply	4	Manufacturing	3
Banking and insurance	1	Mining and quarrying	2	Financial services	2
Trade, hotels, and restaurants	1	Trade, hotels, and restaurants	2	Other services	2
		Real estate, ownership of dwellings, and business services	1	Transport, storage, and communications and services related to broadcasting	2
				Agriculture, forestry, and fishing	1
				Construction	1
No. of States/UTs	32	No. of States/UTs	32	No. of States/UTs	32

Source: Authors' calculations using the CSO data on the GSDP. For the years 2011–12 to 2015–16, data was sourced from RBI's 'The Handbook of Statistics on the Indian Economy' on net state value added by economic activity. Available at: https://rbi.org.in/Scripts/publications.aspx. Last accessed on 12 June 2019.

REFORMS TOWARDS FORMALIZATION
AND DIGITIZATION

Since 2011, and especially post-2014, there have been a number of significant economic changes and reforms. However, it is as yet difficult to quantify their impact on growth and productivity, given the above-mentioned constraints on data comparability and also the lack of requisite time lag. One strand that runs through recent reforms is the trend towards formalization and digitization of the economy, which should have a significant impact on productivity and growth. However, formalization also brings with it higher costs, made worse with little action on the simplification of various compliances. For instance, the two largest shocks to the economy since 2016—demonetization and the introduction of GST—have helped formalization and digitization, but also may have contributed to a significant increase in transaction costs of large and small businesses, including those in the informal sector. As yet, little is understood of these forces, either together or individually. The problem of data comparability makes this task more difficult, reflected in the sparseness of studies using data post-2011.

Nevertheless, the policy changes over the past few years have been substantive and include the following: (*a*) the implementation of a Generalized Sales Tax (GST) and, perhaps more importantly, an efficient institutional mechanism for cooperative federalism, the GST Council; (*b*) overhauling the 'exit' regime via the new Indian Bankruptcy Code (2016) which is a far more efficient mechanism for facilitating 'exit' in a market-driven economy; (*c*) a significant push by the government to increase digital transactions; this included demonetization, an improvement in the digital payment mechanisms, and also reforms to enable new forms, such as payment banks and mobile wallets, to name a few; (*d*) a fillip to infrastructure including road building, rural electrification, and greater investment along with increasing private role for air connectivity in regional airports; (*e*) a rise in the use of LED lights and an incentive-driven growth in solar and wind power, leading in part to achieving a power surplus status in the short run. While each of these can be expected to have a positive impact on the overall productivity, certain changes in the macro-economic regime and economic governance can be expected to have a synergistic impact first on governance and indirectly on the overall productivity. These include: (*a*) rationalization of the subsidy, including LPG, and the expansion of direct benefit transfer; (*b*) targeting a lower fiscal deficit through the Fiscal Responsibility and Budget Management (FRBM) Act and the implementation of the Monetary Policy Committee has brought in more discipline and transparency in the macroeconomic management, though demonetization and the GST implementation in 2016 and 2017 pushed the government away from a steadily reducing deficit path; (*c*) a massive change in the method of sharing of resources between the Centre and the states through the elimination of the Planning Commission in 2014 and the 14th Finance Commission moving towards a larger share for the states in tax collections by the Centre.

These trends can be expected to strengthen with time. However, what we have now already indicates that India of the 2020s will be a different economy, more formal and more digital than ever before.

* * *

This chapter aimed at understanding the underlying factors behind the accelerated growth path of the Indian economy. Trends show that the growth surge after the 1990s was deeper and less volatile than the previous decade, clearly the effect of widespread and more credible reforms. Studies reviewed in this chapter show that growth has been the outcome of productivity, which in turn can be linked to the reforms process in certain sub-sectors. However, a finer analysis that links specific events and reforms to such a process has not been initiated so far. In addition, the puzzle in manufacturing growth that has not responded to industrial reforms in a sustained manner also remains to be answered by researchers.

When it comes to reforms and growth, two points are crucial for further analysis from the point of view of India's future growth trajectory. To begin with, though reforms were directed initially at industry, the sector continues to be plagued by numerous constraints. While on one hand, the manufacturing sector shows a close relation to the global macro-environment and is deeply affected during slowdowns, researchers have identified many domestic factors that possibly have a hand in restraining higher growth, including infrastructure, especially power shortages, labour laws, inspector raj, and lack of foreign investment interest. Clearly, though India does possess the capability of a vibrant manufacturing sector, this sector has not been able to contribute to its potential towards India's growth. This brings us to the second point: why did the services sector take the lead in India, and can this growth be sustained ahead? While studies have attributed the growth surge in the Indian economy to the rise in the services sector's productivity, this chapter notes that the growth in the services sector in India has been broad-based and not confined to any single sub-sector. Over the last 30 years of high growth in the services sector, different sub-sectors have taken the lead across time. The turning point of financial sector productivity improvements is as early as mid-1980s, that of trade and hotels from mid-1990s, and that of transport, storage, and communications since 2000s. *The key tipping point in each case has been some government policy change that facilitated the introduction of new technology or investment in the sector.* Services that started at low bases have responded more than proportionately to the liberalized environment and specific policy moves, and the baton has shifted from one sub-sector to another.

This chapter also finds that different states have responded differently to the reforms process, and there are various reasons for this: favourable initial conditions, political alignments with the central government, and electoral outcomes that defined governance. Interestingly, a few studies have also shown that growth and governance are more crucial for electoral outcomes now than ever before. This despite the fact pointed out by many heterodox economists that the emphasis on reforms, growth, and productivity has pushed to the background more important issues of increasing inequality and persistence of poverty.[19]

Yet, there need not be a dichotomy here, as Rakshit (2007) explains. There are two supply-side initiatives that will increase efficiency for all sectors, particularly the laggard agriculture and industry sectors, as well as provide employment opportunities for low-skill labour. These are: (*a*) putting in place an effective credit delivery system, access to

---

[19] See Nayyar (2006) and Bhaduri (2007).

finance being a major hurdle for productive investment, particularly by small and medium enterprises (in other words, financial inclusion) and (*b*) massive public investment in irrigation, roads, railways, communication, ports, power, and other infrastructure; this is long overdue. With these two in place, productivity and employment will be boosted across the sectors and economy, making for more sustained equitable growth.

As Kochar et al. (2006) argue, India has so far followed an idiosyncratic pattern of development, and the past gives little guidance for the future. Yet, it can be said that reforms have so far led to productivity surges and, therefore, growth across various sectors. What remains is to unblock the infrastructure constraints that are holding back the economy to unleash more broad-based policy changes that will take forward a process that began more than two decades ago.

References

Acharya, Shankar (2002). 'India: Crisis, Reforms and Growth in the Nineties'. Stanford University Center for Research on Economic Development and Policy Reform, Working Paper No. 139.

Aghion, Phillipe, Robin Burgess, Stephen J. Redding, and Fabrizio Zilibotti (2008). 'The Unequal Effects of Liberalization: Evidence from Dismantling the License Raj in India'. *American Economic Review* 98(4): 1397–1412.

Ahluwalia, Montek S. (1994). 'India's Economic Reforms'. Planning Commission Paper. Available at http://planningcommission.nic.in/aboutus/speech/spemsa/msa012.pdf. Last accessed on 10 June 2019.

Bhaduri, Amit (2007). 'Economic Growth: A Meaningless Obsession?'. India Seminar, January 2007. Available at http://www.india-seminar.com/2007/569/569_amit_bhaduri.htm. Last accessed on 10 June 2019.

Bhagwati, Jagdish (1998). 'The Design of Indian Development'. In *India's Economic Reforms and Development: Essays for Manmohan Singh*, edited by Isher Judge Ahluwalia and I.M.D. Little, 23–39. New Delhi: Oxford University Press.

Bhattacharya, B.B. and S. Sakthivel (2004). *Regional Growth and Disparity in India: A Comparison of Pre- and Post-Reform Decades*. Delhi: Institute of Economic Growth.

Bosworth, Barry, Susan M. Collins, and Arvind Virmani (2007). 'Sources of Growth in the Indian Economy'. NBER, Working Paper 12901.

Central Statistical Organization (CSO) (2010). *New Series of National Accounts Statistics (base year 2004–6)*. New Delhi: CSO, Ministry of Statistics and Programme Implementation, Government of India.

Das, Varun Kumar (2016). 'Agricultural Productivity Growth in India: An Analysis Accounting for Different Land Types'. *The Journal of Developing Areas* 50(2) (Spring): 349–66.

DeLong, J. Bradford (2004). 'India since Independence: An Analytic Growth Narrative'. In *Modern Economic Growth: Analytical Country Studies*, edited by Dani Rodrik. Available at http://www.j-bradford-delong.net/.

Desai, Ashok (2006). *India's Telecommunications Industry: History, Analysis, Diagnosis*. New Delhi: Sage.

Dholakia, Bakul (2001–2). 'Sources of India's Accelerated Growth and the Vision of Indian Economy in 2020'. *Indian Economic Journal* 49(4) (April 2001–June 2002): 27–46.

Dholakia, Ravindra and Ameya Sapre (2011). 'Estimating Structural Breaks Endogenously in India's Post-Independence Growth Path: An Empirical Critique'. *Journal of Quantitative Economics* 9(2) (July): 73–87.

Goldar, Bishwanath and Arup Mitra (2007). 'Productivity Increase and Changing Sectoral Composition: Contribution to Economic Growth in India'. Working Paper Series No. E/291/2008, Institute of Economic Growth, New Delhi.

Government of India (2005). *The Report of the Committee on Streamlining the Requirement of Inspection of Industrial Units under Different Acts*. New Delhi: Ministry of Commerce and Industry, Department of Industrial Policy and Promotion.

——— (2007). *Report of the Working Group on Construction for the 11th Five Year Plan (2007–12)*. New Delhi: Planning Commission.

Goldar, Bishwanath, Suresh Aggarwal, Deb Kusum Das, Abdul A. Erumban, and Pilu Chandra Das (2016). 'Productivity Growth and Levels: A Comparison of Formal and Informal Manufacturing in India'. Available at http://www.worldklems.net/conferences/worldklems2016/worldklems2016_Goldar.pdf. Last accessed on 18 January 2018.

Gupta, Poonam and Arvind Panagariya (2011). 'India: Election Outcomes and Economic Performance'. Paper 7, NCAER Conference on Trade, Poverty, Inequality and Democracy, New Delhi.

Jens Matthias, Arnold, Beata Javorcik, Molly Lipscomb, and Aaditya Mattoo (2012). 'Services Reform and Manufacturing Performance Evidence from India'. Policy Research Working Paper 5948, The World Bank.

Joshi, Vijay and I.M.D. Little (1994). *India: Macroeconomics and Political Economy: 1961–91*. Washington DC: The World Bank.

Kar, S. and S. Sakthivel (2007). 'Reforms and Regional Inequality in India'. *Economic and Political Weekly* 42(47).

Kar, Sabyasachi, Debajit Jha, and Alpana Kateja (2010). 'Club-Convergence and Polarisation of States: A Nonparametric Analysis of Post-Reform India'. IEG Working Paper No. 307.

Kathuria, Vinish, Seethamma Natarajan, Rajesh Raj, and Kunal Sen (2010). 'Organized versus Unorganized Manufacturing Performance in India in the Post-Reform Period', MPRA Paper No. 20317.

Kochhar Kalpana, Utsav Kumar, Raghuram Rajan, Arvind Subramanian, and Ioannis Tokatlidis (2006). 'India's Patterns of Development: What Happened, What Follows'. NBER Working Paper No. 12023.

Mitra, Arup, Aristomene Varoudakis, and Marie Ange Veganzones Varoudakis (2002). 'Productivity and Technical Efficiency in Indian States' Manufacturing: The Role of Infrastructure'. *Economic Development and Cultural Change* 50(2): 395–426.

Mohan, Rakesh (2006). Financial Sector Reforms and Monetary Policy: The Indian Experience. RBI Bulletin, July.

Nayyar, Deepak (2006). 'Indians Unfinished Journey Transforming Growth into Development'. *Modern Asian Studies* 40(3): 797–832.

Panagariya, Arvind (2004). 'India in the 1980s and 1990s: A Triumph of Reforms'. IMF Working Papers 04/43, International Monetary Fund.

——— (2008). *India: The Emerging Giant*. USA: Oxford University Press.

Rakshit, Mihir (2007). 'Services-led Growth: The Indian Experience'. *Money and Finance* (February): 91–126.

Reserve Bank of India (2016). 'Disaggregate Industry Level Productivity Analysis for India: The KLEMS'. Available at https://www.rbi.org.in/Scripts/PublicationReportDetails.aspx?UrlPage=andID=855. Last accessed on 18 January 2018.

Rodrik, Dani and Arvind Subramanian (2004). 'From "Hindu Growth" to Productivity Surge: The Mystery of the Indian Growth Transition'. NBER Working Paper 10376.

Sachs, J.D., N. Bajpai, and A. Ramiah (2002). 'Understanding Regional Economic Growth in India'. *Asian Economic Papers* 1(3): 32–62.

Saikia, Dileep (2009). 'Total Factor Productivity in Indian Agriculture: Some Conceptual and Methodological Issues'. MPRA Paper No. 28578.

Singh, Kulwinder (2006). *Foreign Direct Investment in India: A Critical Analysis of FDI from 1991–2005*. New Delhi: Centre for Civil Society.

Singh, Nirvikar, Laveesh Bhandari, Aoyu Chen, and Aarti Khare (2003). 'Regional Inequality in India: A Fresh Look'. *Economic and Political Weekly* 38(11) (15 March): 1069–73.

Singh, Sanjay K. (2006). 'Information Technology in India: Present Status and Future Prospects for Economic Development'. *Directions*, May, IIT Kanpur.

Swaminathan, M.S. (2010). *From Green to Evergreen Revolution: Indian Agriculture: Performance and Challenges*. New Delhi: Academic Foundation.

Trivedi, Pushpa, L. Lakshmanan, Rajeev Jain, and Yogesh K. Gupta (2011). 'Productivity, Efficiency, and Competitiveness of the Indian Manufacturing Sector'. Development Research Group Studies Series No. 37, Reserve Bank of India.

Virmani, Arvind (2004). 'Economic Growth, Governance, and Voting Behaviour: An Application To Indian Elections'. Working Paper No. 138. Delhi: Indian Council for Research on International Economic Relations.

———— (2005). 'India's Economic Growth History: Fluctuations, Trends, Break Points and Phases'. Occasional Paper, January 2005. New Delhi: Indian Council for Research on International Economic Relations.

———— (2005). 'India's Economic Growth History: Fluctuations, Trends, Break Points and Phases'. Occasional Paper, January 2005. New Delhi: Indian Council for Research on International Economic Relations.

Wallack, Jessica Seddon (2003). 'Structural Breaks in Indian Macroeconomic Data'. *Economic and Political Weekly* 38(41) (11 October): 4312–15.

CHAPTER 2

....

AFTER LIBERALIZING
REFORMS

the importance of domestic demand

....

PULAPRE BALAKRISHNAN AND ASHIMA GOYAL[*]

In the early 1990s, it was suggested that India's economy was at a *crossroads* (see Mookherjee 1992). Implicit in this characterization was the understanding that things could not continue as they had for some decades by then. The immediate provocation for such thinking was the unravelling of the former Soviet Union and, with it, the entire communist archipelago of Eastern Europe. This was to have a major implication for India in terms of economic flows, but at that time this was recognized most acutely by political scientists. Economists, on the other hand, being susceptible to the allure of theory, saw the end of the Soviet empire as having immediate implications for the economic model that India was to credibly pursue from then on. Economic reforms aimed at liberalizing the policy regime were launched soon after, in July 1991. It would, of course, be wrong to suggest that these reforms were freely chosen by the Indian policy establishment. India had been under quite severe balance of payments stress for about a year by then. This had led it to approach the International Monetary Fund (IMF) and standard prescriptions had followed. Based on the

* Balakrishnan thanks Reshma Aguiar for exceptional assistance with the data.

perspective from which this chapter is written, however, it is immaterial whether the reforms were imposed or freely chosen. The fact is that those responsible for implementing them in India were quite convinced that the standard reforms package was necessary. Now, more than two decades hence, although the average post-reform growth has risen, its volatility suggests that the high road taken has inadequacies. Choices remain, and Indian policymakers are still at the crossroads. The state of the economy at present, how we got here, and the direction in which the policymakers must now move are the concerns of this chapter.

GENEALOGY OF MARKET REFORMS IN INDIA

Going by the policy statements of the Government of India at the time and the contents of the much-celebrated budget speech of the then Finance Minister Manmohan Singh in July 1991, the guiding principle of policy at that juncture was the integration of India's economy with that of the rest of the world. At the same time, the world over, the inevitability of embracing globalization was assumed by reference to the implosion of the former Soviet Union (FSU). The latter event was itself interpreted as evidence of the unsustainability of the autarkic Soviet economic model upon which India had allegedly based her own. Everything, according to those who held this view, pointed to the imperative of granting freer play to market forces. It is important to flag the rather casual reasoning involved in arriving at this conclusion. First, even as the unsustainability of the Soviet economic model was presented as a predictable outcome after the event, the FSU's collapse had come entirely unexpectedly to economists.[1] Its roots had perhaps lain more in Gorbachev's policy of *glasnost* or openness, a

---

[1] Consider the following:

> Every revolution is a surprise. Still, the latest Russian Revolution must be counted among the greatest of surprises. In the years leading up to 1991, virtually no Western expert, scholar, official, or politician foresaw the impending collapse of the Soviet Union, and with it one-party dictatorship, the state owned economy,

radical regime shift in the sphere of politics, than in *perestroika* or the restructuring of the economy. This had first cut at the foundations of single-party rule by the communists and the vice-like grip of the bureaucracy and the secret police, spreading to dislodge the more than half a century of ethnic Russian hegemony over the so-called 'union' of nationalities. The FSU's unravelling as a political entity had followed, and with it the collapse of the entire Socialist Bloc of Eastern Europe. In hindsight, a potential application of the 'domino theory', albeit in a part of the world far from that for which it had originally been proposed, had remained unimagined for over three decades!

A recognition of politics as the most proximate cause of the collapse of the FSU does not for a moment reinstate its economy as having been dynamic, but it does help us see that the forces making for the disintegration of the European socialist world were largely political, and its timing almost entirely determined by them. It is not irrelevant to note that China had, for at least three decades by then, adhered to a highly *dirigiste* model of import-substituting industrialization which, for a decade and a half from 1950, yielded a growth rate not much higher than that of India's (see Balakrishnan 2010: Table 11.2). The argument advanced here that political liberalization may have been the more important factor in the disintegration of the FSU is strengthened by reference to the experience of China, where the move to a largely capitalist economic model has been underpinned by a severely repressive political regime, which alone could have contained the political disaffection due to a growing inequality of income and regional imbalance. The second reason why the justification of a regime change based on the Soviet experience would be inappropriate is that in 1991, India was quite far from having been a Soviet-style economy ever. Apart from the total absence of the coercive allocation of labour, perhaps the most significant marker

---

and the Kremlin's control over its domestic and Eastern European empires. ... Although there were disagreements over the size and depth of the Soviet system's problems, no one thought them to be life-threatening, at least not anytime soon. (Aron 2011)

The author goes on to provide economic data ranging from the growth rate to the size of the fiscal deficit to argue that there was nothing inevitable about the collapse of the Soviet Union from an economic point of view.

of the erstwhile communist economies, even in 1991, over 80 per cent of the gross domestic product (GDP) in India was generated in a barely regulated private sector, something entirely alien to the FSU. Organized manufacturing had been tightly regulated indeed, but it had comprised a highly developed private sector and constituted less than a fifth of the economy. By 1991, the Indian corporate sector was also highly organized politically and boasted of a lobby with increasing access to the political class. Where India's economy had a strong resemblance to the Soviet economy, however, was with respect to the foreign-trade regime. Here, import quotas were widespread, and when they were absent, there were tariffs which were among the highest in the world. So it can be said that India, as did the FSU, had attempted to industrialize via across-the-board import-substituting industrialization, no matter that some trade liberalization measures had been initiated from the mid-1970s on. However, the broad economic strategy would by itself hardly qualify India as a Soviet clone, for much of East Asia too had pursued what can be termed import-substituting industrialization. But something a little more than mere economic strategy had been in the balance when the policy regime had been chosen by India's political leadership in the 1950s. Foreign capital had not just been discouraged, it had, over time, been more or less expunged from the economy by design. It was this closeness to foreign capital, at times in forms not envisaged in the early 1950s, that was to change in 1991. This was the truly radical shift accomplished by the reforms of that year. There is every indication that it was deliberate and intended to be irreversible. In any case, it is a move that has held for close to 25 years by now and shows no sign of waning.

Within the overarching objective of integrating India with the rest of the world, specific changes to the policy regime were undertaken. For the sake of convenience, these may be grouped under the rubrics 'internal' and 'external', even as we realize that their elements may overlap and need not always be independent of one another. The principal changes in the former group were the scrapping of investment licensing and amendments made to the Monopolies and Restrictive Trade Practices Act of 1969, originally promulgated to regulate 'large industrial houses'. Among the most visible features of the 'policy-scape' for at least a quarter of a century, their disappearance was of considerable symbolic value. As for the changes with respect to India's interface with the rest of the world, three may be noted. First, the tariff rate was reduced across the board, clearly intended to lower the protection enjoyed by the Indian industry. Second, after an early devaluation of the rupee, it was left to float with respect to transactions on the current account. This amounted to allowing a greater role for market forces in determining trade flows. In this context, this could also have been rationalized as necessary to curb a likely influx of imports when quantitative restrictions on imports were being rescinded. Finally, a simplification of procedures for inward foreign direct and portfolio investments was announced. As a signal of the intention to integrate the country with the global economy, this remained unsurpassed. These changes to the external policy regime of the economy were unilateral. Other changes were to come into effect in the mid-1990s, following India's accession to the World Trade Organization (WTO) rules. This was part of a simultaneous move by member countries to a set of rules jointly agreed upon. Prominent elements of this new set were a commitment to phasing-out quotas, legislating a new patent regime granting recognition to product patents, hitherto non-existent in India, and recognizing trade in services. Though these were not ceded unilaterally and came with reciprocal rights—particularly of market access—for India, the move was viewed with deep suspicion by vocal sections of the polity. Arguably, however, it was the trade and industrial policy reforms of 1991 that had constituted a greater shock to the economy and were, in this sense, the more potent of the changes.

The expression 'liberalization, privatization, globalization', or LPG for short, has been used to describe the shift in the policy regime initiated in 1991. But this is misleading and it would be pertinent to demonstrate why.[2] Liberalization, in the form of the trade and industrial policy changes recounted here, was at the forefront of the economic reforms alright, but of privatization there has been relatively very little so far. Evidently, the politics of the public sector run far deeper than the superficially differentiated agendas of India's political parties. This

[2] Admittedly, the usage is found more often in the media than among academic economists, but then in India, by now the media has emerged as an important influence on public opinion.

we can infer from the fact that alliances of nominally both the right and the left have governed India since but have moved little in the direction of privatization. The Indian political class' relationship with the public sector appears to be independent of ideology, the reluctance to privatize perhaps reflecting more an unwillingness to let go of a significant lever of power. That privatization had featured so prominently at all in the policy announcements of governments in the early 1990s, only to be dropped as soon as the crisis of 1991 had passed and the economy had stabilized, has encouraged speculation on the role of some external agencies in its inclusion in the agenda for reforms.

Finally, we come to globalization, the extent of which tends to get exaggerated. User-specificity is a hazard often encountered in the parleying of this term, and not just in India. One might ask if globalization is the adoption of supra-national standards in economic arrangements within a country, or whether it refers to the unrestrained cross-border movement of goods, services, and labour. We can see that either way, far too much by way of globalization is attributed to the reforms of 1991. For a surplus labour economy such as India, true globalization should encompass the possibility of labour emigration. This is restricted by immigration controls in the rest of the world, especially among the labour-scarce economies of the Organization for Economic Cooperation and Development (OECD) which would count as the obvious destination, and not just for Indians, at present. On the other hand, the barriers to adopting certain kinds of global standards are largely internal. Take, for instance, adopting global standards in evaluating the education and health status of the population. For a large country with considerable administrative reach and growing government revenues, which is India, these are not unattainable any longer. However, no move in this direction has been made as part of the reforms of 1991. The reforms themselves were almost entirely in the nature of liberalization and had not initially addressed the issues of either human development or social protection.[3] India lags behind

---

[3] These were to come over a decade after 1991 in the form of the Sarva Shiksha Abhiyan and the National Rural Employment Guarantee Scheme (NREGA) respectively. The budget for 2018–19 introduced Ayushman Bharat, which, the finance minister in his speech asserted, was 'the world's largest government-funded healthcare programme'.

much of the world on almost every indicator of human capital and welfare provision. Therefore, while the share of trade in India's GDP has risen, the extent of globalization—defined more broadly—that has taken place is limited. The one notable move in that direction is that after a gap of four decades or so, India has now once again become exposed to the global flow of financial capital for the first time since 1947.

Another feature of the reforms of 1991 may now be noted. The liberalization that has occurred has taken place mostly in what is constitutionally recognized as the central government's policy space. In the case of foreign trade, central legislation defines policymaking, but this cannot be said of industrial policy. This is so because in India, foreign trade is a 'central subject' and trade policy the preserve of the central government. It is not so with industrial policy. Here, state governments retain substantial powers and a central legislation is not the last word as far as industrial investment is concerned. So, while the Industrial Policy Statement of 1991 may have scrapped industrial licensing, fresh proposals for industrial investment continue to be dependent on state governments for other forms of clearances, especially environmental ones. In practice, some states have turned out to be more attentive to such proposals than others. That this is so is partly revealed by the growing divergence of industrial performance among the states. Yet the scrapping of industrial licensing, once a potential barrier to even a demonstrably profitable capacity expansion, was a significant event, marking the end of an era as far as the policy regime is concerned. Returning to the question of how the reforms of 1991 and after are to be characterized, we might say that we have had liberalizing trade and industrial policy reforms. LPG is not a particularly helpful account of the evolution of the economic policy regime in India.

As may be imagined, the politics of regime change is less sure ground for an economist than is its economics. Judging from their writings, however, it does not appear to be a fully mapped territory for political scientists either.[4] The main 'axis of contestation', an expression favoured by one of them (see Sengupta 2008), is whether the

---

[4] See especially Kohli (2006a, 2006b), Pedersen (2000), and Sengupta (2008).

economic reforms package of 1991 was only an egregious event in a sequence of market reforms that had been experimented with earlier by the domestic leadership or whether it was an imposition by global multilateral agencies, notably the IMF. Political scientists may be expected to bring along the element needed for a fuller understanding of regime change, rendering their perspective invaluable. However, even while they may be united by their interest in the origins of reforms, the question of the factors underlying the regime change in India has not been resolved by them similarly. Among the most recent accounts is that of Sengupta (2008), who rejects the portrayal of reforms 'as the outcome of a linear, cumulative process of "learning"' (Sengupta 2008, 36)[5] among the country's policy elites, preferring instead an account of 1991 as a 'political event'. What is so political about it for her is the defeat of the old paradigm by the Washington Consensus, a manifesto on the ideal economic policy architecture that was ascendant in the 1990s. In this defeat, a significant role is said to have been played by professional economists of the Indian government who subscribed strongly to the worldview that was emerging as dominant globally. Despite a self-conscious effort to provide a political explanation for the reforms, Sengupta's approach lacks a political economy, being without a sufficient role for domestic political parties, global institutions, and historical events.[6] En route to our providing an account that encompasses these, it is instructive to note the views of two other political scientists. One of them sees southern Indian engineering firms with an interest in the global market as constituting an interest group. The managers of these industries had links with the global managerial elite and viewed themselves as positioned differently vis-à-vis the West by comparison with the first generation of Indian industrialists after Independence. Pedersen (2000) sees this

[5] Though reference is made to the career of the idea in political theory, no evidence is advanced for an argument in the Indian context that grants answers to such a description.

[6] However, her characterization of the essence of the regime change is worth noting: 'This was far more than a transition from "state" to "market", since much "market reform" had occurred prior to 1991. The most significant aspect of the 1991 reforms is that they signalled a transition to the political ideology of neoliberalism, and to its attendant assumption of a benign (liberal–capitalist) global order' (Sengupta 2008, 39). The last observation is particularly apposite.

group, which coalesced into the Confederation of Indian Industries (CII), as having been a strong lobby for the kind of reforms which were undertaken in 1991.

Among political analysts, as he describes himself, Kohli's work on the politics of reform is the most grounded, scouring first the policy-scape of the 1980s in order to provide a longer view of the regime change of 1991 (see Kohli 2006a, 2006b). While he is astute in recognizing the role of the newly emerged industry associations, Kohli (2006b) is most insightful when he links the change to the collapse of the Soviet Union. The interpretation that regime change in India was inevitable in that the collapse of the Soviet Union meant that free market was the only solution to India's problem we have already discussed. However, Kohli is referring to something more palpable. This is the ending of the strong economic links that the Indian economy had enjoyed with the FSU for almost four decades. A pivotal feature of this was rupee trade, which had enabled India to buy oil and defence equipment without having to pay foreign exchange, a trade facilitated by the export of tea, textiles, and raw materials. The ending of this possibility, not to mention the drying up of the market constituted by the Eastern European economic block COMECON, had grave implications for the Indian economy. Kohli points to the recognition among India's elites that defence equipment would now have to be sourced from the United States. And, more importantly, that a move in that direction would require the opening up of the Indian economy to American capital and goods, a demand the other developing countries of the world had experienced all along. To this important insight, we might add the following: with the collapse of the FSU, India would have had to export more to an open global market to earn the necessary foreign exchange. And rather like the historically observed relationship between markets and prosperity, it could not but have been apparent to any unbiased observer at that moment that it would be virtually impossible to be a successful exporter while remaining ensconced behind protective trade barriers. The latter has less to do with any ethical element of reciprocity expected in trade relations, having instead everything to do with an exporter needing access to globally competitive technology and capital goods which, in the first instance, can only be imported. Of course, for India in particular, there had all along been present an imperative to export to make up the foreign exchange needed to finance its voracious consumption of oil and gold. We may add that adjustment in the form of reducing oil dependence was politically inconceivable, in that the Indian state is far too populist to restrict consumption.

Having surveyed the views of political analysts, we may now sift through them with reference to the history of the Indian economy since 1947. Some form of incipient reforms of the trade and indus-trial policy regime had begun in the mid-1970s. This continued in dribs and drabs right through till the middle of Rajiv Gandhi's tenure as Prime Minister which lasted till 1989. The intervening two years before 1991 had seen two governments, led by V. P. Singh and Chandrashekhar, respectively, which devoted little attention to mat-ters economic as they were more concerned with political survival. However, except for the Rajiv Gandhi era, liberalizing reforms in some areas were mostly accompanied by enhanced restrictions in others, akin to 'two steps forward, one step back'. For instance, Indira Gandhi's mildly liberalizing initiatives in the mid-1970s and the early 1980s were accompanied by a tightening of labour laws, introducing a major barrier to exit from industry. Earlier, the Janata Party led by the politically conservative Morarji Desai had signalled its intention to liberalize licensing and external commercial policy by appointing the Alexander Committee on Import-Export Policies and Procedures in 1977. However, it granted further concessions to small industry and actively discouraged foreign direct investment (FDI), as may be seen in the highly publicized expulsions of Coca-Cola and IBM. As for the Rajiv Gandhi era, it has been pointed out (see Rodrik and Subramanian 2005) that the effective tariff actually rose during this period, thus neutralizing the removal of import quotas for some products. However, Rajiv Gandhi's role cannot be sufficiently captured by indicators of the restrictiveness of the trade regime. His tenure was on balance a period of reforms. The young prime minister had positioned himself as one who was not afraid of initiating change without rejecting the past in India's economic development. The radical rhetoric talked by Indira Gandhi, and walked by George Fernandes in his brief tenure as the Minister for Industries in the Janata government, was by now a thing of the past. There was a strong sense of using state-of-the-art technol-ogy to transform India. Also, without in any way dismantling the public sector, Rajiv Gandhi had provided room for the private. This was most noticeable with respect to information technology and telecommunications. The, by now extinct, 'STD booth' was at the moment of its first appearance in the mid-1980s, symbolic of some intrepid private entrepreneurs having been allowed to scale the ramparts of a public sector monopoly. Given that after the Nehru-era privileging of the public sector had become a marker of left-wing politics, this was a portent. Further, it could not have been missed by the political class that the move had a widely distributed welfare effect that was not without a significant payoff.

The fact of evidence of a liberalization of the policy regime in the decade before 1991 is not to deny that the reforms package of 1991 may have been influenced by the IMF. Indeed, the influence is there for all to see. However, it is likely to have been more with macroeconomic reforms. Lowering of tariffs, reducing the budget deficit, and restricting credit and devaluation all bear the hallmark of the Fund's standard stabilization package for a balance-of-payments-constrained economy. That the reduction in the fiscal deficit must clearly have been influenced by the IMF is also suggested by the feature that the sharp cuts initiated in the early years of the 1990s were to be followed by a slipping of targets as soon as the programme with the Fund had been wound up. Public savings promptly turned negligible in the second half of the 1990s (see Balakrishnan 2009). On the other hand, it is unlikely though that the Industrial Policy Statement of 1991 abolishing licensing would have been solely at the behest of the Fund, and, even if it was, the reforms for licensing had been contemplated in Indian government circles for close to two decades by then.

In conclusion, it is not particularly difficult to isolate the elements of regime change imposed by external agencies as the price of balance of payments support from those adopted quite willingly by the Indian political leadership, even if it had been hectored to do so. The balance of payments crisis had left India with little alternative but to travel, cap in hand, to Washington. This gave the Fund–Bank combine the perfect opportunity to impose its views of an ideal economic architecture on the last major country that had for long resisted its writ. In fact, an opportunity had been missed in 1981 when having been granted the largest ever loan made by the IMF to a member, India had refused to take the final tranche of the USD 5 billion assistance, as the economy had recovered quickly from the impact of the second oil shock. The recovery itself had been made possible by the then Finance Minister Pranab Mukherjee ingeniously tapping non-resident Indians for foreign exchange support. The end of communism in the FSU and the wooing of the West by China had left India isolated as a practitioner of extensive restrictions on international trade and capital flows. It should not come as a surprise at all that the IMF had weighed-in with its trademark conditionalities, intending that this country's resistance should end forever. However, at least as far an internal liberalization was concerned, this was only the culmination of what had been toyed with hesitantly, for fear of political repercussions, by India's major political parties for some time by then.

The progress of the reforms, both macroeconomic and structural, provides an insight into the role of external agencies relative to that of domestic liberalizing forces. It would be a fair summary to say that next to none of the structural reforms, whether of the 'external' or 'internal' type according to our classification, has been reversed. On the other hand, the principal macroeconomic reforms of permanently reducing the budget deficit, an important element of the IMF package, were more or less abandoned since the end of the IMF programme in the mid-1990s, only to be revived under pressure from foreign outflows in 2011. The Fiscal Responsibility and Budgetary Management Act of 2002 had a shaky start, largely because India's politicians are aware of the restrictions that it places on their established practices, particularly the buying of political allegiance through subsidies while keeping taxes low at the same time. Clearly, budgetary rectitude had been imposed from without in 1991. On the other hand, structural reforms, in evidence at least since the 1980s, were very likely perceived by the political class as potentially contributing to growth, and therefore beneficial to their political future, even if some sectional interests may be hurt in the process. In any case, the role of domestic calculations in at least sustaining structural reforms is evident. However, it is more difficult to place the proposed privatization of public sector enterprises in the perspective offered here. The IMF actually refuses to acknowledge the accrual of revenues from privatization as a legitimate form of fiscal correction.

The liberalizing reforms of 1991 stand out in marked contrast to the liberalization episode of 1966 when, faced with a balance of payments crisis, India had first gone to the IMF. Then, a sharp devaluation and some liberalizing reforms were implemented in return for promised balance of payments support. When this did not materialize, Indira Gandhi, smarting under the ignominy of having been outplayed by the international powers that be and goaded by domestic public opinion, had simply reversed the reforms. On the other hand, since 1991 we have thus far had strongly liberalizing governments of all hues at the Centre, each advancing India's continuing integration with the rest of the world. Clearly, something has altered significantly in the sphere of politics and the work of political scientists discussed here helps us understand that change.

FROM ACCELERATING GROWTH TO DECELERATION WITH INFLATION

Strictly speaking, there never was double-digit growth after 1991, only the promise of it.[7] However, the Indian policy establishment was so confident that this would be attained that they behaved as if the economy had actually achieved double-digit growth. This happened during the five years starting 2003–4 when the economy averaged around 9 per cent growth per annum. It was assumed that the tipping point had been reached. The confidence was soon to evaporate though. Coinciding with the onset of the global financial crisis, the phase of high growth ended in 2007–8. For three consecutive years from 2005–6 the annual growth rate cleared 9 per cent in every year. At that time, there was widespread anticipation in policy circles of the economy crossing the double-digit barrier. However, this was not to be. We see from Table 2.2 that 2008–9 saw a slowing of growth to

---

[7] The average annual growth rate for each decade starting the 1950s and for each year during 2000–9 is presented in Balakrishnan (2010, Table 4.1).

6.7 per cent. A smart recovery may appear to have taken place over the next two years but, as may be seen in the same table, this was aided by a strong fiscal stimulus. However, growth was soon back to 6.7 per cent in 2011–12 and has remained about two percentage points lower on average over 2011–17 compared to 2003–11. Even so, it needs to be acknowledged that this average growth rate of over 6.5 per cent is high by contemporary global standards. Only, it falls well short of the double-digit growth which was expected by the Indian policy establishment in the early 2000s. Be that as it may, the economy clearly shifted to a lower growth path, and this reversal is of interest by itself.

Macroeconomic performance was not characterized by slowing growth alone, however. The deceleration was initially accompanied by a rise in the inflation rate. From a situation of generally low inflation during the high growth phase referred to, it came close to reaching 10 per cent per annum over 2008–11. The decline in the rate of growth of output accompanied by a rise in the inflation rate constituted an unexpected challenge for the policymakers.

The inflationary episode reflected in the data in Table 2.1 provides a clue to understand the slowing of growth in India after 2008. Before moving on to our explanation, however, it may be noted that the data throw out a challenge to two opposing views of the growth–inflation nexus. First, the combination of slowing growth and rising inflation flies in the face of the idea of a Phillips Curve. If there is a trade off, we should have witnessed a decline in inflation as growth slowed. Second, it is contrary to the diagnosis[8] popular among financial economists that inflation reflects 'overheating' of the economy, for we find inflation rising even as growth has slowed substantially. There is, on the other hand, a complete explanation of the observed growth–inflation history that relies on neither account, and we turn to this now.

---

[8] Such a diagnosis of the recent inflation in India made by IMF is contested in Goyal (2012). The author makes her point by referring to the decline in manufacturing growth. Additionally, in Table 2.1 is contained alternative information that makes it difficult to sustain the diagnosis of 'overheating'. The budget deficit of the central government declines quite sharply as inflation accelerates.

Table 2.1 Growth, inflation, and monetary policy

	2009–10	2010–11	2011–12	2012–13	2013–14	2014–15	2015–16	2016–17
GDP growth	8.6	8.9	6.7	5.4	6.1	7.2	7.9	6.6
Inflation (WPI)	3.8	9.6	8.9	6.9	5.2	1.3	–3.7	1.7
Inflation (CPI)	13.5	10.1	8.2	10.1	9.4	5.9	4.9	4.6
Food-price inflation –	15.3	15.6	7.3	10.9	12.3	5.6	2.6	4.0
Relative price of food	126	138	138	146	159	163	171	175
Oil price change	–4.3	16.0	16.9	10.0	9.6	–10.6	–32.0	–0.8
Policy rate	4.8	6.0	7.9	8.0	7.6	7.9	7.1	6.4
Non-food credit growth	17.1	21.3	16.8	14.0	14.2	9.3	10.9	9.0
Industrial growth	5.3	8.2	3.6	3.3	3.4	4.0	3.4	5.0

Source: RBI: 'Handbook of Statistics on the Indian Economy', 'Economic Survey', and the 'RBI Bulletin'; various issues.

Notes: 'Growth rate' is based on the GDP at 2004–5 prices till the year 2011–12 and 2011–12 prices thereafter; the CPI inflation is based on the new combined series from 2012–13.; prior to that, it is taken as a weighted average of the CPI-Agricultural labourers and the CPI-Industrial workers with weights 70:30, reflecting the population distribution; 'Relative price of food' is the ratio of the wholesale price index for food articles to the wholesale price index (WPI) for manufactured goods; 'Policy rate' is the average annual repo rate; 'Food-price inflation' refers to the rate of change of the WPI food articles, and 'Oil price change' is based on the WPI (mineral oils) with the base 2004–5 till 2012–13 and the base 2011–12 thereafter.

There has been a tendency in Indian policy circles to relate the slowing of the economy since 2008 to the global financial crisis. While a priori there is every reason to believe that this is a correct interpretation, we see in Table 2.2 that it is not fully borne out by data. The year-on-year growth in exports is not well correlated with the year-on-year growth of the GDP. On the other hand, there is a reasonable fit between the GDP growth and the year-on-year growth of agriculture. Second, export growth is mostly higher since the ending of the high growth phase in 2007–8, while agricultural growth is mostly lower. Exceptional years do exist in the case of both, however, when there is no correlation.

Of course, exports are not the only way in which the global economic crisis may have affected India's economy. There is also the FDI to consider. The data assembled in Table 2.2 show a cyclical pattern to the FDI. Having declined substantially, it has risen sharply after 2014, and by now is at a level exceeding what was recorded when the crisis had struck. However, this has not restored the GDP growth to its corresponding peak, reflecting fully the share of the FDI in the total capital formation in the economy. Altogether then, we find the tendency to rely on the global slowing as an explanation for the Indian one, less than convincing. On the other hand, the demand-side effect of slowing agricultural growth cannot be ruled out as a factor. Finally, the role of macroeconomic policy: the macroeconomic stance has been contractionary ever since inflation more than doubled in 2010–11 and then remained high for the next three years. This is evident from the movement in the fiscal deficit (see Table 2.2). It is particularly evident with respect to the monetary policy. Comparing the movement of the policy rate to the change in the producer price, namely the WPI inflation, we would observe a severe monetary tightening to have taken place from 2010–11 onwards. Counter-cyclical macroeconomic policy should compensate for negative external demand shocks, but the reverse happened in India after 2011. Unlike the standard expectation, the 2014 fall in oil prices did not increase growth, although there was some pass-through (Table 2.1). Export and agricultural growth were also low (Table 2.2). But this was just the period when real interest rates rose steeply (Table 2.1) with the fall in inflation, thus reducing domestic demand (Goyal 2018).

Table 2.2 Domestic versus global factors in the economic slowdown

	2007–8	2008–9	2009–10	2010–11	2011–12	2012–13	2013–14	2014–15	2015–16	2016–17
GDP growth	9.3	6.7	8.6	8.9	6.7	5.4	6.1	7.2	7.9	6.6
Agricultural growth	5.8	0.1	0.8	7.9	3.6	1.5	5.6	–0.2	0.7	4.9
Export growth	0.2	14.2	–4.7	19.7	15.3	6.8	7.8	1.7	–5.3	0.2
Public investment (% GDP)	8.9	9.4	9.2	8.4	7.7	7.4	7.3	7.0	7.7	7.6
FDI inflow (USD billion)	34.73	41.74	33.11	29.03	32.95	26.95	30.76	35.28	44.91	42.21
Fiscal deficit	2.5	6.0	6.5	4.8	5.9	4.9	4.5	4.1	3.9	3.5

Source: Agricultural growth is from 'Economic Survey', various issues, and export growth is calculated from data in rupees crores from Ministry of Statistics and Programme Implementation (MOSPI); GDP and FDI data are from 'RBI: Handbook of Statistics'.

Notes: All growth figures are based on the GDP at 2004–5 prices till the year 2011–12 and at 2011–12 prices thereafter.

WHAT INFLATION SIGNALS

With the virtual disappearance of inflation from Europe and the United States since the 1970s, the dominant view appears to have been established that inflation is related to central bank action. Money growth is not even mentioned, for apparently central bank announcements—or inflation targets specified in its mandate—are sufficient to assume that inflation signals laxity on the part of the central bank. This view has also been encouraged by the feature that most of the central banks in the western hemisphere have been granted functional autonomy. The facts of the decline of labour militancy and the reduced reliance of the economies of this region on the Organization of the Petroleum Exporting Countries (OPEC), both having been historically relevant to inflation there, tend to get ignored. Non-monetarist explanations of inflation no longer find a place in either Anglo-American textbooks or in the international policy discourse heavily guided by the worldview of the global financial sector.[9] The absence of an inflation theory capable of diagnosing the Indian situation has cost its policy establishment dear. Actually, this cost has been self-inflicted for, as already stated, we have a complete understanding of the inflation episode under study. Such an explanation had originated from a study of the experience of the economies of Latin America observed over some decades. The Western economist who first recognized a universal potential in this approach, which for convenience we may label structuralist, was Nicholas Kaldor (1971). The starting point of the analysis in this tradition is the disaggregation of the economy into sub-sectors according to the rules of price formation and output determination. Thus, in the short-run that is the province of macroeconomics anyway, agriculture is characterized by demand-determined prices and supply-determined output while industry is characterized by cost-determined prices and demand-determined output. Two crucial inter-sectoral links are: agricultural supply is a source of demand for industrial output and agricultural prices are transmitted to industrial prices via wages linked to the cost

---

[9] See, for instance, Romer (2012).

of living. To complete the macro model, money is largely credit, and is thus rendered endogenous due to a central bank's targeting of the interest rate to stabilize the financial system. Introducing dynamics into such a system, any continuing excess demand in the market for agricultural goods leads to rising prices that are generalized across the economy via wage bargaining and cost-determined industrial prices. A flexible exchange rate can aggravate an inflationary situation when depreciation feeds inflation via a rising price of imports. As Kaldor had emphasized, the relative price of agriculture plays a role in driving growth and inflation. A rising relative price of agriculture is inflationary as industrial prices are cost-determined. It can at the same time be recessionary, or at least depressive of output, in that it can impose negative income effects on sections of the population that are not entirely compensated for in the rise in agricultural prices. As food is a necessity, with low-price elasticity of demand, a rise in its price can crowd-out household expenditure on industrial products. A traded goods sector can ameliorate the effects of a slow growth of agriculture by providing imported food and an external market for industrial products. However, competitiveness, which is necessary to be able to import food in exchange for exports, cannot simply be assumed, or ensured by merely depreciating the exchange rate. Kaldor had proposed just such a model to explain the stagflation that had enveloped the economies of Europe and the United States following the first oil shock of the 1970s (see Kaldor 1976). As we shall soon see, it had considerable traction in explaining the growth–inflation nexus in India over 2010–17.

In Table 2.1 are presented data on growth, inflation, and the relative price of food over 2009–17. First, as stated earlier, we can see a pattern of slowing growth and rising inflation. Again, as stated earlier, this is difficult to square with the account of inflation contained in mainstream macroeconomic theory. On the other hand, the structuralist account outlined earlier fares quite well in the context. Note that the course of inflation is fully tracked by the change in the price of food. However, this by itself is insufficient to establish that inflation has been driven by price inflation triggered by agricultural supply shortfall. The rise in the price of food might well be part of a general rise in prices, which is the very definition of inflation. It is the movement of the relative price of food that makes plausible, in the context, a structuralist explanation story. During its high phase, till 2013–14, the inflation rate may be seen to mirror this movement. Since then, inflation has declined even as the relative price of food has continued to rise because of the accompanying decline in the price of oil. Its fall after 2014, evident in both the inflation series presented, was clearly driven by a collapse in the oil prices.[10] Food price inflation also slowed after 2014. The incoming government's policy of restraining[11] the rise in minimum support prices played a role in this. Econometric evidence on the applicability of the structuralist account of inflation to India is available in Balakrishnan (1991) for 1950–80 and in Dash (2012) for 1970–2010.

The data presented is also sufficient for us to infer the limits of macroeconomic policy in eliminating a food-supply-related inflation. Macroeconomic policy can eliminate inflation driven by the rising price of food only by engineering a recession. When industrial output is demand-determined, restrictive macroeconomic policy can lower industrial growth, which in turn lowers the market demand for food and, thus, the inflation rate itself. Since the demand for food is inelastic, this may not be very effective. Moreover, it is an inefficient solution from the point of view of welfare as it is achieved by constricting output and employment growth. Anyhow, the sequence of events is evident from the data in Table 2.1. We find that the Reserve Bank of India has kept the interest (repo) rate high since 2011, with the fall since 2014 not commensurate with the fall in inflation.[12] Industrial output growth has been reduced and so has the inflation rate, though the latter is very likely driven by the fall in oil prices and not the fall in demand.[13] The role of monetary policy in having lowered the output growth is suggested by the reduction in credit growth over the period considered. The rise in the interest rate would be expected to do precisely this. Reduced credit growth affects the availability of capital for

---

[10] The price of crude fell from above USD 100 to USD 40 per barrel by the end of 2014.

[11] At least till the budget of 2018.

[12] Averaging over the year conceals the fact that the interest rate was raised 13 times during 2010–12.

[13] Slowing output growth may not be effective by itself in reducing food inflation because of the low price and income elasticities of the demand for food.

both production and investment. The decline in credit and industrial growth is quite closely aligned with a rise in the real interest rate from 2011–12 onwards, as the policy rate did not fall as much as the rate of inflation fell.

While the anti-inflationary macroeconomic policy in the form of interest rate hikes may have slowed industrial growth all right, it would be placing far too great a burden of explanation on it to suggest that it also accounts for the slowing of the economy itself. As industrial output accounts for only around a fourth of the GDP, a credible explanation must proceed by alluding to some greater economic force. This is to be found in the growth of agriculture and the slowing of public investment, two historically important factors in the growth process in India. It may come as a surprise to many that during the phase of high growth over 2003–8, when it had appeared that the double-digit growth rate barrier was set to be breached, public investment had grown faster than ever since the 1950s (see Balakrishnan 2010: Table 3.4). Public capital formation as a share of the GDP reached a post-reform peak of 9.4 in 2008–9, but now hovers around 7 per cent. Apart from public investment, agriculture has continued to play an important role in determining the annual changes in the rate of growth of the economy. Consider the following evidence: for the first 17 years since 1991, the direction of change in the annual growth in the GDP is correlated more closely with the direction of change in the annual agricultural growth than with that of manufacturing and two out of the three categories of services at the two-digit level (see Balakrishnan 2010). Only the growth of 'community and personal services' is more closely linked to the change in the rate of growth of the GDP during this period. Since services growth is also demand-determined in India (Basu and Das 2017) and is likely to practice cost-plus pricing, it can be considered as part of the manufacturing sector in applying the structuralist model to India.

Coming back to the episode that we have focused on, we have reason to believe that both slow growth and higher inflation have much to do with the record of agricultural growth. Though agricultural growth was impressive in 2011–12, in all other years it remained lower than it was in 2007–8, which was the last year of the high growth phase. Allowing for lags in the impact of agricultural growth on the rest of the economy, its role in influencing the overall growth and inflation trajectory is apparent.

We have already argued that global slowing alone is inadequate to account for the slowing of growth in India recently as the economy had made a swift recovery after 2008–9. In particular, exports—the component of the GDP most likely to have been affected by the slowing—after a bad showing in 2008–9 when the global financial crisis had peaked, continued to do remarkably well right up to 2011–12. But it is the combination of slowing growth and rising inflation that suggests that the global financial crisis and the consequent slowing of the world economy is not the explanation for these outcomes in India. On balance, this can only be explained by reference to domestic developments, and the structuralist approach outlined earlier is effective in such an exercise. Recall that according to it, inflation is caused if agriculture does not grow fast enough in relation to the demand for its output that is generated by growth elsewhere in the economy. Next, if wage incomes are not compensated for inflation, a redistribution takes place and the growth of demand for non-agricultural output is affected adversely. Add to this the possibility that public investment tends to be restrained when inflation rises, monetary policy is tightened, and growth is doubly affected negatively, this time through a restrictive macroeconomic policy.

In this chapter, we do not explore at length the specific factors underlying food-price inflation in India over the past decade, at least not beyond pointing out that agricultural growth has been indifferent since 2012. However, it needs to be emphasized that the relative price of agriculture may rise, with all its consequences for growth and inflation, even if agriculture were to grow. The question is whether it is growing at the rate required for maintaining price stability. Where the income elasticity of demand for high-value foodstuff is greater than 1, double-digit growth of the GDP will require close to double-digit growth in the output of this segment of agriculture. Such a segment comprises vegetables, fruits, eggs, milk, fish, and meat. While the output of these commodities has very likely grown in recent years, it is unlikely to have matched the growth in the demand for these foods, given the rate of non-agricultural growth in 2003–8. Once structural inflation enters the system, it is not easily expunged even after growth slows down.

FOOD PRICE AND DOMESTIC DEMAND

Though it has been argued here that the global financial crisis has had a limited role in the slowing of the Indian economy since 2010, the crisis itself is of import for Indian policymakers. Indeed, it pointed to the need for a fresh approach to public policy. First, and foremost, there is the implication of the slowing of the world economy for the demand side of growth. The only justification for the almost exclusively supply-side-oriented nature of the economic reforms launched in 1991 could have been that growth was predicated on an assumed expansion of world demand. More heroically, it may have been predicated on an assumption of an increasing competitiveness of India's exports which would penetrate world markets. This would then have provided an additional argument for integration with the rest of the world, beyond the anticipated supply-side benefits of access to frontier technologies via imports of intermediate inputs and through the FDI. Even though the global economy has revived since 2015, the question of the future source of demand for double-digit growth aspired to needs to be faced. If internal demand is to be granted a more significant role, then agriculture needs to assume a more important place in the policymakers' agenda. It is not that a strategy for agriculture was not ever considered. In fact, the very act of lowering protection to industry via trade liberalization was meant to boost agricultural growth via a terms-of-trade effect.[14] The shift in the terms-of-trade in favour of agriculture did materialize as predicted by theory, but faster agricultural growth did not. The reasons why trade liberalization may not be a sufficient strategy for an agricultural revival are elaborated on in Balakrishnan et al. (2008). Here, it need only be stated that other measures beyond the opening-up of the economy, central to the reforms launched in 1991, are needed. While public investment is needed, governance in the specific form of ensuring that funds are spent appropriately and that public systems actually function is perhaps more important.

[14] It was laid out with some clarity by Manmohan Singh in a speech made to fellow economists during his tenure as the finance minister. See Singh (1995).

This is most obvious with respect to irrigation (see Balakrishnan et al. 2008).

However, the structuralist approach outlined earlier alerts us to another aspect when it comes to the role of agriculture. Agriculture itself is becoming a shrinking part of the economy, but it crucially impacts the demand for industrial production and for services via the price of food.[15] In the history of the West, the declining real price of food has been a major factor in creating a market for industrial consumer goods. The importance of cheap food to sustained growth is demonstrated by the fact that in the three decades since the Second World War, the real price of food in the United States declined by 75 per cent (see Gopinath and Roe 1997). This was the longest boom enjoyed by Western economies in recorded history. Note that by 1945 the United States was already the world's richest economy. For India, an economy with a low level of per capita income, the beneficial impact of a sustained decline in the price of food may well be imagined. In this context, it is significant that, as may be seen in Table 2.3, this price has actually risen since 1991. Although periods of sharp rise have been followed by slower growth,[16] the movement of food prices in India since 1991 is at variance with that recorded historically in the industrialized economies. It is of relevance to the immediate future of its economy.

The demand-generating role of agriculture has not been sufficiently imagined by India's planners, the term being used here in its broadest sense to include also those in charge of policymaking today. As suggested earlier, for agriculture to play this role, it is not only necessary to elicit more food but also to ensure that it comes forth at a lower real price (which ultimately depends upon lowering the cost of production). Raising yields becomes important now.[17]

---

[15] See Balakrishnan (1991) for evidence of negative impact of the relative price of agriculture on industrial production.

[16] For annual data on the real price of food since 1993–4, see Balakrishnan (2010: Table 4.4).

[17] The Union Budget presented in 2018 promised a minimum support price of 50 per cent above cost of production for 23 crops in order to safeguard farmer income and alleviate farmer distress. While the actual increase will depend on the measure of cost used, the sustainable way to do this is to reduce costs. Table 2.3 shows that a sharp adjustment in the terms of trade cannot normally be maintained over time.

Table 2.3 The real price of food

		Rate of Change
1991–2	98	–
1995–6	101	2.8
2000–1	112	11.2
2005–6	101	–10.0
2006–7	104	2.8
2007–8	106	2.1
2008–9	107	1.0
2009–10	119	11.1
2010–11	125	5.5
2011–12	123	–1.5
2012–13	126	2.4
2013–14	134	6.4
2014–15	140	4.0
2015–16	148	6.1
2016–17	150	1.4

Source: Computed from the price series in RBI: 'Handbook of Statistics on the Indian Economy'.

Notes: 'Real price' is the ratio of the WPI for food articles to the WPI for all commodities. Index base: Figures are to the base 2004–5. Those for 1991–2 to 2000–1 were originally to the base 1993–4 = 100.

How much can trade liberalization contribute to this can well be imagined. This is even before we have factored in the consequences of climate change and declining fertility of land for the global price of food in the future. Finally, the depletion of fossil fuel reserves could lead to the re-allocation of arable land to bio-fuels, which reduces the supply of food. The extent to which technology can keep the possibility of rising food prices at bay globally is yet to be known. But one thing is clear. The episode of slowing growth and rising inflation that we have experienced in India indicates that policymakers must pause. Public policy can no longer be legitimately confined to expanding the ambit of the private sector. In fact, it is when considering the future of agriculture in India that we are able to see this most clearly. There are a few restrictions, other than periodic export caps, on agricultural activity in the country today.

On the other hand, infrastructural bottlenecks abound. Further liberalization is not going to address the issue of cheap food that we have argued is central to faster growth. We had stated that the global financial crisis had two implications for the future of policy in India. The first, having to do with a greater reliance on internal demand, has been discussed. The second is broader and is set within the realm of ideas. The crisis has, to use the expression coined by managerial economist John Kay, revealed via a means which is the closest we can get to a controlled experiment in economics 'the truth about markets' (Kay 2003). Ever since the work of Arrow and Debreu, we have known that the conditions necessary for a Pareto-efficient competitive equilibrium are seldom, if at all, fulfilled in practice. Revolving around the existence of contingent markets, this critique of the market mechanism may appear remote. However, far from being remote to our day-to-day concerns, we have seen market failure on a gigantic scale at work in the case of the financial crisis of 2007–8. The global financial crisis has had the effect of muting the once vocal demand for financial sector reforms in India. The report of a committee[18] set up by the Planning Commission, arguably by somewhat stretching its mandate, was given a quiet burial after the events of 2008. Capital account convertibility is suddenly no longer seen as absolutely vital.

* * *

However, a fundamental rethinking on public policy is yet to take place. We conclude this chapter by proposing the course that this rethinking ought to take.

First, it is necessary to see the role of trade for what it is. The government has alluded[19] admiringly to the fact that trade now accounts for over 50 per cent of India's GDP. It is interesting to note that this statement was made at a time when inflation was close to double-digit and manufacturing growth had almost ground to a halt, for reasons provided earlier in this chapter. A quarter century after 1991, we are able to see what openness to trade and capital

---

[18] 'Report of the Committee on Financial Sector Reforms', New Delhi: Planning Commission, 2009. Available at: http://planningcommission.gov.in/reports/genrep/report_fr.htm. Last accessed on 1 June 2012.

[19] See Government of India, 'Economic Survey 2011–12', p. 4.

flows can in effect do. The foreign exchange constraint, the bugbear of Indian policymakers in the 1950s, appears to have been lifted. This is an achievement indeed. But the wage goods constraint, signalled by rising food prices, appears to be still with us after all these years. As we have seen, the real price of food rose by 50 per cent since the launching of the reforms in1991 (see Table 2.3). And manufacturing, a sector which has been the target of trade liberalization, has not expanded its share of the economy despite the fact that much of the reforms have been addressed at this sector. Clearly, something more than just a liberal policy regime is needed to leave India a manufacturing power to reckon with. East Asia's experience suggests that steady expansion of food supply and the expansion of quality education and infrastructure are likely to be important. Note that apart from food, the set mostly comprises non-tradeables. Focusing on non-tradeables is a strategy countries around the world are adopting in the period of slow post-crisis world growth. There is also less leakage abroad of government expenditure on non-tradeables.

The second element in a necessary rethinking of public policy that is obviously needed now is that the Government must be disabused of the notion that its economic function has been discharged once it has legislated a fixed ideal of a policy regime, if there is one such ideal across economies and over time. The legitimacy of a government draws from its ability to provide and maintain public goods, by definition beyond the aspirational radar of the private sector. The point about public goods is that in the 21st century, they extend beyond roads and parks. We now have to deal with 'public bads' in the form of environmental degradation, climate change, and a depleting water table. Legislating or decreeing policy cannot bring forth the necessary public goods. Governance, which is an expression often encountered but seldom defined in the current discourse on the future of India's economy, must be understood mainly as the provision of public goods. Compressing domestic demand, without paying adequate attention to this aspect, has only resulted in lower rates of growth since 2011. Improving public goods and other cost-reducing measures would boost domestic demand by freeing private income as well as reduce the cost of production. If cost and price inflation are expected to moderate, monetary policy can also support demand.

References

Aron, L. (2011). 'Everything You Think You Know About the Collapse of the Soviet Union Is Wrong'. *Foreign Policy*, July/August. Available at: http://www.foreignpolicy.com/articles/2011/06/20/everything_you_think_you_know_about_the_collapse_of_the_Soviet_Union_is_wrong. Last accessed on 24 October 2013.

Balakrishnan, P. (1991). *Pricing and Inflation in India*. New Delhi: Oxford University Press, pp. 31–55.

———— (2009). 'Macroeconomic Policy, Structural Reforms and Economic Growth'. *Macroeconomic Management and Government Finances*. New Delhi: Oxford University Press for the Asian Development Bank.

———— (2010). *Economic Growth in India: History and Prospect*. New Delhi: Oxford University Press.

Balakrishnan, P., R. Golait, and P. Kumar (2008). 'Agricultural Growth in India since 1991'. DRG Paper No. 27. Mumbai: Reserve Bank of India.

Basu, D. and D. Das (2017). 'Services Sector Growth in India from the Perspective of Household Expenditure'. *Economic and Political Weekly* 52(48): 68–75.

Dash, S. (2012). 'An Empirical Analysis of Inflation in India: 1970–2010'. Unpublished M.Phil. dissertation, Centre for Development Studies, Thiruvananthapuram.

Gopinath, M. and T. Roe (1997). 'Sources of Sectoral Growth in an Economy Wide Context: The Case of U.S. Agriculture'. *Journal of Productivity Analysis* 8: 293–310.

Goyal, A. (2013). 'Propagation Mechanisms in Inflation: Governance as Key'. In *India Development Report 2012–13*, edited by S. Mahendra Dev. New Delhi: IGIDR and Oxford University Press, pp. 32–46.

———— (2018). 'Demand-led Growth Slowdown and the Working of Inflation Targeting in India'. *Economic and Political Weekly*, special issue on Money, Banking, and Finance, 53(13): 79–88.

Kaldor, N. (1971). 'The Role of Industrialisation in Latin American Inflations'. Paper originally read at the Latin American Conference held in Gainsville, Florida, February 1971. Reprinted in *Further Essays on Applied Economics*. London: Duckworth.

———— (1976). 'Inflation and Recession in the World Economy'. *Economic Journal* 86: 703–14.

Kay, J. (2003). *The Truth About Markets*. London: Penguin Books.

Kohli, A. (2006a). 'The Politics of Economic Growth in India, 1980–2005 Part I: The 1980s'. *Economic and Political Weekly* 41: 1251–59.

———— (2006b). 'The Politics of Economic Growth in India, 1980–2005 Part II: The 1990s and Beyond'. *Economic and Political Weekly* 41: 1361–70.

Mookherjee, D. (1992). 'Indian Economy at the Crossroads'. *Economic and Political Weekly* 27: 791–801.

Pedersen, J.D. (2000). 'Explaining Economic Liberalisation in India: State and Society Perspectives'. *World Development* 28: 265–82.

Rodrik, D. and A. Subramanian (2005). 'From "Hindu Growth" to Productivity Surge: The Mystery of Indian Growth Transition'. *IMF Staff Papers* 52: 193–228.

Romer, P. (2012). *Modern Macroeconomics*. New York: McGraw-Hill.

Sengupta, M. (2008). 'How the State Changed Its Mind: Power, Politics and the Origins of India's Market Reforms'. *Economic and Political Weekly* 43: 35–42.

Singh, M. (1995). Inaugural Address, 54th Annual Conference of the Indian Society of Agricultural Economics, Kolhapur, 26 November 1994. Reprinted in *Indian Journal of Agricultural Economics* 50: 1–6.

CHAPTER 3

··

FISCAL AND MONETARY POLICY
outcomes and coordination

··

ROMAR CORREA

Between the time of writing of the first version of this essay and the present occasion of revising it, the need for the Reserve Bank of India and the Government of India to work together has become stronger. Increasingly becoming globalized, the problems facing the country contain universal elements as well. Inflation is not the paramount bugbear here, or anywhere, and thousands of young Indians are added to the workforce regularly. The single macroeconomic bullseye is off and the instrument to strike at its center, the repo rate, is getting blunter by the day. It is true that the magnitude of the policy rate differs from that number prevalent in other countries. It is strictly positive and, indeed, a perennial source of conflict between Mumbai and Delhi, in that the former would see it move northwards, the latter in the opposite direction. In other countries, the zero bound on the interest rate has been breached and it has entered negative territory. In some countries it happened through market forces, in others it was policy-induced. According to one line of thought, the real interest rate has turned negative as well. In that case, according to the Fisher relation, the expected inflation rate becomes rudderless. It can be on either side of the origin on the real number line. At any rate, the natural rate of interest continues to elude capture. All we have is Keynes' theorem that the rate of interest is a monetary phenomenon. The topic is not arcane but helps rebut the 'savings glut' hypothesis of the buildup towards financial crises (Cesaratto 2017). Theory and evidence suggest, instead, off-target monetary policies culminating in a 'financing glut' or 'excess finance'. We reiterate that the interest rate–inflation rate instrument-target policy syndrome is the outcome of a specific model, itself the fruit of holding fast to the belief in price effects. Serious scholars in monetary economics, including members of the old Chicago school, have always insisted that the quantity of money matters and that output and employment are no less important for monetary policy.

We restrain those who would rush off to conclude that 'we are all Keynesians now'. The power exercised by established interests in the neoclassical model is undimmed from real crisis to financial crisis. The theorems on policy neutrality and Ricardian equivalence remained unscathed through the global financial crisis of 2008, quantitative easing, and internal critique. Lars Svensson, one of the high priests of the macroeconomics citadel, for instance, moves quickly to try to crush any model that makes a case for countercyclical policy. The basic issue with mainstream models is that they are locally stable and the classical adjustments mechanisms do not allow for positive feedback. The disastrous effects of positive spillovers is best illustrated by a string of catastrophes all over Europe (Feigl et al. 2016). Banks reduced their credit disbursements particularly during the subprime crisis and the subsequent sovereign debt crisis. At the same time, the demands of firms, small and medium enterprises (SMEs) in particular, collapsed. The negative demand shock was amplified by procyclical fiscal policy. In the context of the impending rollback of quantitative easing in Europe, the advice is that monetary-fiscal coordination should be shored up. The fisc must lead the way through direct support of employment, igniting innovations through imaginative public-private partnerships, target spending in hand-picked social and public projects, and, through all of these, abandon strangleholds such as fiscal rules. The fiscal multiplier is regarded as higher for public investments than government expenditures and higher still for supporting expansionary monetary policy. To be sure, the need of the hour is a 'smart' fiscal rule that supports public investment and flexible budgets that are countercyclical while, at the same time, being sustainable. One of the formulae entertained by the bunch of European scholars referred to is the adoption of the golden rule of public finance that goes back to Richard Musgrave, the founding father of the modern version of the subject. The idea is to deduct public investment from the headline and the structural deficit so that the net public investment is financed *through* deficits. While our framework described below is decidedly unconventional, solidly micro-founded treatments of the 'dire consequences' of the absence of monetary and fiscal coordination, especially in the context of the persistent recession, are being written (Bianchi and Melosi 2017). The benchmark model is one where the Treasury ignores the level of government debt and the Federal Reserve steps away from its inflation stabilization objective. Inflation expectations adjust to determine a stable trajectory of public debt. We summarize this section in the words of two illustrious figures in modern macro, themselves invoking the famous author of the phrase about us all being Keynesians (Mankiw and Reis 2017). 'Central Banks are fiscal agents,' they bluntly instruct us. Students of Indian economics, brought up to believe that monetization of the fiscal deficit is equivalent to the visitation of the plague in our monetary history, would be startled to be educated in the even stronger proposition that money financing of government expenditure should be effected through the instrumentality of 'people's quantitative easing' or the orientation of the people's central bank in the direction of green projects.

In the following sections, we expand on the tension between money and finance in two parts. The first is concerned with the monetary process in historical time and logical time, and the second is the identical format for finance. But first, we recall the methodology we used in the first edition of this volume.

A STOCK-FLOW-CONSISTENT (SFC) FRAMEWORK

If not utility maximization by infinitely lived agents, then what? 'Analytic narratives' is an agenda that amalgamates history and political economy (Mongin 2016). With reference to the former, the strategy partakes of the recent historical practice that moves away from actors and actions while, at the same time, enlarging the space and time of the canvas. The task is to introduce formal models to historical material. While extensively employing game theory and microeconomics in principle, studies need not be confined to the associations illustrated by existing examples. For instance, it is claimed that analytic narratives should be able to absorb both increasing complexity as well as simplicity.

As earlier, we work with the stock-flow-consistent (SFC) framework of Godley and Cripps (1983) [hereafter G&C]. A case for its use, if it might be put that way, is its conformity to applied social accounting matrices (SAMs) (Barbosa-Filho 2017). While input-output matrices originating with Leontief are square in keeping with the norm that, in theory, 'everything depends on everything else', the monetary-real matrices of actual economies are decomposable with causal arrows originating and pointing in particular directions. All the notations and expressions below are from G&C. The strategy is to manipulate sets of macroeconomic identities obeying the precepts of double-entry bookkeeping. The so-called SFC norms connect variables. These are robust social and physical parameters thrown up by the past and the present, and the concatenation of these parameters defines institutional arrangements. Thus, macro-prudential norms are practices that would evolve endogenously. Our concern lies with the zone of stability wherein output and employment can be increased without reaching an upper bound where the threat of inflation reappears. The Phillips curve continues to contort in time and space, and the current macro craftsmen are advised to set it aside in fabricating their models. This time, we introduce asset prices in the macro model. They are captured by a 'time-varying coefficient' in a difference equation. The notational convention followed for change, taking inventories (I) as an illustration, is $\Delta I \cong I - I_{-1}$, where I denotes inventories at the beginning of the current period and I_{-1} stands for the stock of inventories carried forward from the previous period.

The Bank: Central and Commercial—I

Coming to our positive model, an emerging consensus on the emergence of money is that it is emitted in the process of issuing debt. Banks are pivotal here. Only banks create money because only banks can issue debt against themselves. The pure theory of the monetary circuit is indifferent about the appellation, central or commercial, suffixed to the bank. Accordingly, either or both can define money by lending to business. Since repayment is naturally required for the circuit to close, these days we would insist on greater detail concerning the nexus between parties. In particular, a modern social scientist would expect an account of the evolution of trust in the social contrivance of money among strangers in spot and intertemporal transactions (Camera 2016). In possession of it, people accept accounting objects such as bank deposits or notes in exchange for labour, goods, and services. Money is a Nash equilibrium and the non-cooperative outcome is sustained because every player believes every other player would positively value the use of fiat money in payments. Public confidence in the currency, therefore, is a key ingredient in monetary arrangements. It is a small step to take to posit confidence in the issuer of currency as fundamental to durable covenants. Money is a public good. It is non-excludable. It is also non-rival. Indeed, the participation of an individual in a monetary system likely raises the value of currency to others through network effects. A currency that is used more is more valuable than a currency that is used less because more trades are implied. As in the problems of public goods, individuals would be tempted to free ride on the public good. Historically, public confidence in a currency was founded on the quality of the coins that constituted the currency. Governments had an advantage over the private sector in ensuring this quality because they could set and enforce quality standards and, more importantly, because they could internalize the long-term benefits of a stable currency, not falling prey to the temptation to debasement. Since money is a public good, externalities would not be displayed in the supply functions of private issuers. Oversupply would be a real threat. Also, since the central bank is a node in the web of connected institutions of command and control in a society, a government can both control the emission of currency as well as specify the rules of its emission. Results in game theory provide that public monitoring of central bank actions can mitigate deviations from an optimal path. In addition, issuers are likely to renege on promises if the planning horizons are short. Central banks have longer horizons than commercial banks. A sovereign issuer can solve the coordination problem posed by multiple issuers by granting legal tender status to an instrument. It can set a standard by requiring a state-issued currency in the payment of taxes. Second, private issuers of e-cash cannot provide nominal anchors in an economy. Sovereign issuers, in contrast, can provide explicit anchors by accepting their offerings in exchange for government debt.

It is ill-advised for a government/central bank to install many non-trivial frictions or speed breakers in the circulation of bank deposits in the form of pecuniary costs. By instituting a bail in clause in the banking legislation, it is undermining its self-determination. Money, after all, is (cash plus) deposits. Our reading is that the implicit objective is to continue with the transformation of banks into 'wealth managers' and depositors into rentiers. Financial institutions will rely more on wholesale funding for large-scale projects. The latter, in turn, will be supported by a bevy of derivatives, swaps and options, and new-fangled permutations and combinations of vanilla instruments. The view is that since face-to-face banking and long-term credit relationships have come a cropper, contributing mainly to the non-performing assets (NPAs) of the Indian banking system, only finance can contribute to the correct pricing of risk. Second, international finance will only enter for the attraction of sophisticated and diversified portfolios. Infrastructure funding is likely to be included as we observe below.

In the pyramidal structure of the squaring of debts, the central bank has a critical role to play as clearing house at the pinnacle. The function of clearing house as a last resort would be an appropriate point to introduce digital payments into the discussion. The furor and confusion around Bitcoin and the evident volatility generated by that medium of exchange is another motivation. A characteristic of digital currencies is that unlike banknotes and coins, the settlement is not concluded by the simple movement of the instrument initiated by one set of fingers to another. A ledger or a record-keeping system must be in place to establish property rights in the instrument. That is to say, users of digital currencies must establish trust in the financial intermediaries that provide the ledger services. In the case of sovereign digital money or e-money, every financial institution participates in the maintenance and updating of the ledger. The ledger is not public property. Settlement is concluded by adjusting the reserves of commercial banks with the central banks via a system of trustworthy institutions like banks and central banks. Blockchain technology has made secure bookkeeping systems called distributed or public ledgers publicly accessible. The prognosis is that this innovation is poised to sharply increase the speed of settlement times between dealers while, at the same time, reducing the not-inconsiderable costs.

We cannot underline the central bank–commercial bank identity enough. It is always sufficient to fix ideas by referring to the history of the Fed (Hetzel 2018). The real bills doctrine held initial sway during the creation of the central bank of the US in 1912. A bank would never be liquidity constrained because its assets were self-liquidating debt, its loans being automatically repaid in the process of producing and distributing commodities. The founders of the Fed endorsed this view and the attendant eschewing of long-term capital projects because they contained elements of the unknown. The logic led to the creation of regional banks that would supply Federal Reserve credit through the discount window. The opposite of this view was money creation independent of production. The violation of real bills precepts lead to euphoria and depression. Under unduly optimistic expectations about the future, households and firms will hold excessive debt. Comeuppance follows with deleveraging and inactivity. For a contemporary example, a change in the collateral framework of the European Central Bank in 2012 reduced the cost of funding loans to a set of SMEs in France (Cahn, Duquerroy, and Mullins 2017). Directly targeted monetary policy, it transpired, was an effective instrument to increase credit in the recession. The medium was banks with which firms had exclusive long-term and soft relationships. Banks invested in providing continuous finance over the cycle while keeping a close watch on leverage ratios and other stock-flow norms all through. Incentives did not turn perverse, nor were attempts to transfer risk made. The causal efficacy of a drop in the probability of default was observed. The flipside is of significance. Banks that propagate the downturn by reducing lending would prompt defaults in borrowers and the shock would transmit through to their suppliers.

Pathologies result when the link is snapped. Such seems to have become the case of the link between credit and real activity in India. Increased credit disbursements do not result in increased flows in the production of goods and services. Credit instead is directed to the purchase of the stock of existing assets, especially land, and to financing margins on futures and options. The policy option is clear, even if unconventional: the monetary authorities must simply and credibly reassign credit to social welfare–enhancing schemes (Stiglitz 2017). The aftermath of the financial crisis has given birth to a new form of liquidity trap. Despite the monetary authorities expanding manifold the abilities of banks to lend, the latter were paralysed by risk aversion. The propensity to take risks on the part of banks needs to be scrutinized closely. In fact, when they do loosen their purse strings, they lend generously to those they enjoy multi-period contracting relationships with. Succinctly, banks lend to those like themselves. The ongoing connections can be virtuous or vicious. Bad banks will continue to lend to bad borrowers. The tension between installing speed breakers high enough to stall and obstruct, and throttling the legitimate credit needs of businesses has long been understood well. More positively, the ability of bank managers to ferret out a novel and viable idea that does not fall foul of Basel and the Securities and Exchange Board of India (SEBI) norms will have to be probed deeply. The electronic payments system could facilitate direct control by the monetary authorities over the supply and destination of credit. Say the 'government bank' identifies a small firm with an established investment that desires to make a green investment. The bank simply switches on more 'money' into the account of the firm that can then proceed to hire (wo)men and materials. Many, for well-known reasons, would baulk at delegating the discovery of good investment projects to government employees. One solution is the auctioning off of the rights to issue new credit to private parties. The amounts would be added to the 'money supply' in a given period. The winners of the auctions would maximize the value of their asymmetric-information-dependent assets subject to the constraints imposed by the government. Commercial banks would not create this credit. They would merely transfer the money from their accounts to those of the beneficiaries. Now, so as to approach full employment, the amount of credit required to be successfully auctioned might imply a negative price. One way to address this scenario is through state-dependent loans. The amount that a business has to repay depends on the state of the world. A recession becomes stubborn when uncertainty about the future

does not evaporate. Consumers are uncertain about their employment, potential investors about their returns. The situation cumu-
lates: as the downturn persists, unemployment increases and sales
fall further. State-contingent auctions provide a direct route to
ameliorating public risk perceptions. By reducing the amount to be
repaid in the state of a severe downturn, the risk of lending goes
down and the supply of loans goes up.

FINANCE: VIRTUOUS OR VICIOUS—I

The object of a financial instrument is risk minimization and is an
indispensable tool to deal with unknown, even rare, but quantifi-
able events to come. Outcomes are unlikely to be as expected and
agents must write price contracts that hedge the future. At all points
of time, however, the terms of the instrument should include the
conditions of the underlying asset. The aberration that occurred in
our times is that the buying and selling of these instruments took on
a life of their own, disconnected from the characteristics of the commodities or assets on which they had been devised. If the buoyancy
of financial trades matches the vibrancy in commodity and labour
markets, a dynamic equilibrium in all markets would be attained.
However, when the pull of finance seduces the resources away from
the production of goods and services, an economy becomes crisis-
prone. The economy then resembles an inverted pyramid as the base
of activity across sectors gets whittled down and the tapering peak,
perversely, flowers and fattens. At some point during the financial
euphoria, the pieces of paper will be called and found worthless
since the underlying asset base has been hollowed out. The concept
includes the financialization of non-financial institutions like firms
and households. One thesis is that financialization is an offshoot of
marketization defined as increasing energies devoted to the buying and selling of securities on financial markets (Godechot 2016).
Banks now support activities through arms-length interventions
rather than long-term relationships sustained through the vicis-
situdes of the cycle. By introducing a standardization of contracts,

marketization smoothens their comparison. Second, these contracts can be liquidated without even a moment's notice, making liquidity instantaneous. The consequence is the attraction of short-term arbitrage and speculation. The organizational structure of the financial sector transforms from bricks and mortar to virtual trading rooms. A consequence of the shareholder-value-maximization model is that the activities of non-financial firms move significantly in the direction of financial activities. When companies issue debt for the sake of investment in plant and machinery, the debt leverages retain earnings (Lazonick 2017). Increasingly, the development and utilization of productive capacity arises in the face of technological obsolescence and fierce competition. Returns take time and are subject to many imponderables. Firms would prefer to be conservative to avoid cash-flow problems. It is likely that earnings would be depleted in stock buybacks. Productive work is marginalized relative to financial productivity. The share of labour declines in the value added. The financialization of the household sector in the aggregate plays out in the following manner. Richer households borrow at low cost and invest in high-return investments. Low-income households are forced into debt at high interest rates and, more importantly, pay high fees on loans that, through securitization, are owned by their rich comrades. To round off the circle, the financial industry receives an income stream from millions of such contracts.

The Bank: Central and Commercial—II

Money, we have proposed, arises in an engagement with debt (Larue 2017). To recap, though any debtor can, in principle, issue an IOU to a creditor, as an institution only commercial bank deposits come to be accepted as money as a generally-circulating IOU. We also recall the chartalist theory of money according to which the power of the sovereign to borrow vests in its power to collect taxes in common coin. Consequently, government deficits are neither good nor bad as a foundation of monetary macroeconomics. Taxes ensure the acceptance of government debt in an economy. They can even be used to reclaim money in the form of repayment of debts. Governments can raise taxes when inflation is high so as to reduce the quantity of money in the economy. Correspondingly, governments can raise debt in conditions of recession. The sine qua non of this familiar account is that the goods and services underpinning debt must respect the principle of effective demand of an economy. As we return to the basics, we see that money financing of the public sector by central banks is a defining characteristic of money (Mercier 2017). The definition applies as well to commercial bank purchases of government securities. In short, the 'money-issuing sector' is the 'banking sector' comprising of central banks and commercial banks. As a nontrivial embellishment of the central bank–commercial bank continuum, the most bare student-friendly accounting examples are worked out by Mercier, where, for instance, a commercial bank purchases a government bond which is, therefore, recorded on the assets side of its balance sheet. However, the government maintains its current account with the central bank. Thus, the commercial bank reports a blank on the corresponding liability head of its balance sheet, matched by a matching blank on the asset head of the central bank. The gap is filled by the commercial bank accessing the central bank through loans. This is the domain of monetary policy proper. 'Who created the money?' asks Mercier. 'The banking sector' is the answer.

We take up the formalities of drawing out the implications of these remarks using our G&C framework. There are no fresh investment plans below and inventory accumulation/de-accumulation stands for formal and informal activity. The assumption is intended to capture the recessionary conditions prevailing anywhere. Second, while the issue of sources of funding is, consequently, not relevant, firms must retain overdraft facilities with their banks for funding draw-ups or drawdowns. Thus, the total bank loans outstanding, LI, is identical to the current level of inventory stocks, I (G&C 1983, 73). For our purposes, this is the only source of private debt, PD. A breakup of national income, Y, into private income, YP, and government income, YG, is needed. It is time to introduce our first SFC norm. End-period debt, PD, is believed to be connected with disposable income by a debt/income norm, $PD = \beta YP$ (G&C 1983, 149). Government borrowing from banks is *GD*. The net government income is denoted as *YG*, where $YG = \theta Y$ and θ is the tax rate or government share of the income (G&C 1983, 107). For later use, we record that final sales, *FE*, is the sum of private sector purchases, *PE*, and government expenditure, *G* (G&C 1983, 102). Putting it together,

$$Y = YP + YG = \frac{PD}{\beta} + \theta Y \tag{3.1}$$

Summarizing,

$$Y = \frac{PD}{(1-\theta)\beta} \tag{3.2}$$

The subtleties are that while an increase in private debt increases national income, as a proportion of the debt-income norm it does not. We should be wary of a high, or worse increasing, private debt–income norm. The other message is clearer. A higher income tax, as a proportion of private debt, increase the gross national product (GNP). The statement is unoriginal. All macroeconomic identities display the positive correlation between income taxation and output. The opposite case is made on the basis of the tenuous neoclassical theorem of the negative effect of taxation on work. In any event, the latter theory triumphs and all fiscal authorities follow suit.

Coming to government debt, an important norm is given by the steady-state money/income norm α (G&C 1983, 84). Denoting by *FA* the stock of money carried over from the last period, outside of the steady state we have:

$$\Delta FA = \alpha \Delta Y = \Delta GD + \Delta PD \tag{3.3}$$

A straight combination of our expressions gives us the following 'multiplier' for government debt:

$$Y = \frac{GD}{[\alpha - \beta(1-\theta)]} \tag{3.4}$$

As with private borrowing, government borrowing too has a positive effect on national income. An increase in the government deficit must mean, with a downward trend in the income tax, an upward hike in the government expenditure.

What about inflation? G&C dig into production processes and present an assembly of concepts connected with costs and prices. The inflation rate is more than the rate of change in the GDP deflator. A master equation in the literature here is a profit equation. Denoting aggregate profits by Π, the product of the wage rate and the number of people employed (the wage bill) by WB, the sales tax net of subsidies by T, and the rate of interest due on the opening value of inventories in the period under study by R, we have (G&C 1983, 186–7):

$$\Pi \equiv FE + \Delta I - WB - T - R.I_{-1} \tag{3.5}$$

The historic cost of the current period sales, HC, is

$$HC \equiv WB - \Delta I \tag{3.6}$$

The profit markup, λ, is

$$\lambda \equiv \frac{\Pi}{(HC + R.I_{-1})} \tag{3.7}$$

Finally, the average sales tax τ is

$$\tau \equiv \frac{T}{(HC + R.I_{-1} + \Pi)} \tag{3.8}$$

Putting equations 3.5–3.8 together, we get:

$$\tau\, \Pi \left(\frac{1}{\lambda} + 1 \right) \equiv T \tag{3.9}$$

We can read causation from one side to the other in the case of identities. Either we conclude that an increase in the general sales tax increases profits or that a rise in profits increases the volume of sales tax. In Indian parlance, the GST is properly a system-wide variable and not a state subject. Its to-ing and fro-ing and mercurial history is an unfortunate blot on our fiscal history. A fall in the degree of monopoly raises sales tax revenue. Here again, it required the newly-elected chairman of the Fed in 1970 to proclaim that inflation was a non-monetary phenomenon (Hetzel 2018). He championed the cause of incomes policy which included government controls on the degree of monopoly or profit markups. Increasing the level of unemployment so as to control inflation was ruled out.

Finance: Virtuous or Vicious—II

A final flow identity concerns the stock of financial assets, A. With this step, we need to introduce capital gains and losses in a revaluation term, RVA. Since there is no fresh issue of bonds and equities in the period, the term stands for capital gains/losses. If we denote the price of financial assets as p_a, the term is captured by $\Delta p_a A$. The macroeconomic expression is

$$\Delta A = \Delta paA \tag{3.10}$$

The solution of the equation is given by an unchanging asset price level, $p_a = p_{a-1}$. Equating the terms with R, the rate of interest on bank money, we have an arbitrage-free equilibrium money–asset price level. We might even state that the asset markets are efficient. Assets are the sum of private debt and government debt, and we can consider two corner solutions.

In the case of the existence of government debt exclusively, the authorities might buy and sell securities so as to sustain a rising or falling asset price level. 'A new era of central banking' is characterized by using forward guidance in the face of the effective lower-bound policy rate problem and the conjecture that the equilibrium real interest rate is very low (van Reit 2017). The monetary authorities in Europe and elsewhere were forced to stare in the face of secular stagnation and seek fiscal support. An additional reason is that the reverse of maintaining low interest rates would, over time, propel the search for yield with all the horrific implications. As a result, central banks entered uncharted territory in modern times with subsidies and taxes in credit relations with banks, credit allocation, and public-debt management. A well-publicized problem is likely to occur with the large-scale asset purchases by central banks. When short-term interest rates rise, they will have to pay a higher return on their liabilities. There could also be valuation losses on their portfolios. Other questions that arose with the European Central Bank (ECB) concerned the extension of the scope of the Bank even to social projects and environmental concerns. The broad consensus is the implanting of employment and growth policies through a central fiscal capacity. Second, the issue of a

sovereign bond has been recommended that will both facilitate financial integration as well as dovetail with the monetary policy stance.
A safe sovereign asset instrument would aid financial stability as it
would meet the demand of banks for liquid assets.

The G&C model can be extended to allow for bank lending not
oriented exclusively to finance working capital and inventory build-
ups (G&C 1983, 85). Thus, the final expenditure, *FE*, would be the
sum of 'income-generated expenditure', *YFE*, as above, and a new
'loan-financed expenditure', *LFE*. Likewise, new loans, ΔL, or private
debt would now include these loan-financed purchases as well. That
is to say,

$$\Delta PD = \Delta I + LFE \qquad (3.11)$$

The left-hand side and the first term on the right-hand side are bound
by the SFCs, while the new term is unbounded. What about government debt? We only have the fiscal stance defined by the ratio of
government expenditure to the tax rate in the steady state. The matter
can be addressed by considering a non-homogenous extension of
equation 3.10. Assume now that there is a change in the book value
of government debt in the period under consideration, ΔGD, and a
change in private debt, including corporate bonds and equity, at given
issue prices, ΔPD (G&C 1983, 274). That is to say,

$$\Delta A = \Delta GD + \Delta PD + \Delta paA \qquad (3.12)$$

In the overall macroeconomic context, we have

$$YP + \Delta PD - (\Delta GD + \Delta PD) - \Delta I = PE \qquad (3.13)$$

We have isolated the term in brackets for highlighting autonomous
borrowing, finance which is unrelated to endogenous income flows.
Actually, ΔPD stands for *LFE* and something similar applies to ΔGD.
Following a cross-country study of 17 OECD (Organisation for
Economic Co-operation and Development) countries over 1997–2007,
Karwowski et al. (2016) conclude that financialization was connected
with asset price inflation, following the Minsky prognosis, and a debt-
driven demand regime, following Keynes' expectation of the economy
of his grandchildren. Financialization means here the outcomes following the systematic deregulation of financial markets since the 1980s. We

follow the implications on household choices concomitant to the ballooning of the assets of institutional investors, such as pension funds, commercial insurers, and investment companies. Their appetite for paper could not be whetted by the equity offerings of commercial firms. Borrowing more from the Keynes conceptual armoury, this time from Kalecki, we have in 'external markets' the relaxation of the aggregate finance constraint (Cesaratto 2016). A distinction is drawn with 'internal markets' earmarked by endogenous money created to finance private and public production. Banks create money (deposits) when they grant loans. Central banks provide reserves in support. The income flow generated by production is distinguished from 'external markets' which do not create capacity. Consumer credit is the trigger. The so-called autonomous consumption will absorb the portion of the surplus that the capitalists do not consume. The purchasing power, thereby, cycles back to the capitalist as profits. Capitalists become creditors. Thus, the falling savings rates in the 2000s have been explained by the wealth effects generated by increasing asset prices. The dilemma that will remain unresolved is that while credit-financed consumption of households will increase in this milieu, the financialization of nonfinancial firms will lower the investment expenditure. The net effect could go either way. To illustrate, let us return to equation 3.12 and assume the other corner scenario for the fresh issue of autonomous debt this time. Now, $\Delta GD = 0$. Furthermore, in the case of new financial instruments being exclusively driven by speculation, we would have market players depending on the current price exceeding the homogenous driver of the asset market. That is to say, the 'particular solution' of the equation would be $\Delta PD = p_a - (1 + \Delta p_a) A_{-1}$. In that case, we have a bubble solution for the difference equation, $A = p_a$. By the same token, in the event of the first scenario of an exclusively government-debt-dominated regime, we would have the complete crowding out of private debt with the 'particular solution' $\Delta BD = BD - (1 + \Delta p_a) A_{-1}$. The solution now for overall debt is $A = BD$.

We cannot be sanguine about government debt in the shape of government expenditure, even under the rallying cry of infrastructure spending. Close observers of President Trump's programme in the US discern a feedback loop leading from financial innovations to augmenting the wherewithal of the rich in the details. Closer home, Laura Bear (2017) has pointed out that the chants getting louder from government circles the world over concerning roads, railways, ports, and infrastructure more generally bear no resemblance to a New Deal or post-war reconstruction effort of decades gone by. They are, in gross travesty, a manifestation of globalized private and financial infrastructure underwritten by government guarantees and home taxpayers. Our model above, in contrast, suggests the well–known and worked-out implementation of public works through bank loans, taxes, and central bank money. The vicious sequence began in the 1980s with the financialization of sovereign debt, which, in turn, led to the fiscal squeeze of the public sector. The consequence was the hollowing out of public works and the explicit encouragement of short-term private contractual labour for the state. Professor Bear provides a detailed study of the transformation of trade and industry along the Hooghly river in Kolkata to marshal the elements of her case. An austerity regime was imposed by the Kolkata Port Trust in the docks in the 1990s. Jobs were cut to a third by 2000. Licensing and outsourcing of labour mushroomed and the de-unionization of labour proceeded apace. Shipyard workers and European firms offered an alternative model founded on a framework of rights and recognition based on mutual respect. The basis was wealth creation and social reproduction by labour. Imageries drawn from iron-working gods and goddesses and kinship relations were evoked to create and cement solidarity. Instead, since 2012 a massive port has been planned under the joint tutelage of the Kolkata Post Trust and the state government. The port is envisaged as a rentier-landlord construct. The rosy scenarios being written do not include the workers whose pitiable situation continues to worsen. Returning to the beginning of the sequence and connecting with our theme, in keeping with the new mood, governments are no more supported by their independent central banks. Instead, they sell bonds to their central banks at market rates and the central banks, in turn, are supported by dedicated banks that trade the paper.

* * *

The monetary and financial arrangements evolve all of a piece differentially in different economies. The policy makers are both the cause and the effect of these processes. We now know that evolutionary stable strategies and equilibria can be inequitable and growth-retarding. Since institutions are human constructs, governments can intervene and rewrite initial conditions so as to generate less unequal and more balanced growth in the future. Thus, while universal banking seemed to come about in the natural order of things, a string of banking crises led policy makers in England and the US to seriously reconsider ring fencing productive from commercial activity. The sanctity of deposits (money) was sought to be secured from the unknown risks attached to large investment projects. The schemes were shot down by the power of financial interests. In other countries, nationalization of banks is looked at afresh with new scripts written that reflect the lessons learnt from the errors committed in the first flush of governments taking control of the commanding heights of the economies. The monetary and fiscal authorities in India will have to be nimble-footed but, at the same time, grounded in their overall orientation. They might have to rely on their own models more and more rather than the wisdom of international monetary and financial crowds. We have not entered open-economy territory, but here as well basic theorems like the impossible trinity are being scrutinized afresh. The future for fiscal and monetary policy cooperation is exciting and policy models must constantly be dismantled and reconstructed on the worktable.

References

Barbosa-Filho, Nelson H. (2017). 'A Vertical Social Accounting Matrix of the U.S. Economy'. The New School, Schwartz Center for Economic Policy Analysis (SCEPA). Working Paper No. 1, May 2017.

Bear, Laura (2017). 'Alternatives' to Austerity: A critique of Financialized Infrastructure in India and Beyond'. *Anthropology Today*, forthcoming.

Bianchi, Francesco and Leonardo Melosi (2017). 'The Dire Effects of the Lack of Monetary and Fiscal Coordination'. Federal Reserve Bank of Chicago. Working Paper 2017–19.

Cahn, Christophe, Anne Duquerroy, and William Mullins (2017). 'Unconventional Monetary Policy and Bank Lending Relationships'. Banque de France. Working Paper No. 659.

Camera, Gabriele (2016). 'A Perspective on Electronic Alternatives to Traditional Currencies, Economic Science Institute'. Chapman University: WWZ, University of Basel, 16 December 2016.

Cesaratto, Sergio (2016). 'The Modern Revival of the Classical Surplus Approach: Implications for the Analysis of Growth and Crises'. Università Di Siena Quaderni Del Dipartimento Di Economia Politica E Statistica. Working Paper No 735, August 2016.

————— (2017). 'Bofinger and Ries versus Borio and Disyatat: Macroeconomics after Endogenous Money'. Università di Siena Quaderni del Dipartimento di Economia Politica e Statistica n.763.

Feigl, Georg, Markus Marterbauer, Miriam Rehm, Mathias Schnetzer, Sepp Zuckerstäter, Lars Andersen, Thea Nissen, et al (2016). Chapter 3: 'Proposals for a policy mix in the Euro area'. In Revue de l'OFCE, Independent Annual Growth Survey (IAGS 2017), 5th Report, pp. 91–127.

Godechot, Olivier (2016). 'Financialization is Marketization! A study of the respective impacts of various dimensions of financialization on the increase in global inequality'. *Sociological Science* 3: 495–519.

Godley, Wynne and Francis Cripps (1983). *Macroeconomics*. Oxford: Oxford University Press.

Hetzel, Robert L. (2018). 'The Evolution of U.S. Monetary Policy'. Federal Reserve Bank of Richmond. Working Paper 18-01.

Karwowski, Ewa, Mimoza Shabani, and Engelbert Stockhammer (2016). 'Financialisation: Dimensions and Determinants. A Cross-Country Study'. Post Keynesian Economics Study Group Working Paper 1619, December 2016.

Larue, Louis (2017). 'Book Review: The Philosophy of Debt by Alexander Douglas, Abingdon: Routledge, 2016'. Institut de Recherches Économiques et Sociales de l'Université Catholique de Louvain (IRES) Discussion Paper 2017-17.

Lazonick, William (2017). 'Innovative Enterprise Solves the Agency Problem: The Theory of the Firm, Financial Flows, and Economic Performance'. INET Working Paper No. 62, 28 August 2017.

Mankiw, Gregory N. and Ricardo Reis (2017). Friedman's Presidential Address in the Evolution of Macroeconomic Thought (November 2017). NBER Working Paper No. 24043.

Mercier, Paul (2017). 'Public Debt, Central Bank and Money'. Banque Centrale du Luxembourg, Cahier D'Études. Working Paper No. 108.

Mongin, Philippe (2016). 'What Are Analytic Narratives?'. HEC Paris Research Paper No. ECO/SCD-2016-1155, 16 June 2016.

Stiglitz, Joseph E. (2017). 'Macro-Economic Management in an Electronic Credit/Financial System'. NBER Working Paper 23032, January 2017.

van Reit, Ad (2017). 'Monetary Policy Stretched to the Limit: How Could Governments Support the European Central Bank?'. ADEMU Working Paper 2017/075.

CHAPTER 4

MONETARY POLICY TRANSMISSION IN INDIA

interplay of rate and quantum channels[1]

K. KANAGASABAPATHY,

REKHA A. BHANGAONKAR, AND

SHRUTI J. PANDEY

A central bank can use quantity or rate as alternative targets/operating instruments and if it chooses one, the other is determined exogenously. Monetary policy in India seems to operate at both ends, liquidity and interest rates, either by intent or by compulsion due to multiple and, at

[1] This paper was originally prepared for the Oxford University Press edition of 2014 and has been partly updated by Shruti J. Pandey and K. Kanagasabapathy for the 2019 edition.

(Authors wish to place on record their sincere thanks to Professor Ashima Goyal and an anonymous referee for their insightful suggestions on an earlier draft, Thiagu Ranganathan for his valuable suggestions regarding the empirical techniques, Vishakha G. Tilak for her valuable assistance in data analysis and graphs, and Rema K. Nair for page formatting.)

times, conflicting choices. While the rate channel is somewhat straightforward to understand and study, the quantum channel gets blurred
as it operates because of the multiple objectives of complex liquidity
management operations. One of the statements repeatedly finding
place in the monetary policy statements of Reserve Bank of India (RBI)
runs like this: 'The Reserve Bank will ensure that appropriate liquidity is maintained in the system so that all legitimate requirements of
credit are met, particularly for productive purposes, consistent with
the objective of price and financial stability. Towards this end, the RBI
will continue with its policy of active demand management of liquidity
through open market operations (OMO), including the market stabilization scheme (MSS), liquidity adjustment facility (LAF), cash reserve
ratio (CRR), and using all the policy instruments at its disposal flexibly, as and when the situation warrants.'[2] Of late, this seems to be the
case with many central banks in advanced countries too. According to
Benjamin M. Friedman and Kenneth N. Kuttner (2011), central banks
no longer set the short-term interest rates that they target for monetary
policy purposes—the way it is described in standard economics textbooks. The explanation for this phenomenon involves several features
of how central banks actually implement monetary policy decisions
in the current era. Central banks tend to use policy interest rate and
the quantity of reserves not as mutually exclusive operations but in
conjunction with each other; this represents a fundamental departure
from decades of thinking about the scope of a central bank's action.

This chapter fundamentally looks at the interplay between the rate
and quantum channels of monetary operations since 2001 when the
new operating procedure of the LAF was introduced as the principal
liquidity management tool. The literature referred to above and the
position the RBI currently takes is that the policy interest rate should
signal the stance of monetary policy, while liquidity may be managed as
required using discretionary instruments depending upon exogenous
movements in the overall liquidity conditions. The RBI has also recently
taken a stand that rate transmission would work better if the LAF is operated injecting or absorbing liquidity within a band of plus or minus one
percentage point of liability of the banking system. Of late, the RBI also
prefers to keep the system in a deficit mode or liquidity injection mode,

[2] Reserve Bank of India (2007), *Third Quarter Monetary Policy Review*.

as research has shown that rate transmission works better in such a situation. This position has not changed fundamentally since the introduction of inflation targeting in February 2015. But the reality is somewhat different. The LAF is only one of the liquidity managing instruments. There are other discretionary operations such as the OMO, the CRR, and foreign exchange operations, all affecting the bank reserves. Against this backdrop, the chapter addresses the broader question that when an easing or tightening stance is taken with regard to policy rate, in terms of liquidity management operations, whether the movement in liquidity and its impact works complementarily to policy rate changes. With this objective, we look at the transmission mechanism of rate and quantum channels, the former captured by the influence of policy rate on other market rates and the latter assessed through the impact of a measure of total liquidity representing the combined impact of all discretionary use of instruments, such as the LAF, the CRR, the OMO, and foreign exchange operations of the RBI on interest rates and non-food bank credit. The period covered by the study is April 2001 to December 2017 and the data used are on a monthly basis, except for the real gross domestic product (GDP) which is on a quarterly basis.

The chapter is sequenced as follows: following the introduction, the first section briefly narrates the changes in policy framework and operating procedures with reference to rate and quantum channels. The next section makes an effort to divide the reference period into easing and tightening phases of the policy cycle and brings out the stylized facts on several relationships, highlighting the impact of policy rate changes and liquidity conditions on short-term and medium-term market interest rates, output, and prices. The section after that attempts a review of literature. The following section provides the results and analysis of a vector auto regressive (VAR) model built upon Granger's causal relations between a set of variables considered.[3] This model covers relevant data from April 2001 to May 2012. For this purpose, we try to first establish the linkage and transmission from policy rate to other short- and long-term interest rates. Second, we attempt to establish a

---

[3] The Granger causality is a statistical hypothesis test for determining whether one time series is useful in forecasting another, first proposed by Granger, C. W. J. (1969), 'Investigating Causal Relations by Econometric Models and Cross-spectral Methods', *Econometrica* 37(3): 424–38.

relationship between policy rate changes and movement in liquidity, and their combined impact upon the bank lending rate, deposit rate, and non-food credit. The last section provides concluding observations.

POLICY FRAMEWORK AND
OPERATING PROCEDURES

In India, the RBI has historically maintained the twin objectives of designing monetary policy to maintain price stability and ensuring adequate flow of credit to productive sectors of the economy.[4] Since February 2015, the objective of monetary policy is to primarily maintain price stability while keeping in view the objective of growth. While these primary objectives continue to govern the policy, there has been a transformation in the monetary policy framework of India over the years. In that process, the operating instruments and their transmission have become increasingly complex.

Before 1985, the central bank's policy was essentially a credit policy with a plethora of controls on interest rates as also the direction of credit flow to preferred sectors and groups of population. During mid-1980s to 1997–8, a monetary targeting framework with feedback was followed, however, in the mid-1990s, the same framework lost its importance because of several other developments along with economic and financial sector reforms. Taking into account the challenges posed by financial liberalization and the increasing complexities of monetary management, the RBI opted to switch to a multiple indicator approach in 1998–9.[5] This broad-based approach has provided the central bank with enormous flexibility in operating policy instruments. The approach changed further in 2015 to allow flexible inflation targeting and the policy rate is being set by a six-members' Monetary Policy Committee (MPC) since 2016–17.

[4] Financial stability has been loosely added as an objective of monetary policy in the recent years. But this objective is being served more by the macroprudential and regulatory policies of the Reserve Bank of India.

[5] Money supply, M_3, continues to be an informative component, but it is not targeted.

The RBI has also been continuing its efforts to develop the money and government securities markets since the mid-1980s with the introduction of new instruments, such as the commercial paper (CP), certificates of deposit (CD), and later collateralized borrowing and lending obligations (CBLO) which expanded the base of the money market. The RBI also initiated auction methods for primary issuance of government securities, including treasury bills which made the government securities interest rates market related. In parallel, the RBI also strengthened institutional infrastructure for trading and settlements, which contributed to the growth of the secondary market. All these enabled the RBI to use a market-based interest rate and liquidity management with an improved transmission of signals.

A snapshot of growth in money and government securities markets during the last decade and a half is provided in Table 4.1. The deceleration in the growth of call/notice/term money market over the

Table 4.1 Growth in volume of government securities markets

Sr. No.	Nomenclature	Volume (INR crore)			Compound annual growth rate percentage	
		2001–2	2011–12	2016–17	2011–12 over 2001–2	2016–17 over 2011–12
1	Call/notice/term money	5,665,108	4,013,031	4,239,394	−3.39	1.10
2	CDs	1,576	419,530	155,741	74.79	−17.98
3	CPs	7,224	91,190	397,965	28.86	34.27
4	CBLO	976,789#	11,155,428	22,751,895	41.61	15.32
5	Market repo	1,560,510#	3,763,877	11,108,253	13.40	24.17
6	Central government securities	1,138,479	3,151,482	15,178,392	10.72	36.94
7	Treasury bills	66,556	334,136	923,221	17.51	22.54
8	Total government securities (6+7)	1,205,035	3,485,619	16,101,613	11.21	35.81

Source: The RBI and the EPWRF.

period reflects the policy shift from uncollateralized to collateralized money market structure. Reduction in the statutory liquidity ratio by the RBI and expectations of an uptick in the banking sector's credit growth resulted in the subdued CD volumes in recent years.

Against this backdrop, the instruments and the related transmission can be viewed in two broad dimensions: first is the interest rate channel and second the quantum channel; while the former is governed by policy rate changes, the latter is captured by liquidity influencing instruments.

Rate Channel

Bank rate is the standard rate at which the central bank is prepared to buy or discount bills of exchange or other eligible commercial paper. In the early stages of liberalization of interest rates in mid-1990s, the RBI attempted to activate the bank rate as the benchmark rate along with the introduction of prime lending rate (PLR). But with the activation of repo operations, repo rate came to be viewed as a market preferred policy rate. This firmed up further when the RBI introduced the full-fledged LAF in June 2000. The LAF is characterized by repo and reverse repo operations of the central bank at prescribed rates, which provide a corridor within which the short-term interest rates can operate. However, this procedure had some limitations as there was no single policy rate instrument defined as such, and the operating policy rate alternated between repo and reverse repo rates depending upon the prevailing liquidity condition. The absence of a firm corridor led the implicit target rate (call rate) to breach the upper and lower limits under easy liquidity or stress conditions. Taking into consideration these shortcomings, a new operating procedure was put in place in May 2011. Following the recommendations of a Working Group to Review the Operating Procedure of Monetary Policy (Chairman: Deepak Mohanty), repo rate is recognized as the only policy rate. All other associated rates, such as the reverse repo rate, bank rate/ marginal standing facility rate—a kind of Lombard rate—have all been linked to the repo rate at prescribed spreads. The inflation targeting framework since 2015 has also followed this approach and the MPC essentially decides upon the policy repo rate. In the current context and for the purpose of this chapter, repo rate has been used as the policy rate transmitting through other short- and medium-term interest rates.

Quantum Channel

In the pre-reforms period up to the 1980s, the liquidity influencing measures consisted of essentially two instruments—the CRR and refinance facilities. When the monetary targeting approach was followed from 1985 to 1997, these two instruments were used to influence primary liquidity, consistent with the targeted money supply. When the framework was changed to multiple indicators, most of the refinance facilities were withdrawn, though some select facilities are still available. Liquidity operations assumed several complexities, though the primary objective of managing liquidity is implicitly to ensure flow of credit to the productive sectors of the economy. Unless liquidity management operations are used in conjunction and in alignment with the policy stance as reflected through rate signals, such liquidity operations may not only counteract the policy's intentions of tightening or easing, but also negate the signalling effect of policy rate changes. For instance, when the policy rate is on a rising path, a cut in the CRR can send a wrong signal.

First are the LAF operations. Repo is used for injecting liquidity and reverse repo is used for absorption of liquidity. These operations are mostly passive in nature, in the sense that the auctioned amount at the prescribed rates is accepted by the RBI. The policy rate corridor around repo rate has been reduced to ±50 bps since April 2016. The RBI has also introduced term repos since October 2013.

With a view to ensure flexibility and transparency in liquidity management operations, the RBI adopted a revised framework for liquidity management with effect from 5 September 2014. The RBI decided to conduct auctions for overnight fixed rate repos (at repo rate) tenor for a notified amount equivalent to 0.25 per cent of net demand and time liabilities (NDTL) of the banking system. Variable rate 14-day term repo auctions at 0.75 per cent of the system-wide NDTL. For the overnight variable rate repo auction, the auction amount, if any, will be decided by the Reserve Bank, based on an assessment of the liquidity conditions as well as Government cash balances available for auction. For overnight fixed rate reverse repo, there is no restriction on quantity. For overnight variable rate reverse repo auctions, the auction amount, if any, will be decided by the Reserve Bank, based on an assessment of the liquidity conditions, and will be conducted on days when it is considered necessary.

Second is the CRR. In the post-reforms period, the medium-term policy was to gradually reduce the CRR to its statutory minimum.[6] But, in response to an unprecedented surge in foreign capital inflows, the CRR has been reactivated since December 2006 both as a liquidity management tool and as an instrument for sterilization of the liquidity impact of foreign exchange purchases by the RBI. The burden on the LAF turned out to be too high and it tended to affect the RBI balance sheet and profits as well. Hence, an increase in the CRR was a less costly option to sterilize capital flows and the RBI considered that the cost of sterilization should be shared by the banking system as well. Since 2013, the CRR has not changed and continued at 4.0 per cent.

Third major liquidity management tool is the OMO, which involves buying and selling of government securities by the RBI to regulate liquidity in the system. As the RBI is also the debt manager, the OMO has also facilitated a smooth conduct of the government borrowing programme, particularly since 2006 when the RBI was prohibited from participating in the primary issuance of government securities.

Fourth, in the wake of very large and continuous capital inflows and the need for modulating surplus liquidity conditions of an enduring nature, the MSS was introduced in April 2004 to equip the RBI with an additional instrument of liquidity management. Under the MSS, treasury bills (TBs) and dated securities of the Government of India are issued to the market, but these funds were not used for budgetary operations. Money raised under the MSS was held in a separate identifiable cash account maintained and operated by the

---

[6] The statutory minimum was 3 per cent, but an amendment to RBI Act in 2006 removed this ceiling.

RBI and the amount held in this account is appropriated only for the purpose of redemption and/or buyback of TBs and/or dated securities issued under the MSS. But, in the post-global financial crisis period, the MSS securities were de-sequestrated to accommodate the government's higher borrowing needs. Thus, while the MSS was not intended originally as borrowing operations for the government during the crisis, the government exploited the outstanding MSS to expand its budgetary operations through the de-sequestration process. This, to some extent, reduced the rollover problem of government debt that would have necessitated fresh borrowings from the market.

Fifth is the RBI's foreign exchange market intervention. Though the RBI's objective behind such operations is to contain rupee-dollar exchange rate volatility, in effect, it also becomes a part of liquidity management operations, since purchase and sale of foreign exchange have the same influence as the OMO in government securities.

Sterilization is a process that attempts to influence the exchange rate without changing the monetary base. It should, however, be noted that the effectiveness of a sterilized intervention is more controversial and ambiguous. By definition, the sterilized intervention has little or no effect on domestic interest rates, since the level of the money supply is left unchanged. However, according to some literature, a sterilized intervention can influence the exchange rate through two channels: the portfolio balance channel and the expectations or signalling channel. Sterilization in India is generally associated with counteracting the liquidity impact at times of buying foreign exchange by the central bank. In late 2011, when RBI was selling foreign exchange to arrest the depreciation of the rupee, it used the CRR to neutralize the liquidity impact on the system.

For purposes of analysis in this chapter, a measure of 'total liquidity' has been compiled by combining the influence of all these instruments during the reference period.

Thus, in multiple objective and multiple instrument frameworks, a single objective may be served by more than one instrument and a single instrument may aim at fulfilling more than one objective, as shown in Table 4.2. Even after the introduction of inflation targeting since February 2015, the RBI continues to use multiple instruments, though repo continues to be the single policy rate.

Table 4.2 Instruments and their objectives

No.	Instruments	Intended objectives	Other assumed role in practice
1	CRR	To control reserve money and thereby M3 growth	Cost-free sterilization instrument
2	LAF–Repo and reverse repo including term repo	Provide a corridor for short-term money market; in particular call money market	Sterilization instrument at a cost
3	OMO	To supplement LAF	Debt management objective
4	MSS	Sterilization	Liquidity management and debt management objective
5	Forex market interventions	Contain volatility of exchange rate	Reserve accumulation and achieve exchange rate objective

Source: The RBI, compiled by authors.

In a nutshell, given this analysis of operating framework and instruments, the operations of rate and quantum channels in the Indian context may be viewed as in Figure 4.1.

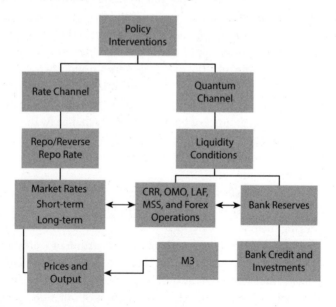

FIGURE 4.1   Schematic representation of monetary policy operations
Source: Authors' presentation.

Trends during Easing and Tightening Phases: Some Stylized Facts

Interest rate cycles follow the changes in the stance of monetary policy and operations from time to time, an easing phase followed by a tightening phase, characterized by falling and rising interest rates respectively. A continuous reduction in the policy rate during a certain period is considered as an easing phase, whereas continued hikes in the policy rate over a period is considered a tightening phase. On this basis, the reference period falls under seven phases— four easing and three tightening phases. Phase I runs from April 2001 to August 2004, an easing phase; Phase II from September 2004 to September 2008, a tightening phase; Phase III from October 2008 to January 2010, an easing phase; Phase IV from February 2010 to April 2012, a tightening phase; Phase V from May 2012 to August 2013, an easing phase; Phase VI from September 2013 to December 2014, a tightening phase; and Phase VII since January 2015, an easing phase. From phase IV onwards, the RBI has used liquidity management tools, such as the CRR, more prominently along with the policy repo rate.

The intensity of easing or tightening can be gauged by the extent of increase in rates in a given cycle, as also from the duration of the cycle. The duration of the cycle was the shortest during the easing phase of the crisis period between October 2008 and January 2010, and the earlier two cycles were much longer at 41 to 49 months from April 2001 to September 2008. The tightening phase after the crisis beginning February 2010 lasted for 27 months up to April 2012 and also during the tightening phase between September 2013 and December 2014. The latter was also a period of external shock. It appears that crisis periods present an aberration from the normal cycles. The easing phase since January 2015 has been a prolonged one.

The policy interest rate has been changed at irregular intervals, sometimes as often as twice a month and at other times as seldom as once in two quarters. Second, the changes have been done in discrete adjustments, typically of 25 basis points (bps).

Liquidity Conditions vis-à-vis Repo Rate Changes

Normally, during an easing phase of interest rates, the liquidity conditions are generally expected to be in surplus and accordingly the RBI is expected to operate on the liquidity absorption mode and vice versa, though there could be some temporary distortions due to frictional factors, such as variations in government cash balances and large payments on income tax due dates. But this was not always the case. The RBI seemed to consistently be in injection mode since about 2010 till 2016 (Table 4.3 and Figure 4.2). It should be noted that while liquidity absorption adds to the cost and reduces the income of RBI, the reverse is the case when the RBI injects liquidity.

It should be noted that absorption/injection of liquidity is captured in terms of a measure of total liquidity in this paper as the combined impact on primary liquidity through the discretionary use of instruments of the CRR, the MSS, the LAF, forex operations, and the OMO.

It can be observed from Figure 4.2 that irrespective of the tightening or easing phases, the RBI was, overall, in a liquidity absorbing mode till mid-2010, allowing huge surplus liquidity conditions in the system. One main reason for this was the enormous capital inflows followed by the RBI's intervention in forex purchases injecting large amounts of liquidity into the system, which in turn needed to be absorbed through various means of sterilization.

The total liquidity in the paper is derived as the combined impact on the primary liquidity through the discretionary use of instruments of the CRR, the MSS, the LAF, forex operations, and the OMO. Through its discretionary operations on liquidity, the RBI periodically ensures liquidity condition reacting to autonomous movements in liquidity caused, for instance, due to the changing government cash balances and currency in circulation. Through its liquidity management operations, the RBI either offsets or complements the autonomous liquidity flows in order to maintain liquidity at the desired level. The chapter attempts to capture how far such discretionary operations on liquidity were consistent with the easing or tightening of policy rates.

During 2002–3, there was a significant increase in capital inflows in India, and the excess capital inflow was managed through day-to-day LAF and OMO, besides other measures, such as building government balances with the RBI, particularly through increased issuances

Table 4.3 Liquidity operations

Phases	Easing Phase	Tightening Phase	Easing Phase	Tightening Phase	Easing Phase	Tightening Phase	Easing Phase
	(Apr '01 to Aug '04)	(Sept '04 to Sept '08)	(Oct '08 to Jan '10)	(Feb '10 to April '12)	(May '12 to Aug '13)	(Sept '13 to Dec '14)	(Jan '15 to Dec '17)
Time durations (months)	41	49	16	27	16	16	36
Change in CRR	8.00 to 4.50	4.75 to 9.00	6.00 to 5.00	5.75 to 4.75	4.75 to 4.00	4.00 to 4.00	4.00 to 4.00
No. of times change	6	13	3	4	3	–	–
Basis points	–350	425	–100	100	–75	0	0
CRR amount (Net Injection (+)/absorption (–))	21,650	–274,000	115,621	–79,669	–25,403	–22,602	–151,842
LAF (Net Injection (+)/absorption (–))	–546,520	–529,746	–1,235,742	1,443,203	1,272,092	546,341	–686,624
OMO (Net Purchase (+)/Net Sales (–))	–121,055	14,123	171,286	259,070	168,297	–27,360	66,218
MSS (Net Injection (+)/absorption (–))	–28,784	–128,001	166,067	7,737	0	0	404,282
Net RBI Intervention in Forex Market (INR crore) (Net Purchases (+)/sales (–))	270,623	490,130	–144,034	–98,371	–77,416	280,053	473,832
Total Liquidity	–404,085	–427,494	–926,802	1,531,970	1,337,570	776,432	105,867

Source: Reserve Bank of India (www.rbi.org.in) & compiled by authors.

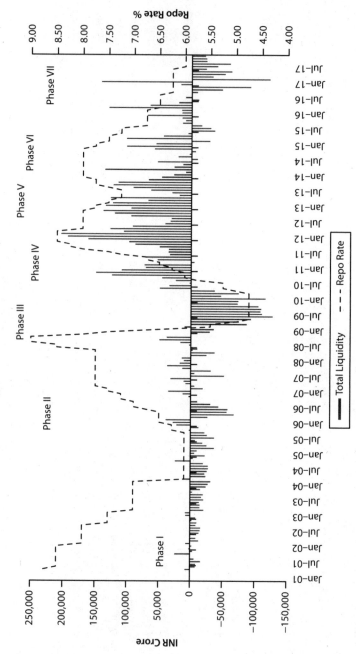

FIGURE 4.2 Movement in liquidity and repo rate

Source: The RBI.

of 91-day TBs and limited forex swaps. Against this backdrop, a Working Group on Instruments of Sterilization recommended that the central government issue a special variety of bills/bonds for sterilization purposes. The Committee recommended that to operationalize such a new instrument of sterilization and ensure fiscal transparency, a new instrument named the MSS be made functional from April 2004. The introduction of the MSS has succeeded broadly in restoring the LAF to its intended function of daily liquidity management. The RBI used multiple instruments, such as the LAF, the OMO, the CRR, and the securities under the MSS, to modulate the liquidity in the system. The RBI also took recourse to increasing the CRR for banks to withdraw excess liquidity from the system.

The period 2004–5 to 2007–8 continued to witness a huge inflow of foreign capital and the RBI had to reckon with its impact on domestic liquidity in several ways. First, the central bank intervened in the foreign exchange market partly to arrest excessive rupee appreciation and partly to build up foreign exchange reserves to more comfortable levels. The foreign exchange reserves increased from USD 18.5 billion in April 2004 to USD 314.6 billion in May 2008. The RBI also used liquidity management tools, such as the CRR and the LAF along with the newly introduced the MSS, to absorb excess liquidity flows into the system through purchase of foreign exchange, termed as sterilization operations. Furthermore, to arrest the inflationary impact, the RBI also hiked the policy repo rate. Thus, the repo rate was raised from 6 per cent in April 2004 to 9 per cent in July 2008.

During 2008–9, after the fall of Lehman Brothers, the impact of the global financial turmoil impacted India too, exploding the myth of decoupling of countries such as India from global shocks. During the crisis period, the RBI had used unconventional instruments to keep the system afloat with abundant liquidity through cuts in the CRR, policy interest rates and through a variety of liberal refinancing instruments.

The system since 2004, therefore, was generally experiencing surplus liquidity conditions and hence the interest rates ruled relatively easy throughout till the last quarter of 2010, though the market interest rates were responding to policy rate changes. The broad objective of RBI's liquidity management operations was to ensure that liquidity conditions do not hamper the smooth functioning of financial markets and disrupt flows to the real economy (Gokarn 2011). According to Patra and Kapur (2012), during the episodes of excess liquidity (2001 through 2006 and again from 2008:Quarter$_4$ (Q_4) to 2010:Q_2, the reverse repo rate was the effective policy rate. On the other hand, during episodes of monetary tightening/liquidity shortage (2007:Q_1 to 2008:Q_3 and 2010:Q_3 to 2011:Q_4), the repo rate became the effective policy rate. Thus, the policy rate, during the post-2003 period, switched between repo and reverse repo rates, but mostly remained closer to the reverse repo rate due to surplus liquidity conditions. Since 2013 for a prolonged period up to 2016, the RBI had been in an injection mode. One reason is that its decision to keep its system in a deficit mode (too much of absorption also puts pressure on the RBI profits). Towards the end of that period, the RBI turned to the absorption mode because of the huge liquidity increase on account of demonetization and capital inflows.

It can be observed from Figure 4.3 that the overnight call money rate for most of the period till mid-2010 hovered around the reverse repo rate. Ghosh and Bhattacharyya (2009) show the dominance of policy interventions in the overnight money market.

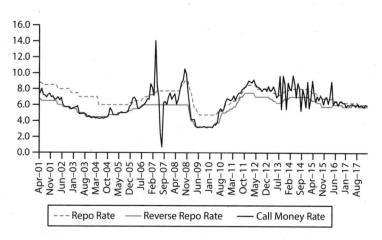

FIGURE 4.3   Repo and reverse repo rate and call money rate
Source: The RBI.

Repo Rate and Market Interest Rates

A hike in policy rate was followed by a rise in short-term market rates, such as the call money, 91-day TBs rate, and one-year government securities (g-sec) rate and vice versa (Table 4.4). While the one year g-sec rate was more elastic, this impact petered out as the maturity increased, showing that longer term rates are influenced by an additional set of factors such as current and future economic activity, output gap, fiscal policy, and the global environment. This was particularly so in the third and fourth phases of the policy cycle. As shown earlier, surplus liquidity conditions that prevailed during most of the reference period also contributed to lower long-term interest rates. However, this trend was not observed during the last three phases. Market rates have not reacted exactly the same way they did during the previous phases. Despite the repo rate hike, market rates saw a declining trend, indicating that they were leading the policy rates and not vice versa. Hence, even before January 2015 when the repo rate was reduced, market rates had already declined.

This could also be attributed to the segmented and still a captive market for government securities from the banking system on account of high statutory liquidity ratio (SLR) and administrative directions applicable to long-term investment institutions, such as insurance companies and provident funds. The ten-year security prices being more sensitive to yield rate changes, markets have a tendency to respond in anticipation to the policy rates changes.

Response of Banking Indicators

Commercial banks were observed to have generally responded to repo rate changes by adjusting both their deposit and lending rates (Figure 4.4).

It appears that while adjusting these rates, the banking system tried to maintain the spread between deposit and lending rates intact. In fact, the spread seems to have widened in the last phase of the easing cycle. Commercial banks also tend to adjust their portfolios of assets

Table 4.4 Short-, medium-, and long-term market rates

	Easing phase (Apr' 01 to Aug' 04)	bps	Tightening phase (Sept' 04 to Sept' 08)	bps	Easing phase (Oct' 08 to Jan' 10)	bps	Tightening phase (Feb' 10 to Apr' 12)	bps	Easing phase (May' 12 to Aug' 13)	bps	Tightening phase (Sept' 13 to Dec' 14)	bps	Easing phase (Jan' 15 to Dec' 17)	bps
Repo rate	8.75 to 6.00	−275	6.00 to 9.00	300	9.00 to 4.75	−425	4.75 to 8.50	375	8.00 to 7.25	−75	7.50 to 8.00	50	7.75 to 6.00	−175
No. of times change was made	5		9		6		12		4		3		7	
91 T-bills	7.53 to 4.59	−294	5.00 to 7.60	260	7.03 to 3.78	−325	3.78 to 8.48	470	8.38 to 10.97	259	10.24 to 8.22	−202	8.18 to 6.22	−196
Call money rate	7.53 to 4.36	−317	3.5 to 14.81	1131	17.89 to 2.99	−1490	3.27 to 8.39	512	8.09 to 5.43	−266	9.65 to 8.91	−74	5.57 to 6.04	47
1-year G-sec	8.94 to 5.26	−368	5.12 to 8.81	369	7.54 to 4.03	−351	4.96 to 8.17	321	8.03 to 10.21	219	9.71 to 8.23	−148	8.16 to 6.64	−152
10-year G-sec	10.24 to 6.37	−387	6.17 to 8.41	223	7.84 to 7.71	−13	7.77 to 8.66	88	8.56 to 8.42	−14	8.49 to 7.93	−56	7.79 to 7.32	−47

bps – basis points

Source: The RBI and the EPWRF.

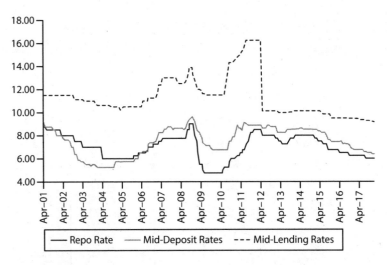

FIGURE 4.4   Trend in mid-deposit rates and mid-lending rates
Source: The RBI.

changing preferences between credit and investments. Monetary policy affecting the willingness of banks to lend is examined either by analysing the portfolio adjustment behavior of banks or the impact on price and non-price term of lending of banks (Bernanke and Blinder 1992: Romer and Romer 1990).

Banks expanded their credit portfolio by reducing their investments during the second phase of the cycle when the system had huge surplus liquidity. But this was also the period of fiscal correction. Later to the global financial crisis, banks seem to have reversed this trend and there is a tendency for investment crowding out bank credit growth (Figure 4.5). During the tightening phase (Feb'10 to April'12), banks seemed to have opted for safer avenues of investment resulting in a compositional shift in their asset portfolios. This can be attributed to increasing non-performing loans and the need for banks to build up additional capital in the run up to compliance with stricter Basel III norms. Lower credit growth can also be partly attributed to lower deposit growth in the period. In recent times, banks' reduced investments in the government securities have resulted in a steep fall in the investment growth.

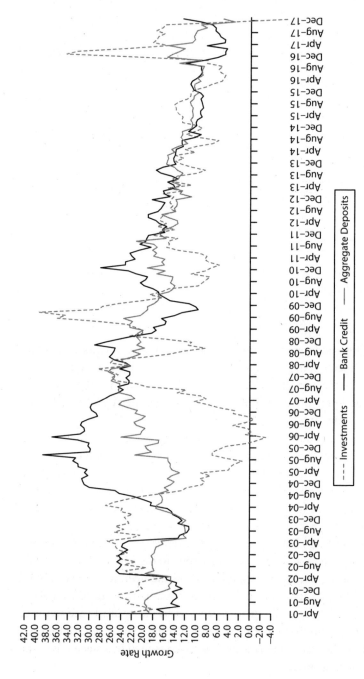

FIGURE 4.5 Trend in deposits, credit, and investments

Source: The RBI.

Commercial banks' investments consist mostly of SLR investments. However, the banks undertake non-SLR investments which comprise commercial papers, shares and bonds/debentures issued by public sector undertakings, private corporate sector, public financial institutions, and other instruments issued by mutual funds. These non-SLR investments are mostly credit substitutes and constituted, on an average, less than 10 per cent of the total investments over the recent period. The total banking assets consist of balances with other banks, money at call and short notice, advance to banks, other assets, investments (SLR), bank credit, loans, cash credit and overdrafts, inland bills, and discounted and foreign bills.

Forex Market Operations and Other Liquidity Operations

If the liquidity management is split into forex market operations and other domestic operations, it is observed that the domestic market operations were more or less a mirror image of forex operations till mid-2008. This signified the counteractive influence of domestic operations to sterilize the impact of forex operations. Since late 2009, however, forex operations had practically been suspended till 2013 when volatility in the forex market compelled RBI to resume forex operations to lift the Rupee from falling steeply (Figure 4.6). Since mid-May 2013, pressure in the foreign exchange market began to increase and in order to curb the excess volatility in the forex market, the RBI instituted various liquidity tightening measures.

CRR and Money Multiplier

A reduction in the CRR impacts the money multiplier as expected with a lower CRR generally leading to a higher money multiplier (Figure 4.7).

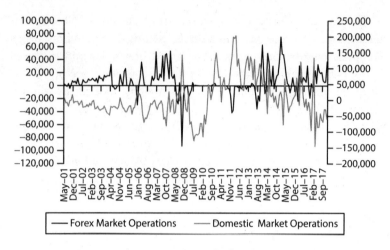

FIGURE 4.6   Forex market operations and other domestic operations
Source: The RBI.

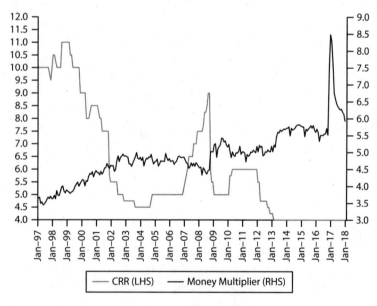

FIGURE 4.7   Movement in CRR and money multiplier
Source: The RBI.

There is an indirect relationship between the CRR and inflation through changes in money supply. A lower CRR leads to a higher money multiplier and thereby higher growth in money supply, higher inflationary pressures and vice versa.

Output and Inflation

Apparently, the impact of easing or tightening of policy is with a lag. A policy-easing phase results in higher growth and higher inflation in the succeeding tightening phase and vice versa. This is reflected both with respect to the GDP growth and growth in the index of industrial production (IIP). With regard to the inflation rate, it is more prominent in the case of wholesale price inflation (WPI); but, the consumer price inflation (CPI) seemed to show some inertia and downward stickiness from October 2008 to August 2013, perhaps contributed by the rising food inflation which has a larger weight in the CPI. During the last phase the consumer price inflation was less than 5 per cent, perhaps due to the generally hawkish stance by the RBI after the introduction of inflation targeting (Table 4.5).

The tight policy stance may not directly address supply-side pressures, but it can certainly help contain the possible spillover from these to a more generalized and entrenched set of inflationary pressures. Oil

Table 4.5 Average monthly and quarterly rates

Phases	GDP*	WPI	CPI	IIP
Easing Phase (Apr 2001 to Aug 2004)	6.32	4.45	3.95	5.48
Tightening Phase (Sept 2004 to Sept 2008)	8.98	6.01	5.88	11.22
Easing Phase (Oct 2008 to Jan 2010)	7.49	3.96	11.05	1.28
Tightening Phase (Feb 2010 to April 2012)	7.75	9.57	10.24	7.04
Easing Phase (May 2012 to Aug 2013)	5.84	6.41	10.53	0.95
Tightening Phase (Sept 2013 to Dec 2014)	6.28	5.27	8.98	1.18
Easing Phase (Jan 2014 to Dec 2017)	6.95	−0.16	4.46	2.29

Source: The RBI; compiled by authors.
*Quarterly average

price shocks appear to have only transitory effects on headline inflation and virtually no impact on measures of underlying trend inflation.

Both directly and via their pass-through, oil price changes have a fairly pronounced impact on the WPI, but not on the CPI (Rakshit 2011). Since prices of petroleum products are fully flexible, but most other prices are fixed on a cost-plus basis, the general price level goes up following a shock, as not only do petroleum prices rise (for clearing the market), but prices of other goods and services also go up (though at a slower rate) due to the oil price pass-through. The northward movement of the general price level as also of relative prices of petroleum products has a contractionary consequence: the former reduces aggregate demand through hardening of interest rates, the latter causes a cutback in expenditure on other products.

It has been well established that a yield spread has a positive influence on output with perhaps some lag, that is, a higher spread is associated with a higher growth and a lower spread with slowdown in growth. It has been observed that the yield spread of one-year and ten-year G-sec evidently has an impact on growth in the IIP (Figure 4.8). It can be particularly seen that the narrowing of the spread around mid-2008–9 is associated with the slowdown in economic activity following the crisis.

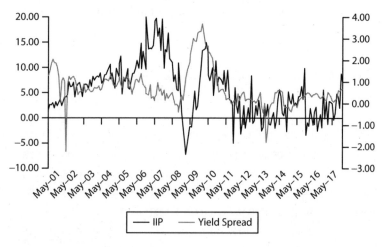

FIGURE 4.8   Movements of IIP growth and yield spread
Source: The RBI.

REVIEW OF LITERATURE

Literature on monetary transmission in India is apparently at a nascent stage mainly due to the under-developed nature of financial markets and quick structural changes. Also, the policy framework and operating procedures are governed by several competing objectives and purposes. Despite these limitations, attempts have been made earlier to study the transmission mechanisms, in particular of rate and credit channels.

Mohanty (2012) used a quarterly structural vector auto-regression (SVAR) model, to find evidence that policy rate increases have a negative effect on output growth with a lag of two quarters and a moderating impact on inflation with a lag of three quarters. The overall impact persists through 8–10 quarters. These results were found to be robust across alternative specifications with different measures of output, inflation, and liquidity. Moreover, significant unidirectional causality was found from the policy interest rate to output, inflation, and various measures of liquidity except broad money (M_3), underlining the importance of the interest rate as a potent monetary policy tool.

Khundrakpam (2011) examined the operation of credit channel of monetary policy transmission in India through changes in policy rate. The period considered was the post-LAF period of $2001{:}Q_3$ to $2011{:}Q_3$. An approach similar to Hendry's general-to-specific method was used for analysis. The paper estimated the lag impact of policy rate on the growth of both nominal and real bank credit. It found that nominal or real bank credit in India is contemporaneously influenced by the corresponding growth in economic activity and nominal or real deposit/money supply growth.

Pandit and Vashisht (2011) examined the transmission of policy rate—repo rate—from the perspective of demand for bank credit in India. Using monthly data during January 2001 to August 2010 in a panel framework of seven emerging market economies including India, they found change in policy interest rate to be an important determinant of a firm's demand for bank credit. Thus, they concluded that monetary policy is an important countercyclical tool for setting the pace of economic activity in India.

Pandit et al. (2006) using a VAR framework on quarterly panel data of banks for 1997 to 2002 found that the changes in the CRR and the bank rate get transmitted to bank lending, with the impact being far more severe on small banks than it is on large banks.

EMPIRICAL ANALYSIS THROUGH VAR MODEL

The continuous evolution of the monetary transmission channel necessitates re-recognizing the interrelation between variables involved in the transmission process. The rate channel, in conventional terms, operates through a short-term rate influencing the term structure of interest rates, including lending rates, in turn influencing the demand for credit and investments, and output and prices thereby. The quantum channel can influence interest rates and also the availability of credit, thereby influencing output and prices. Though the interest rate channel and quantum channel of monetary transmission are thus defined by past literature, we have made an attempt to emphasize the role of the impact of policy rates on market rates and the transmission to output. Similarly from the quantum side, the impact of total liquidity on non-food bank credit and the relationship between the policy rate and total liquidity are attempted to be captured through an empirical analysis. Granger causal relationships among variables were established as a means of deciding the variables involved in the interactive dynamics of monetary transmission. Based on the Granger causal relationship between the variables considered, a VAR model was applied to arrive at the results.

The ability of the VAR framework that treats all variables as simultaneous and endogenous fetches merit in an analysis of monetary transmission (Pandit et al. 2006). Akaike information criterion (AIC) was used to ascertain lag length pertaining to the model. In considering lag length as suggested by the Bayesian information criterion

(BIC), the system suffered from auto correlation in residuals. The stability of the VAR estimates are checked through the Eigen value stability condition. With a stable VAR, impulse response function (IRF) graphs are plotted and the Cholesky forecast-error variance decomposition (FEVD) tables are arrived at. The variables suffered from unit root and hence were corrected for unit root using the first difference.

The structure of the method adopted and the general form equations are as follows.

$$Y_t = \sum_{i=1}^{n} \alpha_{11} Z_{t-i} + \sum_{j=1}^{n} \alpha_{12} Y_{t-j} + u_{1t} \tag{a}$$

$$Z_t = \sum_{i=1}^{n} \alpha_{21} Z_{t-i} + \sum_{j=1}^{n} \alpha_{22} Y_{t-j} + u_{2t} \tag{b}$$

$$Y_t = \beta_{10} + \beta_{11} Z_{t-1} + \beta_{12} Y_{t-1} + \gamma_{12} Z_{t-2} + \varepsilon_{y_t} \tag{c}$$

$$Z_t = \beta_{20} + \beta_{21} Z_{t-1} + \beta_{22} Y_{t-1} + \beta_{23} Y_{t-2} + \varepsilon_{z_t} \tag{d}$$

As the Granger causal relations involve bi-directional estimation of the variables,

Y_t = Response variable

Z_t = Policy variable

$\sum_{i=1}^{n} \alpha_{11} Z_{t-i} = n$ is the lag length, and α_{11} is coefficient matrix of lagged observation of Z_t

$\sum_{j=1}^{n} \alpha_{12} Z_{t-j} = n$ is the lag length, and α_{12} is coefficient matrix of lagged observation of Y_t β = representing the co-efficient values.

The analysis covers the period from May 2001 to May 2012. The frequency of the data is monthly and the data have been sourced from various sources of the RBI and as compiled by the EPW Research Foundation.

In Model I, the variables used are repo (*repo rate*), one-year government security rate (*Onegs*), ten-year government security rate (*Tengs*), the mid-bank lending rate (*Lend*), the mid-bank deposit rate (*Deposit*), and call money rate (*Call*). In building a relationship between short-term and long-term interest rates derived from market and non-market sources, variables were grouped as block 1: *Repo*,

Onegs, and *Tengs*; block 2: *Repo*, *Lend*, and *Deposit*; and block 3: *Repo* and *Call*. The blocks were independently estimated and the Granger causal relationship was derived. Further, the blocks were integrated and their Granger causal relation was re-estimated. Based on the Granger causal results in the blocks' integrated estimation, the VAR equations were re-estimated. As the variables *Lend* and *Deposit* are collinear in nature, they were integrated with other blocks independently.

Model I The system of equations: Rate channel of monetary transmission

$$Onegs_t = f(Onegs_{t-n}, Repo_{t-n}, Call_{t-n}) \qquad \text{Eq.1}$$

$$Tengs_t = f(Tengs_{t-n}, Repo_{t-n}, Deposit_{t-n}) \qquad \text{Eq.2}$$

$$Lend_t = f(Lend_{t-n}, Repo_{t-n}) \qquad \text{Eq.3}$$

$$Deposit_t = f(Deposit_{t-n}, Lend_{t-n}, Repo_{t-n}) \qquad \text{Eq.4}$$

$$Repo_t = f(Repo_{t-n}, Lend_{t-n}) \qquad \text{Eq.5}$$

$$Call_t = f(Call_{t-n}, Repo_{t-n}) \qquad \text{Eq.6}$$

$$LnNonFood_t = f(LnNonFood_{t-n}, Deposit_{t-n}) \qquad \text{Eq.7}$$

Table 4.6 Granger causal results: Model I

Variable 1	Granger causes	Variable 2
Repo **	Granger Causes	Onegs
Call **	Granger Causes	Onegs
Repo ***	Granger Causes	Tengs
Deposit **	Granger Causes	Tengs
Repo***	Granger Causes	Lend
Lend **	Granger Causes	Deposit
Repo ***	Granger Causes	Deposit
Lend ***	Granger Causes	Repo
Repo ***	Granger Causes	Call
Deposit **	Granger Causes	LnNonFood

Note: *** Significant at 1 per cent; ** Significant at 5 per cent; * Significant at 10 per cent.

Source: The RBI.

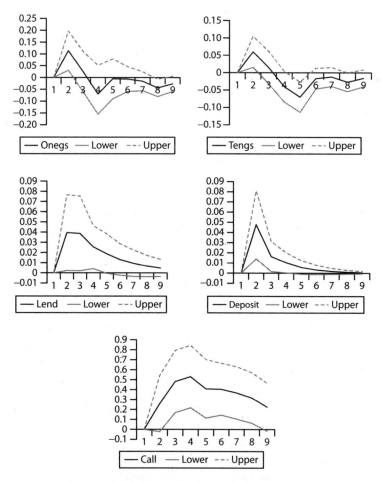

FIGURE 4.9 Impulse response function to change in repo rates: Rate channel (Model I)

Source: The RBI, computed by authors.

The important observations are as follows:

1. One-year government securities and ten-year government securities respond immediately to a shock in repo rates with both showing a peak effect with a similar time lag. The peak effect occurs in the second month from the shock. However, the magnitude of change, as observed, is higher in case of one-year government securities than in the case of ten-year

government securities. The FEVD table explains that lagged values of ten-year government securities have a stronger impact on the current value of ten-year government securities rate in comparison to the lagged values of one-year government security. Eq.1 and Eq.2 were estimated for four lag periods as suggested by the AIC. At the fourth lag, when lagged values of ten-year government securities explained 92 per cent changes in it, only 87 per cent of the changes in one-year government securities could be explained by the lagged values of one-year government securities. The ten-year government securities therefore exhibit inertia to movement, given a policy rate shock.

2. In the short-term interest rate market, the linkage between one-year government security and call money rates is significant as indicated by the Granger causal relation. However, guided by a variance decomposition, the impact of call rate on one-year government securities surfaces only from the third lag. About 6 per cent of the changes in one-year government security is caused by call money rates.

3. Similar to short-term interest rates, in the long-term interest rate market also, ten-year government securities are linked to the deposit rates. But the impact of deposit rates on the ten-year government security market is visible only after the fifth month. Even then, only about 3 per cent of the changes in ten-year government security can be explained by the deposit rate, emphasizing rigidity to movement caused by other factors.

4. Thus, the impact of policy rate on call and one-year government securities which are short-term market rates is clearly established. The influence of policy rate on ten-year government security is weak, perhaps because of the influence of debt management objective being formed through liquidity management by the central bank.

5. The Granger causal relationships suggest that the lending rate influences the deposit rate, but reciprocation of the same is not observed. Both lending and deposit rates peak at the second lag to a shock in repo rate, but both rates behave quite differently. When the lending rate achieves a stable position lasting for about over a month, the deposit rate drops immediately after it reaches the peak effect.

6. Repo rate influences the lending rate only from the third lag, explaining 5 per cent of the changes in lending rates. With about 97 per cent changes in lending rates being explained by their own lagged values, lending rates are stubborn to policy rates changes. In the case of deposit rates, at the second lag when the peak effect is observed, 5 and 4 per cent of the changes are attributed to repo rate and deposit rate. In other words, of the peak effect, only 91 per cent of the changes in deposit rate are contributed by its lagged values. This renders the lagged values and the deposit as rates that are insignificant factors in influencing the prevailing lending rates.

7. A widely spread response curve is observed for call money rates with the peak effect observed after the fourth month. At the peak effect, about 86 per cent of the changes in call money are explained by the lagged values of call money and 14 per cent of the changes are explained by repo rate. This indicates that call money and repo rates operate in close nexus with each other, with repo rates influencing call rates in a unidirectional manner as indicated by the Granger causal relation. This shows that the new operating target of the weighted call money rate introduced recently can be successfully pursued by the central bank.

8. In considering the VAR relationship between non-food credit and deposit rates, the lag length as suggested by the AIC was two time periods. The impact of repo rates on non-food credit, however, is steady at 3 per cent through eight lag periods.

In Model II, the variables used are repo (*repo rate*), total liquidity (*TLq*), and the natural log value of non-food credit (*LnNonFood*). The relationships developed between variables are guided by the Granger causal relationship.

Model II The system of equations: Quantum channel of monetary transmission

$$Repo_t = f(Repo_{t-n}, Tlq_{t-n}) \qquad\qquad \text{Eq.8}$$

$$TLq_t = f(TLq_{t-n}, Repo_{t-n}, LnNonFood_{t-n}) \qquad \text{Eq.9}$$

$$LnNonFood_t = f(LnNonFood_{t-n}, Repo_{t-n}, TLq_{t-n}) \qquad \text{Eq.10}$$

Table 4.7 Granger causal results: Model II

Variable 1	Granger Causes	Variable 2
Repo***	Granger Causes	TLq
TLq*	Granger Causes	Repo
LnNonFood**	Granger Causes	TLq
TLq*	Granger Causes	LnNonFood
Repo**	Granger Causes	LnNonFood

Source: The RBI.

Notes: *** Significant at 1 per cent   ** Significant at 5 per cent
* Significant at 10 per cent

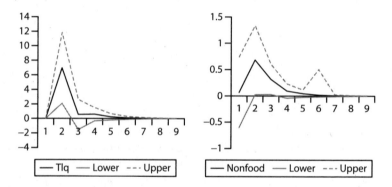

FIGURE 4.10   Impulse response function of repo rate: Quantum channel (Model II)

Source: The RBI, computed by authors.

The important observations are as follows:

1. A bi-causal relation is observed between the total liquidity and repo rates; however, repo has a stronger causal relationship with total liquidity. Total liquidity is estimated as a function of repo rate and non-food credit. From the variance decomposition table, during the peak effect, both the repo rate and non-food credit together explain 9 per cent of the changes in total liquidity.

2. Non-food credit also reaches a peak effect in the second lag with 95 per cent of the changes being explained by the lagged values. Only 5 per cent of the changes are explained by total liquidity

and repo rate together. An insignificant result was obtained between non-food credit and repo rate, indicating that non-food credit remains insulated from the influence of changes in repo rate. Convention suggests a negative relationship between repo and non-food credit; however, in this study, the sign of the non-food coefficient was positive. This is, to a certain extent, reflective of some disharmony between the rate and the quantum/liquidity channels. Even while keeping the repo rate high or while raising the repo rate, liquidity is made available liberally through the use of various instruments, such as the CRR, the OMO, and the LAF, and credit growth is less affected through policy rate changes.

3. This confirms the stylized fact that liquidity, for most part of the reference period, was in surplus mode and bore no relationship with the tightening or easing phase marked by repo rate changes.

* * *

Monetary policy in India operates through a combination of adjustment in policy rate/s and a complex set of liquidity management tools. This chapter captures the interplay between the rate channel and the quantum channel and addressed the issue whether they work complementary to each other. The study covered the period April 2001 to December 2017 through a set of monthly data series (excepting the GDP available on a quarterly basis). The empirical model is, however, restricted up to the end of May 2012. The study of stylized facts after dividing the period into easing and tightening phases showed that:

1. For most of the period, liquidity conditions remained in a surplus mode during both easing and tightening phases, up to 2011, but since then the RBI seemed to have left the system in deficit mode till about 2016 when the system turned to surplus mode again because of demonetization and capital flows. As a result, the interest rate conditions ruled relatively easy during most part, since call money rate hovered around the reverse repo rate.

2. The elasticity of short-term interest rates, such as call and one-year government securities rates to repo rate changes was higher compared to ten-year government securities till 2013. Since then, elasticity has shown a mixed picture.

3. Bank deposit and lending rates showed concomitant changes to the repo rate and banks seemed to have been anxious to maintain their spread between deposit and lending rates.

4. Domestic market operations generally mirrored forex operations due to sterilization attempts by the RBI. Forex operations seemed to have contracted during mid-2008 to mid-2011 due to the hands-off policy of the RBI in the foreign exchange market. Since 2013, the RBI again became active in foreign exchange operations.

5. The CRR impacted money multiplier as expected.

6. Output growth seemed to have responded with a lag to policy easing and tightening. The easing phase resulted in higher growth in the GDP and industrial production in the subsequent tightening phase and vice versa. The WPI inflation showed generally similar responses. The CPI inflation, however, remained sticky in the middle of the reference period and fell significantly in the last two phases.

7. The yield spread between one- and ten-year g-sec seemed to have anticipated growth in industrial production.

8. An empirical analysis using a combination of Granger casual relationships and the VAR model confirmed that short-term responses to a change in policy rate—repo—attains a peak effect in two months' time. While one-year government securities showed a sharp response with a sudden rise and a steep fall, call money rates tend to have a distributed effect with the peak effect occurring only after four months. The long-term interest rate, ten-year government security, also responds to policy shock in two months, but the ten-year government security rate is dependent more on the lagged values of the variable, than on the repo rate.

9. Both the lending and deposit rates reach a peak effect in two months; lending rates hover around an interest rate achieved as a result of the policy shock, but the deposit rates drop immediately.

10. Both total liquidity and non-food credit take a two-month lag for the peak effect to occur. While total liquidity is explained by repo rate and non-food credit, non-food credit is dependent

on the lagged values of the variable. An insignificant positive relationship was observed between the repo rate and non-food credit.

Appendix

Table 4A.1 Cholesky forecast–error variance decomposition table: Model I

Equation 1 Onegs

Lags	FEVD (Onegs)	FEVD (Repo)	FEVD (Call)
1	1	0	0
2	0.94563	0.048281	0.006089
3	0.92953	0.049773	0.020691
4	0.874311	0.063282	0.062407
5	0.875071	0.059415	0.065514
6	0.868341	0.05893	0.072726
7	0.868343	0.059294	0.072364
8	0.859148	0.064351	0.076501

Equation 2 Tengs

Lags	FEVD (Tengs)	FEVD (Repo)	FEVD (Deposit)
1	1	0	0
2	0.948622	0.049168	0.00221
3	0.946051	0.051741	0.002208
4	0.923334	0.071331	0.005335
5	0.842763	0.12303	0.034207
6	0.839156	0.125855	0.034989
7	0.839104	0.126095	0.034802
8	0.8326	0.132979	0.034426

Equation 3 Lend

Lags	FEVD (Lend)	FEVD (Repo)
1	1	0
2	0.970278	0.029722
3	0.944799	0.055201
4	0.934954	0.065046
5	0.929637	0.070363
6	0.927115	0.072885
7	0.92579	0.07421
8	0.925127	0.074873

Equation 4 Deposit

Lags	FEVD (Deposit)	FEVD (Repo)	FEVD (Lend)
1	1	0	0
2	0.904604	0.051083	0.044312
3	0.885652	0.055272	0.059076
4	0.879615	0.056998	0.063388
5	0.87773	0.057517	0.064753
6	0.877131	0.057682	0.065186
7	0.876941	0.057735	0.065324
8	0.87688	0.057752	0.065368

Equation 5 Repo

Lags	FEVD (Repo)	FEVD (Lend)
1	1	0
2	0.933966	0.66034
3	0.92213	0.07787
4	0.911984	0.088016
5	0.908594	0.091406
6	0.906476	0.093524
7	0.90553	0.09447
8	0.905016	0.94987

Equation 6 Call

Lags	EVD (Call)	FEVD (Repo)
1	1	0
2	0.980021	0.019979
3	0.922876	0.077124
4	0.863374	0.136626
5	0.838173	0.161827
6	0.832466	0.187534
7	0.791183	0.208817
8	0.775602	0.224398

Equation 7 LnNonFoodCr

Lags	FEVD (LnNonFoodCr)	FEVD (Deposit)
1	1	0
2	0.964103	0.035897
3	0.964276	0.035724
4	0.96337	0.03663
5	0.963315	0.036785
6	0.963061	0.036939
7	0.963044	0.036956
8	0.963028	0.036972

Table 4A.2 Cholesky forecast–error variance decomposition table: Model II

Equation 9 TLq

Lags	FEVD (Tlq)	FEVD (Repo)	FEVD (LnNonFood)
1	1	0	0
2	0.911754	0.05038	0.037866
3	0.909084	0.0505	0.040416
4	0.908724	0.050831	0.040445
5	0.908677	0.050881	0.040443
6	0.90867	0.05887	0.040443
7	0.908869	0.050888	0.040443
8	0.908869	0.05889	0.040443

Equation 10 LnNonFood			
Lags	FEVD (LnNonFood)	FEVD (Repo)	FEVD (TLq)
1	1	0	0
2	0.953154	0.027043	0.019803
3	0.947642	0.03267	0.019688
4	0.947067	0.33159	0.019774
5	0.94694	0.033278	0.019782
6	0.946921	0.033296	0.01783
7	0.946917	0.033299	0.019784
8	0.946917	0.0333	0.019784

References

Banerjee, Rituparna and Saugata Bhattacharya (2008). 'The RBI's Monetary Policy Reaction Function: Does Monetary Policy in India Follow an Inflation Targeting Rule?'. Mumbai: Indira Gandhi Institute of Development Research (IGIDR).

Bernanke, Ben and Mark Gertler (1995). 'Inside the Black Box: the Credit Channel of Monetary Transmission'. National Bureau of Economic Research (NBER) Working Paper No. 5146.

Bhattacharya, Indranil and Partha Ray (2007). 'How Do We Assess Monetary Policy Stance?: Characteriation of a Narrative Monetary Measure for India'. *Economic and Political Weekly* 42(13) (31 March–6 April): 1201–10.

Bhattacharyya, Rudrani, Ila Patnaik, and Ajay Shah (2010). 'Monetary Policy Transmission in an Emerging Market Setting'. Working Paper No. 11/5, International Monetary Fund.

Bhaumik, Sumon Kumar, Vinh Dang, and Ali M. Kutan (2010). 'Implication of Bank Ownership for the Credit Channel of Monetary Policy Transmission: Evidence from India'. Working Paper No. 988, May. Ann Arbor: William Davidson Institute, University of Michigan.

Dua, Pami and Nishita Raje (2010). 'Determinants of Weekly Yields on Government Securities in India'. Working Paper No 187, Centre for Development Economics.

Enders, Walter (2004). *Applied Econometric Time Series*, 4th edition. USA: John Wiley & Sons Inc.

EPW Research Foundation (2011). 'Liquidity Management Gaining Ground'. Money Market Review, *Economic and Political Weekly* 46(53) (31 December): 69–75.

_____ (2011). 'Cyclical Responses to Monetary Policy'. Money Market Review, *Economic and Political Weekly* 46(12) (19 March): 76–82.

_____ (2009). 'Downward Sticky Lending Rates'. Money Market Review, *Economic and Political Weekly* 46(25) (20 June): 25–31.

_____ (2009). 'Upward Sticky Bank Lending'. Money Market Review, *Economic and Political Weekly* 46(47) (21 November): 27–33.

Friedman, Benjamin M. and Kenneth N. Kuttner (2011). 'Implementation of Monetary Policy: How Do Central Banks Set Interest Rates?'. NBER Working Paper No. 16165, p. 63.

Ghosh, Saurabh and Indranil Bhattacharyya (2009). 'Spread, Volatility and Monetary Policy: Empirical Evidence from the Indian Overnight Money Market'. Macroeconomics and Finance in Emerging Market Economies, *Taylor and Francis Journals* 2(2): 257–77.

Jadhav, Narendra (2005). 'Dynamics of Monetary Policy in Emerging Market Economies: A Case Study of India'. Monograph No. 1.

Joshi, Himanshu (2004). 'The Inter-bank Money Market in India: Evidence on Volatility, Efficacy of Regulatory Initiatives and Implications for Interest Rate Targeting'. Occasional Papers 25(1, 2, and 3 [summer, monsoon, and winter]). Mumbai: Reserve Bank of India.

Kapur, Muneesh and Harendra Behera (2012). 'Monetary Transmission Mechanism in India: A Quarterly Model'. Working Paper Series (WPS) (DEPR), 9 June. Mumbai: Reserve Bank of India.

Kashyap, A.K. and Stein, J.C. (2000). 'What do a Million Observations on Banks Say About the Transmission of Monetary Policy?'. *American Economic Review* 90(3): 407–28.

Khundrakpam, Jeevan Kumar (2011). *Credit Channel of Monetary Transmission in India: How Effective and Long is the Lag?*. Mumbai: Reserve Bank of India.

Khundrakpam, Jeevan Kumar, and Rajeev Jain (2010). 'Monetary Policy Transmission in India: A Peep inside the Black Box'. Reserve Bank of India, Working Paper series, June.

Kramer, Charles F., Hélène K. Poirson, and A. Prasad (2008). 'Challenges to Monetary Policy from Financial Globalization: The Case of India'. IMF Asia and Pacific Department, Country Report No. 08/52, January.

Kumar, Sunil and N.R.V.V.M.K. Rajendra Kumar (2012). 'Sovereign Debt Management and Monetary Policy in India: An Empirical Investigation of Conflict of Interest Argument'. Working Paper Series (WPS) (DEPR), 15 July. Mumbai: Reserve Bank of India.

Mahadeva, L. and P. Sinclair (2002). Introduction: 'The Transmission Mechanism and Monetary Policy'. In *Monetary Transmission in Diverse*

Economies, edited by L. Mahadeva and P. Sinclair, 1–27. Cambridge: Cambridge University Press. doi:10.1017/CBO9780511492488.002.

Mitra, A.K., and Abhilasha (2012). 'Determinants of Liquidity and the Relationship between Liquidity and Money'. Working Paper Series No. 14. Mumbai: Reserve Bank of India.

Mohan, Rakesh (2008). 'Capital Flows to India'. Reserve Bank of India, Bank for International Settlements (BIS), Paper No. 44.

———— (2006a). 'Coping With Liquidity Management in India: A Practitioner's View'. Address at the 8th Annual Conference on 'Money and Finance in the Indian Economy' at Indira Gandhi Institute of Development Research (IGIDR), March 27.

———— (2006b). 'Monetary Policy and Exchange Rate Frameworks: The Indian Experience'. Presentation at the Second High Level Seminar on 'Asian Financial Integration', organized by the International Monetary Fund and Monetary Authority of Singapore, Singapore.

———— (2004). 'Challenges to Monetary Policy in a Globalising Context'. Mumbai: Reserve Bank of India Bulletin, January.

Mohanty, Deepak (2010). 'Implementation of Monetary Policy in India'. Speech delivered by Deepak Mohanty, Reserve Bank of India, at the Bankers Club in Bhubaneswar on 15 March 2010.

———— (2011). 'How does the Reserve Bank of India Conduct Monetary Policy?' Speech delivered by Shri Deepak Mohanty, Executive Director, Reserve Bank of India, at the Indian Institute of Management (IIM), Lucknow, on 12 August. Available at https://www.rbi.org.in/scripts/BS_SpeechesView.aspx?Id=590.

———— (2012). 'Evidence on Interest Rate Channel of Monetary Policy Transmission in India'. WPS (DEPR), 18 May. Mumbai: Reserve Bank of India.

Mohanty, Deepak, A.B. Chakraborty, and S. Gangadaran (2012). 'Measures of Nominal and Real Effective Lending Rates of Banks in India'. Reserve Bank of India, Working Paper Series (WPS) (DEPR) No. 7, 18 May.

Mohanty, M.S. (2002). 'Improving Liquidity in Government Bond Markets: What Can Be Done?' Reserve Bank of India, Bank for International Settlements (BIS), Paper No. 11.

Pandit, B.L., Ajit Mittal, Mohua Roy, and Saibal Ghosh (2006). 'Transmission of Monetary Policy and the Bank Lending Channel: Analysis and Evidence for India'. Study No. 25, January 16. Mumbai: Reserve Bank of India.

Pandit, B.L. and Pankaj Vashisht (2011). 'Monetary Policy and Credit Demand in India and Some EMEs'. Working Paper No. 256, May. New Delhi: Indian Council for Research on International Economic Relations.

Patra, Michael Debabrata and Muneesh Kapur (2010). 'A Monetary Policy Model without Money for India'. Working Paper No. 10/183, August. Washington DC: International Monetary Fund.

Reddy, Y.V. (2002). 'A Short Term Liquidity Forecasting Model for India'. Reserve Bank of India, June 24. Available at https://www.rbi.org.in/Scripts/PublicationReportDetails.aspx?ID=287.

Thorat, Usha (2003). 'Report of the Working Group on Instruments of Sterilisation'. Reserve Bank of India. Available at https://rbidocs.rbi.org.in/rdocs/PublicationReport/Pdfs/40661.pdf.

Virmani, Vineet (undated). 'Examination of Credit Channel of Monetary Transmission in India: Results from Response of Commercial Banks' Balance Sheet to a Monetary Policy Shock'. Working Paper (WP) 2004/09/03. Ahmedabad: Indian Institute of Management (IIM).

CHAPTER 5

··

OPENNESS AND GROWTH IN THE INDIAN ECONOMY

··

SOUMYEN SIKDAR

Since the initiation of economic reforms in 1991, India's economic policy has shifted continuously to outward orientation and market incentives. Imparting a big push to an economy struggling on a low growth trajectory must have been among the main objectives of the architects of policy change. Their expectations were not belied.

If we go back to 1950 and look at the performance over three successive decades, the following picture emerges. Gross domestic product growth rates (at constant prices) for the decades 1950–60, 1960–70, and 1970–80 were 3.9 per cent, 3.7 per cent, and 3.1 per cent respectively; a pretty depressing picture all through. Then came the first noticeable break away from the trend. Over 1980–90, growth jumped to 5.8 per cent and continued at this rate over the next decade too. But the miracle came later. The nine years spanning 2000–9 witnessed uninterrupted growth at 7.2 per cent and China ceased to be the sole poster boy of market reforms and globalization. In the sub-period 2003–9, the growth was actually up there at 8.3 per cent, second only to China's. There was a short but sharp downturn in 2008–9 when the GDP grew by 6.7 per cent but the recovery was fairly quick. It was hoped that India would soon regain its position on the path of dazzling performance. Unfortunately, that did not happen and the slideback continued. Over the last three years or so, the growth engine has slowed down considerably and advance estimates of the Central Statistical Organization (CSO) have put down 6.9 per cent as the most that can be hoped for. This is not good news for sure, but the very fact that 6.9 per cent can cause dejection speaks volumes for what we have managed to achieve over the past quarter century. What was once unthinkable has come within the realm of possibility.

Openness and growth have proceeded in tandem. The trade–GDP ratio (export + import/GDP), the most widely used measure of openness, increased from as low a value as 8 per cent in 1970 to 22 per cent in 2000–1, and to 48 per cent at present. Along with this current account openness, Indian policymakers have taken significant steps to open up the capital account too. There are far fewer restrictions now on the movement of investible funds in and out of the country.

The objective of this chapter is to understand to what extent openness (on both current and capital accounts) has contributed to the Indian growth miracle. As is well known, the link between free trade and growth is a hotly discussed issue and no consensus has emerged from the debate. In this context, the experiences of the newly industrializing countries (NIC), Hong Kong, South Korea, Singapore, and Taiwan, have been intensely studied with mixed conclusions. For some observers, the key element was the successful export of labour-intensive manufactured products throughout the 1970s and 1980s. This, it is maintained, refutes the conventional wisdom that industrial development and growth must take place via import substitution. Others point out that the spectacular export success was actually facilitated by previous import substitution and careful policy planning. There is a plethora of cross-country studies that investigate the growth-openness linkage. They have produced mixed results, with Sachs and Warner (1995), Frankel and Romer (1999), and Dollar and Kraay (2000, 2002) on the supportive side and Harrison (1996) and Rodriguez and Rodrik (2001) strongly on the other. One major conclusion of the last study mentioned is that the robustness of the correlation between openness and growth declines as other variables are included in the model. Dodzin and Vambakidis (2004) use a panel of 92 developing countries over 1960–2000 and conclude that greater openness in trade raises the share of industry in value added at the expense of the agricultural sector. Thus, trade actually facilitates industrialization, contrary to the conventional infant industry argument. Rodrik, Subramanian, and Trebbi (2004) considered the simultaneous effects of institutions, geography, and trade on per capita income and concluded that the quality of institutions matters a great deal for a positive trade-income nexus.

The trade-growth link for India after liberalization has been explored by many economists. Instead of listing them separately, we shall refer to them in the course of our discussion.

Openness–Growth Link

The major channels through which greater openness is supposed to stimulate an economy are as follows:

1. *Demand pull and cost reduction effect* Net exports form an important component of aggregate demand in an open economy. A sustained rise in this component has historically played an important role in the success stories of Japan, the NICs, and more recently China, which has become the workshop of the world. Besides getting an additional source of demand, home producers can import cheaper and better quality inputs and capital equipment from abroad after trade liberalization. Rising demand and falling costs give a strong boost to profits and encourage capital formation and other expansion plans.

2. *Competition effect* Exposure to foreign competition forces domestic firms to improve efficiency for survival. A protected domestic market tends to shelter too many firms. The car industry in Argentina in the 1980s and 1990s is a classic example. Examples from India and other developing countries can be multiplied at will. Greater competition raises the average efficiency by forcing the less efficient firms to contract or shut down. Even the more efficient ones feel the compulsion to pay careful attention to the choice of products, production

locations, and techniques. The industrial structure experiences salubrious 'rationalization'.

3. *Learning effect* Ongoing contact with partners operating with better technology, managerial skills, and marketing networks induces learning that boosts efficiency and competitiveness over time. Historically, this has been one of the most prominent sources of *dynamic* gains from trade. The efficiency improvement due to combined competition and the learning effect is supposed to show up in improvement in total factor productivity (TFP) of an open economy. TFP growth as an index of efficiency has many limitations, but it remains the most widely used measure nevertheless.

   The strength of the learning effect depends on the quality and other characteristics of the trade basket of an economy. For countries seeking to move up the value ladder in the international network of production and distribution, changing the export composition from resource-based (RB) low technology (LT) to medium technology (MT) or high technology (HT) products is essential.

4. *Capital inflow effect* Openness involves freer movement of both commodities (and services) and investible funds. Capital inflow may be either long term foreign direct investment (FDI) or short term foreign portfolio investment (FPI). Of the two, FDI has the potential to act as a vehicle for transnational transfer of technological knowledge and managerial skills. This has a positive supply-side effect and tends to pull in local investments. The benefit once again should show up in the growth of TFP. The benefits of FPIs, on the other hand, are supposed to flow by improving the depth and liquidity of the stock market and by stimulating investments through a reduction in the cost of capital.

Let us now take a look at how effective these channels have been for the Indian economy. Though I shall mostly concentrate on the period since 1991, it is worthwhile to pause briefly to consider the 1980s. The general consensus seems to be that the first noticeable departure from a dismal trend happened in the early years of that decade.

The next section surveys the 1980s. Subsequent sections follow the openness-growth story in the following sequence: (*a*) the performance of the three sectors—services, agriculture, and industry; (b) the product structure of trade, (c) competition and productivity effects, (d) capital inflows and exchange rate policy, and (e) regional growth. The penultimate section gives a brief description of the impact of the global financial crisis (GFC) on India and the final section presents the conclusions in summary form.

THE 1980S

The growth spurt over the 1980s may safely be taken as domestically driven. Policy reforms during this period mainly focused on domestic industrial liberalization rather than foreign trade. Hardly anything was done to expose the industry to external competition. Import liberalization related to inputs and components, which actually raised the effective protection of final products. According to Rodrik and Subramanian (2005), in the early 1980s there was a significant attitudinal change on the part of the national leadership, signaling a shift in favour of the private sector. The fillip to business confidence and profitability stimulated investment in a big way. As a proportion of the GDP, investment accounted for 18.27 per cent over 1971–80, but for 1981–90 the figure was significantly higher at 22.04 per cent. Public investments over the latter period grew at 6.89 per cent per annum, while the rate for private investments was 7.60 per cent. The jump in the investment ratio was accompanied by improvements in productivity of capital as reflected in the drop in the incremental capital–output ratio (ICOR) from 5.98 to 3.65 over the same periods (Rakshit cited in Basu 2006). Sectoral contributions to the GDP growth during the latter period were: 27.5 per cent (agriculture), 28.9 per cent (industry), and 43.6 per cent (services). International trade accounted for a small part of the economy with the trade ratio standing stagnant at around 14 per cent over the 1980s, an increase of a mere 4 per cent over the previous decade. Moreover, the bulk of the trade, almost 80 per cent, was in goods and this was actually in deficit. Services trade was more or less balanced. All this suggests that the degree of integration with the global market was rather weak and that the growth boost was largely due to increase in domestic investments and the productivity of capital. There was to be a drastic deceleration in public investments (with an absolute decline in three successive years) in the second half of the 1990s and private investments would follow suit. In India, there is strong evidence of complementarity or 'crowding in' between public and private investments, so that changes in government investments can have a significant impact on the economy's overall investment ratio and growth. No wonder then that with the deceleration in public investments, continuing the domestic engine of growth became weaker and weaker. The consequences would have been really dire but for the emergence and growing power of an external engine in the form of services exports.

Many studies have econometrically examined the exports–growth nexus for the Indian economy. Pradhan (2011) may be taken as typical. Considering the period 1970–1 to 2008–9, he found evidence for both short-run and long-run relationships between exports and output growth. The direction of causality ran from export growth to GDP growth, but there was no reverse causation. Also, a long-run relationship could be detected between net capital flows and non-agricultural GDP.

We now turn to the narrative of sectoral performances in foreign trade, starting with the star of the show.

SERVICES

In the 1990s, the speed and depth of integration went on increasing. The trade–GDP ratio had already reached 22.1 per cent by 2000–1. In sharp contrast to the 1980s, goods exports now failed to keep pace with imports and ran into persistent deficit while the net export of services accelerated. The chief contributory factor was our ability to capitalize on a great change in the technology of production and distribution. IT-aided modularization and fragmentation led to a dramatic reversal of the process of vertical integration and enabled the MNCs to bring together resources, ideas, and skills from different regions of the world to lower the cost of producing a good or delivering a service. India, with its huge stock of scientific and technical manpower and significantly lower wage rate, naturally emerged as a leader in the export of business services. From an average of 6.2 per cent in 1980–95, the growth rate of such services rose to 21 per cent during 1996–2004 and further to 27 per cent during 2005–11. The share in world exports of commercial services climbed steadily to reach the value of almost 4 per cent in 2011. Over the same period, agriculture was nearly stagnant and industry grew at a much slower pace. Sectoral shares have been deeply impacted as a result of this pattern of uneven sectoral growth. The services component swelled and swelled and commands about 57 per cent share in the GDP at present.

Export oriented services are not the only type that have witnessed rapid growth since the early 1990s. Rate of expansion of telephone services or miscellaneous communications services have over some periods, 1992–6 for example, actually exceeded that of business services (Nagaraj 2008). But since 2006, business services have continued to dominate.

It is worth noting at this point that the Indian services sector is not homogeneous and displays a distinctive dual character. The unorganized part of it that is not directly linked to external demand actually accounts for no less than two-thirds of the total output. But recent growth (in terms of value added) in the sector has undoubtedly been dominated by growth in the organized component that responds positively to the growing global demand. In terms of growth of output, however, the unorganized sector has not been negligible. For most periods in the past two decades, it has actually outpaced the manufacturing sector. These traditional services are usually provided by small enterprises and are likely, in recent times, to have been gaining in importance as subcontractors to large firms. There are indications of significant spillover of the telecommunications revolution into the unorganized segment. This intra-services interlinkage is still awaiting careful empirical investigation.

AGRICULTURE AND INDUSTRY

The GDP share of agriculture has been declining continuously and quite steeply since the 1950s. In the course of the last two decades, it has fallen from around 40 per cent to almost 15 per cent. This decline is the direct consequence of a persistently low rate of growth relative to the other two sectors. Greater openness of the economy has failed to provide a stimulus because agricultural exports never really picked up in the era of greater global integration. In our reforms program, industry was taken up first, then trade, and then finance. Agriculture got the least attention. On the external front too, prospects were fairly depressing. Yielding to the pressure of their immensely strong farm lobbies, the developed countries did not (and still have not) opened up their markets to agricultural imports from the developing world. At home, the pressure on fiscal consolidation coupled with the inability to bring down subsidies and other unproductive populist transfers led to sharp cutbacks in public investments. Agriculture and infrastructure were the worst sufferers. A possible diversification into horticulture and livestock was hampered by the poor state of cold storages, refrigerated transport, insurance, and organized marketing. Thus, the negative effect of stagnant external demand has been reinforced by persistent decline in domestic investment and serious deficiencies in infrastructural facilities. Indeed, with the domestic supply-side constraints being so severe, it would be foolish to hope that better access to the markets of developed countries will automatically provides the necessary fillip to dynamism and growth. For the major crops, both acreage and yield have tended to stagnate, as noted by the Economic Survey of 2011–12 (GOI 2012) in detail. The Survey contains a long list of 'options for addressing supply-side constraints', but all action seems to end there. Nothing is said about a sustained government initiative (actual or planned), either at the central or the state level, for easing or removing these constraints.

As a proportion of the agricultural GDP, subsidies have been rising steadily since the 1970s while public investment has declined almost continuously since around 1980. The bulk of public investments in agriculture is in surface irrigation. As in education, expenditure in rupee terms is a poor index of addition to real productive capacity. And whatever real capacity is created fails to be properly utilized due to inefficient local level management and poor maintenance. Spending on rural electrification, roads, storage facilities, and provision of extension services has declined sharply over the years.

Given its strong complementarity with private capital formation, the slowdown in public investment has had very serious negative consequences for the overall GDP growth in general and agricultural performance in particular. The expectation of the government that enough private sector funds will flow into the areas it was withdrawing from proved wildly off the mark. The explanation lies in a conjunction of factors. The public goods nature of most infrastructural services, return uncertainty, lumpiness of investment, and heightened difficulties of procuring finance in the new deregulated environment all played their part in discouraging private entry into the field. It is important to keep in mind in this context that India's emergence as a major provider of IT services undoubtedly owed much to the unleashing of private energy through deregulation and external sector liberalization, but equally important were the availability of skilled scientific and technical manpower in the major metropolitan centres and the massive extension and improvement in telecommunication facilities. In all this, planned public investment played a decisive role. Fund and infrastructure requirements of most IT units are considerably smaller than those of capital-intensive manufacturing, but in no way does it detract from the government's positive role in laying the foundations of our glorious 'services revolution'.

The relative stagnation of the manufacturing sector (it has managed to hold its sectoral share at an average of 22–3 per cent over 1980–1 to 2009–10) can be explained by the increased competition from China in the global market, larger import penetration in some important segments, persistent inefficiency, and, very crucially, serious deficiencies in such basic infrastructural facilities as ports, roads, and power. Deceleration in public investments has acted as a major damper on private capital accumulation. While managing to avert the fate of agriculture, manufacturing has failed to keep pace with the burgeoning tertiary sector.

Even external capital has failed to provide adequate succour. After a brief period in the early 1990s when foreign companies took a lively interest in investing in Indian manufacturing, the FDI flows dramatically shifted towards newly emerging tertiary activities in which the problems of outdated technology, poor supporting infrastructure, and inflexible labour laws (and militant trade union-ism) were far less serious. In China, the workshop of the world, manufacturing continues to account for more than 70 per cent of the net FDI every year. In respect of the FDI in manufacturing, Thailand, Malaysia, and the Philippines are all substantially ahead of us.

In their work on the FDI and the Indian economy Dua and Rashid (1998) took the index of industrial production as the measure of economic activity. Causality tests suggested that FDI flows (approved and actual) respond to the level of industrial production, but actual flows do not cause industrial output.

The overall health and dynamics of manufacturing have also been adversely affected by the absence of a broad industrial base in the rural areas. Here, the contrast with China is remarkable. The Chinese Township and Village Enterprises (TVEs) formed an integral part of a vibrant rural enterprise boom triggered by the initiation of reforms in the late 1970s. Trade liberalization was successfully decentralized to provincial and local levels and the TVEs participated vigorously in the growth of exports. Their efficiency, already higher than that of state owned enterprises, was boosted by sustained gains in the TFP over time (Bardhan 2010; Lardy 1992). The absence of anything comparable in our countryside has without a doubt weakened the ability of foreign trade to bring about broad-based industrial transformation and is also responsible in a big way for the much-lamented muted impact of reforms on rural poverty.

PRODUCT STRUCTURE OF TRADE

It is not merely export growth that is important but its quality as well. Stimulus to growth through exports will be stronger if the composition changes in favour of more skill-intensive and more technologically sophisticated products. The following table presents the export and import shares of four broad product groups.

Table 5.1 Product structure of export and import

Product groups	1985		1996		2000		2006	
	Export	Import	Export	Import	Export	Import	Export	Import
Labour and resource intensive	42.2	8.2	48.5	9.7	55.9	23.8	31.2	10.8
Low skill and technology intensive	2.5	8.9	6.2	5.6	5.1	3.7	9.4	10.1
Medium skill and technology intensive	5.8	17.0	6.3	16.6	6.2	7.4	7.9	7.9
High skill and technology intensive	4.2	17.0	8.6	20.4	12.3	34.7	10.1	37.3

Source: Bhat (2011).

In exports, the share of labour and resource-intensive goods fell substantially between 1996 and 2006. Medium and high skill products gained in importance, though not very dramatically. Table 5.2 tells a similar story.

Table 5.2 Export composition (percentage share in exports)

Product Groups	2000–1	2010–11
Engineering goods	12.4	23.63
Petroleum products	1.66	16.59
Gems and jewellery	16.75	13.75
Textiles	24.26	9.34
Agriculture and allied	8.8	6.97
Ores and minerals	2.62	4.42
Leather and leather goods	4.41	1.59
Electronic goods	2.54	3.36
Chemical and related products	14.61	12.93

Source: Bhat (2011).

The shares of engineering goods and petroleum products have gone up and those of textiles and leather goods have come down substantially. The share of petroleum products has undergone a quantum leap from 1.6 to 16.5 over the last decade. Compared to their status in 1990–1 (8 per cent, not given in Table 5.2), chemical and related products have grown in importance. Electronic goods have looked up, but only marginally. The surge in demand from China explains the rise in ores and minerals. Gems and jewellery have held their position steady.

Though the movement up the value ladder of industrial exports has been encouraging, there is much scope for improvement here. In manufacturing, our comparative advantage has remained mostly stable over four decades. As part of the global supply chain, China, Malaysia, and the Philippines import components, assemble and re-export high and medium technology products on a big scale. India remains a marginal player in this field. This has slowed the process of technology upgradation and skill improvement in the industry. To benefit more substantially from globalization India needs to broaden its trade beyond a narrow category of services. For that to happen, our manufacturing-cum-export-oriented infrastructure has to be expanded and improved. The incentive regime still favours the domestic market and the protection of inefficient industries still persists, though at a lower level compared to the pre-reform days. The involvement of MNCs in the Indian export activities is still relatively low and has limited our ability to utilize their marketing networks and skills. Affiliates of multinationals in India contribute less than 5 per cent of our total exports, whereas the corresponding contributions exceed 50 per cent for China and Malaysia.

Import composition has also undergone significant change. Though petroleum and related products continue to dominate (30 per cent on average), there has been a perceptible shift away from petro-products towards crude imports following significant rise in refinery capacity. Actually from 2001–2, India has transformed itself from a net importer of finished petroleum products to a net exporter. At the same time, the shares of capital goods and export related items have displayed a more or less upward trend since the 1990s. All these factors are positively correlated with growth.

A detailed study by Goldberg, Khandelwal, and Pavcnik (in Bhagwati and Panagariya 2013) examined the role of imported inputs and product scope expansion in India during the period of trade reforms. It is shown that a large proportion of Indian manufacturing firms added new products to their production lines and these products contributed substantially to manufacturing output growth. A key driver of the process was the expansion in the range of imported intermediate inputs in the wake of substantial tariff harmonization and reduction.

It is also relevant in this context that there have been important changes in India's *export destinations* with the share of the developing countries increasing at the cost of the Organization for Economic Cooperation and Development (OECD). And within the developing countries it is developing Asia (China, South Korea, Hong Kong (China), Malaysia, Thailand, and Singapore) that is gaining in importance. This augurs well because these countries constitute the fastest growing region of the world economy today.

Within the category of business services, there has been a noticeable shift towards more sophisticated, higher value added activities over the last decade. The share of routine programming work and maintenance accounted for 68.9 per cent of the total export revenue in 2001, this had fallen to 33.7 per cent by 2008. Share of software products and the RDES (research, development and engineering services) went up from 10 per cent to 21 per cent over the same period (Dossani cited in Ghani 2010).

An internal study (see GOI 2012) of our exports of the world's top import items using the latest UN commodity trade data shows that: (*a*) in the top 100 imports of the world in 2010, India has only six items with a share of 5 per cent and above and only 15 items with a share of 2 per cent and above, (*b*) among the top 100 items, there are many where the country has acquired competence, but the share continues to be very low. Most of these are simple items like taps, cocks, valves, suitcases, briefcases, school satchels, musical instrument cases, various types of containers, flat rolled iron and steel products, simple electric motors, and generators.

Clearly, there is enormous scope for greater export basket diversification and movement into more sophisticated, more valuable industrial products. A lot needs to be done to have a perceptible share in the leading items of world trade. This may, however, be difficult to achieve without greater involvement of multinationals.

COMPETITION AND PRODUCTIVITY EFFECTS

A large number of studies for developing economies have concluded that increased exposure to foreign competition causes profit margins or price-cost mark-ups to decline, with the largest effect in the most concentrated industries. Thus, liberalization imposes discipline on domestic business and forces it to develop its competitive muscle. Has the disciplining device worked for India?

Balakrishnan et al. (2002) worked with data on more than 3,000 firms over 1988/9–97/8 and found that in the post-reforms period the mark up declined for some types of products (rubber, plastic, petro products, machinery, and transport equipment) while it increased for others (food products, chemicals, basic metals, and metal products). Kambhampati and Parikh (2003) covered 280 firms over 1980–98. Their conclusion is that for firms with an above average export-sales ratio the profit margins improved during 1992–8 compared to 1980–90, but fell in the relatively less export oriented firms. In Goldar and Aggarwal (2005), the competitive effect of the lowering of tariff and non-tariff barriers to manufacturing imports was examined in detail. Evidence for a significant pro-competitive impact (decline in the price-cost margin) was found, particularly for the more concentrated industries. Concomitantly, there was a significant drop in labour's share in value added in the post-reforms years beyond what can be explained by changes in capital intensity.

It is to be noted that even if in the short run the impact of trade liberalization on profitability is adverse, over a longer horizon the damage may be repaired, partially or even fully, if the affected firms succeed in raising their efficiency through restructuring of production, closures and relocations, scaling down of the labour force, mergers and amalgamations, and improvements in organizational management (reduction in X-inefficiency) in general. Such adjustments, if successful, should show up in improvements in the TFP (or its rate of growth), which, despite serious limitations (see Balakrishnan 2011a), continues to be widely used as the indicator of efficiency gain in almost all empirical work.

What is the evidence for India? Table 5.3 gives an idea.

Table 5.3 Sources of growth by major sectors (percentage change per annum)

Period	Output	Output per worker	Factor productivity
Agriculture			
1978–93	2.7	1.3	1.0
1993–2004	2.2	1.5	0.5
Industry			
1978–93	5.4	2.1	0.3
1993–2004	6.7	3.1	1.1
Services			
1978–93	5.9	2.1	1.4
1993–2004	9.1	5.4	3.9

Source: Bardhan (2010).

Annual rate of growth of industrial output between 1978 and 1993 was 5.4 per cent and was 6.7 per cent between 1993 and 2004. The corresponding TFP growth rates were 0.3 per cent and 1.1 per cent. There was considerable expansion of the varieties of imported inputs as well as of new domestic products following reductions in import tariffs on inputs. Goldberg et al. (2013) contains a detailed discussion of this very important gain reaped by Indian firms after trade liberalization. In Harrison et al. (2011), all of the estimated increase in sectoral productivity is due to the scaling down of input tariffs. According to Topalova and Khandelwal (2011), a 10 per cent reduction in tariff leads to a 0.5 per cent increase in the TFP of a typical firm.

Table 5.3 shows that the service sector in India experienced the most significant growth. The TFP in this field jumped from an annual average of 1.4 per cent in 1978–93 to 3.9 per cent in 1993–2004. So, there is a strong correlation between openness and productivity in this vibrant area of the economy.

Balakrishnan et al. (2000) failed to find any significant rise in productivity growth in manufacturing since 1991. Goldar and Kumari

(2003) concluded that the post-reforms deceleration in TFP growth in industry should not be attributed to import liberalization. They suggested gestation lags in industrial projects, underutilization of capacity, and fall in agricultural growth as possible factors contributing to the deceleration.

In principle, the FDI is capable of transforming a developing economy by promoting capital formation and boosting efficiency by bringing over knowledge of new techniques and managerial methods. These beneficial effects, real as they are, are notoriously difficult to isolate and capture in empirical work. Serious as it is, data availability may not be the major problem here. Usually, external sector liberalization forms just one component of a whole gamut of policy reforms that may directly or indirectly impact productivity at the firm level. Disentangling the contribution of foreign investment becomes very difficult as a result. Also, fuzziness of results may be due to the imprecision of the measures of openness or foreign investment or efficiency. A detailed study by Pallikara (2002) contained in a survey report brought out by the Asian Productivity Organization failed to find any significant link between the FDI and TFP growth in India. There was little evidence that openness had any significant implications for R&D expenditure. It is interesting to report in this context Ng's (2006) work on eight East Asian countries. Over 1970–2000 there was evidence of the FDI causing the TFP growth in only two of them. Replacing the TFP by other measures of efficiency also did not change the results much. Actually, most studies on East Asian economies have failed to find much evidence for a significant TFP growth in their years of miraculous growth.

Several studies have demonstrated that the power to assimilate new technology and ideas require a critically high stock of human capital that determines the absorptive capacity of an economy (Easterly 2001). Only beyond that level of human capital does the FDI's impact on growth become discernible. This seems to be a good explanation of the weak FDI-growth link in India (and much of Africa). Also, it is the *quality* of human capital that is critical. Conventional measures of education, such as literacy or school enrollment or expenditure on education, are generally very poor guides to the quality of education imparted.

CAPITAL INFLOWS AND EXCHANGE RATE POLICY

Despite sincere efforts by the Government of India to encourage FDI, capital inflows into the country remain heavily tilted in favour of portfolio investment by foreign institutional investors. The share of FPI in the total net foreign investment in 2009–10 was almost 58 per cent; in 2010–11, the total was lower, but FPI's share was more than 70 per cent of that. In 2008–9, in the wake of the global crisis, the net portfolio inflow actually turned negative while the FDI stood practically steady. In 2010, however, the FPI was the first to recover from the shock and continued on more or less an upward trend till it swerved dramatically down again in the second half of 2011. This underscores the volatility of such flows.

A closer look at the FDI inflows reveals that on average a substantial portion (as high as 29 per cent between 2004 and 2007 according to Nagaraj 2008) goes into acquiring managerial control in domestic companies, which does not add to the real capital stock. Also, a high percentage consists of 'reinvested earnings', which does not represent a fresh flow of funds. Our national accounts show that both the gross domestic saving ratio and the gross investment ratio have been rising steadily over time in close correspondence with each other. Over 2006–7 to 2009–10, for example, both rates hovered around an average value of 33–4 per cent with the investment rate maintaining a slender lead over most of the years. The implication of this close match between the two critical ratios is that the increases in domestic investment have been almost entirely financed by domestic resources with foreign capital playing a modest role at best. It is worthy of note in this context that it is the household segment, and not the private corporate sector, that is chiefly responsible for the sharp rise in domestic savings and investments.

Given the prominence of portfolio funds in the total funds inflow into the economy, an important question concerns their contribution to the nation's growth. The beneficial effects of greater portfolio flow into underdeveloped financial markets are supposed to operate through three main routes: (*a*) it lowers the cost of capital by raising

stock prices (and hence the price-earning ratio) and thereby stimu-
lates new investment, (b) it lowers transaction costs by enhancing
the depth of the stock market, and (c) it encourages savings by providing a new equity instrument to the savers. What is the scenario
for India?

The doors of the Indian capital market were thrown open to
portfolio flows in 1992. It was followed by a considerable stock
market growth. Both the Sensex and the 'depth index' (stock
market capitalization/GDP) rose steadily during the early 1990s.
Rising share prices combined with rising rates of interest (which
were deregulated under financial liberalization) induced a big shift
in corporate financing towards equity. But the trend did not last
long. Using a dataset for three hundred companies over 1990–2001,
Khanna (2002) found that cost of capital declined initially but
started on a reverse trend after 1994. In 2001, it was back at its 1991
level. Meanwhile, interest rates had started to fall. Rising cost of
capital and falling interests restored the previous status of debt as
a more attractive source than equity. The study by Chandrasekhar
and Pal (2006) concludes that the promised benefits of portfolio
inflow have failed to materialize for the Indian economy. Over
time, Foreign institutional investment (FII) activities have come
to mostly be confined to the secondary market for blue chip company shares and direct contact with the real sector seems to have
been lost. Empirical research has failed to unearth any strong link
between stock indices and private corporate investment in the
Indian context.

It was hoped that development of the stock market would encourage the household sector to save and invest more in the newly available equity instruments, but this hope too was belied. After an initial
burst of enthusiasm, domestic savers began to lose interest in the
stock market rapidly, chiefly because they became aware of the widespread malpractices in share trading and company audits. In recent
years, the scenario has changed for the better under the Securities
and Exchange Board of India's (SEBI's) stricter supervision, but
the general public's confidence in stock related activities has failed
to revive. Large swings in stock prices continue to act as a damper
on the enthusiasm of individual investors. As a result, the domestic
investor base remains weak and, instead of gaining in maturity and

depth, our stock market continues to be unhealthily dominated by a small number of big players.

Short-term portfolio flows driven mainly by the prospect of capital gains have enhanced the *volatility* of the stock market. This has been reflected in the volatility of the exchange rate. As a precaution against sudden outflow of short-term capital (hot money) and the consequent turmoil in the foreign exchange market, the RBI has decided to maintain a large stock of foreign reserves mainly invested in low-yielding US T-bills. The paradoxical implication is that capital poor India is providing cheap loan to capital rich USA. Obviously, this perversity is creating serious growth costs. China is doing the same on a much bigger scale. There is an important difference though. Most of China's reserves are 'earned' through a positive trade balance whereas our reserves are basically 'borrowed', generated by surplus in the capital account.

The growth costs of reserves are, however, counterbalanced by their insurance or buffer value in an environment of highly volatile cross-border flow of short-term funds (hot money). A comfortable position in respect of foreign assets is taken by international credit rating agencies as an indicator of good health and enables the country to access the international capital market on more favourable terms.

Addition to the stock of foreign reserves directly translates into growth of high powered money. Fear of inflation led the RBI to undertake sterilization on a substantial scale to sever the balance of payments–money supply link. But sterilization entails significant costs. In particular, contraction of domestic credit on a big scale in a situation of excess capacity and demand constraints has had a serious adverse impact on growth. Over the past few years, the RBI has scaled down its foreign exchange intervention considerably and this negative effect of the exchange rate policy has been mitigated to that extent.

On the important issue of the impact of capital inflows on the volatility of stock returns, international evidence is mixed. In the Indian context, Coondoo and Mukherjee (2004) considered three aspects of the volatility implicit in a given time series data: strength (S), duration (D), and persistence (P). The sample period is from January 1999 to May 2002. The S measure is consistently the largest for the FIIS (sale by the FIIs), followed by the FIIN (net FII) and the FIIP (purchase by the FIIs). In terms of D, the FIIN tended to be in a volatile state for the largest proportion of days in a given period. In terms of P, volatility for all the variables is found to persist for a small spell only.

Openness bestows on an economy the capability to invest beyond its domestic savings by utilizing the savings of foreigners through the current account deficit. Under a flexible exchange system, greater capital inflows potentially boost investment by widening the deficit. A policy that reduces the flexibility of the exchange rate blocks this route or makes it narrower. From this perspective, RBI's policy of heavy intervention in the forex market has entailed some growth cost. This, however, is not easy to quantify. It is worth repeating that the intervention was undertaken primarily to counter volatility and 'maintain orderly conditions' in the forex market. Volatility and the consequent need for RBI action would have been much lower had the flows come to our shores more in the form of long term, stable FDI.

The experience of East Asia has amply demonstrated that inflows intermediated through commercial banks may lead to credit expansion which, instead of stimulating investment, may trigger a consumption boom (with a strong import bias) or a speculative asset bubble (mainly in equity or real estate). Capital takes flight en masse when the bubble inevitably bursts. To avert disasters of this type, the RBI has kept a close watch on bank intermediation of inflows. Kohli (2010) examined the impact of inflows on India's banking sector and found that it has not been very strong. Bank assets as a proportion of the GDP underwent a modest growth of 3 per cent over 1990–2000 and has not risen significantly thereafter. The new prudential norms have induced banks to enlarge their holding of safe government securities to improve the quality of their portfolios, but actual investments in such securities is substantially in excess of prudential requirements. Heightened risk aversion in an environment of heightened financial turbulence has undoubtedly played an important role here. Private domestic credit has expanded much more slowly. Bank financed asset speculation and the resultant banking crises have been successfully prevented, but large-scale fund diversion to safe government bonds has impacted private investment adversely. The drying up of credit has been particularly disastrous for small-scale enterprises. Their export operations have suffered heavily in consequence.

REGIONAL GROWTH

An overwhelming majority of studies in the vast trade-growth literature have worked with country-level income or per capita income.
On the other hand, research on regional growth in India has for
the most part concentrated on issues of convergence or divergence
without paying attention to the role of external sector integration in
the process. Dholakia (2011), for example, analyses regional sources
of growth acceleration in considerable detail without bringing in the
factor of openness at all.

In a novel attempt, Maiti and Marjit (2009) constructed three
indices—the export intensity index, the import intensity index, and
the regional openness index—to scrutinize the impact of export
orientation and import penetration on regional trade and disparity
across 15 major Indian states during 1980–2004. It is indeed very
important for a massively heterogeneous country like India to know
whether greater openness has had an equalizing impact or not. Their
major conclusion is that more open states grew faster by 1–1.5 per cent
per annum. States that were able to change their production structure
towards export production showed greater change in growth. And
this ability was strongly correlated with the quality of institutions
and the prevailing investment climate. Per capita net state domestic
products all grew over the period but at different rates, exacerbating
regional inequality. Dispersion in regional openness seems to have
been a major contributory factor.

INDIA AND THE GLOBAL CRISIS

Initially, India and other emerging economies were hit hard by the
GFC or the Great Recession that originated in the sub-prime housing
market in the USA and then spread rapidly to the rest of the world.
Their recovery was remarkably rapid and spectacular, only to be followed by a sharp downturn since 2010. This was particularly so for

India where the growth rate jumped from 3.89 per cent in 2008–9 to 8.48 per cent in 2009–10 and to 10.26 per cent in 2010–11, but collapsed thereafter to 6.64, 4.74, and 4.98 per cent respectively over the next three years.

To get an idea of the differential impact of the crisis, we note that over 2008–11 the developed countries averaged a growth rate of -4 per cent. Under the eurozone crisis that followed the US sub-prime crisis, the average growth in the euro area was 0.7 per cent. This was far below India's average growth over the decade covering the two crises. The reasons for the remarkably muted impact will become clear in the discussion that follows.

Before touching briefly on the slowdown, let us first have a broad idea about the GFC's impact on India.

(a) *Capital outflow and value of the Indian currency*   The main blow emanated from significant changes experienced in the capital account. While there was no slowdown in the FDI flows, portfolio investments by foreign institutional investors witnessed a net outflow of about USD 6.4 billion in April–September 2008 as compared to the net inflow of USD 15.5 billion in the corresponding period the previous year. This was primarily a flight-to-safety phenomenon. (There was such a flight within the country too as investors shifted from stocks to mutual funds and other safer assets and from private to public sector banks.) External commercial borrowings of the corporate sector also declined sharply between April–June 2008 to April–June 2009.

The heavy capital outflow led to the most precipitous fall in the value of rupee in more than two decades. The possible inflationary impact was muted by the fall in oil prices in the global market. On the positive side, this depreciation had a role in cushioning, to some extent, the drop in our net exports triggered by the drop in the US GDP. The adverse balance sheet effect did not take a devastating form chiefly because of the low share of dollar denominated debt in the liabilities of banks and the corporate sector.

(b) *Impact on the stock market*   Stock prices were severely affected by the withdrawals of the foreign institutional investors.

Huge FIIs between January 2006 and January 2008 drove the Sensex past 20,000 over the period. Equally massive withdrawals caused it to tumble below 9,000 the year after. Both primary and secondary markets got severely disrupted and corporate plans for raising resources for all types of projects, major or minor, had to be either abandoned or put on hold.

(c) *Impact on the banking sector*   Thanks to the RBI's close supervision and oversight, the Indian banking system did not experience any serious contagion. It did not suffer any direct exposure to the sub-prime mortgage assets and even indirect exposure was low. This was generally true of most of the emerging economies. The average capital to risk weighted assets ratio (CRAR) for the Indian banking system in March 2008 was 12.6 per cent, as against the regulatory minimum of 9 per cent and the Basel norm of 8 per cent.

In the aftermath of the turmoil following the bankruptcy of Lehman Brothers, the RBI promptly announced a series of measures, including the provision of additional liquidity support to distressed banks, to prevent a serious disruption of financial activities.

To counteract the fall in net exports and other components of aggregate demand, fiscal stimulus was also initiated promptly and on a substantial scale. The budget deficit, quite naturally, temporarily overshot the limits of Fiscal Responsibility and Budgetary Management (FRBM) Act. But, as a result of these concerted and well-planned efforts, the Indian economy succeeded in averting any major catastrophe.

Regarding the subsequent slowdown in India (and China), according to the IMF (2013), it was caused by the operation of both demand- and supply-side factors. While supply-side constraints have reduced the potential growth, part of the slowdown—in fact, one half for India by IMF's estimates—is due to demand-side factors. The RBI's findings are also similar. Various measures were suggested and tried to reverse the trend.

Interesting as this slowdown is from the macroeconomist's point of view, it does not fall within the purview of our present essay. We conclude this section by noting once again that although the Indian economy is considerably open now, it could escape the global crisis relatively unscathed chiefly due to quick and appropriate action, both on fiscal and monetary fronts, within a tight regulatory structure.

* * *

The major ideas of this chapter can be summarized as follows. Openness to current account trade has indeed played a significant role in India's growth surge. The main drivers have been the lowering of trade restrictions on a wide range of imported technologies and inputs and a spectacular acceleration in the export of commercial IT-enabled services in more recent times. The pull effect of foreign demand has been much weaker for manufacturing and non-existent for agriculture. Manufacturing has suffered from intense Chinese competition no doubt, but domestic deficiencies, such as inadequacy and low quality of basic infrastructure (barring telecommunications), persistence of inefficiency and declining public investments (in both industry and agriculture) have been more important contributors.

On the export front, a movement up the value ladder is noticeable and import composition too has broadly changed for the better. But there is considerable scope for improvement along both dimensions.

Supply-side effects of greater openness working through heightened competition and efficiency improvement have been rather muted and difficult to measure. But there is evidence to show that TFP growth has been stimulated and the boost given by reduction in the cost of importing inputs and technical knowledge has been substantial. Inefficient domestic firms continue to enjoy protection by the government. But for this the dynamic efficiency gains would have been greater.

The FDI has failed to effect any major supply-side change. This is not surprising, given its low share and the deficiencies of complementary local inputs, such as physical infrastructure and human capital. The FPI has been confined mostly to the secondary market and has, on the whole, not succeeded in stimulating real capital formation through any significant reduction in the cost of capital. The stock market remains shallow, dominated by a few big sellers. In spite of better regulation and lower frequency of scams, participation of domestic agents continues to be low and the promised stimulus to household savings has not materialized. On the positive side, a strict supervision of banks in their handling of foreign funds has successfully prevented the occurrence of financial crises that have caused terrible growth disruption in a large number of developing countries.

The objectives of maintaining orderly conditions in the forex market in the face of a volatile FPI and sustaining the confidence of global investors in the Indian economy have led the RBI to run up huge foreign reserves. Attendant sterilization programmes generated by fear of inflation have had a negative impact on growth. Overall, lifting of capital account restrictions has been less beneficial than greater openness on the current account.

The gains from openness have not been shared evenly by the heterogeneous regions of the country. External liberalization may have added to regional disparity.

With better infrastructure, better human capital, less corruption, better management of credit supply to the small scale sector, a broader industrial base in the countryside, a more diversified export basket, closer integration with the global supply chain, and a more favourable FDI-FPI mix, the positive impact of greater openness on growth would have been much higher, more solidly founded, and the fruits of prosperity more evenly shared throughout the economy. A nagging anxiety over the sustainability of the current export-led growth would also have been far less acute in that case.

References

Balakrishnan, P. (2011a). *Economic Growth in India*. New Delhi: Oxford University Press.

———— (ed.) (2011b). *Economic Reforms and Growth in India: Essays from the Economic and Political Weekly*. New Delhi: Orient Blackswan.

Balakrishnan, P., K. Pushpangadan, and S. Babu (2000). 'Trade Liberalization and Productivity Growth in Manufacturing: Evidence from Firm Level Panel Data'. *Economic and Political Weekly* 35 (41, October): 3679–82.

———— (2002). *Trade Liberalization, Market Power and Scale Efficiency in Indian Industry*. Centre for Development Studies, Working Paper (WP) 336.

Bardhan, P. (2010). *Awakening Giants, Feet of Clay*. Princeton, New Jersey: Princeton University Press.

Basu, K. (ed.) (2006). *India's Emerging Economy*. New Delhi: Oxford University Press.

Bhagwati, J. and A. Panagariya (eds) (2013). *Reforms and Economic Transformation in India*. New York: Oxford University Press.

Bhat, T.P. (2011). *Structural Changes in India's Foreign Trade*. New Delhi: ISID, November.

Chandrasekhar, C.P. and P. Pal (2006). 'Financial Liberalization in India: An Assessment of Its Nature and Outcomes'. *Economic and Political Weekly* 41(11) (March): 975–85.

Coondoo, D. and P. Mukherjee (2004). 'Volatility of FII in India'. *ICRA Bulletin* 2: 85–102.

Dholakia, R. (2011). 'Regional Sources of Growth Acceleration in India'. In Balakrishnan (2011b).

Dodzin, S. and A. Vambakidis (2004). 'Trade and Industrialization in Developing Countries'. *Journal of Development Economics* 75: 319–28.

Dollar, D. and A. Kraay (2002). 'Trade, Growth and Poverty'. *Economic Journal* 114(493): F22–49.

Dossani, R. (2010). 'Software Production: Globalization and Its implications'. In *The Service Revolution in South Asia*, edited by E. Ghani, Chapter 4. New Delhi: Oxford University Press.

Dua, P. and A. Rashid (1998). 'Foreign Direct investment and Economic Activity in India'. *Indian Economic Review* 33(2): 153–68.

Easterly, W. (2001). *The Elusive Quest for Growth*. Boston, Massachusetts: MIT Press.

Frankel, J. and D. Romer (1999). 'Does Trade Cause Growth?'. *American Economic Review* 89(3): 379–99.

Ghani, E. (ed.) (2010). *The Service Revolution in South Asia*. New Delhi: Oxford University Press.

Goldberg, P.K., A. Khandelwal, and N. Pavcnik (2013). 'Variety In, Variety Out'. In *Reforms and Economic Transformation in India*, edited by J. Bhagwati and A. Panagariya, Chapter 7. New York: Oxford University Press.

Goldar, B. and A. Kumari (2003). 'Import Liberalization and Productivity Growth in Indian Manufacturing in the 1990s'. *The Developing Economies* 41(4): 436–60.

Goldar, B. and S. Aggarwal (2005). 'Trade Liberalization and Price-Cost Margin in Indian Industry'. *The Developing Economies* 43(3): 346–73.

Harrison, A. (1996). 'Openness and Growth: A Time Series Cross-country Analysis for Developing Countries'. *Journal of Development Economics* 48(2): 419–47.

Harrison, A., L. Martin, and S. Nataraj (2011). 'Learning vs Stealing: How Important are Market-share Reallocations to Industrial Productivity Growth?' NBER Working Paper No. 16733.

Indian Monetary Fund (2013). *World Economic Outlook.* Washington DC: IMF.

Kambhampati, U. and A. Parikh (2003). 'Disciplining Firms: The Impact of Trade Reforms on Profit Margins in Indian Industry'. *Applied Economics* 35(4): 461–70.

Khanna, S. (2002). 'Has India Gained from Capital Account Liberalization? Private Capital Flows and the Indian Economy in the 1990s'. Paper presented at a conference on International Money and the Developing Countries in Tamil Nadu, December.

Kohli, R. (2010). *Liberalizing Capital Flows; India's Experience and Policy Issues.* New Delhi: Oxford University Press.

Lardy, N. (1992). *Foreign Trade and Economic Reform in China, 1978–1990.* Cambridge, UK: Cambridge University Press.

Maiti, D. and S. Marjit (2010). 'Regional Openness, Income Growth and Disparity across Major Indian States during 1980–2004'. Institute of Economic Growth, Working Paper 304.

Nagaraj, R. (2008). 'India's Recent Economic Growth: A Closer Look'. *Economic and Political Weekly* 43(15): 55–61.

Ng, T. (2006). 'Foreign Direct Investment and Productivity: Evidence from the East Asian Economies'. UNIDO Working Paper No. 03.

Pallikara, R. (2002). Chapter on India in *TFP Growth: Survey Report.* Tokyo: Asian Productivity Organization.

Pradhan, N. (2011). 'Openness and Growth of the Indian Economy: An Empirical Analysis'. EXIM Bank Occasional Paper 150.

Rakshit, M. (2006). 'Some Macroeconomics of India's Reform Experience'. In *India's Emerging Economy,* edited by K. Basu, Chapter 5. New Delhi: Oxford University Press.

Rodriguez, F. and D. Rodrik (2001). *Trade Policy and Economic Growth: A Sceptic's Guide to the Cross-national Evidence.* NBER Macroeconomics Annual.

Rodrik, D., A. Subramanian, and F. Trebbi (2004). 'Institutions Rule: the Primacy of Institutions over Geography and Integration in Economic Development'. *Journal of Economic Growth* 9(2): 131–65.

Rodrik, D. and A. Subramanian (2005). 'From "Hindu Growth" to Productivity Surge: The Mystery of the Indian Growth Transition'. IMF Staff Papers 52(2).

Sachs, J. and A. Warner (1995). 'Economic Convergence and Economic Policies'. Brookings Papers on Economic Activities No. 1.

Topalova, P. and A. Khandelwal (2011). 'Trade Liberalization and Farm Productivity: the Case of India'. *Review of Economics and Statistics* 93(3): 995–1009.

CHAPTER 6

....

REFORMS AND GLOBAL ECONOMIC INTEGRATION OF THE INDIAN ECONOMY[1]

emerging patterns, challenges, and future directions

....

NAGESH KUMAR

A major liberalization of trade and investment regimes has taken place since 1991 as a part of the package of reforms undertaken to deepen the integration of the Indian economy with the world economy as a whole. Peak tariff rates came down from 150 per cent in the early 1990s to just 10 per cent by 2007. The quantitative restrictions on imports

[1] This chapter is an updated version of an earlier UNESCAP-SSWA' development paper published in the first edition of *A Concise Handbook of the Indian Economy*, edited by Ashima Goyal. The author is grateful to Chris Garroway for some computations reported, to Helene Meurisse, Quentin Roblin, Neha Aggarwal, Vinod Soman, the ESCAP-SSWA interns in 2012 for their competent research assistance, and to Joseph George and Takuma Imamura, who assisted with the updating of tables. The views expressed are those of the author alone and should not be attributed to the United Nations or its member states.

were phased out and a bulk of the tariff lines (over 70 per cent) have been bound under the World Trade Organization (WTO). Most sectors of the economy are open to foreign direct investment (FDI) today with up to 100 per cent foreign ownership, although sectoral ownership limits apply in service sectors. Since 1992, foreign institutional investors (FIIs) have also been allowed to invest in India. The Indian rupee was made convertible in the current account and the capital account is being opened gradually, including a gradual liberalization of the regime governing outward FDI from India.

These economic reforms have led to industrial restructuring in the country with a focus on competitiveness and global economic integration. The growing economic integration of the Indian economy is reflected in various indicators including the rising share of trade in the economy. The structure and direction of trade have changed over time along with growing magnitudes. An important and more dynamic aspect of India's integration with the world economy is through the growing trade in services. India has emerged as a hub for outsourcing of IT software and other business services, such as business process outsourcing (BPO). India is also attracting attention from major multinational enterprises (MNEs) around the world wishing to make India a hub for knowledge-based services to tap the availability of high-quality–low-cost trained human resources as well as scientific and technological infrastructure. Another aspect of growing global integration is through the FDI—both inward and outward. With a liberal FDI policy regime and a large and growing domestic market among other advantages, India is attracting increasing attention of the MNEs even as Indian enterprises develop global ambitions and undertake outward investments in increasing numbers and with growing magnitudes.

India is known for an impressive turnaround of the external sector from a foreign exchange crisis faced in 1991, when the current account deficit touched 3 per cent of the GDP, to a current account surplus during 2001–4 and the buildup of large foreign exchange reserves. However, the balance of payments situation is yet to become sustainable and continues to face occasional periods of stress linked to the fluctuations in oil prices. This calls for harnessing the opportunities for geographical and product diversification besides deepening the industrial base of the country through strategic import substitution, leveraging the large domestic market. Through a visionary Look East policy (LEP) pursued since 1992, India has taken steps to deepen its engagement with the dynamic East Asian economies through a growing web of free trade agreements (FTAs). Indeed, India is an important part of an incipient broader regional economic arrangement bringing together 16 of the region's largest and fastest growing economies. Therefore, regional economic integration is likely to play an increasingly important role in the global economic integration of the Indian economy in the coming years.

Against that backdrop, this chapter considers the changing trade and investment profile of the Indian economy, highlighting major emerging trends and patterns, the external sector challenges faced, and concludes with a few policy lessons to address them.

MERCHANDISE TRADE

Growth of Merchandise Trade

The reforms of the 1990s led to a rapid expansion of India's trade. The growth rates of India's exports and imports averaged over 10 per cent during the 1990s but stepped up to an average of 22 per cent during 2001/2 to 2008/9. Imports have generally grown at faster rates (25.8 per cent) than exports (20 per cent), as shown in Table 6.1 and Figure 6.1. The global financial crisis, which started with the collapse of the Lehman Brothers in 2007, is a structural break for the world trade, having brought down its growth rate. India's trade has also been affected significantly from it as the average rate of growth of exports and imports has come down during 2009/10 to 2016/17 to 6 and 4 per cent respectively, which is only a fraction of the pre-crisis rates. The values of trade actually shrunk in the four years following the financial crisis. As a result, the current trade magnitudes are actually lower than the peak levels of USD 314 billion for exports (2013/14) and USD 490.7 billion for imports (in 2012/13). This calls for a geographical diversification of trade away from the traditional trade partners and in favour of more dynamic economies in East Asia.

The other noticeable trend is the widening deficit in the balance of trade with imports growing at a faster rate than exports, especially in the pre-crisis period. The trade deficit has snowballed from USD 7–8 billion a year at the turn of century to USD 190 billion in 2012–13, amounting to around 10 per cent of the GDP. Since then, however, trade deficit came down gradually to USD 108 billion in 2016–17 as the oil prices cooled down.

Table 6.1 India's merchandise trade growth rates and balance, 2001–17 (in million USD)

Year	Exports	Imports	Trade balance	Per cent change	
				Export	Import
2001–2	43,827	51,413	−7,587	−0.6	2.9
2002–3	52,719	61,412	−8,693	20.3	19.4
2003–4	63,843	78,149	−14,307	21.1	27.3
2004–5	83,536	111,517	−27,981	30.8	42.7
2005–6	103,091	149,166	−46,075	23.4	33.8
2006–7	126,414	185,735	−59,321	22.6	24.5
2007–8	163,132	251,654	−88,522	29.0	35.5
2008–9	185,295	303,696	−118,401	13.6	20.7
Average growth rate				20.0	25.8
2009–10	178,751	288,373	−109,621	−3.5	−5.0
2010–11	251,136	369,769	−118,633	40.5	28.2
2011–12	305,964	489,319	−183,356	21.8	32.3
2012–13	300,401	490,737	−190,336	−1.8	0.3
2013–14	314,405	450,200	−135,794	4.7	−8.3
2014–15	310,338	448,033	−137,695	−1.3	−0.5
2015–16	262,290	381,007	−118,717	−15.5	−15.0
2016–17	275,852	384,356	−108,504	5.2	0.9
Average growth rate				6	4

Source: Prepared by the author based on data from Economic Survey 2017–18, Statistical Appendix.

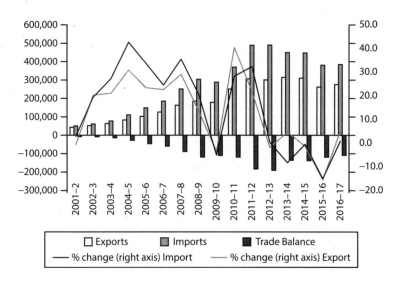

FIGURE 6.1   Growth rates of India's trade 2001–17

Source: Prepared by the author based on data from *Economic Survey 2017–18*, Statistical Appendix.

Changing Structure of Trade

The export structure is expected to change with the level of development from one dominated by primary products to one dominated by products with greater value added. Diversification of the export structure also makes the exporting country less vulnerable to external shocks compared to a country with a more concentrated export structure. Table 6.2 summarizes some important shifts in the patterns of India's export structure over 2000–17. First, as expected, the share of primary products, including agricultural and mineral products, declined steadily from nearly a quarter of India's merchandise exports in the 1990s to 16 per cent at the turn of the century and to just 12 per cent in 2016/17. But, the declining share of India's manufactured exports from a peak of 77 per cent of merchandise exports in 2000/1 to 62 per cent in 2009/10 was a matter of concern, before they recovered to 70 per cent in 2016/17. However, this decline can be seen as a statistical artifact due to the emergence of India as a petroleum refining

Table 6.2 Structure of India's exports from 2000 to 2017

Commodity/Year	2000–1	Share	2005–6	Share	2009–10	Share	2016–17	Share
I. Primary products	7,126	16	16,377	16	23,203	13	33,450	12
Agriculture and allied products	5,973	13	10,214	10	14,727	8	28,388	10
Ores and minerals	1,153	3	6,164	6	8,476	5	5,062	2
II. Manufactured goods	34,335	77	72,563	70	111,327	62	194,356	70
Leather and manufactures	1,944	4	2,698	3	3,278	2	5,183	2
Chemicals and related products	5,886	13	14,770	14	18,147	10	35,071	13
Engineering goods	6,819	15	21,719	21	39,233	22	73,092	26
Textile and textile products	11,285	25	16,402	16	20,611	12	33,711	12
Gems and jewelry	7,384	17	15,529	15	28,639	16	43,510	16
Other manufactured goods	356	1	984	1	1,419	1	3,789	1
III. Petroleum products	1,870	4	11,640	11	28,192	16	31,622	11
IV. Others	1,229	3	2,511	2	16,030	9	17,119	6
Total exports	44,560	100	103,091	100	178,751	100	276,547	100

Source: Extracted from RBI's Handbook of Statistics on Indian Economy, 2017. See www.rbi.org.in.

Note: The figures for 2009/10 onwards follow the revised commodity classification.

hub. Exports of refined petroleum products rose from just 4 per cent of India's exports at the turn of the century to 16 per cent by 2009/10 and accounted for 11 per cent of India's exports of merchandize in 2016/17. If refined petroleum products are considered as value added products like other manufactured and processed products, then the share of manufactured goods in exports comes out to be nearly 81 per cent in 2016/17.

There is also a reorganization of exports of manufactured products as the share of conventional products such as textiles and clothing has declined from 25 per cent in 2000/1 to just 12 per cent in 2016/17. Gems, Jewellery, and leather products have also either stagnated or declined in terms of their share in exports. On the other hand, engineering goods have increased their share from 15 per cent to 26 per cent over 2000–17. Chemicals and related products have maintained their share of 13 per cent in this period. The two broad sectors of engineering and chemicals now account for nearly two fifths of India's merchandise exports and over 55 per cent of manufactured exports.

Among engineering goods, exports of transport equipment rose very fast from less than a billion dollars in 1995 to nearly USD 21 billion by 2011–12. Besides exporting vehicles and two wheelers, India has emerged as a competitive exporter of auto parts and a number of procurement groups of auto companies, such as Delphi Systems (for General Motors) and Visteon (of Ford), have set up procurement subsidiaries in India. This emergence owes itself to a particular strategic intervention by the government in the form of an erstwhile performance requirement that required foreign-owned companies to balance imports by foreign exchange earnings (Kumar 2005).

Chemicals and related products is another group of manufactured products that has improved its share in the total merchandise exports even if only marginally from 10 to 13 per cent over 2009/10 to 2016/17. But among chemicals and allied products, the chemicals and pharmaceuticals group has gained the most. This is due to India's emergence as a major exporter of generic medicines in the world, accounting for a third of global pharmaceuticals exports by volume. A major supplier of cost-effective generics to developing countries and multilateral organizations such as the World Health Organization (WHO) for their health care programmes in developing countries, India is sometimes referred to as the pharmacy of the developing world. This success owes itself to another strategic intervention by the government in terms of the adoption of a patent law that abolished product patents for pharmaceuticals in 1970, which encouraged the development of generics by Indian companies (Kumar 2003).

It is clear that India's export structure has continued to move away from the export of primary and conventional products such as textiles and clothing, leather products, and gems and jewelry towards products with a greater value added, such as transport equipment, generic pharmaceuticals, and refined petroleum products. However, primary commodities and conventional products together still account for as much as 42 per cent of the total merchandise exports. Second, the share of high-technology exports in India's export basket was only 7.5 per cent compared to 25.2 per cent for East Asian countries (World Bank 2017). India has also not been able to make a mark in fast-growing high value added segments of manufacturing, such as electronic and telecom equipment (Kumar and Joseph 2007). In fact, the growing imports of electronic equipment and other hardware are straining India's trade balance, as observed later. India has also not been able to exploit the job-creating potential of exports and has been unable to develop highly labour-intensive export-oriented industries such as toys and electronic assembly, among others (RIS 2006).

India's import structure has also changed over the years, as summarized in Table 6.3. First, bulk imports comprising crude oil, raw materials, and certain foods accounted for as much as 45.7 per cent of the total merchandise imports in 2012/13, but declined to 36.4 per cent in 2016/17 as the oil prices came down. As oil prices have begun to rise again in 2018, their share is likely to go up again. In recent times, imports of coal, coke, and briquettes, etc. have also risen sharply from USD 3.9 billion to USD 15.7 billion as some Indian business houses invested in coal mines in other countries such as Indonesia and Australia to secure reliable and stable supplies of coal for their thermal power plants. Considering that the demand of bulk imports that are mainly raw materials and foods is relatively price-inelastic, one needs to pay attention to the rising imports of capital and other manufactured goods in the context of the rising

Table 6.3 Structure of India's imports from 2005 to 2017

Commodity/Year	2005–6	per cent	2012–13	per cent	2016–17	per cent
I. Bulk Imports	61,086	41	224,238	45.7	139,314	36.4
A. Petroleum, crude, and products	43,963	29.5	164,041	33.4	86,866	22.7
B. Bulk consumption goods	2,766.6	1.9	13,995	2.9	17,865	4.7
C. Other bulk items	14,357	9.6	46,203	9.4	34,583	9
II. Non-bulk imports	88,080	59	266,498	54.3	243,427	63.6
A. Capital goods	37,666	25.3	95,234	19.4	96,970	25.3
Machinery and machine tools	11,086	7.4	34,485	7.1	31,698	8.3
Electronic goods	13,242	8.9	32,906	6.7	41,941	11
Transport equipment	8,838.5	5.9	21,289	4.3	21,224	5.5
Project goods	882.7	0.6	6,554	1.3	2106	0.6
B. Mainly export related items	18,641	12.5	40,866	8.3	41,928	11
C. Others	31,772	21.3	96,759	19.7	71,218	18.6
1. Gold and silver	11,318	7.6	55,679.3	11.3	29,329	7.7
2. Artificial resins and plastic materials, et cetera	2,267.7	1.5	9,989.6	2	11,961	3.1
3. Professional, scientific controlling instruments, photographic optical goods	1,972.7	1.3	3,756	0.8	3,849	1
4. Coal, coke, and briquettes, and so on.	3,868.7	2.6	15,438	3.1	15,715	4.1
5. Medicinal and pharmaceutical products	1,027.9	0.7	5,465	1.1	4,998	1.3
6. Chemical materials and products	1,052.5	0.7	4,862	1	5,367	1.4
D. Other commodities	9,643.2	6.5	33,639	6.9	33,311	8.7
Total imports	149,166	100	490,737	100	382,741	100

Source: RBI's *Handbook of Statistics on Indian Economy, 2017*. See www.rbi.org.in.

trade deficit. Among the capital goods, major categories included machinery accounting for USD 32 billion, electronic goods worth USD 42 billion, and transport equipment making up USD 21 billion in 2016/17. In particular, imports of electronic goods are rising rapidly and are expected to grow to USD 400 billion in a few years, according to some projections.[2]

In this context, it is also worth looking at the trends and patterns in India's import dependence for final consumption. Using the input-output tables for India, Kumar (2018) finds a sharp rise in the share of imports in final consumption over 2001–11, particularly in Electrical and Optical Equipment (from 20 per cent to 52.2 per cent), Machinery, n.e.c. (from 5.9 per cent to 15.1 per cent), Transport Equipment (from 0.5 per cent to 4.7 per cent), and Other Non-Metallic Minerals (8.3 to 37.1 per cent). Given the weight of these sectors in the manufacturing value added, he concludes that the country was witnessing a premature deindustrialization or 'hollowing out' of the industry during the period. The demise of India's fledgling electronic hardware industry can partly be explained in terms of India's premature signing of the WTO's Information Technology Agreement 2000. It exposed Indian manufacturers to direct competition with established rivals in East Asian countries that have massive scales of production due to their links with multinational supply chains. It is in these categories of imports that an attempt needs to be made to pursue strategic import substitution to leverage sizeable domestic markets to develop domestic supply capabilities that will also generate value added and jobs while helping to moderate the trade deficit (Kumar 2018).

Changing Geography of Trade

A major transformation has taken place in the direction of India's trade in terms of declining dependence on conventional trade partners, such as the European Union and the United States, and diversification of trade in new and emerging markets. As Table 6.4 shows, the share

---

[2] See http://www.thehindubusinessline.com/industry-and-economy/electronic-goods-import-up-30-to-rs-157-lakh-cr-in-201112/article4512418.ece?homepage=true&ref=wl_home. Last accessed on 12 June 2019.

Table 6.4 Changing direction of India's trade, 1990–2016

	Per cent share in	1990	2000	2010	2016
North America	Imports	12.66	7.05	6.05	6.55
	Exports	16.14	23.34	11.50	18.01
	Trade	**14.14**	**14.58**	**8.34**	**11.41**
European Union	Imports	33.67	21.20	6.05	11.13
	Exports	28.87	24.47	18.64	17.60
	Trade	**31.62**	**22.78**	**14.64**	**13.87**
Association of Southeast Asian Nations (ASEAN)	Imports	6.77	8.72	8.46	10.76
	Exports	4.27	6.47	10.33	10.18
	Trade	**5.70**	**7.69**	**9.19**	**10.51**
South Korea	Imports	1.36	1.97	2.83	3.43
	Exports	0.92	1.08	1.63	1.36
	Trade	**1.17**	**1.56**	**2.37**	**2.55**
Japan	Imports	7.51	4.01	2.36	2.76
	Exports	9.30	4.16	2.16	1.46
	Trade	**8.27**	**4.08**	**2.28**	**2.21**
China	Imports	0.13	2.88	11.78	16.99
	Exports	0.10	1.79	7.86	3.42
	Trade	**0.12**	**2.38**	**10.26**	**11.24**

(cont'd)

Table 6.4 (cont'd)

Per cent share in		1990	2000	2010	2016
Australia	Imports	3.15	2.12	3.44	2.45
	Exports	1.03	0.95	0.74	1.12
	Trade	2.25	1.59	2.39	1.89
ASEAN+6 subtotal	Imports	19.17	19.87	29.07	36.54
	Exports	15.73	14.6	22.80	17.65
	Trade	17.70	17.46	26.63	26.92
South Asia	Imports	0.46	1.10	3.59	4.03
	Exports	3.06	4.29	5.00	6.48
	Trade	1.57	2.48	2.30	5.07
Middle East	Imports	17.82	8.45	26.76	19.94
	Exports	6.74	11.05	19.96	18.26
	Trade	13.10	9.64	24.11	19.23
Africa	Imports	2.89	6.09	8.58	7.05
	Exports	1.84	4.28	7.04	7.76
	Trade	2.44	5.26	7.98	7.35
Latin America and Caribbean	Imports	2.24	1.53	3.88	5.15
	Exports	0.44	2.26	4.18	3.95
	Trade	1.47	1.86	3.99	4.64
World	Imports (in million USD)	23,991	50,260	350,780	356,320
	Exports (in million USD)	17,811	42,464	222,907	261,862
	Total trade (in million USD)	41,803	92,723	573,687	618,182

Source: Extracted from International Monetary Fund (IMF), Direction of Trade Statistics 2017, available at www.imf.org.

of the EU in India's trade in 2016 was less than half of what it was in 1990. Similarly, North America's share came down from 14 per cent to 11 per cent over the same period. Japan's share in India's trade is now only a fourth of what it was in 1990. The trade structure is gradually diversifying in favour of emerging countries in the Asia-Pacific region and beyond. The most impressive rise is that of China from a negligible share in 1990 to over 11 per cent of India's trade by 2016, making China the single largest trade partner of India.

ASEAN's share in India's trade also went up from 5.7 per cent to nearly 10.5 per cent in 2016. China and ASEAN's emergence explains the rising share of ASEAN+6 countries, namely China, Japan, Republic of Korea, Australia, and New Zealand that are India's partners in the East Asia Summit (EAS), in India's trade from 17.70 per cent to nearly 27 per cent between 1990 to 2016. The shift in the geography of India's trade from the advanced economies of the West to East Asian economies did not happen automatically but was a result of a conscious and well thought out strategic policy pursued since 1992 called the Look East policy. However, India's trade with China is heavily tilted in favour of imports, unlike that with other trade partners in ASEAN+6. Another region rising in prominence as a trade partner is the Middle East with its share in India's trade nearly doubling between 1990 and 2010 to 18.9 per cent, mainly on account of India's high dependence on the region for fuels. But trade with the Middle East is also increasing because of India's growing exports of manufactures, sometimes trans-shipped through the region to other countries like Pakistan. Shares of South Asia, Africa, and Latin America and the Caribbean have also risen very fast from rather low bases. In particular, it is worth noticing that the share of South Asian countries in India's trade not only doubled between 2000–16 but is also much more balanced across imports and exports, unlike in 2000 when the share in exports was more than four times as much as in imports. With unilateral offers of market access on a duty-free-quota-free basis to the least developed countries (LDCs) in South Asia, abolition of the negative list for the LDCs under the SAFTA, and a bilateral FTA with Sri Lanka, South Asian countries have been able to expand their exports of value added products to India, sometimes through India's outward FDI. Yet, the potential of intra-regional trade is far from being realized because of high cost of trade due to poor land transport connectivity and facilitation (UNESCAP 2013, 2018).

Decomposing Sources of Growth of India's Exports

A country's exports grow due to the growth of global markets in the products it exports (growth effect), due to improved competitiveness of its exports (competitiveness effect), due to diversification into new markets (markets effect), or due to diversification into new products (products effect). The constant market share (CMS) analysis is a technique applied to decompose the possible role of these factors in explaining the export growth of countries (Tyszynski 1951; in India's context, see Tiwari 1986). In what follows, we examine the results of an exercise done to analyse the factors contributing to India's export growth over 2000–10. The exports were grouped into 10 1-digit Standard International Trade Classification (SITC) categories and the time series was divided into two 5-year averages to suppress random yearly fluctuations. Exports to major markets, namely the EU, USA, Japan, East Asia, ASEAN, China, SAARC, Africa, and Central and South America, and the Caribbean, that absorb 80 per cent of India's exports, are analysed using data from the United Nations Conference on Trade and Development (UNCTAD).

Table 6.5 summarizes the decomposition of different effects in the CMS analysis. The most important contributor to exports growth was the growth effect explaining 44 per cent of export growth, indicating the fact that India was able to benefit from the expansion of world trade over the past decade. This also explains the declining magnitudes of India's exports in recent years with the declining

Table 6.5 Sources of India's export growth, 2000–10

	Size of the effect (in million USD)	Percentage share
Growth effect	56,700	44.30
Competitiveness effect	47,600	37.19
Product effect	13,200	10.31
Market effect	10,500	8.20
Total change	128,000	100

Source: ESCAP calculations based on UNCTAD statistics. See UN-ESCAP-SSWA (2013).

rates of world trade in the aftermath of the global financial crisis. The next most important effect accounting for 37 per cent of export growth was increased competitiveness in the products it has been exporting. The contribution of product diversification and market diversification is positive but relatively modest. Therefore, the potential for the diversification of the export structure and of geography remains to be fully exploited. Although the share of East Asia in India's trade has improved, it is more in terms of imports than exports. Similarly, although the product structure has changed, the share of conventional products such as agricultural and mineral raw materials and textiles and clothing continues to be quite significant, as observed earlier. Furthermore, India has not been able to move up the value chain in the export of conventional products—whether it is the export of iron ore, tea or textiles and clothing. One exception includes Tata Tea that acquired the Tetley brand in the UK and integrated its operations to control the entire value chain in-house (see Kumar 2008). Going forward, it would be critical for India to exploit the potential of geographical and product diversification in view of the anemic growth of world trade, as the traditional trade partners in advanced countries deal with global imbalances in the aftermath of the global financial crisis.

Services in India's Trade

The emergence of the services sector as the most dynamic sector driving India's growth has been accompanied by its growing importance in trade. The share of trade in services in India's GDP quadrupled from 3.3 per cent to 20 per cent between 1990 and 2016. Table 6.6 shows that unlike in goods trade, the growth rate of services exports was higher than that for imports. There has been a striking transformation of India as a net exporter of services from being a net importer in 2005. Exports of USD 162 billion worth of services in 2016 left a surplus of USD 28 billion after imports. Growth of trade in services in India was also faster than in other countries, leading to a 69 per cent increase in India's share in the global services exports over 2005–16.

Table 6.6 Services trade balance

	2005	2016	Avgerage Annual Growth Rate (2005–16), per cent
Exports (in million USD)	52,179	161,845	12 per cent
Share in global exports (per cent)	1.97	3.32	
Imports (in million USD)	60,636	133,710	8 per cent
Share in global imports (per cent)	2.33	2.79	
Balance of services trade	−8,457	28,135	

Source: Based on UNCTAD, Online database, www.unctad.org (last accessed 01/03/18).

The transformation of India's services trade has attracted attention in a number of studies (see Verma 2008 and Raychaoudhuri and De 2012).

The dynamism of services trade is a result of India's emergence as a hub for IT software development and other IT-enabled services, also referred to as business process outsourcing (BPO) services. In these services, India is recognized as the global leader. According to the Indian Ministry of Information Technology, India's exports of IT and ITES services were of the order of USD 117 billion in 2016/17.[3] In the Global Services Location Index by AT Kearney, a global consultancy organization, India was ranked first globally in 2017 (Table 6.7), a position it has consistently retained since the inception of the index in 2004. Among the sources of its strength in the sector are people skills and their abundance, given the large youthful workforce of the country. India's success in IT services has been attributed to, among other factors, a far-sighted government policy to spot emerging opportunities and create high-end education and training facilities and computing infrastructure way back in the late 1970s (Kumar 2001). In future, this strength in Information and Communication Technology (ICT) services can and should be leveraged to build a globally competitive electronic goods industry.

[3] See http://meity.gov.in/content/performance-contribution-towards-exports-it-ites-industry. Last accessed on 12 June 2019.

Table 6.7 Ranks of Asian countries in global services location
index

Country	2004	2007	2011	2017
India	1	1	1	1
China	2	2	2	2
Malaysia	3	3	3	3
Indonesia	–	6	5	4
Thailand	13	4	7	8
Vietnam	20	19	8	6
Sri Lanka	–	29	21	11
Pakistan	–	30	28	30
Singapore	5	11	32	51

Source: Based on atkearney.com.

CURRENT ACCOUNT BALANCE

India faced a major balance of payments crisis in 1991 when its current account deficit crossed 3 per cent of GDP and the government had to mortgage its gold reserves to borrow foreign exchange to stave off a liquidity crisis. However, subsequent reforms and structural adjustment led to a major turnaround of the external sector with India running current account surpluses during the 2001–2 to 2003–4 period. But since 2004–5, the current account situation has again turned adverse with widening deficits.

Despite significant surpluses in services trade, current account deficits have been widening due to a steadily worsening merchandise trade deficit. As Table 6.8 shows, the merchandise trade deficit of India widened steadily from 2.1 per cent of the GDP in 2002–3 to 10.5 per cent in 2012–13, an unprecedented level in India's post-Independence history. One of the reasons for this widening was the faster growth rate of imports compared to that of exports, especially during 2002–3 to 2008–9. Rising import intensity of Indian economy in this period, as indicated earlier, could be resulting from an appreciating exchange

Table 6.8 Current account balance indicators, 2000–17

| Year | Trade | | | Net invisibles/ | Current account | | |
	Exports/GDP	Imports/GDP	Trade balance/GDP	GDP	Current Account Deficit (CAD)/GDP	Foreign investment/GDP	Import cover of reserves (in months)
2000–1	9.6	10.9	–1.3	2.1	–0.6	1.3	10.0
2001–2	9.2	10.7	–1.5	3.1	0.7	1.4	12.6
2002–3	10.4	12.1	–1.7	3.4	1.2	0.8	14.9
2003–4	10.6	13.0	–2.4	4.6	2.3	2.3	17.3
2004–5	11.9	15.9	–4.0	4.4	–0.4	1.9	15.2
2005–6	12.7	18.4	–5.7	5.2	–1.2	1.9	12.2
2006–7	13.7	20.2	–6.5	5.5	–1.0	1.6	12.9
2007–8	13.6	20.9	–7.3	6.1	–1.3	3.6	14.8
2008–9	15.6	25.6	–10.0	7.5	–2.3	0.7	10.0
2009–10	13.5	21.8	–8.3	5.9	–2.8	3.8	11.6
2010–11	15.2	22.3	–7.1	5.0	–2.7	2.5	9.9
2011–12	16.8	26.8	–10.0	6.0	–4.2	2.2	7.2
2012–13	16.4	26.9	–10.5	5.8	–4.8	2.6	7.1
2013–14	16.9	24.2	–7.3	6.2	–1.7	1.4	8.1
2014–15	15.2	22.0	–6.8	5.8	–1.3	3.6	9.2
2015–16	12.6	18.2	–5.6	5.2	–1.1	1.5	11.3
2016–17	12.2	16.9	–4.7	4.3	–0.7	1.9	11.6

Source: RBI's Handbook of Statistics on Indian Economy, 2017, and www.rbi.org.in.

rate, besides trade liberalization. In terms of the real effective exchange rate, the rupee appreciated by 14.5 per cent over 2004–5 to 2016–17, as is evident from Table 6.9. By making imports cheaper in relative terms, this trend of appreciation pushed Indian enterprises to outsource the manufacturing of a number of their products to cheaper locations, such as China, in addition to affecting the competitiveness

Table 6.9 Indices of the real effective exchange rate (REER) of the Indian rupee (36-Currency Bilateral Weights) (Financial Year–Annual Average)

Year	REER	
	Export-based weights	Trade-based weights
(Base:1993–4 = 100)		
1997–8	103.07	100.77
1998–9	94.34	93.04
1999–2000	95.28	95.99
2000–1	98.67	100.09
2001–2	98.59	100.86
2002–3	95.99	98.18
2003–4	99.07	99.56
2004–5	98.30	100.09
(Base: 2004–5 = 100)		
2005–6	102.01	102.38
2006–7	100.47	100.76
2007–8	109.23	109.20
2008–9	99.72	99.65
2009–10	104.97	103.88
2010–11	115.02	112.68
2011–12	113.18	110.27
2012–13	108.71	105.57
2013–14	105.48	103.27
2014–15	111.24	108.94
2015–16	114.44	112.07
2016–17	116.44	114.50

Source: Extracted from RBI's *Handbook of Statistics on Indian Economy, 2017*; and updated from www.rbi.org.in.

of India's exports. The appreciating exchange rate has promoted a premature hollowing out of the Indian economy (Kumar 2018). It is strange, however, that the exchange rate of the country should be appreciating while it has a widening current account deficit. Normally, a country with a widening current account deficit should face a depreciating exchange rate, which would help in bringing down the deficits by enhancing the competitiveness of exports and by making imports more expensive. The culprit has been the short-term capital flows as those by foreign institutional investors (FII) that have pushed the exchange rate while the current account deficits were widening.

Even though the current account deficit touched an alarming level of 4.8 per cent of the GDP in 2012/13, it came down gradually and was in a comfortable range of around 1 per cent of the GDP in recent years, helped by the low oil prices. However, as the oil prices have started to harden again since 2018, the balance of payments situation may worsen in the coming years. Despite that, a comforting factor is that India has built sizeable foreign exchange reserves of over USD 400 billion over the years. There should be no room for complacency though, given the fact that India's foreign exchange reserves are primarily made up of highly volatile short-term capital flows.

Foreign Institutional Investment Inflows and Exchange Rate Instability

What explains the appreciation of the rupee despite the fact that India has been running trade and current account deficits for so long? The rapid rise in inflows of portfolio investments in India since 2003–4 is summarized in Table 6.10. Large magnitudes of portfolio investments in the form of short-term equity investments by foreign institutional investors (FII) flowed in as the Indian economy gathered momentum and capital markets started giving attractive returns. The annual net inflows, however, are highly volatile.

FII inflows rose to a sizeable USD 27 billion in 2007–8 that not only led to stock prices booming, with the Bombay Stock Exchange (BSE) Sensex more than doubling from under 10,000 to 20,000, but also to the rupee exchange rate appreciating sharply from 47 rupees to a US dollar in 2006 to 38 rupees in 2008. In 2008–9, in the wake

Table 6.10 The FDI and foreign portfolio investment flows to India

Year	Gross inflows/ gross invest- ments	Direct invest- ment to India	FDI by India	Net foreign direct invest- ment	Net portfolio invest- ment	Total (in million USD)
2000–1	4,031	4,031	759	3,272	2,590	5,862
2001–2	6,130	6,125	1,391	4,734	1,952	6,686
2002–3	5,095	5,036	1,819	3,217	944	4,161
2003–4	4,322	4,322	1,934	2,388	11,356	13,744
2004–5	6,052	5,987	2,274	3,713	9,287	13,000
2005–6	8,962	8,901	5,867	3,034	12,494	15,528
2006–7	22,826	22,739	15,046	7,693	7,060	14,753
2007–8	34,844	34,729	18,835	15,893	27,433	43,326
2008–9	41,903	41,738	19,365	22,372	−14,030	8,342
2009–10	37,746	33,109	15,143	17,966	32,396	50,362
2010–11	36,047	29,029	17,195	11,834	30,293	42,127
2011–12	46,552	32,952	10,892	22,061	17,170	39,231
2012–13	34,298	26,953	7,134	19,819	26,891	46,711
2013–14	36,047	30,763	9,199	21,564	4,822	26,386
2014–15	45,147	35,283	4,031	31,251	42,205	73,456
2015–16	55,559	44,907	8,886	36,021	−4,130	31,891
2016–17	60,220	42,215	6,603	35,612	7,612	43,224

Source: Extracted from RBI's *Handbook of Statistics on Indian Economy, 2017*, and www.rbi.org.in.

of the global financial crisis, there was a net outflow of the FIIs to the tune of USD 14 billion dollars that brought down the BSE Sensex from nearly 20,000 points to less than 9000 points in the early part of 2009. Much more importantly, it led to a sharp depreciation of the rupee by nearly 25 per cent in early 2009. The depreciation would have been greater if the Reserve Bank of India had not intervened in the market by selling dollars. This depleted the RBI's foreign exchange reserves by USD 58 billion to about USD 252 billion from USD 310 billion from 2007–8 to 2008–9. However, FIIs returned rapidly to the market with the onset of recovery and the FII inflows to the country in 2010 were of the order of USD 32 billion, bringing the Sensex back

above 20,000 points in October 2010. Despite the RBI's market intervention to offset the subsequent exchange rate pressure, the rupee
appreciated by nearly 8 per cent, although foreign exchange reserves
were augmented to about USD 284 billion. FII inflows have become
primary determinants of movements in the stock exchange indices
and the exchange rate of the rupee (see Kumar 2011). As there are
sharp movements in these inflows linked to global developments,
they become channels of transmission of instability to the country's
financial system. As a result, the rupee has been on a roller coaster
ride: from Rs 44 per dollar in January 2007 to Rs 39 in January 2008
to an increase again to Rs 49 per dollar in January 2009 to Rs 44
in October 2010. The rupee fluctuated around Rs 54 in 2012 as the
FIIs showed a lukewarm response to the Indian capital markets. As
the capital flows started to decline due to the improving economic
prospects of the US economy and the expectation of withdrawal of
monetary stimulus by the Fed between May and September 2013, the
rupee depreciated substantially, touching an all-time low of Rs 68.80
before appreciating in the second half of September 2013 as the Fed
announced a delay in the tapering of the quantitative easing. The
postponement of tapering by the Fed provides a short reprieve to the
country, but the recent episodes have exposed the country's vulnerability in view of the high current account deficit, foreign exchange
reserves built up of short-term capital flows, and the declining FDI
inflows. The volatility of FII inflows has continued in the recent years
with magnitudes fluctuating between a high of USD 42 billion in
2014/15 to a net outflow of USD 4.1 billion in 2015/16 and an inflow
of USD 7.6 billion in 2016/17.

Perils of High Exposure to FII Inflows

Besides being highly volatile, FII inflows have a very high servicing
burden. Among foreign resources such as the FDI, foreign borrowings,
non-resident Indian (NRI) deposits, American depositary receipts
(ADRs), and global depositary receipts (GDRs), FII investments are
the most expensive in terms of the servicing burden (Kumar 2011).
This is because they come to chase primarily good returns at the stock
markets and the exchange rate speculation. As they tend to be stock
price makers rather than takers, they manage to exit safely before the
markets' major crashes, thereby precipitating the declines. They are

fair-weather friends and pro-cyclical in nature. They cannot be relied upon when the country needs them most.

One may argue that FII inflows help a country build foreign exchange reserves. What is not appreciated very well is the fact that exposure to these inflows also enhances the need to have large foreign exchange reserves due to their highly volatile nature. Therefore, developing countries such as India should rely more on FDI inflows for their foreign resource needs and raise the ADRs/GDRs and deposits from NRIs, where possible, rather than relying on the FIIs. In view of their high cost and other deleterious effects, such as volatility, a number of emerging economies such as Brazil, South Korea, Thailand, and Indonesia imposed capital controls in 2010 to moderate their volatility. The unprecedented injection of liquidity by the governments in developed countries in the wake of the global financial crisis has exposed emerging economies of Asia such as India to a much larger volatility through capital flows. There is now a growing consensus on the relevance of capital controls as elements of the policy tool kit for the governments in emerging economies (UN-ESCAP 2010; Ostry et al. 2010). The benefits of maintaining open capital accounts, if any, are ambiguous. However, capital controls need to be exercised when the economy is on the upswing and net capital flows are positive rather than when they are negative as their imposition may further precipitate the crisis.

Foreign Direct Investment (FDI) Flows and Their Quality

Trends in Inward FDI Flows

Besides the liberalization of trade, 1991 was also the time for substantial liberalization of the FDI policy regime for both inward as well as outward FDI. The key features of the FDI policy regime of India include up to 100 per cent foreign ownership in most sectors except those due to sensitivities and security concerns, such as arms and ammunition. Sectoral caps also apply to services sectors. Full repatriation of capital and remittances of profits, dividends, technical fees, and royalties is permitted.[4]

The FDI inflows to India have been growing since 1991, but the big break came in 2006 when annual inflows to the country nearly tripled in one year from USD 7.6 billion to USD 20 billion and increased from that level peaking to USD 47 billion in 2008 before declining to USD 24 billion in 2010 in the wake of the global financial crisis but recovering to USD 44 billion by 2015 (Table 6.11). India's share in the global FDI inflows nearly doubled over 2005–6 and again between 2006 and 2009 before moderating to around 2.5 per cent by 2015. The relative importance of the flows in relation to gross fixed investment also rose from 2.9 per cent in 2005 to 6.8 per cent in 2016. The share of FDI in gross fixed investments in India has been lower than that for other developing countries, but is catching up. In 2008 when FDI inflows peaked in India, this ratio was at 10.1 per cent—quite close to that for developing Asia at 10.4 per cent—indicating the potential for a rise in the future.

The rise in FDI inflows since 2006 reflected an improving investment climate in India with the acceleration of growth rate since 2003, the rise of a sizeable middle class with purchasing power, and the recognition of India's comparative advantage in knowledge-based industries. This is not only evident from the rising magnitudes of FDI inflows but also from investor surveys conducted by global consultancy organizations. In the *FDI Confidence Index* published by AT Kearney, covering the 25 top destinations for FDI, India has remained within the top six or seven ranks for the past decade. Similar upgrading in India's ranks has been reported by surveys of investors conducted by the Japanese Bank of International Cooperation (JBIC) as well as in UNCTAD's *World Prospects Surveys*, where India is ranked among the most preferred FDI locations (UNCTAD 2012). Recent reforms also helped improve India's ranking from 130 to 100 in 2017 in the World Bank's studies on *Ease of Doing Business* based on perception surveys. As the economy recovers from the recent disruptive reforms of currency in 2016 and introduction of the GST

---

[4] See consolidated FDI policy of India at http://www.makeinindia.com/documents/10281/0/Consolidated+FDI+Policy+2017.pdf. Last accessed on 12 June 2019.

Table 6.11A Inward foreign direct investment flows, annual, 2005–16 (in million USD)

Year	2005	2006	2007	2008	2009	2010	2011	2012	2013	2014	2015	2016
World	958,516	1,411,171	1,909,234	1,499,133	1,190,006	1,383,779	1,591,146	1,592,598	1,443,230	1,323,863	1,774,001	1,746,423
Developing economies	339,992	411,896	537,894	592,713	473,893	642,690	687,511	670,998	674,658	703,780	752,329	646,030
Developing economies: Asia	224,921	292,959	358,389	378,847	321,519	410,424	425,657	401,177	421,500	460,316	523,641	442,665
Southern Asia	14,182	28,590	34,595	56,597	42,479	34,912	44,327	32,317	35,629	41,417	50,848	53,735
India	7,622	20,328	25,350	47,102	35,634	27,417	36,190	24,196	28,199	34,582	44,064	44,486
Share of India in developing Asia (%)	3.39	6.94	7.07	12.43	11.08	6.68	8.50	6.03	6.69	7.51	8.41	10.05
Share of India in developing economies (%)	2.24	4.94	4.71	7.95	7.52	4.27	5.26	3.61	4.18	4.91	5.86	6.89
Share of India in world (%)	0.80	1.44	1.33	3.14	2.99	1.98	2.27	1.52	1.95	2.61	2.48	2.55

Source: Author's compilation from UNCTAD online data base (2017), www.unctad.org.
Note: Data unavailable for 2016.

Table 6.11B FDI inflows as a percentage of gross fixed capital formation, 2005–15

	2005	2006	2007	2008	2009	2010	2011	2012	2013	2014	2015
World	9.5	12.8	15.1	12.5	9.1	9.7	10.3	7.8	7.7	6.8	9.6
Developing economies	12.1	12.9	14.3	13.3	10.1	10.2	9.8	9.1	7.5	7.5	8.1
Developing economies: Asia	10.9	11.8	11.9	10.6	7.9	8.3	7.4	6.5	5.9	6.1	6.9
Southern Asia	3.9	6.8	6.4	9.4	6.9	4.6	5.2	3.9	4.1	4.7	5.8
India	2.9	6.6	6.2	10.8	7.9	4.8	5.6	4	4.4	5.2	6.8

Source: Author's compilation from UNCTAD online data base (2017), www.unctad.org.

Note: Data unavailable for 2016.

in 2017 and returns to its high growth trajectory, FDI inflows are likely to grow further in the coming years. FDI inflows may also assist in manufacturing-oriented structural transformation of the economy and technological upgrading of exports that India needs by working together with local entrepreneurs and bringing in technologies and other resources as a part of the 'Make in India' programme of the NDA government.

Quality of FDI Inflows

There can be several indicators of the quality of FDI inflows, capturing different aspects of direct and indirect impacts on the development of the host country (see Kumar 2002). In what follows, we discuss India's performance in terms of a few such indicators.

Sectoral Composition

One of the indicators of quality is the sectoral composition of FDI inflows. It matters whether the FDI is going to the modern technology-intensive sectors and building productive capabilities or to the conventional sectors, crowding out domestic investments. In terms of the sectoral composition of FDI inflows, there has been a shift since 1991 in India's case. Earlier, the bulk of FDI inflows were directed to manufacturing especially the high technology industries through a selective policy. Since liberalization, a substantial proportion of FDI inflows has been directed to services. Manufacturing accounted for only about 40 per cent of inflows in the post-1991 period with services accounting for about 35 per cent share. Furthermore, among the manufacturing sub-sectors, FDI stock in the post-1991 period is also more evenly distributed between food and beverages, transport equipment, metals and metal products, electricals and electronics, chemicals and allied products, and miscellaneous manufacturing. This stands in contrast to the situation prior to 1990 when there was a very heavy concentration in relatively technology-intensive sectors, that is, machinery, chemicals, electricals, and transport equipment (Kumar 2005a).

In China, on the other hand, the bulk of FDI inflows have been directed by government policy to manufacturing (of the export-oriented type) and very little has gone to services (Yongding 2006). Of the FDI in manufacturing in China, 11 per cent went to electronics and telecommunication equipment, helping the country emerge as the leading producer and exporter of these products. A policy guiding FDI inflows to manufacturing helped China to emergence as a global factory. Therefore, FDI inflows in China have been directed to assist in the development of the industry that has made China a global factory, generating billions of dollars of output and exports and millions of jobs in the process.

Impact of FDI on Growth and Domestic Investment

FDI inflows could contribute to growth rate of the host economy by augmenting the capital stock as well as with infusion of new technology. However, high growth rates may also attract more FDI inflows by enhancing the investment climate in the country. Therefore, the FDI-growth relationship is subject to causality bias given the possibility of two-way relationship. What is the nature of the relationship in India? A study has examined the direction of causation between the FDI and growth empirically for a sample of 107 countries for the 1980s and 1990s period. In the case of India, the study finds a Granger neutral relationship as the direction of causation was not pronounced (see Kumar and Pradhan 2005, for more details of the methodology and results).

It has also been shown that FDI projects may sometimes actually crowd out or substitute domestic investments from product or capital markets with the market power of their well-known brand names and other resources and may thus be immiserizing (see Fry 1992 and Agosin and Mayer 2000 for evidence). Therefore, it is important to examine the impact of the FDI on domestic investment to evaluate its impact on growth and welfare in the host economy. An earlier study to examine the effect of the FDI on domestic investment in a dynamic setting, however, did not find a statistically significant result in the case of India (see Kumar and Pradhan 2005). It appears, therefore, that FDI inflows received by India have been of a mixed type, combining some inflows crowding-in domestic investments while others crowding them out, where no predominant pattern emerged. In the case of East Asian countries such as South Korea and Thailand, the relationship clearly indicated the FDI crowding-in domestic investments

(Kumar and Pradhan 2005). Therefore, the quality of the FDI in India with respect to its impact on growth and domestic investment is of a mixed type and leaves scope for improvement.

Empirical studies on the nature of the relationship between the FDI and domestic investments suggest that the effect of the FDI on domestic investments depends on the policies of the host government. Governments have extensively employed selective policies and imposed various performance requirements such as local content requirements (LCRs) to deepen the commitment of the MNEs towards the host economy. The Indian government, in the past, had imposed a condition of phased manufacturing programmes (or LCRs) in the auto industry to promote vertical inter-firm linkages and encourage the development of the auto component industry (and the crowding-in of domestic investments). A case study of the auto industry where such a policy was followed shows that these policies (in combination with other performance requirements, that is, foreign exchange neutrality) have succeeded in building an internationally competitive vertically integrated auto sector in the country (see Kumar 2005). The Indian experience in this industry, therefore, is in tune with the experiences of Thailand, Brazil, and Mexico, as documented by Moran (1998).

FDI and Export-Platform Production

A number of developing countries have used FDI to exploit the resources of MNEs, such as globally recognized brand names, best practice technology or by increasing integration with their global production networks, among others, for expanding their manufactured exports. In this respect, China has had considerable success in exploiting the potential of FDI for export-oriented production. A very substantial (55 per cent) proportion of China's manufactured exports are undertaken by foreign invested enterprises, which account for as much as 80 per cent of all technology-intensive exports (UNCTAD 2005). Foreign enterprises, while setting up export-oriented production bases, had created 23 million jobs by 2003, making China a global factory. Export-oriented FDI also helps in bringing the world's best practice technology as the affiliate has to compete globally right from the beginning. It also enhances the chances of FDI inflows crowding-in domestic investments and reducing the chances of crowding-out as the foreign affiliate will mainly be catering to outside markets rather than eating into domestic firms' markets. It will also create fresh possibilities of market information spillovers for domestic firms on export possibilities.

Unlike East Asian countries, India has not been able to exploit the potential of the FDI for export-oriented production. The bulk of FDI inflows in India are market-seeking, coming to tap the domestic market, with the share of foreign affiliates in exports being around 10 per cent. Therefore, the quality of FDI in respect of export orientation is poorer compared to the FDI received by East Asian countries. In this respect, two observations can be made. The first is that recent studies of export-performance are beginning to indicate a relatively superior performance of foreign enterprises in terms of export orientation compared to early studies suggesting a poorer performance of foreign companies (see Kumar and Joseph 2007). Therefore, the MNEs are beginning to exploit the potential of India as base for export-oriented production.

The second observation is about the role of host country policies in exploiting the potential of FDI for export-oriented production. A quantitative study analysing the determinants of the patterns of export-orientation of MNE affiliates across 74 countries in seven branches of the industry over three points of time has shown that in host countries with large domestic markets, export-obligations were effective for promoting export-orientation of foreign affiliates to third countries (see Kumar 1998).

Export-obligations have also been employed fruitfully by many countries to prompt the MNE affiliates to exploit the host country's potential for export platform production. For instance, in China, which has succeeded in expanding manufactured exports with help from the MNE affiliates, regulations stipulate that wholly owned foreign enterprises must undertake to export more than 50 per cent of their output (Rosen 1999: 63–71). As a result of these policies, the proportion of foreign enterprises in manufactured exports has steadily increased to over 55 per cent as observed above.

India has not imposed export obligations on the MNE affiliates, except for those entering the products reserved for the SMEs. However, indirect export obligations in the form of dividend balancing have been imposed for enterprises producing primarily consumer goods (since phased out in 2000). Under these policies, a foreign enterprise was obliged to earn the foreign exchange that it wished to remit abroad as dividend so that there was no adverse impact on host country's balance of payments. Sometimes a condition of foreign exchange neutrality has been imposed where the enterprise is required to earn enough foreign exchange to cover the outgo on account of imports. Therefore, these regulations have acted as indirect export obligations prompting foreign enterprises to export to earn the foreign exchange required by them. The available evidence suggests that such regulations have prompted foreign enterprises to undertake exports. In the case of the auto industry, in order to comply with their export commitments to comply with the foreign exchange neutrality condition, foreign auto majors undertook the export of auto components from India, which not only opened up new opportunities for the Indian component manufacturers but also in that process found profitable business opportunities (Kumar 2005). Hence, exports of auto components from India are now growing rapidly as was observed earlier. These regulations have acted to remove the information asymmetry existing about the availability of quality components in India among foreign auto majors. In that respect, India's experience is very similar to that of Thailand that has emerged as a major auto hub of South East Asia (as documented by Moran 1998 and Kumar 2005).

R&D and Other Knowledge-Based Activities and Local Technological Capability

A comparison of the R&D intensity of foreign firms in India and in other countries has not been possible due to lack of data. Within the country, foreign firms appear to be spending more on R&D activity than the local firms, although the gap between their R&D intensities has tended to narrow down. A study analysing the R&D activity of Indian manufacturing enterprises in the context of liberalization found that after controlling for extraneous factors, the MNE affiliates reveal a lower R&D intensity compared to local firms, presumably on account of their captive access to the laboratories in their parent and associated companies. The study also observed differences in the nature or motivation of R&D activity of foreign and local firms. Local firms seem to be directing their R&D activity towards absorption of imported knowledge and provide a backup to their outward expansion. The MNE affiliates, on the other hand, focus on the customization of their parents' technology for the local market (Kumar and Agarwal 2005).

An important issue is the diffusion and absorption of technology brought by foreign firms in the host countries. Some governments have imposed technology transfer requirements on foreign enterprises, for example Malaysia. However, such performance requirements do not appear to have been very successful in achieving their objectives (UNCTAD 2003). Instead, other performance requirements such as local content requirements or domestic equity requirements may be more effective in the transfer of technology. As mentioned above, local content requirements and export performance requirements have prompted foreign enterprises to transfer and diffuse some knowledge to domestic enterprises in order to comply with their obligations. Similarly, the domestic equity requirements may facilitate the quick absorption of the knowledge brought in by foreign enterprises, which is an important pre-requisite of the local technological capability, as is evident from case studies of the Indian two-wheelers industry where Indian joint ventures with foreign firms were able to absorb the knowledge brought in by the foreign partner and eventually become self-reliant, not only to continue production but even to develop their own world-class models for the domestic market and for exports on their own (see Kumar 2005). Some have expressed the view that domestic equity requirements may adversely affect the extent or quality of technology transfer (Moran 2001). However, it has been shown that the MNEs may not transfer key technologies even to their wholly owned subsidiaries abroad, fearing the risk of dissipation or diffusion through mobility of employees. Furthermore, even if the content and quality of technology transfer is superior in the case of a sole venture as opposed to a joint venture, from the host country's point of view, the latter may have more desirable externalities in terms of local learning and diffusion of the knowledge transferred.

Trends and Patterns in Outward FDI by Indian Enterprises

FDI flows no longer represent a one way street in India's case. In fact, outward investments from Indian enterprises have been growing fast especially since the turn of the century and have become quite significant in magnitude. As a part of economic reforms since 1991, the policy governing outward investments was also liberalized in 1992 when an automatic approval system for overseas investments was introduced. In a significant liberalization of the policy governing outward investments in March 2003, the government allowed Indian companies to invest under automatic route upto 100 per cent of their net worth, which was gradually raised to 400 per cent of their net worth in 2008 and more to facilitate large acquisitions including those for securing access to natural resources. Although Indian companies have been investing abroad since the early 1970s, the magnitude of investments was quite little until the mid-1990s when the investment limits were raised. However, the magnitude as well as number of outward investments have suddenly swelled since 2000 to around USD 1.5 billion per annum. Since 2006, the outward investments have climbed new heights, as apparent from Table 6.12. In 2006, the magnitude of outward investments by Indian companies more than tripled from the 2005 levels to USD 14 billion and peaked at USD 21 billion in 2008. Since then, it has gradually declined in the wake of the global financial crisis with the slowdown of the world economy. In recent years, outward flows from India have been in the range of USD 5–7 billion. In 2016, Indian companies had a total stock on outward FDI of USD 144 billion, which is substantial compared to just USD 1.7 billion at the turn of the century. It accounts for 2.47 per cent of the total stock of outward FDI from developing countries (UNCTAD 2017).

In putting the magnitude of Indian outward FDI (OFDI) in a global comparative perspective of other emerging economies, one finds that China has emerged as a significant source of outward FDI in recent years as a part of its 'going global' strategy. However, outward investments from Brazil have fluctuated like those of India and have been comparable in magnitude. The share of outward FDI as a percentage of gross fixed capital formation (GFCF) was higher for India than for China in 2006–10, before it declined in the recent years. It is likely that the recovery of the Indian economy to its growth trajectory will also lead to greater outflows as Indian enterprises pursue assets-seeking strategies, acquire access to markets, technology, brands, and sources of raw materials that have dominated their recent investments (see Kumar 2008, 2016).

Table 6.12 The FDI outflows from India in a global comparative perspective, 2001–16 (in millions USD)

Region/economy	2001	2005	2006	2010	2015	2016
World	684,972.5	841,091.5	1,360,036.1	1,386,061.2	1,594,317.2	1,452,462.6
Developed economies	623,262.2	704,694.3	1,120,552.6	961,715.4	1,172,867.1	1,043,884.4
Developing economies	59,187.0	118,350.8	209,329.6	373,905.7	389,267.0	383,429.3
Asia	56,633.8	88,807.4	149,399.3	290,746.4	338,682.6	363,057.5
China	6,885.4	12,261.2	17,634.0	68,811.3	127,560.0	183,100.0
India	1,397.4	2,985.5	14,285.0	15,947.4	7,572.4	5,120.3
Brazil	−2,257.6	2,516.7	28,202.5	22,059.9	3,091.7	−12,433.8
FDI Outflows as percentage of gross fixed capital formation						
Developing economies	3.3	3.9	5.9	5.7	4.2	4.2
Asia	4.4	4.0	5.7	5.8	4.4	4.7
China	1.5	1.3	1.6	2.5	2.6	3.8
India	1.2	1.2	4.8	3.0	1.2	0.8
Brazil	−2.2	1.7	14.8	4.9	0.9	−4.2

Source: Extracted from UNCTAD, FDI/MNE database. Available at www.unctad.org/fdistatistics. Last accessed on 12 June 2019.

A detailed examination of the quality of outward FDI flows from India from a host country's perspective is yet to be made. Kumar and Chadha (2009), while comparing the OFDI from India and China, observed that the Indian enterprises active abroad are typically privately managed enterprises seeking to globalize their operations, compared to the much larger state-owned enterprises in China going abroad to secure their natural resource supplies. This stylized fact was corroborated by the case study of the steel industry, where leading Indian enterprises had undertaken green field investments as well as acquisitions of established global firms in the Western world to acquire global footprints. Whereas, Chinese enterprises in the industry were found to have focused their outward investments primarily on raw material–seeking activities. From a host country's point of view, green field investments in value-adding downstream activities generate more favourable direct and indirect impacts compared to just extractive activities.

REGIONAL ECONOMIC INTEGRATION

India has generally pursued multilateralism faithfully in its trade policy with very few exceptions till the end of the last century. However, it has increasingly begun to pay due respect to regionalism in its trade policy since the turn of the century, following the emerging trend globally. Among the early schemes for regional cooperation, India has been a member of one of the earliest preferential trading arrangements in Asia-Pacific, namely the Asia-Pacific Trade Agreement (APTA), earlier known as the Bangkok Agreement, negotiated under the auspices of ESCAP in 1975. India has also been a member of the South Asian Association for Regional Cooperation (SAARC), formed in 1985, that adopted SAARC Preferential Trading Agreement (SAPTA) in 1993 that eventually evolved into the SAARC Free Trade Agreement (SAFTA) in 2004, implemented in the decade starting from 2006. In 1998, India also signed a bilateral FTA with Sri Lanka that has been operational since 2000. India also has trade and transit agreements with Bhutan and Nepal that provide them non-reciprocal free access to the Indian market.

Since 1992, in the wake of the economic reforms, a new thrust was given to India's approach to regional cooperation as a part of what is called the Look East policy. As a part of this policy, India became a sectoral dialogue partner of ASEAN. India was made a full dialogue partner by ASEAN in 1995 and was accorded a membership of the ASEAN Regional Forum in 1996. The ASEAN-India dialogue partnership was further upgraded to an annual summit-level dialogue from 2002. Therefore, the India-ASEAN partnership saw a remarkable transformation from being a sectoral dialogue partnership to a summit-level interaction within the decade of 1992–2002. At their second summit in October 2003, ASEAN and India signed a framework agreement on Comprehensive Economic Cooperation (CEC), allowing for a free trade arrangement. At the Laos Summit in 2004, they signed a long-term Partnership for Peace, Progress and Shared Prosperity based on the work done by the think tanks of ASEAN and India. CEC is usefully complemented by a Comprehensive Economic Cooperation Agreement (CECA) signed between India and Singapore in 2005. Since 2004, the early harvest scheme of the India–Thailand bilateral Free Trade Agreement has been operational. India has also signed a bilateral FTA with Malaysia and is negotiating one with Indonesia. The India–ASEAN FTA was also concluded in 2009. Subsequently, a services agreement was also signed. The India–ASEAN partnership is also complemented by the Mekong–Ganga Cooperation (MGC), and the Bay of Bengal Initiative for Multisectoral Techno-Economic Cooperation (BIMSTEC) which combines seven South and Southeast Asian countries. India has been assisting the new ASEAN countries, namely Cambodia, Laos, Myanmar, and Vietnam (CLMV), as part of ASEAN's Initiative for ASEAN Integration (IAI). India is assisting them particularly with capacity-building by setting up centres for entrepreneurship development, ICT, and English language training among other areas. The high-level interactions between India and ASEAN countries have steadily grown in both directions. In January 2018, India hosted an India–ASEAN Commemorative Summit in New Delhi to commemorate the 25th anniversary of their summit-level dialogue.

India's Look East policy started with its engagement with ASEAN but is not confined to it. As a part of it, India has also engaged East Asian countries like the Republic of Korea and Japan, concluding the CEPA with both of them. Negotiations are on with Australia and New Zealand. The engagement of ASEAN and the East Asian countries by India led to her inclusion in the East Asia Summit (EAS) established in 2005 as an annual summit-level forum between ASEAN and its six dialogue partners (Kumar et al. 2008). In 2011, the EAS was joined by the US and Russia. Within the framework of the EAS, a Comprehensive Economic Partnership of East Asia (CEPEA) that brought together ASEAN and its six FTA partners into a single trade agreement was proposed and accepted in principle in the 2009 Hua Hin Summit and four working groups were set up to take the negotiations forward. In 2011 at the Bali Summit, ASEAN proposed a framework on Regional Comprehensive Economic Partnership of East Asia (RCEP) with the six partners. The RCEP was formally launched at the Phnom Penh Summit of ASEAN in November 2012. The RCEP negotiations have continued and twenty-one rounds have been completed. India hosted the 17th round of RCEP negotiations in New Delhi. Bringing together key dynamic Asian economies of China, India, Japan, and ASEAN in one single trade agreement, the RCEP is among the largest such arrangements in the world and has the potential of becoming the third and more dynamic pillar of the world economy alongside the EU and NAFTA.

In a new and changed post-crisis international context where the advanced economies of the West are not able to play their role as the engines of growth in view of the compulsions of unwinding their huge debt accumulations, a rebalancing of external orientation in favour of regional economic integration is clearly important with the Asia-Pacific region emerging as the centre of gravity of the world economy (ESCAP 2012). In that respect, the Indian Look East policy, now reinforced as 'Act East Policy', of turning attention to East Asia was farsighted. Hopefully, the business enterprises of the country will be able to take advantage of the preferential markets access, made available through the emerging RTAs in some of the fastest growing markets of the world, in the coming years to address the balance of trade concerns.

Towards a More Inclusive and Sustainable Integration

The reforms pursued since 1991 have led to a much deeper integration of the Indian economy with the global economy in terms of a rising share of merchandise trade, an even more dramatic transformation of services trade, and the emergence of the country as one of the most attractive destinations for FDI as well as an important source of FDI outflows. The trade structure has changed in terms of product composition and destinations. However, the analysis presented suggests that much of the export growth benefited from the expansion of world trade, while the potential of product diversification and market diversification remains to fully be exploited. India needs to leverage the opportunities of product and geographical diversification of the export structure and strategic import substitution through deepening her industrial structure and reversing the trend of premature deindustrialization. In that context, the Make in India programme launched by the NDA government is timely. Besides the compulsion of creating decent jobs for India's burgeoning youthful workforce, Make in India is critical also for making India's balance of payments situation more sustainable. Despite healthy trade surpluses earned by services exports with India emerging as a global hub for ICT outsourcing, the balance of payments situation continues to face periodic stress depending on the oil price fluctuations. With the rising oil prices and the growing threat of protectionism and trade wars against the backdrop of the anaemic growth of world trade, such a strategy is becoming increasingly critical.

The growth and sizeable imports of electronic goods, non-electrical machinery, and other equipment—including those for defence, among others—provide fruitful opportunities for strategic import substitution. To exploit these opportunities, policy measures normally grouped as industrial policy—including infant industry protection (to leverage the domestic market for exploiting the economies of scale), pioneer industry programmes, public procurement preferences, a proactive FDI policy, and exchange rate management—as employed extensively by the industrialized countries and East Asian countries in the past may be fruitful in the context of 'Make in India', while avoiding the pitfalls of the earlier import substitution regime (see Kumar 2018 for a detailed analysis).

Finally, in the context of the dramatically changed international scenario in the aftermath of the global financial crisis, when advanced economies are not able to provide a growth stimulus to Asian economies, a rebalancing of growth in favour of domestic and regional sources of demand is imperative. India has already moved towards integration with East Asian economies with a number of bilateral and regional FTAs and is a part of the incipient Regional Comprehensive Economic Partnership (RCEP) of East Asia that seeks to create a broader Asia-Pacific regional trade arrangement, covering 16 of the region's largest and fastest growing economies. Indian industry should aggressively exploit the export opportunities of preferential access to East Asian markets provided by these agreements rather than only using these FTAs to import duty free from the partners.

REFERENCES

Aggarwal, Aradhna and Nagesh Kumar (2012). 'Structural Change, Industrialization and Poverty Reduction: The Case of India'. ESCAP-SSWA Development Papers 1206. Available at: http://sswa.unescap.org/meeting/documents/Dev-Challenges/SSWA_Development_Papers_1206_October2012.pdf. Last accessed on 11 June 2019.

Agosin, M.R. and Ricardo Mayer (2000). 'Foreign Investment in Developing Countries: Does it Crowd in Domestic Investment?'. UNCTAD Discussion Paper No.146. Geneva: UNCTAD.

Ahluwalia, I.J. (2008). 'Rapid Economic Growth: Contributing Factors and Challenges Ahead'. *Asian Economic Policy Review* 3(2): 180–204.

Ahluwalia, Montek S. (2006). 'India's Experience with Globalization'. *The Australian Economic Review* 39(1): 1–13.

AT Kearney (2012). FDI Confidence Index 2012. Available at: www.atkearney.com.

Battat, Joseph, Isiah Frank, and Xiaofang Shen (1996). 'Suppliers to Multinationals: Linkage Programmes to Strengthen Local Capability in Developing Countries'. Foreign Investment Advisory Service Occasional Paper No. FIAS 6. Washington DC: The World Bank.

Freire, C. (2012). 'Structural Transformation for Inclusive Development in South and South-West Asia'. ESCAP-SSWA Development Papers 1204. Available at: http://sswa.unescap.org/meeting/documents/Dev-Challenges/SSWA_Development_Papers_1204_August2012.pdf. Last accessed on 11 June 2019.

Fry, Maxwell J. (1992). 'Foreign Direct Investment in a Macroeconomic Framework: Finance, Efficiency, Incentives and Distortions'. PRE Working Paper. Washington DC: The World Bank.

Gordon, J. and Poonam Gupta (2004). 'Understanding India's Services Revolution'. IMF Working Paper No. WP/04/171. Washington DC: IMF.

Huang, Yasheng and Tarun Khanna (2003). 'Can India Overtake China?'. Foreign Policy. Available at: http://www.foreignpolicy.com/story/story.php?storyID=13774. Last accessed on 16 June 2019.

Kumar, Nagesh (1998). 'Multinational Enterprises, Regional Economic Integration, and Export-Platform Production in the Host Countries: An Empirical Analysis for the US and Japanese Corporations'. Weltwirtschaftliches Archiv 134(3): 450–83.

———— (2001). 'National Innovation Systems and Indian Software Industry Development'. Paper prepared for UNIDO. Available at: http://www.unido.org/fileadmin/import/userfiles/hartmany/idr-kumar-paper2.pdf. Last accessed on 16 June 2019.

———— (2002). Globalization and the Quality of Foreign Direct Investment. Delhi: Oxford University Press.

———— (2003). 'Intellectual Property Rights, Technology and Economic Development: Experiences of Asian Countries'. Economic and Political Weekly 38(3) (January): 209–26.

———— (2005). 'Performance Requirements as Tools of Development Policy: Lessons from Experiences of Developed and Developing Countries'. In Putting Development First: The Importance of Policy Space in the WTO and International Financial Institutions, edited by Kevin Gallagher, 179–94. London: Zed Press.

———— (2005a). 'Liberalization, Foreign Direct Investment Flows and Development: Indian Experience in the 1990s'. Economic and Political Weekly 40(14) (2 April 2005): 1459–69.

———— (2008). 'Internationalization of Indian Enterprises: Patterns, Strategies, Ownership Advantages and Implications'. Asian Economic Policy Review 3(2): 242–61.

———— (2011). 'Capital Flows and Development: Lessons from South-Asian Experiences'. In Handbook of South Asian Economies, edited by Raghabendra Jha. London and New York: Routledge.

_____ (2016). 'Competitive Advantages of Indian Multinationals'. In *Emerging Indian Multinationals: Strategic Players in a Multipolar World*, edited by M. Thite, A. Wilkinson, and P. Budhwar, 102–29. New Delhi: Oxford University Press.

_____ (2018). 'Reversing Premature Deindustrialization for Job-creation: Lessons for Make-in-India from Industrialized and East Asian Countries'. In *Economic Theory and Policy amidst Global Discontent: Essays in Honour of Deepak Nayyar*, edited by A. Ghosh-Dastidar et al., 389–415. London and New York: Routledge.

Kumar, Nagesh and Alka Chadha (2009). 'India's Outward Foreign Direct Investments in Steel Industry in a Chinese Comparative Perspective'. *Industrial and Corporate*. Oxford: Oxford University Press.

Kumar, Nagesh and Aradhna Agarwal (2005). 'Liberalization, Outward Orientation and In-house R&D Activity of Multinational and Local Firms: A Quantitative Exploration for Indian Manufacturing'. *Research Policy* 34(4): 441–60.

Kumar, Nagesh and J. Pradhan (2005). 'Foreign Direct Investment, Externalities and Economic Growth in Developing Countries: Some Empirical Explorations'. In *Multinationals and Foreign Investment in Economic Development*, edited by Edward M. Graham, 42–84. USA: Palgrave.

Kumar, Nagesh and Kevin P. Gallagher (2007). 'Relevance of "Policy Space" for Development: Implications for Multilateral Trade Negotiations'. RIS Discussion Papers 120. Available at: http://www.ris.org.in/publications/discussion-papers/508. Last accessed on 16 June 2019.

Kumar, Nagesh and K.J. Joseph (eds) (2007). *International Competitiveness and Knowledge Based Industries*. New Delhi: Oxford University Press and RIS.

Kumar, Nagesh, K. Kesavapany, and Yao Chaocheng (eds) (2008). *Asia's New Regionalism and Global Role: Agenda for the East Asia Summit*. New Delhi and Singapore: ISEAS and RIS.

Moran, Theodore H. (1998). *Foreign Direct Investment and Development*. Washington DC: Institute for International Economics.

_____ (2001). *Parental Supervision: The New Paradigm for Foreign Direct Investment and Development*. Washington DC: Peterson Institute of International Economics.

Ostry, Jonathan D., Atish R. Ghosh, Karl Habermeier, Marcos Chamon, Mahvash S. Qureshi, and Dennis B.S. Reinhardt (2010). 'Capital Inflows: The Role of Controls'. IMF Staff Position Note SPN/10/04.

Panagariya, A. (2008). *India: The Emerging Giant*. New York: Oxford University Press.

Raychaudhuri, Aajitava and Prabir De (2012). *International Trade in Services In India*. New Delhi: Oxford University Press.

Research and Information System (2006). *Towards an Employment-Oriented Export Strategy: Some Explorations*. New Delhi: Research and Information System for Developing Countries.

Reserve Bank of India (2012). *Handbook of Statistics on Indian Economy 20012*. Mumbai: RBI. Available at: www.rbi.gov.in. Last accessed on 11 June 2019.

Rodrik, D. (2004). 'Industrial Policy for the Twenty-First Century'. CEPR Discussion Paper 4767, November.

Rosen, D. (1999). *Behind the Open Door: Foreign Enterprise Establishment in China*. Washington DC: Institute for International Economics.

Tiwari, T.S. (1986). 'Constant Market Share Analysis of Export Growth: the Indian Case'. *The Indian Economic Journal* 33(3): 70–80.

Tyszynski, H. (1951). 'World Trade in Manufactured Commodities, 1899–1950'. *The Manchester School* 19(3): 272–304.

United Nations Conference on Trade and Development (2003). *Use and Effectiveness of Performance Requirements: Select Case Studies*. New York: United Nations.

⸻ (2005). *World Investment Report 2005*. New York: United Nations.

⸻ (2012). *World Investment Report 2012*. New York: United Nations.

United Nations Economic and Social Commission for Asia and the Pacific (2010). *Economic and Social Survey of Asia and the Pacific*. Bangkok: UN-ESCAP.

⸻ (2012). *Growing Together: Economic Integration for an inclusive and sustainable Asia-Pacific Century*. Bangkok: UN-ESCAP.

⸻ (2012). *Regional Cooperation for Inclusive and Sustainable Development: South and South-West Asia Development Report 2012-13*. New York, New Delhi, and London: UN Publications and Routledge.

⸻ (2017). *Unlocking the Potential of Regional Economic Cooperation and Integration in South Asia*. Bangkok and New Delhi: UNESCAP South and South-West Asia Office.

Verma, R. (2008). 'The Service Sector Revolution in India: A Quantitative Analysis'. Research Paper No. 2008/72. Helsinki: United Nations University, UNU-WIDER, September.

Yongding, Yu (2006). 'The Experience of FDI Recipients: The Case of China'. In *Multinationals and Economic Growth in East Asia*, edited by Shujiro Urata, Chia Siow, and Fukunari Kimura, 423–52. London and New York: Routledge.

CHAPTER 7

....

POVERTY AND INEQUALITY

redesigning intervention[1]

....

RAGHBENDRA JHA AND ANURAG SHARMA

Poverty and inequality are issues of enduring concern in India. In particular, there is substantial disquiet about the persistence of mass poverty and perceived rising inequality even in the presence of accelerated rates of economic growth, particularly since about 2001. An oft-repeated question in academic and policy circles has been: 'Have reforms led to an accelerated fall in poverty?' The evolution of economic inequality in India has followed the first half of the Kuznets curve pattern, that is, inequality has risen with the rising per capita income. Will this rise be moderate and will the second half of the Kuznets curve, that is, a falling trend in inequality with further increases in the per capita income, come sooner rather than later?

Needless to say, there is voluminous literature on these concerns. For recent analyses of these issues, see The World Bank (2011), Kurosaki (2011), and Jha (2004). Some basic statistics on the growth

[1] We are grateful to Raj Bhatia for expert statistical help and to Ashima Goyal and three anonymous referees for helpful comments on an earlier draft. The usual caveat applies.

and poverty performance of the Indian economy (using international poverty lines given by The World Bank) are reported in Table 7.1A which reports decadal growth rates of real gross domestic product (GDP), real GDP per capita, and their respective standard deviations along with head count ratios (HCR) and poverty gaps at USD 2 purchasing power parity (PPP) a day and USD 1.25 PPP a day. With the onset of economic reforms, growth rates have, by and large, accelerated and become more stable over time. During a particularly high growth phase of 2005–10, the HCR at USD 2 PPP per day fell by about 7 points, whereas the HCR at USD 1.25 PPP per day fell by about 9 points. These figures lend strong credence to the hypothesis that higher economic growth leads to a sharp reduction in poverty. Table 7.1B reports on the comparable HCRs for India and China for various years and makes clear the role that the much higher economic growth rates in China (as compared to India) have had in reducing poverty in China at an accelerated rate.

However, The World Bank's global poverty lines, like those reported in Table 7.1, have been widely criticized. Thus, Pogge and Reddy (2010) argue that this poverty line is arbitrary and unrelated to any conception of what poverty is. The measure of purchasing power used is also deemed to be an inaccurate measure of purchasing power 'equivalence' and extrapolates incorrectly from limited data, rendering its estimates highly prone to error. Srinivasan (2010) is also sharply critical of The World Bank's poverty lines. This leads us to explore inequality and poverty using national poverty lines.[2]

TWO CONTROVERSIES RELATING TO THE NATIONAL POVERTY LINE

As indicated by Srinivasan (2007) the original poverty line for India developed by Dadabhai Naoroji in the late 19th century was based on calorie requirements. After Independence, the poverty line using

---

[2] Part of Table 7.1A also shows HCR in 2011–12 according to the national poverty line.

Table 7.1A Real GDP growth, real GDP per capita growth, and poverty in India: Track record of economic growth and poverty reduction in India

	Real GDP growth (average)	Standard deviation of real GDP growth	Real GDP per capita growth (average)	Standard deviation of real GDP per capita growth	Poverty HCR at USD 2 a day (PPP) (percentage of population)	Poverty HCR at USD 1.25 a day (PPP) (percentage of population)	Poverty gap at USD 2 a day (PPP) (percentage)	Poverty gap at USD 1.25 a day (PPP) (percentage)
1961–70	6.519	5.811	4.281	5.690				
1971–80	3.086	4.279	0.699	4.172				
1981–90	5.567	1.847	3.252	1.826				
1991–2000	5.475	2.065	3.519	2.070				
2001–10	7.689	2.181	6.085	2.197				
2011–12 to 2016–17	6.890	0.998	5.550	0.970				
1978					88.97	65.89	44.59	23.22
1983					84.79	55.51	38.20	17.24
1988					83.77	53.59	36.74	15.81
1994					81.73	49.40	34.11	13.56
2005					75.62	41.64	29.49	10.51
2010					68.72	32.67	24.45	7.49
2011–12					21.90			

Source: Authors' compilation based on the data from World Development Indicators, 2017.

Notes: GDP data for 2011–12 to 2016–17 use 2011–12 prices as base. Computations based on data from the Reserve Bank of India's Handbook of Statistics on the Indian Economy. Poverty data for 2011–12 use the Tendulkar poverty line and are based on data from Niti Aayog. The rest are authors' computations based on The World Bank database.

Table 7.1B Real GDP growth, real GDP per capita growth, and poverty in India: Comparable head count ratios in India and China

Year	1983	1987	1993	2004	2009	2011	2012
HCR (India)	53.86	44.76	45.91	38.21	31.1	21.23	20.0
Year	1984	1987	1993	2005	2008	2011	2012
HCR (China)	75.76	60.84	57	18.75	14.65	7.9	6.47

Source: Authors' compilation based on the data from World Development Indicators 2017.
Note: Poverty line is USD 1.90 PPP per capita 2011 dollars.

calorie requirement was recast in 1961 and extended over time. Thus, in 1973–4, based on a survey of consumer behaviour by the National Sample Survey Office (NSSO), a consumption basket was proposed that would ensure, on an average, 2,100 calories per person per day in urban areas and 2,400 calories per person per day in rural areas. The poverty lines established for 1973–4 were INR 49 per person per month for rural areas and INR 57 per person per month for urban areas. These poverty lines were regularly updated using the consumer price index for agricultural labourers (CPI-AL) for rural areas and the consumer price index for industrial workers (CPI-IW) for urban areas. State-level poverty lines were also determined and poverty rates were routinely calculated using these measures.

These poverty lines were heavily criticized for concentrating exclusively on food consumption norms, with no allowance being made for expenditure on health, education, and other basic needs. The Tendulkar Committee Report (TCR) submitted in 2009 was geared towards addressing this shortcoming. However, prior to that another controversy had affected the computation of poverty rates—in the 55th round of the NSS conducted in 1999–2000. This survey marked a departure from the earlier practice in two important ways—first, food items were canvassed on a dual recall period of seven days as well as the standard 30 days. Second, items on which only infrequent expenditures are made, such as medical goods, were only canvassed on a 365 day recall instead of the dual 30 day and 365 day recall in the previous 'thick' round. Earlier experiments with reference periods indicated this change could potentially halve the measured rate of poverty. Further, this change came exactly as reliable statistics were required to gauge the impact of India's 1991 economic reforms on the poor. A wide literature has evolved analysing and correcting the data from this round. Morten (2006) and, particularly, Deaton and Kozel (2005) provide a review of this literature. In the next 'thick' round of the NSS (the 61st round conducted in 2004–5) and subsequently, recall periods were set as per previous norms, making results from this round comparable to those from rounds earlier than the 55th.

Reacting to the TCR, the Planning Commission fixed the poverty line based on the data relating to the 66th round of the NSS, conducted in 2009–10, for the country at INR 672.8 per person per month (that is, INR 22.42 per person per day) for rural areas and INR 859.6 per person per month (that is, INR 28.65 per person per day) for urban areas. In 2011, this was revised to be INR 26 per day for rural areas and INR 32 per day in urban areas in view of the price inflation between 2009–10 and 2011.

When these figures were released, there was an immediate outcry from both the press and economists as these figures did not guarantee even bare subsistence. The ensuing course of events is well known, with the Government of India appointing a new committee (under the chairmanship of C. Rangarajan) to construct a new poverty line to replace the recommendations of the TCR.

It now behooves us to enquire what is wrong with the recommendations of the TCR. A result in this prolonged process is, of course, that we do not yet have an accurate idea of the extent and depth of poverty in India since we do not have a widely accepted poverty line.

The TCR is an attempt to address these deficiencies of the traditional approach. The TCR suggests that the old urban poverty line for 2004–5, when suitably adjusted, is adequate to meet today's requirements, both rural and urban, with respect to nutrition, education, and health. The TCR then makes a major methodological change by constructing new price indices to compare rural and urban prices in different states and the state-level price indices with the all-India price indices. Using the existing urban poverty line for 2004–5 and these 'new' prices, a revised rural poverty line is calculated. This raised the proportion of the poor in the rural population below the official poverty line, but it worked with a very flawed methodology. The poverty line that it proposes actually amounts to a reduced calorie consumption, and fails to provide for reasonable household expenditures on schooling and health. A deeper issue is that divesting the poverty line of its calorie requirement moorings robs it of any policy significance. Indeed, some people have legitimately argued that the poverty line is so low that it could barely buy one or two items of a subsistence basket.

Another related but distinct argument is that the delinking of subsistence requirements from calorie norms is mistaken, if not misguided. If the poverty line is anchored to a calorie norm, given changes in activity patterns and lifestyles, and improvements in the epidemiology of infectious diseases, it will have greater credibility in identifying the poor.

The TCR's claims about education and health are also fallacious. The TCR states that in 2004–5, 90 per cent of the children aged 5–14 years and belonging to households at the poverty line level of expenditure in urban areas were in school. The TCR then assumes that the median cost of sending a child to school sets a desirable level of expenditure on a child in school but little justification is provided for this assumption except to say that the average expenditure on education per child among households in the poverty line expenditure class was higher than the median cost of schooling per child. On this basis, the TCR surmises that the actual expenditure is adequate to ensure that children are in school. However, in actual practice, the median cost may be completely inadequate to cover all the costs of proper schooling for all children. It should also be noted that, given the high degree of inequality of expenditure on education in urban India, the median cost is likely to be lower than the mean cost. If the TCR had used the mean cost of education, the poverty line would have been higher and so would be the head count ratio of poverty. Moreover, the mere fact that a child is in school does not guarantee that all his/her schooling requirements, including learning materials, school uniform, etc., are met.

Exactly the same criticism applies to the TCR's arguments with respect to health expenditure. Using the data for 2004, the TCR calculates the median cost of non-institutional health care and institutional healthcare/hospitalization. The TCR again relies on median health care expenses but, just as in the case of educational expenses and given the significant inequality in health expenditure, the median health expenditure is likely to be well below the mean health expenditure. Further, median health expenditures may not guarantee adequate healthcare.

Thus, both generalizations of the traditional poverty line by the TCR are deeply flawed and, therefore, misleading. In reality, the TCR methodology actually underestimates the number of poor (Swaminathan 2010).[3]

HUNGER, INEQUALITY, AND POVERTY IN INDIA

Against this background, we are justified in asking the question: What of calorie deprivation (hunger)—the original motivation behind constructing the poverty line? Deaton and Dreze (2009) have shown that despite rapid economic growth in India, the per capita calorie intake has declined, as has the intake of many other nutrients. More than three quarters of the population lives in households whose per capita calorie intake is less than 2,100 in urban areas and 2,400 in rural areas—calorie intakes regarded as 'minimum requirements' in India. Anthropometric indicators tell an equally dismal story, while some of these indicators are the worst in the world. For instance, according to the National Family Health Survey, the proportion of underweight children remained virtually unchanged between 1998–99 and 2005–6—from 47 to 46 per cent for the age-group of 0–3 years. Yet, the government has occasionally permitted thousands of tonnes of food grains to rot in granaries of the Food Corporation of India (FCI).

Apart from its nutritional and human costs, such hunger also has strong implications for productivity, wages, and economic growth. If workers are nutritionally deprived, they will have low productivity, from whence they will get low wages. Low wages, in turn, will mean that the workers will be unable to buy the entire nutritional intake they need, which will then complete this vicious cycle. In the economics literature, this is called the poverty nutrition trap (PNT). Jha et al. (2009) establish the existence of a PNT with respect to calories and various micronutrients for various types of agricultural operations by

---

[3] See also Subramanian (2011).

male and female workers in rural India. In particular, women, more than men, are subject to the PNT.

In the poorer districts of India, the incidence of hunger is far more acute. For 2007–8, Jha et al. (2011a) collected primary data for 500 households in Rajasthan, Maharashtra, and Andhra Pradesh (AP) each and showed that the incidence of deprivation of both macronutrients (calories and protein) as well as a number of micronutrients is very high, in several cases 80 per cent or above. Hence, there is a huge hunger crisis in India which is not being picked up by 'falling' poverty—no matter which poverty line is used. This reaffirms the case for rooting poverty lines on nutritional norms to discover what the people of India probably already know—that nutritional deprivation is widespread and deep and probably worsening!

Against this background,[4] Table 7.2 depicts the evolution of inequality, measured by the Gini coefficient, in the rural and urban sectors of major individual states and the country as a whole between 1993–4 and 2009–10. Comparable figures for 1993–4, 2004–5, and 2009–10 are given, while the states and the country are ranked on the increasing inequality recorded for them. Figures for 1999–2000 and 2004–5 are also given, the latter being comparable to the former in magnitude. In the rural sector for the country as a whole, the Gini coefficient rose between 1993–4 and 2004–5 and stayed unchanged in 2009–10. For the urban sector, however, there was a steady rise in the Gini coefficient from 0.34 in 1993–4 to 0.37 in 2004–5 and 0.39 in 2009–10. Thus, the rise in urban inequality in the five-year period 2004–05 to 2009–10 was comparable to that in the 11-year period 1993–4 to 2004–5.[5] Hence, urban inequality has become a concern.

There has been a wide spatial variation in the evolution of inequality. Thus, in 1993–4, rural inequality was higher than the national Gini in AP, Kerala, Haryana, Maharashtra, and Tamil Nadu, whereas it was below the national Gini in Assam, Bihar, Jammu and Kashmir (JK), Gujarat, Orissa, West Bengal (WB), Punjab, Rajasthan, and Karnataka. Urban inequality was higher than the national Gini in

---

[4] The results on poverty and inequality that follow are subject to the critique of the traditional poverty line discussed earlier.

[5] Gini coefficient estimates for the 2011-12 NSS database are unavailable at the time of writing and hence not reported.

Table 7.2 Gini coefficient of distribution of consumption for select states and all India

State/India	1993–4 (50th Round) Rural State/India	Urban State/India	1999–2000 (55th Round) Rural State/India	Urban State/India	2004–5 (61st Round) Uniform reference period (comparable with 1993–94) Rural State/India	Urban State/India	2004–5 (61st Round) Mixed reference period (comparable with 1999–00) Rural State/India	Urban State/India	2009–10 (66th round) (comparable with 1993–4 and 2004–5 uniform reference) Rural State/India	Urban State/India	Urban
Assam	0.18 Haryana	0.28 Jammu & Kashmir	0.17 Jammu & Kashmir	0.22 Assam	0.19 Jammu & Kashmir	0.24 Assam	0.17 Jammu & Kashmir	0.24 Bihar	0.23 Jammu & Kashmir	Jammu & Kashmir	0.31
Bihar	0.22 Jammu & Kashmir	0.28 Assam	0.20 Rajasthan	0.28 Bihar	0.20 Gujarat	0.31 Bihar	0.17 Himachal Pradesh	0.26 Rajasthan	0.23 Assam	Assam	0.33
Jammu & Kashmir	0.23 Punjab	0.28 Bihar	0.21 Gujarat	0.29 Jharkhand	0.22 Assam	0.32 Jharkhand	0.20 Assam	0.30 Jammu & Kashmir	0.24 Bihar	Bihar	0.34
Gujarat	0.24 Assam	0.29 Rajasthan	0.21 Haryana	0.29 Jammu & Kashmir	0.24 Himachal Pradesh	0.32 Jammu & Kashmir	0.20 Rajasthan	0.30 Karnataka	0.24 Gujarat	Gujarat	0.34
Orissa	0.24 Gujarat	0.29 West Bengal	0.22 Orissa	0.29 Rajasthan	0.25 Uttarakhand	0.32 Rajasthan	0.20 Uttarakhand	0.30 West Bengal	0.24 Karnataka	Karnataka	0.34
West Bengal	0.25 Rajasthan	0.29 Gujarat	0.23 Punjab	0.29 Karnataka	0.26 Bihar	0.33 Uttarakhand	0.22 Bihar	0.31 Assam	0.25 Tamil Nadu	West Bengal	0.34
Punjab	0.26 Orissa	0.30 Himachal Pradesh	0.23 Himachal Pradesh	0.3 Gujarat	0.27 Jharkhand	0.35 Karnataka	0.23 Gujarat	0.32 Gujarat	0.26 Haryana	Tamil Nadu	0.37
Rajasthan	0.26 Bihar	0.31 Andhra Pradesh	0.24 Andhra Pradesh	0.31 Madhya Pradesh	0.27 Orissa	0.35 Uttar Pradesh	0.23 Punjab	0.32 Maharashtra	0.27 Madhya Pradesh	Haryana	0.37
Karnataka	0.27 Andhra Pradesh	0.32 Haryana	0.24 Assam	0.31 West Bengal	0.27 Haryana	0.36 Andhra Pradesh	0.24 Jharkhand	0.33 Orissa	0.27 Uttar Pradesh	Madhya Pradesh	0.37
Himachal Pradesh	0.28 Karnataka	0.32 Karnataka	0.24 Bihar	0.32 Orissa	0.28 Karnataka	0.36 Madhya Pradesh	0.24 Orissa	0.33 Tamil Nadu	0.27 Punjab	Uttar Pradesh	0.38
Madhya Pradesh	0.28 Uttar Pradesh	0.32 Madhya Pradesh	0.24 Karnataka	0.32 Punjab	0.28 Tamil Nadu	0.36 Chhattisgarh	0.24 Andhra Pradesh	0.34 Uttar Pradesh	0.27 Andhra Pradesh	Punjab	0.39
Uttar Pradesh	0.28 Madhya Pradesh	0.33 Orissa	0.24 Kerala	0.32 Uttarakhand	0.28 Andhra Pradesh	0.37 West Bengal	0.24 Tamil Nadu	0.34 Andhra Pradesh	0.29 Rajasthan	Andhra Pradesh	0.39

(cont'd)

Table 7.2 (cont'd)

State/India	1993–4 (50th round) Rural State/India	Urban State/India	1999–2000 (55th Round) Rural State/India	Urban State/India	2004–5 (61st Round) Uniform reference period (comparable with 1993–94) Rural State/India	Urban State/India	2004–5 (61st Round) Mixed reference period (comparable with 1999–00) Rural State/India	Urban State/India	2009–10 (66th round) (comparable with 1993–4 and 2004–5 uniform reference) Rural State/India	Urban
India	0.28 West Bengal	0.33 Punjab	0.24 Madhya Pradesh	0.32 Andhra Pradesh	0.29 Maharashtra	0.37 Gujarat	0.25 Uttar Pradesh	0.34 Madhya Pradesh	0.30 West Bengal	0.39
Andhra Pradesh	0.29 Kerala	0.34 Uttar Pradesh	0.25 Uttar Pradesh	0.33 Chhattisgarh	0.29 Rajasthan	0.37 Orissa	0.25 Kerala	0.35 Punjab	0.30 India	0.39
Kerala	0.29 Tamil Nadu	0.34 Maharashtra	0.26 West Bengal	0.34 Uttar Pradesh	0.29 Uttar Pradesh	0.37 India	0.25 Chhattisgarh	0.35 India	0.30 Orissa	0.40
Haryana	0.30 India	0.34 India	0.26 India	0.34 Himachal Pradesh	0.30 India	0.37 Himachal Pradesh	0.26 Maharashtra	0.35 Haryana	0.31 Himachal Pradesh	0.41
Maharashtra	0.30 Maharashtra	0.35 Kerala	0.27 Maharashtra	0.35 India	0.30 West Bengal	0.38 Punjab	0.26 India	0.35 Himachal Pradesh	0.31 Maharashtra	0.42
Tamil Nadu	0.31 Himachal Pradesh	0.43 Tamil Nadu	0.28 Tamil Nadu	0.38 Maharashtra	0.31 Madhya Pradesh	0.39 Tamil Nadu	0.26 Haryana	0.36 Kerala	0.44 Kerala	0.52
Jharkhand	Jharkhand	Jharkhand	Jharkhand	Haryana	0.32 Punjab	0.39 Maharashtra	0.27 Karnataka	0.36 Jharkhand	Jharkhand	
Chhattisgarh	Chhattisgarh	Chhattisgarh	Chhattisgarh	Tamil Nadu	0.32 Kerala	0.40 Kerala	0.29 West Bengal	0.36 Chhattisgarh	Chhattisgarh	
Uttarakhand	Uttarakhand	Uttarakhand	Uttarakhand	Kerala	0.34 Chhattisgarh	0.43 Haryana	0.31 Madhya Pradesh	0.37 Uttarakhand	Uttarakhand	

Source: For 1993–94, 1999–2000, and 2004–5: Planning Commission, Government of India, Databook for DCH, April 2012.

Himachal Pradesh (HP) and Maharashtra and below the national Gini in Haryana, JK, Punjab, Assam, Gujarat, Rajasthan, Orissa, Bihar, AP, Karnataka, Uttar Pradesh (UP), Madhya Pradesh (MP), and WB. In 2004–5, rural inequality was lower than the national Gini in Assam, Bihar, Jharkhand, JK, Rajasthan, Karnataka, Gujarat, MP, WB, Orissa, Punjab, Uttarakhand, AP, Chhattisgarh, and UP. Urban inequality was higher than the national Gini in Maharashtra, Haryana, Tamil Nadu, and Kerala. In 2009–10, rural inequality was lower than the national Gini in Bihar, Rajasthan, JK, Karnataka, WB, Assam, Gujarat, Maharashtra, Orissa, Tamil Nadu, UP, and AP, whereas it was higher than the national HCR in Haryana, HP, and Kerala. Urban inequality was below the national Gini in JK, Assam, Bihar, Gujarat, Karnataka, Tamil Nadu, Haryana, MP, UP, and Punjab, whereas it was higher than the national Gini in Orissa, HP, and Maharashtra.

Table 7.2 does not give information on the inequality between the rural and the urban sectors. Further, it gives an indication of the consumption inequality and not the income or wealth inequality, essentially because household-level income and wealth data for India are mostly unavailable and notoriously unreliable. Typically, income and wealth inequalities are higher than consumption inequality.

Table 7.3 reports on the evolution of poverty in India using the traditional poverty line. HCRs are reported for 1993–4, 2004–5, as well as 2009–10 along with poverty gaps and the squared poverty gap. Table 7.4 reports the Planning Commission/Niti Aayog data on HCR for 2004–5 and 2009–10 using the TCR criterion. Poverty rates are arranged in an increasing order of magnitude.

The HCR for the rural sector has fallen steadily from 37.3 per cent in 1993–4 to 28.3 per cent in 2004–5 and, more rapidly, to 22.2 per cent in 2009–10. In the urban sector, poverty fell from 32.4 per cent in 1993–4 to 25.7 per cent in 2004–5 and, more rapidly, to 22.2 per cent in 2009–10. In the rural sector in 1993–4, Maharashtra, MP, WB, UP, Assam, Orissa, and Bihar had an HCR higher than the national HCR, whereas Punjab, AP, Gujarat, Kerala, Rajasthan, Haryana, Karnataka, HP, JK, and Tamil Nadu had a lower HCR than the national average. In the urban sector in 1993–4, Bihar, Maharashtra, UP, AP, Tamil Nadu, Karnataka, Orissa, and MP had higher poverty than the national

Table 7.3 Poverty estimates using traditional poverty line methodology for select states and all India

State/India	1993-4 (50th Round)				2004-5 (61st Round)				2009-10 66th Round											
									Head Count Ratio				Poverty Gap				Square Poverty Gap			
	State/India	Rural	State/India	Urban	State/India	Rural	State/India	Urban	State/India	Rural	State/India	Urban	State/India	Rural	State/India	Urban	State/India	Rural	State/India	Urban
Punjab	Assam	12	Jammu and Kashmir	7.7	Assam	4.6	Jammu & Kashmir	3.3	Punjab	4.36	Punjab	6.27	Punjab	0.42	Punjab	0.92	Punjab	0.067	Punjab	0.21
Andhra Pradesh	Himachal Pradesh	15.9	Punjab	9.2	Himachal Pradesh	9.1	Punjab	3.4	Assam	4.90	Jammu & Kashmir	6.93	Jammu & Kashmir	0.66	Jammu & Kashmir	1.09	Assam	0.19	Assam	0.23
Gujarat	Jammu and Kashmir	22.2	Himachal Pradesh	9.2	Punjab	10.7	Andhra Pradesh	7.1	Jammu & Kashmir	6.40	Andhra Pradesh	7.91	Assam	0.97	Himachal Pradesh	1.10	Jammu & Kashmir	0.26	Jammu & Kashmir	0.23
Kerala	Punjab	25.8	Andhra Pradesh	11.4	Jammu and Kashmir	11.2	Himachal Pradesh	7.9	Himachal Pradesh	6.80	Himachal Pradesh	8.01	Haryana	1	Haryana	1.42	Haryana	0.27	Haryana	0.36
Rajasthan	Haryana	26.5	Kerala	16.4	Andhra Pradesh	13.2	Kerala	13	Haryana	9.60	Rajasthan	9.69	Himachal Pradesh	1.20	Rajasthan	1.60	Himachal Pradesh	0.28	Himachal Pradesh	0.42
Haryana	West Bengal	28	Haryana	22.4	Kerala	13.6	Rajasthan	14.8	West Bengal	10.40	Gujarat	12.31	Gujarat	1.50	Gujarat	2.18	Gujarat	0.30	Gujarat	0.56
Karnataka	Kerala	29.9	Rajasthan	24.6	Haryana	18.7	Haryana	15.1	Gujarat	11.30	Kerala	12.76	West Bengal	1.63	West Bengal	2.37	West Bengal	0.48	West Bengal	0.68
Himachal Pradesh	Gujarat	30.3	Gujarat	27.9	Rajasthan	19.1	Gujarat	20.2	Andhra Pradesh	12	Haryana	15.44	Andhra Pradesh	1.80	Andhra Pradesh	2.78	Andhra Pradesh	0.49	Andhra Pradesh	0.77
Jammu and Kashmir	Rajasthan	30.3	Karnataka	30.5	Gujarat	20.8	Jharkhand	20.2	Kerala	13.46	Maharashtra	16.06	Kerala	2.22	Kerala	3.23	Kerala	0.53	Kerala	0.95
Tamil Nadu	India	32.5	Assam	32.4	Karnataka	22.3	Tamil Nadu	22.2	Rajasthan	14.67	Tamil Nadu	18.49	Tamil Nadu	2.23	Tamil Nadu	3.48	Tamil Nadu	0.56	Tamil Nadu	1.01
India	Bihar	37.3	Tamil Nadu	34.5	Tamil Nadu	22.8	Maharashtra	25.7	Tamil Nadu	14.70	Karnataka	19.84	Rajasthan	2.70	Karnataka	3.60	Rajasthan	0.76	Rajasthan	1.09
Maharashtra	Maharashtra	37.9	India	35.2	India	28.3	India	28	India	22.20	India	20.67	India	4.29	India	4.53	India	1.04	India	1.48
Madhya Pradesh	Uttar Pradesh	40.6	West Bengal	35.4	Uttar Pradesh	28.6	West Bengal	30.6	Maharashtra	24.61	Assam	22.43	Maharashtra	4.30	Maharashtra	5.55	Maharashtra	1.26	Maharashtra	1.91

West Bengal 40.8	Andhra Pradesh 38.3	Maharashtra 29.6	Maharashtra 32.2	Madhya Pradesh 26.50	Karnataka 23.45	Karnataka 4.59	West Bengal 5.84	West Bengal 1.27	Uttar Pradesh 1.96
Uttar Pradesh 42.3	Tamil Nadu 39.8	Uttar Pradesh 33.4	Karnataka 32.6	Assam 27.30	Uttar Pradesh 27.69	Uttar Pradesh 5.30	Uttar Pradesh 6.17	Uttar Pradesh 1.45	Karnataka 2.01
Assam 45	Karnataka 40.1	Madhya Pradesh 36.9	Rajasthan 32.9	Uttar Pradesh 30	Madhya Pradesh 31.97	Bihar 5.60	Madhya Pradesh 8.36	Madhya Pradesh 1.70	Bihar 2.84
Orissa 49.7	Orissa 41.6	Chhattisgarh 40.8	Bihar 34.6	Orissa 34.48	Orissa 32.46	Madhya Pradesh 8.20	Bihar 8.54	Bihar 2.60	Orissa 3.02
Bihar 58.2	Madhya Pradesh 48.4	Uttarakhand 40.8	Uttarakhand 36.5	Bihar 39.30	Bihar 36.35	Orissa 8.40	Orissa 8.80	Orissa 2.80	Madhya Pradesh 3.17
Chhattisgarh	Chhattisgarh	Bihar 42.1	Chhattisgarh 41.2	Chhattisgarh	Chhattisgarh	Chhattisgarh	Chhattisgarh	Chhattisgarh	Chhattisgarh
Jharkhand	Jharkhand	Jharkhand 46.3	Madhya Pradesh 42.1	Jharkhand	Jharkhand	Jharkhand	Jharkhand	Jharkhand	Jharkhand
Uttarakhand	Uttarakhand	Orissa 46.8	Orissa 44.3	Uttarakhand	Uttarakhand	Uttarakhand	Uttarakhand	Uttarakhand	Uttarakhand

Sources: For 1993–4 and 2004–5: Planning Commission, Government of India, Databook for DCH, April 2012. For 2009–10: Authors' computations.

Table 7.4 Poverty in India and states 2004–5, 2009–10, and 2011–12 using TCR methodology

2009–10 Rural			2009–10 Urban			2009–10 Total			2004–5 Rural			2004–5 Urban			2004–5 Total		
State/India	Percentage of persons	No. of persons (lakhs)	State/India	Percentage of persons	No. of persons (lakhs)	State/India	Percentage of persons	No. of persons (lakhs)	State/India	Percentage of persons	No. of persons (lakhs)	State/India	Percentage of persons	No. of persons (lakhs)	State/India	Percentage of persons	No. of persons (lakhs)
Puducherry	0.2	0	A & N Islands	0.3	0	A & N Islands	0.4	0	Lakshadweep	0.4	0	A & N Islands	0.8	0	A & N Islands	3	0.1
A & N Islands	0.4	0	Puducherry	1.6	0.1	Puducherry	1.2	0.1	Daman & Diu	2.6	0	Nagaland	4.3	0.2	Lakshadweep	6.4	0
Delhi	7.7	0.3	Lakshadweep	1.7	0	Lakshadweep	6.8	0	A & N Islands	4.1	0.1	Himachal Pradesh	4.6	0.3	Nagaland	8.8	1.7
Jammu & Kashmir	8.1	7.3	Sikkim	5	0.1	Goa	8.7	1.3	Nagaland	10	1.5	Mizoram	7.9	0.4	Daman & Diu	8.8	0.2
Himachal Pradesh	9.1	5.6	Goa	6.9	0.6	Chandigarh	9.2	1	Meghalaya	14	2.9	Puducherry	9.9	0.7	Chandigarh	11.6	1.1
Chandigarh	10.3	0	Chandigarh	9.2	0.9	Jammu & Kashmir	9.4	11.5	Jammu & Kashmir	14.1	11.6	Chandigarh	10.1	0.9	Delhi	13	19.3
Goa	11.5	0.6	Tripura	10	0.9	Himachal Pradesh	9.5	6.4	Delhi	15.6	1.1	Jammu & Kashmir	10.4	2.9	Jammu & Kashmir	13.1	14.5
Kerala	12	21.6	Mizoram	11.5	0.6	Kerala	12	39.6	Kerala	20.2	42.2	Lakshadweep	10.5	0	Puducherry	14.2	1.5
Punjab	14.6	25.1	Kerala	12.1	18	Sikkim	13.1	0.8	Punjab	22.1	36.7	Delhi	12.9	18.3	Mizoram	15.4	1.5
Uttarakhand	14.9	10.3	Himachal Pradesh	12.6	0.9	Delhi	14.2	23.3	Puducherry	22.9	0.8	Daman & Diu	14.4	0.1	Meghalaya	16.1	4.1
Meghalaya	15.3	3.5	Jammu & Kashmir	12.8	4.2	Punjab	15.9	43.5	Mizoram	23	1.1	Dadra & Nagar	17.8	1.1	Kerala	19.6	62
Sikkim	15.5	0.7	Tamil Nadu	12.8	43.5	Meghalaya	17.1	4.9	Haryana	24.8	38.8	Kerala	18.4	19.8	Punjab	20.9	53.6
Haryana	18.6	30.4	Delhi	14.4	22.9	Tamil Nadu	17.1	121.8	Himachal Pradesh	25	14.3	Punjab	18.7	16.9	Himachal Pradesh	22.9	14.6

Value	State	Value	State	Value	Value	State	Value	Value	State	Value	Value	State	Value	Value	State	Value	Value
19.3	Nagaland	2.8	Andhra Pradesh	17.7	48.7	Tripura	17.4	6.3	Goa	28.1	1.8	Tamil Nadu	19.7	59.7	Haryana	24.1	54.6
19.8	Tripura	5.4	Dadra & Nagar	17.7	0.3	Uttarakhand	18	17.9	Sikkim	31.8	1.5	Gujarat	20.1	42.9	Goa	24.9	3.4
21.2	Tamil Nadu	78.3	Gujarat	17.9	44.6	Haryana	20.1	50	Andhra Pradesh	32.3	180	Assam	21.8	8.3	Tamil Nadu	29.4	194.1
22.2	Lakshadweep	0	Punjab	18.1	18.4	Nagaland	20.9	4.1	Arunachal Pradesh	33.6	3.2	Goa	22.2	1.7	Andhra Pradesh	29.6	235.1
22.8	Andhra Pradesh	127.9	Maharashtra	18.3	90.9	Andhra Pradesh	21.1	176.6	Chandigarh	34.7	0.2	Haryana	22.4	15.9	Sikkim	30.9	1.7
26.1	Karnataka	97.4	Karnataka	19.6	44.9	Mizoram	21.1	2.3	Uttarakhand	35.1	23.1	Tripura	22.5	1.5	Arunachal Pradesh	31.4	3.8
26.2	Arunachal Pradesh	2.7	Rajasthan	19.9	33.2	Gujarat	23	136.2	Rajasthan	35.8	166.4	Andhra Pradesh	23.4	55	Gujarat	31.6	171.4
26.4	Rajasthan	133.8	India	20.9	764.7	Karnataka	23.6	142.3	Assam	36.4	89.4	Arunachal Pradesh	23.5	0.6	Uttarakhand	32.7	29.7
26.7	Gujarat	91.6	West Bengal	22	62.5	Maharashtra	24.5	270.8	Karnataka	37.5	134.7	Jharkhand	23.8	16	Karnataka	33.3	186.5
28.8	West Bengal	177.8	Madhya Pradesh	22.9	44.9	Rajasthan	24.8	167	Tamil Nadu	37.5	134.4	West Bengal	24.4	60.8	West Bengal	34.2	288.3
29.5	Maharashtra	179.8	Haryana	23	19.6	Arunachal Pradesh	25.9	3.5	West Bengal	38.2	227.5	Meghalaya	24.7	1.2	Assam	34.4	97.7
31.1	Mizoram	1.6	Chhattisgarh	23.8	13.6	West Bengal	26.7	240.3	Gujarat	39.1	128.5	India	25.5	814.1	Rajasthan	34.4	209.8
33.8	India	2,782.10	Meghalaya	24.1	1.4	India	29.8	3,546.80	Manipur	39.3	6.7	Maharashtra	25.6	114.6	India	37.2	4,072.20
34.2	Daman & Diu	0.2	Arunachal Pradesh	24.9	0.8	Daman & Diu	33.3	0.8	India	42	3,258.10	Karnataka	25.9	51.8	Manipur	37.9	9
39.2	Orissa	135.5	Nagaland	25	1.4	Madhya Pradesh	36.7	261.8	Uttar Pradesh	42.7	600.5	Sikkim	25.9	0.2	Maharashtra	38.2	392.4

(cont'd)

Table 7.4 (cont'd)

2009–10 Rural			2009–10 Urban			2009–10 Total			2004–5 Rural			2004–5 Urban			2004–5 Total		
State/India	Percentage of persons	No. of persons (lakhs)	State/India	Percentage of persons	No. of persons (lakhs)	State/India	Percentage of persons	No. of persons (lakhs)	State/India	percentage of persons	No. of persons (lakhs)	State/India	percentage of persons	No. of persons (lakhs)	State/India	percentage of persons	No. of persons (lakhs)
Uttar Pradesh	39.4	600.6	Uttarakhand	25.2	7.5	Orissa	37	153.2	Tripura	44.5	11.9	Uttarakhand	26.2	6.6	Tripura	40	13.4
Assam	39.9	105.3	Orissa	25.9	17.7	Uttar Pradesh	37.7	737.9	Maharashtra	47.9	277.8	Chhattisgarh	28.4	13.7	Uttar Pradesh	40.9	730.7
Jharkhand	41.6	102.2	Assam	26.1	11.2	Assam	37.9	116.4	Jharkhand	51.6	116.2	Rajasthan	29.7	43.5	Jharkhand	45.3	132.1
Madhya Pradesh	42	216.9	Jharkhand	31.1	24	Jharkhand	39.1	126.2	Madhya Pradesh	53.6	254.4	Uttar Pradesh	34.1	130.1	Madhya Pradesh	48.6	315.7
Manipur	47.4	8.8	Uttar Pradesh	31.7	137.3	Dadra & Nagar	39.1	1.3	Chhattisgarh	55.1	97.8	Manipur	34.5	2.3	Dadra & Nagar	49.3	1.3
Bihar	55.3	498.7	Daman & Diu	33	0.5	Manipur	47.1	12.5	Bihar	55.7	451	Madhya Pradesh	35.1	61.3	Chhattisgarh	49.4	111.5
Dadra & Nagar	55.9	1	Bihar	39.4	44.8	Chhattisgarh	48.7	121.9	Orissa	60.8	198.8	Orissa	37.6	22.8	Bihar	54.4	493.8
Chhattisgarh	56.1	108.3	Manipur	46.4	3.7	Bihar	53.5	543.5	Dadra & Nagar	63.6	1.1	Bihar	43.7	42.8	Orissa	57.2	221.6

Source: Planning Commission, Government of India, Databook for DCH; April 2012.

Notes: 1. Population as on 1 March 2010 has been used for estimating the number of persons below poverty line (interpolated between the 2001 and 2011 population census).

For population in 2004–5, data as on 1 March 2005 has been used for estimating the number of persons.

2. The poverty line of Tamil Nadu is used for Andaman and Nicobar Islands; the Urban Poverty Line of Punjab is used for both rural and urban areas of Chandigarh.

3. The poverty line of Maharashtra is used for Dadra & Nagar Haveli as well; the poverty line of Goa is used for Daman & Diu as well.

HCR, whereas Assam, HP, JK, Punjab Haryana, WB, Kerala, Gujarat, and Rajasthan had lower poverty than the national average.

In the rural sector in 2004–5, JK, Punjab, HP, AP, Kerala, Haryana, Rajasthan, Gujarat, Karnataka, Assam, and Tamil Nadu had lower poverty than the nation as a whole, whereas WB, Maharashtra, UP, MP, Chhattisgarh, Uttarakhand, Bihar, Jharkhand, and Orissa had higher poverty than the national average. In the urban sector in 2004–5, Assam, HP, Punjab, JK, Gujarat, WB, Haryana, Jharkhand, Kerala, and Tamil Nadu had lower poverty than India as a whole, whereas AP, UP, Maharashtra, Karnataka, Rajasthan, Bihar, Uttarakhand, Chhattisgarh, MP, and Orissa had higher poverty than the national average.

In 2009–10 in the rural sector, JK, Punjab, AP, HP, Kerala, Rajasthan, Haryana, Gujarat, Tamil Nadu, Karnataka, and Maharashtra had lower poverty than the national HCR, whereas WB, MP, Assam, UP, Orissa, and Bihar had higher poverty than the national HCR. In the urban sector in 2009–10, Punjab, Assam, JK, HP, Haryana, WB, Gujarat, AP, Kerala, Rajasthan, and Tamil Nadu had lower poverty than the national HCR, whereas Maharashtra, Karnataka, UP, MP, Bihar, and Orissa had higher poverty than the national HCR.

In 2011–12 for their rural sectors, Uttarakhand, Assam, Bihar, Nagaland, Maharashtra, Punjab, Meghalaya, Arunachal Pradesh, Karnataka, Chhattisgarh, and Delhi had HCRs higher than the national level. In urban areas, A&N islands, Kerala, Delhi, Orissa, Punjab, Arunachal Pradesh, Assam, Maharashtra, Daman and Diu, Chhattisgarh, Karnataka, Uttarakhand, Bihar, and Meghalaya had higher HCRs than the national level. For the combined data, Uttarkahand, Maharashtra, Assam, Punjab, Bihar, Arunachal Pradesh, Meghalaya, Karnataka, Delhi, and Chhattisgarh had higher HCRs than the national level.

For the sake of completeness, Table 7.3 also reports the poverty gap and the squared poverty gap as indicators of the depth of poverty and Table 7.4 reports on the computations of the HCR[6] by the methodology of the TCR for 2004–5, 2009–10, and 2011–12. Table A7.1 in the Appendix to this chapter provides information on the poverty lines used by the Planning Commission in its approach to implement the TCR for 2009–10 and 2011–12. As many as 354,680,000 Indians (278,210,000 in the rural sector and 76,470,000 in the urban sector) were poor in 2009–10 according to the Planning Commission.

---

[6] These are subject to the critique of the TCR discussed earlier.

National Institution for Transforming India (NITI) Aayog data revealed that 269,780,000 Indians, consisting of 216,660,000 people from the rural sector and 53,120,000 from the urban sector, were poor. Thus, there have been significant declines both in the HCRs as well as the number of poor. With respect to the persistence of poverty, Jha et al. (2012) indicate that, at least in rural India, there is very high incidence of transient poverty, with only 10 per cent of the population chronically poor. Thus, covariate and idiosyncratic shocks form a good proportion of the explanation for poverty.

Our analysis here has shown that the aggregate GDP growth matters in poverty alleviation, measured traditionally or as per the TCR, but agricultural growth matters more (despite a sharp reduction in its contribution to the GDP) since most of the poor are in agriculture. Agricultural growth makes four contributions to poverty alleviation: its direct growth component, its indirect growth component, the participation of the poor in the growth of this sector, and its size in the overall economy.

REDUCING POVERTY, INEQUALITY, AND HUNGER: POLICY AND TARGETING ISSUES

There is ample literature on the association between economic growth and poverty reduction. Just as a tide raises all the boats higher, economic growth makes everyone better off—so goes the refrain, to which James Tobin had responded: not if the boats have leaks! India's anti-poverty policy certainly has had more than its fair share of leaks. Two basic principles of an effective anti-poverty strategy, even against the backdrop of high rates of economic growth, are fairly straightforward. Since a huge majority of the poor reside in the rural sector, any successful anti-poverty programme must focus on the agricultural sector and, second, since the poor have only one asset—their labour—any anti-poverty strategy must involve a sharp and sustained increase in the demand for labour, particularly in the rural sector. The performance of the Indian economy with regard to both has been lacklustre. Balakrishnan et al. (2008) consider stagnant public

Table 7.5 Tendulkar poverty head count ratios and number of poor in 2011–12

Rural			Urban			Combined		
State/UT	HCR	No. of poor (lakhs)	State/UT	HCR	No. of poor (lakhs)	State/UT	HCR	No. of poor (lakhs)
Lakshadweep	0	0.0	Dadra & Nagar Haveli	0	0	Dadra & Nagar Haveli	1	0.0
Puducherry	0	0.0	Puducherry	3.4	0.02	Puducherry	2.8	0.0
Dadra & Nagar Haveli	1.6	0.0	Tamil Nadu	3.7	0.1	Gujarat	5.1	0.8
Daman & Diu	1.6	0.0	Gujarat	4.1	0.4	Madhya Pradesh	7.1	23.9
Gujarat	6.8	0.4	Jammu & Kashmir	4.3	0.3	Jammu & Kashmir	8.1	5.6
Rajasthan	7.7	13.4	Madhya Pradesh	5	8.5	Tamil Nadu	8.2	0.5
Jammu & Kashmir	8.5	5.3	Andhra Pradesh	5.8	17	Rajasthan	8.3	23.2
Madhya Pradesh	9.1	15.5	Chandigarh	6.3	0.6	Andhra Pradesh	9.2	78.8
Tamil Nadu	9.9	0.4	Nagaland	6.4	0.4	Chandigarh	9.7	1.2
Andhra Pradesh	11	61.8	Tripura	6.5	23.4	Goa	9.9	17.0
Jharkhand	11.5	10.7	Jharkhand	7.2	2.5	Lakshadweep	9.9	0.3
Himachal Pradesh	11.6	19.4	Uttar Pradesh	7.4	0.8	Jharkhand	10.3	13.3
West Bengal	11.6	8.2	Manipur	9.1	47.4	Himachal Pradesh	11.2	28.8
Mizoram	12.5	3.0	Rajasthan	9.2	9.8	Tripura	11.3	82.6
Goa	12.9	0.5	Mizoram	9.3	0.6	West Bengal	11.3	11.6
Tripura	15.8	59.2	Goa	9.8	16.5	Mizoram	11.9	3.6
Sikkim	16.1	84.2	Haryana	10.1	26.9	Uttar Pradesh	14	5.2

(cont'd)

Table 7.5 (cont'd)

Rural			Urban			Combined		
State/UT	HCR	No. of poor (lakhs)	State/UT	HCR	No. of poor (lakhs)	State/UT	HCR	No. of poor (lakhs)
Uttar Pradesh	16.5	4.5	Himachal Pradesh	10.3	9.4	Sikkim	14.7	102.9
Chandigarh	17.1	0.7	West Bengal	10.5	3.4	Haryana	16.6	102.2
Orissa	19.9	2.8	Sikkim	10.7	18.7	Manipur	17.4	197.9
Haryana	21.5	75.4	Lakshadweep	12.6	0.3	Orissa	18.9	3.8
A & N Islands	22.5	141.1	India	13.7	531.2	A & N Islands	20	185.0
Manipur	24.2	150.6	A & N Islands	14.7	43.8	Nagaland	20.4	2.3
Kerala	24.5	92.8	Kerala	15.3	37	Kerala	20.9	129.8
All India	25.7	2,166.6	Delhi	15.4	0.3	Daman & Diu	21.8	2.3
Uttarakhand	30.4	479.4	Orissa	16.5	1	India	21.9	2,697.8
Assam	33.9	92.1	Punjab	17.3	12.4	Uttarakhand	29.4	598.2
Bihar	34.1	320.4	Arunachal Pradesh	20.3	0.7	Maharashtra	31.6	234.1
Nagaland	35.4	1.9	Assam	20.5	9.2	Assam	32	101.3
Maharashtra	35.7	191.0	Maharashtra	21	43.1	Punjab	32.6	138.5
Punjab	35.7	126.1	Daman & Diu	22.3	2.3	Bihar	33.7	358.2
Meghalaya	38.8	7.4	Chhattisgarh	24.8	15.2	Arunachal Pradesh	34.7	4.9
Arunachal Pradesh	38.9	4.2	Karnataka	24.8	20.2	Meghalaya	36.9	10.2
Karnataka	40.8	104.1	Uttarakhand	26.1	118.8	Karnataka	37	124.3
Chhattisgarh	44.6	88.9	Bihar	31.2	37.8	Delhi	39.3	1.4
Delhi	62.6	1.2	Meghalaya	32.6	2.8	Chhattisgarh	39.9	104.1

Source: Planning Commission, Government of India, Databook for DCH, April 2012.

investment in agriculture, even as agricultural subsidies have gone up, and continuous fragmentation of landholdings as two of the principal reasons for the lagging productivity and employment in agriculture. These trends must be reversed. The quality of public investment, in particular, must be improved and a new blueprint for engaging the private sector in meaningful public–private partnerships must be evolved. Agricultural growth is important for its own sake since it employs more than 60 per cent of the labour force despite accounting for a relatively small portion of the GDP. Further, agricultural growth would have dampened the double digit food price inflation that occurred recently, thereby furthering the cause of macroeconomic stabilization. In addition, non-agricultural growth both in the rural and the urban sectors should be enhanced and labour markets made more flexible to ensure rapid growth of employment. Not surprisingly, the golden age of rural poverty reduction was the 1980s when the adoption of Green Revolution technology led to sharp rises in agricultural growth, employment, and incomes.

The NSS estimated aggregate unemployment at 8.28 per cent on a current daily status (CDS) basis for 2004–5, but the first survey on employment and unemployment (Ministry of Labour and Employment 2010) estimated 2009–10 unemployment in the economy as a whole at 9.4 per cent, with 7.3 per cent of the urban labour force unemployed while the rural unemployment stood at a staggering 10.1 per cent. Further, there is the burden of large-scale underemployment. Hence, a basic problem with the current growth experience is that not enough productive jobs for unskilled and semi-skilled workers are being created. Unless this problem is attacked front and centre, rapid reduction of mass poverty will remain a mirage for India, although gradual and slow improvements will take place.

India has instituted a number of anti-poverty measures, but a large number of them are subject to considerable errors of targeting, that is, Tobin's leaking boats. Thus, Jha et al. (2009b) showed that one of the most popular and widely discussed anti-poverty intervention, the National Rural Employment Guarantee Scheme (NREGS), was subject to capture by wealthier elements in a relatively well-off state such as Andhra Pradesh.

The government's own statistics indicate that the performance of the National Rural Employment Guarantee Scheme (NREGS) across the four criteria has been very disappointing and has deteriorated over time (Jha and Gaiha 2012): (*a*) average number of days of employment per household; (*b*) percentage of households completing 100 days of employment under the NREGS; (*c*) percentage of expenditure against total available funds; and (*d*) percentage of work completed in 2009–10 and 2011–12.

The NREGS is an example of a broad class of rural public works (RPWs) programmes. The RPWs have been widely cited as a crucial tool for poverty alleviation, particularly in the rural sector (World Bank 2001). Properly designed RPWs provide employment to the unemployed (hence reducing poverty) and build the much-needed rural infrastructure. Besides, as the RPWs are designed to peak in seasonally slack periods, they help stabilize incomes. Since they stimulate rural incomes and, therefore, demand, the RPWs have the potential of stimulating the rural economy and, hence, act as a counterfoil to contracting demand during recessions. RPWs have been used in many countries. But Jha et al. (2011b) compare the capture of the RPW and the Food for Work (FFW) programmes for the 1993–4 and 2004–5 NSS and find a high degree of capture of programmes meant essentially for the poor, by non-poor groups. This capture is often in return for contributions made by the rural rich to politicians. These programmes are often meant to target socially backward groups such as Scheduled Castes (SC) and Scheduled Tribes (ST). In particular, targeting among SC worsened significantly between 1993–4 and 2004–5. Since these results are based on all-India samples, they call into question the entire basis for targeting by social class; income-based targeting is likely to yield much better results.

Since the introduction of Aadhaar cards, identification of the recipients of government subsidy has, however, become much easier. Direct Benefit Transfer of subsidies for food, kerosene, LPG, and fertilizers among others has led to a considerable diminution of leakages from the system. A recent report indicated that the government expected the reduction to be of the order of 35 to 40 per cent.[7] The rationalization of fuel subsidies following the dismantling of the Administered Price

---

[7] See http://www.livemint.com/Politics/nCiltUfKCOodusoBesE85M/Govt-expects-DBT-to-plug-3540-leakage-in-PDS.html. Last accessed on 10 January 2018.

Regime in a number of cases, accompanied by voluntary relinquishing of the LPG subsidy by the better-off sections of the society, facilitated the Ujawla programme whereby free gas connections were given to the below poverty line (BPL) households. By July 2017, 25 million households had benefited from this program.[8] Apart from the direct subsidy implied in this program, there is also the huge benefit of the women in these households not being exposed to toxic fumes from burning firewood. Aadhaar cards are linked to bank accounts. Through the Jan Dhan Yojana, the world's largest financial inclusion program, 30.84 crore bank accounts had been opened by 9th January 2018 with INR 72,266.94 crore deposited in them.[9] Bank accounts are now linked to Aadhaar cards whereby payments under the NREGS scheme are directly transferred into the beneficiary accounts. This has substantially reduced the large number of middlemen who used to siphon off portions of the NREGS earnings of workers. This must have a positive impact on poverty reduction, which should reflect in the household consumption data collected in the future.

Further, there is an urgent need to increase low-skill manufacturing employment. India has a natural comparative advantage in low-value-added manufacturing but, because it has not taken advantage of international production networks, this sector of the Indian economy has stagnated. This is particularly true in comparison with China, although India has a substantial labour-cost advantage. Thus, Anukoonwattaka and Mikic (2011) report that the monthly wage of a typical manufacturing worker in India was USD 23.80 in 2002, while for China the figure was USD 110.80. This wage gap has only widened since then because wages in China have grown substantially in the aftermath of a long period of rapid economic growth. Indeed, other economies, such as the Philippines, have stepped in to take advantage of the high labour costs in China and become integral parts of the international production network. Thus, it appears that India has not yet utilized its labour cost advantage to create more employment opportunities in the manufacturing sector. Two policy

[8] See http://www.livemint.com/Industry/cTycVe4kwGtmRNjvowf8BO/Ujjwala-scheme-for-LPG-connections-now-has-25-crore-benefic.html. Last accessed on 10 January 2018.

[9] See https://www.pmjdy.gov.in/. Last accessed on 10 January 2018.

measures are urgently needed to facilitate India's rapid integration into such networks: a) assured infrastructural services, and b) flexible labour laws, so that small- and medium-sized firms can plan production in response to changes in the international patterns of demand.

India's Targeted Public Distribution System (TPDS) is another programme notorious for its inefficiency, leakages, incompetent targeting of the poor, and a huge food subsidy bill. Consequently, for 2010–11 the food subsidy bill jumped by 27 per cent over the previous year to INR 742.310 billion (USD 16.495 billion at INR 45 = USD 1). However, Khera (2011) has indicated that there is considerable variation across states in the efficiency of the TPDS. In relation to the functioning of the TPDS, essentially the leakages from the TPDS and some other characteristics revealed by household data collected over 1993–4 to 2004–5, states could be categorized into three groups: (i) functioning (all the southern states, HP, and Maharashtra); (ii) reforming (Chhattisgarh, MP, Orissa, and UP); and (iii) languishing (mostly eastern states including Bihar, WB, and Jharkhand). States with 'functioning' TPDS systems had low leakages throughout this period, whereas 'reforming' states improved their performance on these criteria. 'Languishing' states performed poorly over 1993–4 to 2004–5. The improved performance of the 'reforming' states was itself driven by two factors: (*a*) increased food subsidy contribution from the central government, and (*b*) a rising gap between the open market price and the TPDS price of foodgrains, which led to an increased off-take from the TPDS. High food-price inflation makes a significant contribution to the persistence of poverty and it would be unfair to characterize the whole PDS as dysfunctional. However, if the impact of food price inflation is not addressed, any recent gains in poverty alleviation could be reduced if not wiped out entirely.

Careful attention must be given to reducing transaction costs—long distances to be travelled, long queues and waiting periods, and under-weighing by fair price shops (FPS). A better network of the FPS, higher margins, and adequate supplies would go a long way in making the TPDS more cost-effective. A real culprit is the FCI with its abysmal inefficiency in procuring, storing, and distributing food. Above all, top priorities include livelihood expansion opportunities in rural areas and food price stabilisation—two areas in which the government's track record has been and continues to be unimpressive. Indeed, a revamped TPDS on a smaller scale combined with more sensible policies that aim to augment productivity in agriculture, avoid market imperfections that come in the way of remunerative farm gate food prices, and expand livelihood options may lead to the fulfilment of food entitlements in a more economical and effective manner.

Further, best practices in the TPDS need to be adopted on a subnational level for the TPDS to improve. In line with the economist Raj Krishna who once advocated that Sikh farmers be asked to relocate to all parts of the country to teach others the benefits and practices of adopting the Green Revolution technology, it may be advisable to relocate bureaucrats from the states where the TPDS is functioning well to the states where the TPDS is reforming or languishing. A complementary policy initiative would be to raise the margin made available to retailers in the FPS so as to reduce their incentive to divert the TPDS stocks to the open market.

To address the hunger crisis, first and foremost food entitlements must be increased and guaranteed. For various reasons, most importantly that it would reduce farmers' incentives to expand output and grossly inflate the food subsidy bill, the Food Security Bill is not an answer to this issue. Ensuring rapid and efficient supply of foodgrains and eliminating all waste of food is certainly a part of the answer. Nutrition science suggests that one-third of the nutritional status of a child is determined in the mother's womb, before the child is born. Hence, ensuring adequate nutrition for women is a critical issue and must be addressed on a war footing. Social safety nets, if properly administered, can have a very strong impact on under-nutrition. Thus, Jha et al. (2011a) show for a household data set for 2007–8 for the states of Andhra Pradesh, Maharashtra, and Rajasthan that a transfer of as little as INR 100 per capita per month through the TPDS and, in many cases the NREGS, can substantially reduce under-nutrition in all major categories of macro and micro nutrients. Hence, the potential impact of social safety nets is very high—a fact that strongly underscores the importance of proper targeting and avoidance of leakages. Administrative reforms in these areas and active involvement of the private sector and civil society organizations are the key to success.

Some economists have advocated replacing the TPDS with food stamps or even cash payments to the BPL households. Under this scheme, instead of going to the FPS, households would buy from regular stores and get compensated by transfers to their bank accounts, which much of the poor do not yet have. However, study after study has indicated that directly subsidized food improves nutrition more than an equal amount of cash or food stamps (Gentilini 2007). Moreover, the value of such a cash aid can easily be eroded by inflation. In some cases, food stamps can be used to supplement a successful TPDS programme but should not replace it. Digital targeting in the manner discussed above for NREGS earnings would help improve the impact of the TPDS.

Finally, when it comes to inequality, India's excessive reliance on regressive commodity taxation and the handing out of current subsidies, which are largely garnered by the non-poor, need to be addressed. Moreover, the public provision of services, including essential services such as health and education, is stagnating, if not in decline, under fiscal pressure. The spectre of increasing inequality does not bode well for an increasing political support for the economic reforms programme. Here, too, there are some signs of hope. As a result of the drive to improve tax compliance through programmes such as demonetization and the GST along with subsequent tax reforms, redistributive taxation may become more effective in India.

* * *

This chapter has argued that more than 20 years since the current phase of economic reforms programme was initiated, inequality has grown and poverty has fallen according to the existing yardsticks of assessment. However, legitimate questions have been raised about the accuracy of these yardsticks. There is widespread spatial variation in both inequality and poverty. Having adequate nutrition—the traditional rationale for the poverty line—has not recorded impressive gains.

We have indicated that the most important means of lowering poverty is by creating jobs for poor, unskilled, and semi-skilled workers in both rural and urban sectors. The chapter advances arguments and suggestions for better targeting of anti-poverty interventions, for improving nutritional outcomes, and for reducing inequality.

Appendix

Table 7A.1 State-specific poverty lines for 2009–10 and 2011–12 (INR per capita per month)

State/India	2009–10 Rural	2009–10 Urban	State/India	2011–12 Rural	2011–12 Urban
Andhra Pradesh	693.8	926.4	Andhra Pradesh	860	1,009
Arunachal Pradesh	773.7	925.2	Arunachal Pradesh	930	1,060
Assam	691.7	871	Assam	828	1,008
Bihar	655.6	775.3	Bihar	778	923
Chhattisgarh	617.3	806.7	Chhattisgarh	738	849
Delhi	747.8	1040.3	Goa	1,090	1,134
Goa	931	1025.4	Gujarat	932	1,152
Gujarat	725.9	951.4	Haryana	1,015	1,169
Haryana	791.6	975.4	Himachal Pradesh	913	1,064
Himachal Pradesh	708	888.3	Jammu & Kashmir	891	988
Jammu & Kashmir	722.9	845.4	Jharkhand	748	974
Jharkhand	616.3	831.2	Karnataka	902	1,089
Karnataka	629.4	908	Kerala	1,018	987
Kerala	775.3	830.7	Madhya Pradesh	771	897
Madhya Pradesh	631.9	771.7	Maharashtra	967	1,126
Maharashtra	743.7	961.1	Manipur	1,118	1,170
Manipur	871	955	Meghalaya	888	1,154
Meghalaya	686.9	989.8	Mizoram	1,066	1,155
Mizoram	850	939.3	Nagaland	1,270	1,302
Nagaland	1016.8	1147.6	Orissa	695	861
Orissa	567.1	736	Punjab	1,054	1,155
Puducherry	641	777.7	Rajasthan	905	1,002
Punjab	830	960.8	Sikkim	930	1,226
Rajasthan	755	846	Tamil Nadu	880	937
Sikkim	728.9	1035.2	Tripura	798	920
Tamil Nadu	639	800.8	Uttar Pradesh	768	941
Tripura	663.4	782.7	Uttarakhand	880	1,082
Uttar Pradesh	663.7	799.9	West Bengal	783	981
Uttarakhand	719.5	898.6	A & N Islands		
West Bengal	643.2	830.6	Chandigarh		

(cont'd)

Table 7A.1 (cont'd)

	2009–10			2011–12	
State/India	Rural	Urban	State/India	Rural	Urban
A & N Islands			Dadra & Nagar Haveli		
Chandigarh			Daman & Diu		
Dadra & Nagar Haveli			Delhi	1,145	1,134
Daman & Diu			Lakshadweep		
Lakshadweep			Puducherry	1,301	1,309
India	672.8	859.6	India	816	1,000

Source: Planning Commission, Government of India, Databook for DCH, April 2012 and www.niti.gov.in.

REFERENCES

Anukoonwattaka, W. and M. Mikic (eds) (2011). 'India a New Player in Asian Production Networks'. UNESCAP Studies in Trade and Investment 75, Bangkok.

Balakrishnan, P., R. Golait, and P. Kumar (2008). 'Agricultural Growth in India since 1991'. Development Research Group Study No. 27, Department of Economic Analysis and Policy. Mumbai: Reserve Bank of India.

Deaton, A. and J. Dreze (2009). 'Food and Nutrition in India: Facts and Interpretations'. *Economic and Political Weekly* 44: 42–65.

Deaton, A. and V. Kozel (2005). 'Data and Dogma: The Great Indian Poverty Debate'. *World Bank Research Observer* 20(2): 177–99.

Gentilini, U. (2007). *Cash and Food Transfers: A Primer*. Rome: World Food Programme.

Jha, R. (2004). 'Reducing Poverty and Inequality in India: Has Liberalization Helped?'. In *Inequality, Growth and Poverty in an Era of Liberalization and Globalization*, edited by G.A. Cornia, 297–326. Oxford and New York: Oxford University Press.

Jha, R., R. Gaiha, and A. Sharma (2009a). 'Calorie and Micronutrient Deprivation and Poverty Nutrition Traps in Rural India'. *World Development* 37(5): 982–91.

———— (2009b). '"Capture" of Anti-Poverty Programs: An Analysis of the National Rural Employment Guarantee Program in India'. *Journal of Asian Economics* 20(2): 456–64.

_____ (2011a). 'Social Safety Nets and Nutrient Deprivation: An Analysis of the National Rural Employment Guarantee Program and the Public Distribution Scheme in India'. *Journal of Asian Economics* 22(2): 189–201.

_____ (2011b). 'Temporal Variations of Capture of Anti-poverty Programs: Rural Public Works and Food for Work Programs in Rural India'. *International Review of Applied Economics* 25(3): 349–62.

Jha, R. and R. Gaiha (2012). 'India's National Rural Employment Guarantee Program as It is—Interpreting the Official Data'. Australia South Asia Research Centre, Working Paper 2012/12.

Jha, R., W. Kang, H. Nagarajan, and K. Pradhan (2012). 'Vulnerability as Expected Poverty in Rural India'. Australia South Asia Research Centre, Working Paper 2012/04.

Khera, R. (2011). India's Public Distribution System: Utilisation and Impact'. *Journal of Development Studies*. Online publication DOI: 10.1080/00220388.2010.506917. Last accessed on 3 May 2017.

Kurosaki, T. (2011). 'Economic Inequality in South Asia'. In *Routlege Handbook of South Asian Economics*, edited by Raghbendra Jha, 61–75. London and New York: Routledge.

Ministry of Labour and Employment (2010). *Report on Employment and Unemployment Survey (2009–10)*. New Delhi: Labour Bureau, Government of India.

Morten, M. (2006). 'Indian Poverty during the 1990s: Resolving Methodological Issues from the 55th NSS Round'. Australia South Asia Research Centre Working Paper: 2006/07, Australian National University.

Pogge, T. and S. Reddy (2010). 'How Not to Count the Poor'. In *Debates in the Measurement of Poverty*, edited by S. Anand, P. Segal, and J. Stiglitz, 42–85. Oxford: Oxford University Press.

Srinivasan, T. (2007). 'Poverty Lines in India: Reflections after the Patna Conference'. *Economic and Political Weekly* 42(41): 4155–65.

_____ (2010). 'Irrelevance of the USD 1 a Day Poverty Line'. In *Debates in the Measurement of Poverty*, edited by S. Anand, P. Segal, and J. Stiglitz, 143–53. Oxford: Oxford University Press.

Subramanian, S. (2011). 'The Poverty Line: Getting It Wrong Again'. *Economic and Political Weekly* 46 (48): 37–42.

Swaminathan, M. (2010). 'The New Poverty Line: A Methodology Deeply Flawed'. *Indian Journal of Human Development* 4(1): 121–5.

World Bank, The (2001). *World Development Report 2000*. New York: Oxford University Press.

_____ (2011). *Perspectives on Poverty in India: Stylized Facts from Survey Data*. Washington DC: The World Bank.

CHAPTER 8

....

CASTE, CLASS, GENDER

dynamism or stasis?

....

ASHWINI DESHPANDE

The Indian economy, in the last three decades, has seen rapid and far-reaching changes resulting from globalization and liberalization. Given the multiple axes along which Indian society is divided, an investigation into how these fissures are changing in response to the growing integration of the Indian economy with the global economy is an extremely complex exercise. This chapter makes an attempt to capture a few key economic dimensions of the contemporary nature of caste, class, and gender disparities, with a larger focus on caste, while recognizing at the outset that there are many other critical identities, such as religion and region, which shape economic outcomes of individuals as well as group antagonisms just as significantly. The reason for focusing on three social identities is that affirmative action programmes in India are designed along caste and gender lines, thus providing an official acknowledgement of their salience. A strict space constraint has not allowed the discussion to go beyond these three, and has also precluded a comprehensive, in-depth assessment of each of these three fissures.

There is a view that as the Indian economy liberalizes, becomes more market-oriented, and increases its integration with the global economy, inter-group disparities are likely to reduce because of several reasons. One, labour market discrimination on account of social identity is expected to decline, and two, the creation of new and varying types of jobs is likely to provide an impetus to members of marginalized groups to acquire new skills and break out of traditional, caste-based, dead-end, oppressive, and stigmatizing occupations. The argument that discrimination is likely to reduce is based on the belief that market-orientation is likely to give primacy to profit maximization, and more generally, to efficient allocation of resources on the part of employers—a process in which the social identity of workers ought to be irrelevant. The implicit assumption in this argument is that foreign agents, especially, are less likely to be concerned with local hierarchies and the accompanying prejudices. The argument that employment avenues will expand and become more diverse is based on the premise that globalization will provide an impetus to certain sectors which will grow faster. This will induce a demand for skilled labour, among other things, which will open up avenues of employment, hitherto either limited or unavailable to the domestic population and, given the local labour market discrimination, out of reach for the marginalized groups in society.

Contrary to this set of arguments is the view that traditionally marginalized groups might be at a disadvantage even in this new scenario, given the legacy of exclusion from the kind of education that would be needed to take advantage of these emerging opportunities. Also, multinational corporations (MNCs) do not work in a vacuum; their hiring decisions are taken by local managers who are as aware of local social cleavages and are driven by the same prejudices as hiring managers of domestic firms. Foreign agents are not likely to disturb domestic norms and practices, or rock the boat, unless it is absolutely essential, since their bottom line is earning profits. Economic theory shows how maximization of profits and discrimination on account of social identity are not incompatible.[1] Indeed, research in

---

[1] See, for instance, Arrow (1971), Becker (1957), and Akerlof (1984).

the mechanics of the hiring process in urban formal labour markets (Deshpande and Newman 2007; Jodhka and Newman 2007) indicates that lip-service to merit notwithstanding, managers show a deep awareness of the overlapping and complex categories of caste, class, religion, and gender and of the strong stereotypical beliefs that merit is distributed along axes defined by these social identities. This is as true for private domestic firms as it is for MNCs.

Additionally, cross-national comparisons of inter-group disparities have highlighted that there seems to be no straightforward relationship between the relative prosperity of a country (or the level of its market orientation) and the severity of disparities (or the prevalence of discrimination). Darity and Deshpande (2003) summarise the major general findings that have emerged from these comparative inquiries. Specifically, they point out that intergroup disparity is persistent and significant in countries at all levels of development, whether the development is measured narrowly by per capita income or more broadly by a more encompassing index of well–being, such as the human development index (HDI). Also, higher rates of economic growth do not invariably close the economic gaps between racial and ethnic groups, nor does lower economic growth inevitably widen the gaps. This is relevant to the Indian discussion in that it suggests that India's high rate of growth in the post-liberalization era is not sufficient to close the gaps, just as a lower rate of growth would not necessarily widen the gaps.[2] We can apply this analogy to different states in India. We find lack of a clear pattern: intergroup disparity does not seem to be systematically related with growth, or the lack of it (Deshpande 2017).

In what follows, we briefly assess a few economic aspects of three contemporary group divisions—caste, class, and gender. The discussion is aimed to provide an overview of the critical aspects, and interested readers can follow the references at the end for more discussion on specific aspects.

---

[2] At the time of writing, the Indian economy has experienced a distinct slowdown in its aggregate rate of growth, thus highlighting the fact that greater integration with the global economy is not an unmitigated bonus. It also makes the domestic economy more vulnerable to international trends, for example, recession.

CASTE

Each renewed controversy over affirmative action inevitably rekindles the debate over the continued relevance or otherwise of caste as a category shaping *economic* outcomes in contemporary India. There is also the related issue of whether the primacy accorded to caste in public discourse actually keeps the (presumably considerably weakened, even dying) institution alive, whereas it needs to be given a quiet burial (Beteille 2012). This question also illustrates an interesting contrast between discussions on religion and caste: for some inexplicable reason, the legitimacy of the former is not questioned, either on the grounds of the institution being antiquated or on the grounds of promoting sectarian, communal mind-sets. This is despite the fact that religious schisms have erupted into extremely violent conflicts, with disturbing regularity, in virtually all parts of the country. The contrast between the discourse on caste and religion is reflected, for instance, in the collection of macro data. Starting with the national census, all data sets have data for individual religions but not for castes. At the moment, the availability of data on caste categories is dictated by the needs of the affirmative action policy, such that data are collected by broad aggregate groups which contain within them several diverse jatis and tribes, not separately enumerated: Scheduled Castes (SCs), Scheduled Tribes (STs), Other Backward Classes (OBCs), and Others (the residual).[3] Interestingly, till 2011 the Indian census did not count the OBCs separately, even though affirmative action for the OBCs had been a part of individual state policies for decades and had become a part of central government policies in 1991. That is, perhaps, the only instance of affirmative action anywhere in the world where a group being recognized as deserving affirmative action was not counted in the national census.

---

[3] The 2011 census has conducted an accompanying socio-economic and caste census but the data are not available yet.

Caste Disparities and Discrimination

The primary source of economic disparities between castes is the traditional link between caste and occupation. The caste system, since its inception, has seen enormous mutations as new castes got created through fission, fusion, migration, inter-marriages, and so forth. The operative form of contemporary caste divisions is jati and it shares some of the characteristics of the ancient varna system, but jatis are not clear subsets of varnas. The occupational distribution inherent in the varna system indicates a rudimentary economy; the jati system is more complex, but over the centuries, while occupational divisions have undergone a complete transformation with the modernization of the Indian economy, the mutations in jati divisions have not kept pace. Additionally, since Indian Independence in 1947, there is supposed to be no link between caste and occupation legally, in that it is illegal to deny a job to an applicant simply on the basis of caste (for that matter, on account of any social identity, for example, religion or gender). Thus, formally, the link between caste and occupation is broken and indeed a whole range of occupations in the modern economy, both in the public and private sectors, are not caste-based. However, an examination of the persistence or weakening of the link between caste and occupation has to be done at two levels: one, are traditional caste-based jobs, especially at the top and bottom ends of the traditional hierarchy (for example, scavengers, sweepers, or priests in temples), being allocated randomly, with no clear caste pattern? Two, is there any overlap between positions in the traditional caste hierarchy and the modern occupational spectrum? Data indicate that such an overlap between caste and status in the modern occupational spectrum persists. Castes that are lower in the traditional hierarchy are disproportionately represented in lower-paying modern occupations, whereas the opposite is true of high castes (Deshpande 2017). Thus, one finds persistent disparities in occupational attainment, with inter-state variations, between the broad caste groups of SC (or ST) and Others. It should be noted that any disparity based on this broad comparison actually *understates* the disparity between the top and bottom ends of the caste hierarchy, as Others is an omnibus and extremely heterogeneous category, containing castes and communities only marginally higher than the SCs in the social and economic hierarchy.

Given that income data are notoriously difficult to collect in India, one of the standard ways to examine disparities is to look at differences in education, occupation, consumption expenditure, and wages as indicators of the material standard of living. Hnatkovska et al. (2012) find a strong convergence between the SCs and Others in educational and occupational attainment as well as in consumption and wages and suggest that the convergence is driven by the narrowing of educational gaps. The picture, however, is complicated, not the least because while educational attainment at lower levels is converging, gaps from secondary education onwards are not necessarily converging. In Deshpande and Ramachandran (2016), we documented changes in caste disparities over time by splitting the data into age cohorts and comparing the average outcomes between cohorts across castes and time. We find that caste groups have been converging towards each other in terms of literacy rates and primary and middle school completion rates. However, for education levels higher than middle school, we find a divergence between caste groups over time, which is reflected in the divergence in access to prestigious white-collar jobs as well as consumption expenditure.

Elsewhere, I have created a 'caste development index' (CDI) based on five indicators of standard of living (educational attainment, occupational attainment, land ownership, livestock ownership, and consumer durable ownership) (Deshpande 2001), and calculated the CDI values using the three rounds of the National Family Health Survey (NFHS) data for each of the caste groups, by state. The gap between the CDI for the SCs and the CDI for 'Others' can be seen as a rough measure of inter-caste disparity (Deshpande 2011). Table 8.1 (Deshpande 2011: 90–1) shows the ranking of some major states by three measures: per capita (PC) state domestic product (SDP), CDI for the SCs, and disparity between the SCs and Others.

This table illustrates the lack of a clear pattern in the relationship between the material prosperity of a state, the material well-being of SCs, and inter-caste disparity.[4] Tamil Nadu is ranked number 6 in the per capita real SDP rankings in all the three years, qualifying it as a

---

[4] The same lack of relationship can be seen if one uses rate of growth of different states instead of the real SDP.

Table 8.1 Per capita SDP, CDI for SCs and disparity between SCs and others, major Indian states

Ranks	PC Real SDP			Disparity			CDI SC		
	1993–4	1998–9	2002–3	1992–3	1998–9	2003–4	1992–3	1998–9	2003–4
1	Delhi	Delhi	Delhi	Haryana	Tamil Nadu	Tamil Nadu	Himachal Pradesh	Delhi	Delhi
2	Punjab	Punjab	Maharashtra	Delhi	Madhya Pradesh	Rajasthan	Jammu	Maharashtra	Gujarat
3	Maharashtra	Maharashtra	Punjab	Punjab	Karnataka	Madhya Pradesh	Rajasthan	Punjab	Maharashtra
4	Haryana	Gujarat	Haryana	Bihar	Bihar	Bihar	Delhi	Gujarat	Assam
5	Gujarat	Haryana	Gujarat	Himachal Pradesh	Andhra Pradesh	Delhi	Punjab	Jammu	Himachal Pradesh
6	Tamil Nadu	Tamil Nadu	Tamil Nadu	Jammu & Kashmir	Haryana	Gujarat	Assam	Haryana	Jammu & Kashmir
7	Kerala	Karnataka	Himachal Pradesh	Madhya Pradesh	Orissa	Uttar Pradesh	Madhya Pradesh	Himachal Pradesh	Haryana
8	Himachal Pradesh	Himachal Pradesh	Karnataka	Maharashtra	Punjab	Punjab	Gujarat	Assam	Punjab
9	Karnataka	Kerala	Kerala	Orissa	Delhi	Andhra Pradesh	Haryana	Kerala	Rajasthan

10	Andhra Pradesh	Andhra Pradesh	West Bengal	Andhra Pradesh	Gujarat	Orissa	Uttar Pradesh	Madhya Pradesh	Madhya Pradesh
11	West Bengal	West Bengal	Andhra Pradesh	Tamil Nadu	Uttar Pradesh	Haryana	Maharashtra	Rajasthan	Uttar Pradesh
12	Madhya Pradesh	Rajasthan	Rajasthan	Karnataka	Rajasthan	Kerala	Karnataka	Uttar Pradesh	Kerala
13	Jammu & Kashmir	Madhya Pradesh	Madhya Pradesh	Rajasthan	Kerala	Himachal Pradesh	West Bengal	Tamil Nadu	Tamil Nadu
14	Rajasthan	Jammu and Kashmir	Assam	Gujarat	West Bengal	Jammu & Kashmir	Orissa	Karnataka	West Bengal
15	Assam	Assam	Orissa	West Bengal	Himachal Pradesh	Maharashtra	Andhra Pradesh	West Bengal	Andhra Pradesh
16	Uttar Pradesh	Orissa	Uttar Pradesh	Kerala	Assam	Karnataka	Kerala	Andhra Pradesh	Karnataka
17	Orissa	Uttar Pradesh	Bihar	Assam	Jammu & Kashmir	West Bengal	Bihar	Bihar	Orissa
18	Bihar	Bihar	N/A	Uttar Pradesh	Maharashtra	Assam	Tamil Nadu	Orissa	Bihar

Source: Deshpande (2011: 90–1).

Notes: Source of PC SDP: www.indiastat.com: table 51676.
Disparity and CDI are author's own calculations from NFHS I, II and III. Only those states that are common to all 3 rounds have been retained in this table.

relatively richer state among the 18 states. However, with no change in its relative ranking in the per capita real SDP, its ranking on disparity (gap in the CDI between Others and the SCs) was 11 in 1992–3 and increased to 1 (implying highest disparity) in the other two years. In terms of the CDI for the SCs (the indicator for the absolute standard of living for the SCs), it was the lowest among the Indian states in 1992–3 and rose to number 13 in the next rounds. These movements seem to be independent of the SDP levels; moreover, despite being a relatively rich state, it fares poorly on the CDI for the SCs and has fairly high disparity.

Uttar Pradesh, with a ranking of 16, 17, and 16 in the per capita real SDP rankings across the three rounds, is one of the poorest states in India. However, inter-caste disparity has steadily increased across the three rounds: from being the state with the lowest inter-caste disparity, it moved up to number 11 by 1998–9 and to number 7 in 2004–5, demonstrating that just as being a relatively rich state (for example, Tamil Nadu or Delhi) is no guarantee for lower disparity, being poor is not a guarantee either (witness Uttar Pradesh or Bihar). In terms of the CDI for the SCs, its ranking remains relatively stable: 12, 14, and 13, respectively, across the three rounds. One can find other examples to illustrate the basic point being made here: the relative prosperity of a state (or the lack of it) does not appear to be a good predictor either of inter-caste disparity or of the absolute level of development of the SCs.

Deshpande (2011: 93) also reports correlations between the CDI-SC and the per capita real net SDP, which is positive and has become stronger over the three NFHS rounds, from 0.09 to 0.72, and between the CDI-SC and the rate of growth of the per capita real NSDP, which was very low but positive in the first round, but turned negative in the latter two rounds, with the strength of the negative correlation declining from 0.09 to −0.27 to −0.16. The correlation between disparity and the per capita NSDP was positive in the first round (0.54), but declined to an insignificant -0.03 in the third round; the correlation between disparity and the rate of growth of the real per capita NSDP fluctuated in direction and magnitude and was ambiguous overall. Deshpande (2011) also discusses the relationship between overall inequality (as measured by the Gini coefficient calculated over the monthly per capita expenditure (MPCE) and both the CDI-SC and disparity. States with higher disparity not only have a higher Gini but a higher CDI-SC too.

Foreign Direct Investment and Intergroup Disparities

Coming back to the debate outlined in the beginning of this section about the possible impact of liberalization and globalization on intergroup disparities, one of the possible ways to examine this relationship is through an assessment of the foreign direct investment (FDI) data. Disaggregated data, which would allow us to identify the location of the project, are available only for the FDI approvals, not for the realised FDI.[5] An examination of this data, where the location of the proposed project can be identified by district, reveals a great deal of spatial clustering.[6] Thus, whatever the magnitude of new jobs created, they are limited to a small number of geographical clusters, limiting access to the local population or those who are willing to migrate. The next question is whether this employment generation is evenly distributed across social groups and between men and women, according to their share in the state's populations. The NCAER (2009: 18) suggests that India's attractiveness as an investment destination rests on the following factors: 'a large and growing market, world-class scientific, technical, and managerial manpower, cost-effective and highly skilled labour, ... a large English speaking population.' Sectoral distribution of the FDI projects confirms this picture in that the labour demand generated by the FDI is for workers with a specific educational and skill profile, and especially with a knowledge of English. Given the existing educational disparities by caste, prima facie, it appears that a large section of Dalits and women would not be prime candidates for these jobs.[7] Additionally, research into the pathways through which caste plays a role in urban, formal sector labour markets suggests that

[5] A large part of FDI comes in through the automatic route and does not require prior approval.

[6] I am grateful to the Ministry of Commerce, Government of India, for allowing me access to this data.

[7] The designation of English as the new 'Dalit goddess', as the vehicle which will eventually lead to Dalit emancipation is easier to understand in the context of the huge advantage that knowledge of English gives in the labour market. Available at http://www.indianexpress.com/news/happy-birthday-lord-macaulay-thank-you-for-dalit-empowerment/15423/0. Last accessed on 27 February 2011.

Dalits face direct and indirect discriminatory barriers even after they acquire higher education from reputed, elite institutions (Deshpande and Newman 2007).

Of course, this static picture could change. Growth in certain kinds of jobs could provide the requisite incentives to acquire higher education and English-language skills over time. The educational levels of the labour force could thus be both a cause and an effect of FDI (for example, certain kinds of FDI tend to get concentrated in areas that already have the labour force with requisite education and English skills, which then provide further incentives for increasing this skill acquisition). Unless the dynamic spreads to other areas, this could lead to further clustering of the FDI. Deshpande (2018) finds that, based on district level data for FDI approvals between 1995 and 2010, a greater number of FDI approvals were associated with *lower* relative wages of Dalits versus Others. This result is obtained after controlling for the relative proportions of Dalits versus Others with secondary education or more (the section which is eligible for FDI-induced jobs), and the relative proportion of those in regular wage/salaried jobs, as well as district-specific fixed effects. This suggests that earnings' gaps are more likely to widen, rather than diminish, controlling for other factors.

The Larger Impact of Globalization

The creation of new types of jobs through FDI is only one channel through globalization and liberalization that is likely to affect caste disparities, either positively or negatively. The broader argument for the emancipatory effect of globalization has several contours; it hinges on the fact that globalization will make the market salient as well as unleash competition between Indian and foreign firms, impacting Dalits positively in many dimensions. FDI and the MNCs will be an implicit and important, but not the only, part of this process. It has been argued that one of the ways in which globalization empowers Dalits is by 'universalising access to aspirations'. The reference is to the process of certain consumer goods being plentifully and cheaply available (for example, colour televisions, mobile phones, refrigerators, air conditioners, and so on) and within the reach of the Dalits, goods that are supposed to be 'material markers of pride'. It is argued that this has broken the exclusivity of the 'predominantly Upper Caste Consumer Club', a process aided also by the rise of Dalit entrepreneurs.[8] Omvedt (2005) argues that globalization is inevitable, already a reality for India, and has many positive aspects. Thus, instead of taking a blind anti-globalization position (as she argues the Left and ecologists in India take), she suggests that we need to think about a comprehensive and nuanced response of Dalits and Adivasis to these changing realities. This sentiment is echoed by others in that Dalits are asked to view globalization as an opportunity rather than as a threat.[9]

Kapur et al. (2010, 39), on the basis of a survey of all Dalit households in two blocks of two districts in Uttar Pradesh, argue that the shift from a state-led to a market-led path of development has changed patterns of interaction between castes, leading to a 'rapid erosion in discriminatory practices that stigmatized Dalits'. They also find large shifts in the pattern of economic life, both within and away from the village. They see this change manifesting itself both in terms of a change in occupational patterns, with Dalits moving away from traditional occupations, as well as in the nature of contracts between Dalits and upper castes, such that practices such as bonded labour that tied Dalits to generations of servitude appear to have become obsolete.

It is not immediately apparent to what extent the study of two blocks in one state can be generalized to the rest of the country. There has undoubtedly been significant changes in consumption patterns in contemporary India over the last two to three decades,[10] but these changes are neither confined to Dalits, nor is it clear that Dalits exhibit a differential pattern of *changes* in consumption compared to upper castes.

Another channel through which liberalization will have implications for caste disparity is privatization. At the moment, affirmative action in India takes the form of quotas for the SCs, the STs, and the

---

[8] Availabe at: http://www.chandrabhanprasad.com/frmGlobalization.aspx. Last accessed in February 2011.

[9] Chandra Bhan Prasad, see http://www.chandrabhanprasad.com/frmGlobalization.aspx. Last accessed in February 2011.

[10] See, for instance, Meenakshi (1996).

OBCs in public sector jobs and government-run educational institutions. As the economy privatizes and more jobs get created in the private sector, the scope of affirmative action in its present form is likely to shrink. Deshpande (2013) discusses the impact of the affirmative action programme in detail; suffice it to say here that while affirmative action has not been able to eliminate inter-caste disparity, partly because it is not designed for that purpose and partly because of inadequate implementation, there are compelling reasons to believe that the gaps would be larger in the absence of affirmative action.

Overall, the impact of globalization on caste disparities is complex, and contains many inter-woven strands, not necessarily easy to disentangle. What is noteworthy is that this debate over whether globalization will be favourable to Dalits or not, by and large, is *not* backed by hard empirical facts. Much more empirical work, based on smaller studies in different parts of India as well as on macro all-India data, needs to be undertaken before we can etch out the contours of the multidimensional impact of globalization on caste disparities.

CLASS

The rapid growth of the economy in the last two decades has resulted in a noticeable expansion in the group of 'high net worth individuals' (HNIs, individuals with investible assets of USD 1 million or more), or extremely affluent Indians. India's HNI population grew at 20.8 per cent to 1,53,000 in 2010 compared with 1,26,700 in 2009, according to the 2011 Asia-Pacific Wealth Report by Merrill Lynch Global Wealth Management and Capgemini. The cumulative wealth of Indian HNIs grew by 22 per cent in 2009–10 to INR 28,60,000 crore from a year ago.[11] These are globally connected individuals who enjoy lifestyles comparable to the elite in developed countries, and visibly shape patterns of conspicuous consumption in urban India, especially in metropolitan cities.

---

[11] Availabe at: http://businesstoday.intoday.in/story/india-high-networth-hni-population-grows-by-20-per-cent/1/19634.html. Last accessed in July 2012.

The growth of this elite segment, which is small in proportion but large in numbers and purchasing power, should be separated from the growth of the Indian middle class. A lot of attention has been given to the growth of the middle class, signalling the rapid growth of a domestic market; however, it should be noted that there is no official estimate of the size of the Indian middle class and estimates vary from 25 to 300 million. The variations in estimates come from different databases, but more importantly from how the middle class is defined. The middle class, by definition, should be defined as having an income within some interval which includes the median. Ravallion (2009) discusses the diverse and ad hoc ways in which the upper and lower bounds of this interval have been defined and suggests that a common way to define the middle class in developed countries is those having incomes between 75 and 125 per cent of the median of that country.[12] A key issue in the definition of the middle class is whether it is appropriate to use the same definition for both rich and poor countries.

Ravallion (2009: 6) suggests a 'developing world's middle class' defined as those who are not poor by the standards of developing countries but might be poor by the standards of developed countries. He suggests a lower bound of USD 2 a day, which is double the official poverty line of India (and also China). His upper bound is USD 13 a day, which is the US poverty line at the 2005 purchasing power parity (PPP).[13] A person will have entered the 'Western middle class' if earning more than the US poverty line. Using this definition for India, based on the National Sample Survey (NSS) data, he finds only 3 million people not poor by the US standards. Correcting for possible under-reporting of consumption expenditure in the NSS data by increasing all consumption expenditures by 50 per cent, the count of Indians who are not poor by the US standards rises to only six million (Ravallion 2009: 9). However, the growth of the segment which he defines as the 'developing country middle class' (proportion living between USD 2 and USD 13 a day) has been substantial

[12] This is a relative definition; Ravallion (2009) discusses other definitions which have absolute lower and upper bounds.

[13] These bounds are similar to those suggested by Banerjee and Duflo (2008).

between 1990 and 2005: an extra 117 million people joined this group in India. He argues that this is linked to a reduction in poverty, as the bulk of the increase in the middle class came from an increase in the USD 2 to USD 6 segment, rather than from an increase in the upper middle class.

Inequality and Class Conflict: Growth of the Maoist Movement

One side of the Indian growth story is reflected in the growth of the super-rich and the middle class. However, the other side of the story is rising inequality reflected in the growing class discontent, which found expression through the rise of the Maoist movement that has spread to several states in India, including Bihar, Jharkhand, Chhattisgarh, Madhya Pradesh, Orissa, Maharashtra, and Karnataka. Today, this movement, christened 'left wing extremism' (LWE) by the Indian state, poses a challenge major enough for the former Prime Minister Manmohan Singh to express concern about the fact that 'not a day passes without an incident of Left Wing Extremism taking place somewhere or the other … [making LWE] probably the single biggest security challenge to the Indian state.'[14]

The rapid spread of the movement over large parts of central and southern India in the last decade reinforces the need for a rigorous assessment of both the causes and consequences of this conflict. In one of the early empirical exercises, Borooah (2008) finds that the probability of Naxalite activity in a district increased with a rise in its poverty rate, and decreased with a rise in its literacy rate. In addition, districts with a smaller coverage of safe drinking water were more likely to have Naxalite activity, compared to districts where a greater proportion of the habitants had access to safe drinking water, clearly hinting at high poverty and lack of development as factors contributing to Maoist violence.

---

[14] Prime Minister Manmohan Singh's speech to the Conference of Chief Ministers on Internal Security, 20 December 2007. Available at: http://www.satp. org/satporgtp/countries/india/document/papers/20071220pmspeech.htm.   Last accessed on 13 May 2012.

In a cross-country study of violence in South Asia (not only Maoist conflict but including all other conflicts in the region), Iyer (2009) finds a clear divergence between 'leading' and 'lagging' regions in the post-2001 period, in that incidents of violence increased sharply in the lagging regions, while they remained steady in the leading regions. She defines regions as leading or lagging based on per capita income levels in 2004. According to this definition, the lagging regions in India were Assam, Bihar, Chhattisgarh, Jharkhand, Madhya Pradesh, Manipur, Mizoram, Meghalaya, Nagaland, Orissa, Rajasthan, Uttar Pradesh, Uttarakhand, and West Bengal. She finds that this trend further intensified after 2004, with lagging regions displaying a continued increase in conflict and leading regions showing a slight decline. This is mirrored in counter-terrorism activities, proxied by the number of terrorists killed by security forces, which has been declining in leading regions after 2005, possibly a reflection of lower levels of extremist activity in those areas, whereas the trend in lagging regions continues to rise.

Going further into the causes of conflict (again, note that her analysis is not confined to, but includes, the Maoist conflict) using district level data, Iyer finds that conflict is higher in poorer regions, with a large effect: an increase in poverty by 10 percentage points is associated with 0.26 incidents of conflict per district. This is quite high compared to an average of 0.77 incidents per district. A 10 percentage point increase in poverty is associated with 0.39 more deaths for an average district (compared to the mean level of 0.60 deaths per district). She also finds a significant positive relationship between intensity of conflict and the extent of mountain and forest cover. Exploring the impact of social diversity (proxied by the relative presence of members of disadvantaged groups in the population [fractions of SCs, STs, and Muslims]) and institutional quality (proxied by a measure of historical property rights based on whether land tenure was historically controlled by landlords), she finds that areas with lower historical land inequality have a lower incidence of conflict, but the relationship is not statistically significant and the presence of disadvantaged communities is not significantly associated with conflict intensity.

Thus, evidence suggests that poverty, illiteracy, or (more broadly) underdevelopment, combined with inequality in land ownership are the key factors responsible for the sustained growth of the Maoist movement in the last decade or so. Geography plays a role in two ways: one, that forested terrains facilitate guerrilla activity and two, these are the regions where tribals form a substantial proportion of the population, but where there is disaffection due to lack of control over forest land and/or mineral wealth. The question which remains to be answered is whether the movement is working as a Robin Hood state, redistributing to the poor what they believe is justly due, given the perception that the state is an instrument to protect the interests of the rich landlords; or whether the movement is more like an extortionist mafia, which, in return for extortion, provides protection and some community services, again hinting at state failure. Also, whether the Maoist strategy of individual annihilation (of those deemed to be class enemies) will fundamentally alter the material conditions of the marginalized and the dispossessed can be debated; the point being made is that there is sufficient material deprivation to fuel further growth of Maoism.

Official Response to the LWE

Official references, including journalistic accounts in the print media, regard LWE as an extremist menace, with frequent references to 'Naxalite-infested' areas. The speech in 2007 by the then Prime Minister, as quoted earlier, confirms this official view by resolving that 'we cannot rest in peace until we have eliminated this *virus*' [emphasis added]. While the movement and its sympathisers view themselves as spearheading a revolution for radical social transformation in response to deprivation and inequality, the official view inverts the cause and effect and sees the movement as *causing* deprivation in order to sustain its ideology.

This assertion of the Indian government is not unique to the LWE context. Indeed, the idea that conflict *causes* deprivation has been forcefully made in other international contexts. For instance, it has been suggested in the cases of Rwanda, Angola, Congo, and Sudan that war has resulted in a destruction of physical infrastructure as well as human capital, leading to a lowering of per capita incomes in war-affected countries; this being one of the factors in the growing gap between the world's richest and poorest nations (Blattman and Miguel 2009: 3).

Following directly from this view, the mainstream official view is towards the elimination of the movement through force. Increased Maoist activity has been met by increased police repression, resulting in heavy casualties on both sides. Since 2005, the Chhattisgarh state government has sponsored a counter-insurgency operation called 'Salwa Judum' (literally, the purification hunt), which is touted as a spontaneous people's reaction to the excesses of Naxalism (Sundar 2006). This outfit has killed several suspected Maoists and displaced thousands of people. There have been several reports of the terror unleashed by Salwa Judum, including sexual attacks on women. What is especially dangerous is that this is supposedly a civil society initiative but is completely state-sponsored and not accountable to any agency.

State-sponsored counter-violence, bypassing the due process of law and justice, is now a matter of serious concern as, in addition to Salwa Judum, there are suspected underground counter-insurgency forces acting in several states. Additionally, special counter-insurgency forces targeted towards the Maoists have been created. In Andhra Pradesh, an elite security force called the Greyhounds was launched in 1989. Though the size of the force is small, it consists of a highly trained cadre, and to match the highly trained force, all police capacities have been augmented. Harris (2010: 12) describes how the Greyhounds operate very much like the Naxalites' own squads and are 'bound by no law, including the constitution of India'. Thus, the approach is very clearly one of suppression by sheer force, reflecting the state's attitude that regards Maoism as a menace or, at best, a 'law and order' problem.

While this is the dominant approach, attempts have been made through the appointment of commissions, most notably through the formation of an expert group set up by the Planning Commission in 2008, to examine the 'Development Challenges in Extremist Affected Areas' (Planning Commission 2008). The report of this group comprehensively outlines the multi-faceted sources of discontent in areas of Maoist activity, with a detailed outline of the multiple class–caste–gender disadvantages of Dalits, Adivasis and women. It highlights, in particular, the sources of tribal alienation and a deep sense of exclusion, since a majority of the Scheduled Tribes live in conditions of serious deprivation and poverty despite several special and targeted policies. The conflict between the Adivasis and the Indian state is seen not only in the Maoist areas but in the North-Eastern states as well, such that the deep-rooted discontent gets manifested in various insurgent forms. In addition to poverty and illiteracy, the expert group highlighted the following causes of tribal discontent: 'absence of self-governance, forest policy, excise policy, land related issues (forced evictions from land, displacement) ... political marginalization' (p. 8). The report also points out that 'failure to implement protective regulations in Scheduled Areas, absence of credit mechanism leading to dependence on money lenders and consequent loss of land and often *violence by the State*' is rampant (emphasis added).

The right to forest land is a central part of the tension between the Adivasis and the State. The lip service to symbiotic relationships not-withstanding, the actual use of forests by communities traditionally dependant on forests for livelihoods, with traditional practices which preserve the ecological balance, has been regularly circumscribed. A related issue is large-scale displacement of tribals due to large development projects. Orissa, Jharkhand, and Chhattisgarh, in particular, have seen massive displacement of tribals on account of mining projects, and these have led to widespread protests. The expert group points out that unless tribals are resettled in scheduled areas, they will lose their special rights and are likely to be further marginalized.

Each of these issues is vital and complex, and will need to be assessed separately in complete detail, taking all the nuances into account. The point of this brief discussion is that the Indian state has access to a perspective which highlights the multiple causes of discontent and suggests very forcefully that the Maoist 'menace' is a political problem, not only a law-and-order one. Yet, the mainstream approach continues to be a security-based one. The danger with this approach is that the discontent can actually multiply manifold as, in addition to the already existing dissatisfaction against material deprivation and the resulting alienation, the local populations will now have to deal with the consequences of repression and violence by the state too.

It would be useful to recall that there have historically been specific episodes during the Naxalite movement that have seen political solutions. For instance, at the time of the first Naxalbari uprising, the United Front government was in power in West Bengal. The revenue minister Hare Krishna Konar of the Communist Party of India (Marxist) (CPI[M]) used Mao Zedong's theory of 'fish in water'—the disgruntled peasantry was the water in which the fish of militancy was bound to grow as long as the distress of the peasantry continued. Thus, the strategy to move the peasantry away from the militants took the form of acquisition of ceiling-surplus land of zamindars and big landlords by the government and its redistribution among the landless peasants. This was an important part of the anti-Naxalite strategy that proved effective in weaning a section of the peasantry away from the Naxalites; of course, this was accompanied by conventional law-and-order measures.

Gender

Gender disparities in educational and occupational attainment have been a persistent feature of the Indian society and the subject of a great deal of academic and policy attention (Rao et al. 2010). Considerable concern and attention is also centred on the adverse and declining sex ratio, the phenomenon of sex-selective foeticides and infanticides, and an overall neglect and malnutrition of the girl child. In the limited space of this chapter, I would like to focus on one specific aspect—that is, gender wage gaps—in order to comment on the nature of economic discrimination faced by women workers.

A standard way of estimating discrimination in labour markets is by decomposing the average wage gap into an 'explained' (by wage earning characteristics) part and the 'residual', which is part of the wage gap that remains even after all possible explanatory factors are accounted for. The residual is taken as the measure of discrimination in the labour market. Both the average wage gap as well as its decomposition are useful in that they provide a summary measure of discrimination. However, a newer technique of quantile regressions allows us to assess how returns to wage earning characteristics vary over different quantiles or over different parts of the wage distribution (so it allows us to answer questions, such as 'what happens where'). Using quantile regressions, we can see if wage gaps are higher at the top or bottom ends of the wage distribution. In other words, do women face a 'glass ceiling' or a 'sticky floor'? Estimating quantile regressions

separately for men and women also allows for separate decompositions for each quantile. Specifically, these quantile decompositions
allow us to answer the following question: do high earning women
face greater discrimination (greater residual or a greater unexplained
part) as compared to low wage earning women?

In Deshpande et al. (2018), we use nationally representative data
from the employment–unemployment schedule (EUS) of two large
rounds of the NSS, for 1999–2000 and 2009–10 respectively, in order
to explore gender wage gaps among the regular wage/salaried (RWS)
workers. We focus on this segment for two reasons. One, this is a segment of the workforce where jobs are presumed to be allocated on
meritocratic lines. Two, part of the reason underlying the low-reported
labour force participation rates of women in developing countries
such as India is under-reporting, that is, women underestimate and/
or under-report their involvement in productive work. This underes-
timation is likely to be minimal among the RWS workers. We examine
wage gaps at the mean as well as along the entire distribution. We
then decompose the gaps into an 'explained component' (due to gender differences in wage earning characteristics) and an 'unexplained
component' (due to gender differences in the labour market returns
to characteristics); the literature treats the latter as proxy for labour
market discrimination. We perform the standard mean decomposition as well as quantile decompositions.

We then evaluate changes in each of these over the ten-year time
period. Our study presents the latest comprehensive empirical evidence on gender wage gaps and labour market discrimination in
India. This is among the earliest studies of gender discrimination
along the entire wage distribution for India and the first to focus
on regular salaried workers. Our main findings are as follows: There
are significant gender gaps among the RWS workers who constitute
about 17 per cent of the Indian labour force. The raw (unconditional)
gender wage gap at the mean changed from 55 per cent to 49 per cent
between 1999–2000 and 2009–10, but this change is not statistically
significant. In both the years, even after accounting for differences in
observable characteristics, the average female wages were less than
those for males. The Blinder-Oaxaca (BO) decompositions indicate
that the bulk of the gender wage gap at the mean is unexplained, that
is, possibly discriminatory. While the educational and occupational

attainment for women improved relative to men over the decade, the discriminatory component of the wage gap also increased. In fact, in 2009–10, had women been paid like men, they would have earned more than men on account of their superior characteristics.

Moving beyond the mean for both years, male wages are still higher than female wages across the entire wage distribution. In both years, the gender wage gaps are higher at lower deciles and decline thereafter. In 2009–10, the gap is the highest at the first decile at 105 per cent and declines to about 10 per cent at the ninth decile, indicating the existence of the 'sticky floor', in that gender wage gaps are higher at lower ends of the distribution and steadily decline over the distribution. This is true for all the RWS workers, as well as for rural and urban workers separately. Using standard definitions, we find that the sticky floor became 'stickier' for the RWS women over the decade. Like the mean decomposition, the quantile decompositions also reveal that the bulk of the gender wage gaps are discriminatory and that the discriminatory component is higher at lower ends of the distribution.

We focus on the most recent decade, as this has been a period of rapid growth, new job openings, greater integration with the global economy, and an increasing domestic privatization in India. While this chapter is not a causal analysis of these changes in gender wage gaps and gender discrimination, it raises questions about the likely association between these structural changes, wage disparities, and, more broadly, about discrimination. Seguino (2000), in a cross-country study, finds that gender inequality, which lowers women's wages relative to men's, is actually a stimulus to growth in export-oriented economies. This runs counter to the conventional wisdom that greater inequality (based on household income as a unit of measurement, obliterating gender gaps) is inimical to growth because it fuels social conflict. Seguino suggests that inequality is 'less likely to produce social conflict if the burden is borne by women, a group traditionally socialized to accept gender inequality as a socially acceptable outcome' (p. 1212). In India, we note that high growth has not been accompanied by an increase in female labour force participation rates (LFPRs). Also, in 2009–10, only about 10 per cent of women in the labour force were in RWS jobs (as opposed to 16 per cent for men), and an overwhelming share of the RWS jobs were held by men (83 per cent). Equally, if not more, worrying is the fact that women face adverse returns to their characteristics. In 2009–10, women were recorded to earn less than men throughout the wage distribution due to labour market discrimination, even though they had better characteristics than men. Moreover, at the lower end of the wage distribution, for the bottom 10 per cent where women face higher discrimination, the wage gaps have increased.

An important reason for the high gap at the lower ends of wage distribution is the fact that as many as 42 per cent of women (amounting to 43 lakh women) in the *regular wage/salaried category* earn less than the statutory minimum wage. One can imagine how much worse this situation would be among the casual and informal workers. So, a clear and straightforward lesson from this picture would be strict implementation of minimum wages.

* * *

The recent slowdown notwithstanding, the Indian economy has been characterized by momentous changes over the last two decades. The translation and impact of these changes on inter-group disparities has been uneven. Caste inequality shows very strong inter-state variations and some convergence, but no clear relationship between growth and convergence. In other words, it is not necessarily the case that richer or faster-growing states have seen lower caste disparity (or vice versa). Gender wage gaps are substantial and surprisingly greater for the lower part of the wage distribution. A decomposition of these gaps between 'explained' and 'residual' components indicates that the discriminatory component is greater among the bottom four wage deciles, indicating the presence of a 'sticky floor', rather than a 'glass ceiling', for women. While the incidence of poverty has reduced, class inequality has increased sharply, particularly in certain parts of the country, leading to protracted armed insurgency, which has brought to the fore questions of control over forests and natural resources. Ironically, as the economy becomes more market oriented, it appears that the state has to step in decisively to act on a strategy of redistribution in order to quell discontent and to ensure that the gains from growth are distributed more equitably across the diversity of India's population. While this is a longer-term need, the state needs to immediately improve provision of public goods and make the policy framework as well as governance structures accountable, transparent, and inclusive.

REFERENCES

Akerlof, George (1984). 'The Economics of Caste and of the Rat Race and Other Woeful Tales'. *An Economic Theorist's Book of Tales*. Cambridge: Cambridge University Press, pp. 23–44.

Arrow, Kenneth J. (1971). 'The Theory of Discrimination'. Working Paper 403, Princeton University, Department of Economics, Industrial Relations Section.

Banerjee, Abhijit and Esther Duflo (2008). 'What is Middle Class about the Middle Classes Around the World?'. *Journal of Economic Perspectives* 22(2): 3–28.

Becker, Gary S. (1957). *The Economics of Discrimination*. Chicago: The University of Chicago Press.

Beteille, Andre (2012). 'The Peculiar Tenacity of Caste'. *Economic and Political Weekly* 47(13) (March): 41–8.

Blattman, Christopher and Edward Miguel (2009). 'Civil War'. National Bureau of Economic Research Working Paper Series, Working Paper 14801. Available at http://www.nber.org/papers/w14801. Last accessed on 11 June 2019.

Borooah, Vani K. (2008). 'Deprivation, Violence, and Conflict: An Analysis of Naxalite Activity in the Districts of India'. MPRA Paper No. 19425. Available at http://mpra.ub.uni-muenchen.de/19425/. Last accessed on 17 March 2012.

Deshpande, Ashwini (2001). 'Caste at Birth? Redefining Disparity in India'. *Review of Development Economics* 5(1) (February): 130–44.

———. (2011). *The Grammar of Caste: Economic Discrimination in Contemporary India*. New Delhi: Oxford University Press. (2017 paperback).

———. (2013). 'Affirmative Action in India'. *Oxford India Short Introductions*. New Delhi: Oxford University Press.

———. (2018). 'Foreign Direct Investment and Intergroup Disparities in India'. In *The Right to Development: Making it Work in India*, edited by Ashok Kotwal, Moshe Hirsh, and Bharat Ramaswami. University of British Columbia Press, forthcoming.

Deshpande, Ashwini and Katherine Newman (2007). 'Where the Path Leads: The Role of Caste in Post University Employment Expectations'. *Economic and Political Weekly* 42(41) (October 13–October 19): 4133–40.

Deshpande, Ashwini and Rajesh Ramachandran (2016). 'The Changing Nature of Intergroup Disparities and the Role of Preferential Policies in a Globalising World: Evidence from India'. Centre for Development Economics, Working Paper No. 267, December 2016.

Deshpande, Ashwini, Deepti Goel, and Shantanu Khanna (2018). 'Bad Karma or Discrimination? Male-Female Wage Gaps Among Salaried Workers in India'. *World Development* 102: 331–44.

Harris, John (2010). 'The Naxalite/Maoist Movement in India: A Review of Recent Literature'. ISAS Working Paper No. 109, Institute for South Asian Studies, National University of Singapore.

Hnatkovska, Viktoria, Amartya Lahiri, and Sourabh Paul (2012). 'Castes and Labour Mobility'. *American Economic Journal: Applied Economics* 4(2): 274–307.

Iyer, Lakshmi (2009). 'The Bloody Millennium: Internal Conflict in South Asia'. Working Paper 09-086, Harvard Business School.

Jodhka, Surinder and Katherine Newman (2007). 'In the Name of Globalisation'. *Economic and Political Weekly* 42(41, October 13–October 19).

Kapur, Devesh, Chandra Bhan Prasad, Lant Pritchett, and D. Shyam Babu (2010). 'Rethinking Inequality: Dalits in Uttar Pradesh in the Market Reform Era'. *Economic and Political Weekly* 45(35) (August): 39–49.

J.V., Meenakshi (1996). 'How Important are Changes in Taste? A State-Level Analysis of Food Demand'. *Economic and Political Weekly* 31(50): 3265–9.

National Council of Applied Research and Training (NCAER) (2009). *FDI in India and Its Growth Linkages.* New Delhi: NCAER.

Planning Commission (2008). *Development Challenges in Extremist Affected Areas: Report of an Expert Group to the Planning Commission.* New Delhi: Planning Commission, Government of India.

Omvedt, Gail (2005). 'Capitalism and Globalisation: Dalits and Adivasis'. *Economic and Political Weekly* 40(47) (November 19): 4881–5.

Rao, Nitya, Ashwini Deshpande, Arjan Verschoor, and Amaresh Dubey (2010). 'Gender Caste and Growth Assessment: India, Report to Department for International Development'. DEV Reports and Policy Paper Series, School of International Development, University of East Anglia, UK.

Ravallion, Martin (2009). 'The Developing World's Bulging (But Vulnerable) "Middle Class"'. Policy Research Working Paper 4816, World Bank Policy Research Group.

Seguino, S. (2000). 'Gender Inequality and Economic Growth: A Cross-Country Analysis'. *World Development* 28(7): 1211–30.

Sundar, Nandini (2006). 'Bastar, Maoism and Salwa Judum'. *Economic and Political Weekly* 41(29): 3187–92.

··

CHAPTER 9

A GOVERNANCE ANALYSIS OF TRANSPORTATION IN INDIA

··

S. SRIRAMAN

In an earlier version of the chapter, which dealt with governance issues in transportation in the Indian context (Sriraman 2014), the author of the current chapter had attempted to understand governance practices in transportation in India, given an ideal framework of governance arrangements that are required to maximize efficiency in the sector so as to promote growth objectives of the economy. The objective was to understand how the institutional arrangements for the operation of two modes of transport, railways and roads, were effective in terms of the policy framework that was developed and the extent to which the elements of this framework were properly and effectively implemented through existing governance practices. Further, an analysis of governance issues in the urban context was undertaken with the experience of Mumbai in mind. In the current version, to begin with, an attempt is made to examine whether some of the issues brought out earlier, which were in need of governance-related changes for useful solutions, have been addressed seriously in some form or the other. An effort has also been made to identify new initiatives that have been proposed with a view to examine the extent to which challenges that are emerging in terms of urban transport-sector governance are being handled effectively.

Transportation System Governance in India: Some Recent Initiatives to Improve Governance

The efficiency of any transportation system is always on the radar of policymakers due to its contribution to the national economic growth objectives, especially the dynamic growth of metropolitan areas. According to Christodoulou and Finger (2012), governance determines the relationships between the main agents involved in the transport system and those with the economy in general and emphasized that these relationships need to be represented and indicated clearly in order to understand the mechanisms that lead to better performing systems. It was clearly stated in Sriraman (2014) that the central purpose of the policy and planning coordination mechanisms for transport is to help generate technical, economic, and other conditions (relationships) for its growth while, at the same time, initiating distribution of traffic between different modes such that the process helps in ensuring that facilities in each mode are developed and operated within a framework that keeps in view the need to satisfy the overall requirements of traffic at minimum cost to the community. More specifically, it was emphasized that such a framework would require certain considerations to be fulfilled. One such consideration related to the correct forecast of the volume of traffic demand, not just in terms of tonnages involved but also by way of traffic leads (distance that a unit of goods moves in average terms), which becomes significant in a vast country such as India. Neglect of the spatial dimension (which determines leads) in a detailed way during the planning exercises of the past led to inadequate provisions for investment in the transport sector, especially in

the context of movement of bulk commodities across the country by
the railways. The result was a most disconcerting development in the
Indian transport scenario, namely the emergence of road transport as
a very dominant mode. It is in this context that it would be useful to
examine whether policy initiatives are in place to stem this trend and
help the railways regain their lost position with regard to the modal
split to some extent in the years to come. The following three sections
critically examine three major initiatives that have been proposed in
the context of railway operations, specifically to reverse the trend of
diversion towards highways. One of them relates to the development
of Dedicated Freight Corridors (DFCs), which is currently under
implementation with a section of this network to be completed by
the end of 2019, while the other concerns the policy of promotion of
a multi-modal system, with the railways serving as the backbone of
such a system. Further, the next section outlines an (feeble) attempt to
tweak the fare policies of the railways—this aspect being connected to
the overall governance at the policy and implementation levels.

DEDICATED FREIGHT CORRIDORS
OF THE INDIAN RAILWAYS

The Need

According to Hope and Cox (2015), the concept of freight corridors
has arisen from the larger idea of a 'transport corridor' that has both
a physical and a functional dimension. In terms of physical components, a corridor includes one or more transport routes that connect
centres of economic activity. These routes will have different alignments but with common transfer points and will be connected to the
same end nodes. A basic transport corridor will typically impact only
the area immediately adjacent to the corridor. The economic potential
of a basic transport route, along with the hard infrastructures of one
or more transport modes, can then be harnessed to develop it into a
transport corridor and as more freight and people move along the
corridor, the soft infrastructure (logistics and institutions) can also

improve in order to maintain, or increase, efficiency. Such efficient corridor operations normally encourage further economic activity that leads to further investments and, ultimately, the corridor evolves into an 'economic corridor'. But the evolution into a fully fledged economic corridor requires broader investments in the area served by the corridor. As Srivastava (2011) observed that for corridors to be viable, they must make economic sense through encompassing actual or potential economic growth.

The GOI (2006a) had observed that the competitive pressure on Indian Railways would increase with further upgradation of the National Highways on the Golden Quadrilateral in terms of six-laning. To compete with the highways, it was necessary to not only be price-competitive but also improve performance by way of the quality and quantity of services offered, catering especially to the requirement of the clientele. Also, there were major constraining factors on the existing High Density Network (HDN) routes (Golden Quadrilateral) of Indian Railways with 161 out of a total of 247 sections, that is, 65 per cent of the sections, running at 100 per cent or above line capacity (GOI 2015a). This limited throughput required dedicated freight corridors to be constructed on new alignments.

The National Transport Development Policy Committee (GOI 2014) had recommended that by 2020 Indian Railways (IR) must accommodate 46 per cent of the total freight traffic from the then estimated existing share at 31 per cent to balance the modal mix. Only a strategy involving DFCs could be expected to result in an improvement towards an optimal split, which would then ensure long-term sustainability of freight movement at competitive costs. In other words, with a view to retain and even increase market share, Indian Railways needed to reposition itself differently in order to meet the competition from the road sector in terms of a market focus in its operations. This could only possibly be addressed more effectively by an independent organization operating services on dedicated freight corridors than from within a very large organizational set up. Accordingly, a major initiative that was set into motion was one related to the development of new Dedicated Rail Freight Corridors connecting the four metropolitan centres (with diagonals), which are currently connected by sections on the Golden Quadrilateral.

A Brief on Projects under Implementation

The Dedicated Freight Corridor Corporation of India (DFCCIL) is a special purpose vehicle (SPV) set up under the Ministry of Railways to undertake planning, mobilization of financial resources, construction and development, maintenance, and operation of the DFCs. The currently sanctioned projects involve construction of 3,322 kms of dedicated freight lines, efficiently linking ports on the western side to the industrial hubs across the states of Mumbai, Gujarat, Rajasthan, Madhya Pradesh, Delhi, and western Uttar Pradesh and the coal and steel production centres on the eastern side to the northern hinterland. Each corridor would provide for a capacity of 150 to 180 freight trains each way each day against a maximum of 50/60 freight trains each way today on trunk routes. This traffic would mostly consist of bulk items such as coal, iron, and steel on the eastern corridor and containers, fertilizers, and coal on the western corridor. According to the concession agreement with the railways, at least 70 per cent of the existing freight traffic on their track that is running on the same alignment as the DFC will be transferred to the new facilities. Thus, after the diversion of freight traffic from the existing routes, additional capacity is expected to be available for introducing more trains.

The Expectations

Freight train movement in India has always suffered as high speed, express trains and even other passenger trains get priority to use the tracks which are common to all. Both industry and the railways have suffered as a result. This has led to a sharp decline in the share of freight carried by railways from 86 per cent in 1950–1 to 36 per cent by 2011–12, even as the total freight traffic has grown exponentially. In comparison, in many countries, about 50 or more per cent of freight (especially bulk items) moves through the railway network. It is expected that providing separate and exclusive tracks for freight trains would reverse the trend over time. To begin with, freight trains will run according to a timetable and as fast as express trains. The new tracks being laid for the freight corridor will be able to handle heavier trains, which will increase the freight handling capacity of the railways. Freight train capacity is proposed to be more than doubled the current capacity, that is, 13,000 tonnes as opposed to 6,000 tonnes before. The western corridor would primarily cater to containerized traffic, mostly exports and imports, while the eastern corridor will mostly be used to move coal from mines in east India to power plants in the north. It has also been proposed to operate double stack container trains, thereby increasing the handling capacity of the railways and also helping decongest ports when the consignments arrive. Also expected is a sharp increase in the average speed of freight trains—from the current speed of 25 kilometres per hour to 70 kmph with the maximum speed of these trains reaching 100 kmph or more. Moving most freight trains to the new corridor will also benefit passengers by reducing congestion on the main tracks and enabling passenger trains to move faster.

The strategy of DFCs that is being implemented constitutes a significant departure from what Indian Railways has been doing historically, that is, running mixed traffic (freight as well as passenger) across its entire network. Though the primary objective of building new rail corridors is to dedicate them exclusively to freight trains, it will not be limited to just that. In many ways, the dedicated freight corridors will have the same impact that rivers and highways had in the process of development.

It is expected that the DFCs will induce large volumes of additional traffic, which is likely to be generated by industrial corridors that are coming up with the aim of creating high impact development areas spanning a distance of 150 kms on either side of the corridors, such as the Delhi Mumbai Industrial Corridor (DMIC) on the Western Dedicated Freight Corridor (WDFC).

It is to be noted that the development of DFCs is being promoted keeping in mind the effective coordination between land-use planning and transportation planning. Thus, a more integrated approach in terms of effecting better governance is being attempted within a dynamic planning framework that explicitly recognizes the spatial relationships between the major freight hubs and transport links to and from distribution centres, which is important not only to provide large volumes but also to ensure that the system is time-sensitive in terms of schedule. It is suggested that the corridor can help the railways gain an increased access to high potential markets such as consumer durables, fast moving consumer goods, and containerized cargo if the necessary institutional arrangements can be made to cater to the parcel business, which is expanding and thriving in a big way.

Issues in Governance

It has been pointed out that elements related to the governance of the facilities being developed have proved to be difficult to handle even at their initial stages. These include problems relating to land acquisition, which can be the biggest hurdle besides the development of linkages to provide the first and last mile connectivity, policy issues concerning complicated procedures, tax regimes, and so on. Some of the reasons for delay in execution of the project are issues of land acquisition including court cases/arbitration, environment clearances, law and order problems in a few locations, etc. Even as on 1 March 2018, a total of 98.1 per cent of land required for the Eastern and Western Dedicated Freight Corridors has been acquired. An improved framework to deal with these issues could possibly ensure a timely delivery of the projects in order to realize the full potential of the DFC strategy. Even within the transportation sector, there is a need to adopt structural reforms by increasing private sector penetration, especially in roads, to provide the first and last mile connectivity and connectivity to ports, thus generating the synergies to improve inter-modal coordination.

Though the understanding is that a major portion of the movement on existing corridors will be diverted to the DFCs in the future, it should not happen that this agreement is not really kept in spirit and word as it happened in the case of Konkan Railways Corporation, which has continuously been denied traffic that would have turned its fortunes around in a big way (Sriraman and Roy 2009; Banerjee et.al. 2000).

The GOI (2006a) had considered a number of variants of the DFC's organizational governance structure in order to capture the best practices and benefits from the different models that existed in the world then, including the one in which the SPV would not only own the infrastructure but would also be the dominant operator, allowing Indian Railways and other qualified operators to conduct the business of freight movement and run trains in competition with it. However, the consensus in the end was that the SPV would be responsible only for the infrastructure and the movement of trains on its system, while Indian Railways and other qualified private and public operators would run trains on the tracks owned by the SPV. It would allow non-discriminatory access to Indian Railways and other qualified private- and public-sector operators of goods trains within a regulatory framework.

In a critique of the proposed organisational structure of the DFCs, Agarwalla and Raghuram (2012) argued that the structuring of the DFCs has been a lost opportunity in terms of the opening of a new railway sector in India, while pointing out emphatically that the autonomy of the DFCCIL has been reduced so as to make the IR their sole owner and customer, as per their draft business plan. By virtue of it being the single owner of DFCCIL and controlling its board, the IR would be in a position to influence all policy decisions, including the charges payable by it to the DFCCIL. A key reason provided for the IR being the sole owner of the DFCCIL is that the former's underutilized assets, especially in terms of land, could be offered to the latter without much complexity. The authors felt that a part of the above problem could be resolved if there is a separation between the Ministry of Railways (MOR) (policy making institution) and the IR (implementation arm), in that such a separation can rule out the under-utilization of IR's assets by making sure that their value can be unlocked through alternate use. While it is admitted that a part of the assets may have no opportunity cost since an excess of assets have been vested over the decades with the IR, it being viewed as a government body providing critical infrastructure, part of the assets may have some opportunity cost in terms of possible expansion of activities, which can be commercially determined and explicitly tapped by making necessary provisions in the concession agreement. To conclude, it is stated that the unbundling that has happened in other infrastructure sectors (aviation, maritime, and road) to bring in greater autonomy and accountability, which was expected to begin in a significant way for the DFCCIL, cannot really happen since there appears to be no clear sign as yet of unbundling of roles in terms of policy making and licensing, operations, and regulations on the part of the IR. In another critique on the governance elements of the emerging DFCs, Pangotra and Shukla (2012) point out that the current proposed organization structure of the DFCCIL Corporate Office is a conventional one based on functional classifications, which is common in government organizations, that leads to less-than-efficient coordination across departments. A programme-based structure, they feel, on the other hand, can lead to better coordination and better performance management. Therefore, coordination for a greater programme effectiveness would be an important management challenge for the DFCCIL, especially when operating within a conventional structure. Pangotra and Shukla (2012) also examined the potential for reduction of carbon emissions that was envisaged from the operations of the proposed projects in terms of developing elements of a sustainable transport system. Their analysis showed that large transport infrastructure projects such as the DFCs could have a significant impact on CO_2 emissions, which can thereby provide an additional dimension of sustainability to the efficiency gains for which these transportation projects have been undertaken, thus recognising the substantial environmental benefits. In other words, the low-carbon characteristics of such large infrastructure projects make their case even more compelling. However, it is emphasized that this strategy of transport investments that can benefit the economy in terms of low-carbon emissions needs to be aligned with low-carbon sustainable actions on several other fronts, in terms of proposed developmental activities, in order to maximize social welfare gains.

Containerized Multi-modalism as a Significant Governance Initiative

Transportation is one of the major infrastructure sectors that has changed over the years as a result of technological changes due to the sector's long-term relationship with economic growth, which has remained a high priority in the development of transport policy objectives in many countries, especially through the late 20th century. Transportation plays a key role in the economic success of a country by allowing for safe and efficient distribution of goods and services throughout the supply chain. Transportation links various elements in this chain to provide for integrated logistics activities. Without transportation, the integrated logistics system breaks down. One of the challenges of transportation today is to increase capacity and reduce costs. Transportation has a significant logistics function for all industries and therefore has a large impact on the escalation or reduction of logistics cost. It is against this background that multi-modalism or inter-modalism (the terms are used interchangeably for the specific purpose of this chapter) in terms of transportation components has emerged.

Intermodal transportation includes a type of displacement with mutual links and effects that covers more than one mode of transportation. A key feature of intermodal freight transportation is the use of consolidation to obtain economies of scale. Standardized cargo units, such as containers, have been a great technical invention for improving the efficiency and effectiveness of international transport chains. Perhaps the biggest advantage of these units comes from their modularity. Modularization can also be seen as a prerequisite for future transport systems while integrating the physical cargo flows and related information more closely with each other. In this context, containerization is one of the most salient aspects of the development of multimodal transport. Containerization contributes to a higher efficiency in the development of multimodal transport operations.

Container traffic in the country has grown at a compound annual growth rate (CAGR) of nearly 15 per cent as compared to 8 per cent globally, driving its share of the global container traffic from 0.6 per cent in 1991 to 1.8 per cent in 2012. Currently, the top three container ports, that are, Jawaharlal Nehru Port Trust (JNPT), Mundra, and Chennai together account for almost 75 per cent of India's total container traffic.

A large share of break-bulk commodities are now sent in containers. Kadam (2017) observed that a period of recent growth had been boosted by rapid growth in the containerization of general cargo, which has increased from 60 per cent in 2001 to around 68 per cent in 2011, and projected that container penetration in India could reach up to 72 per cent by 2020. Presently, containerized cargo represents about 30 per cent of India's external trade value and this proportion is likely to grow as containerization increasingly penetrates the general cargo trades and increases its share from the current 68 per cent to near international levels of around 75–80 per cent (World Bank 2007). With multiple advantages of multimodal transportation yet to be tapped, the introduction of more containerization movement can prove to be a major business driver for the overall logistics sector in the years to come. Containerization is considered to be one of the most vital factors in the context of multimodal transportation as it combines the advantages resulting from the consistency of rail movement, the flexibility of road movement, the cost-effectiveness of shipping, and the speed of air transport.

Kadam (2017) examined whether multimodal containerized movement is cost-efficient or not when compared to only rail movement or road movement. Using a range of models, the author attempted to point out the advantages that can accrue from a multimodal system, especially one that involves containerized movement. The author concludes on the basis of a comprehensive empirical modelling exercise that multimodal transport is a comprehensive approach in utilising the advantages of different modes of transport. At the same time, it must be recognized that by the integration of various modes of transport, one does not merely achieve a simple addition of the strong points of all modes concerned. There is, in fact, a synergetic effect in integrating different modes of transport into a multimodal system that needs to be tapped. India has witnessed good growth in multimodal movement in the recent decades and an integrated transport sector is still evolving where containerization is not yet seen as a major process of movement.

Current Issues of Containerized Multimodal Transportation in India

Currently, Indian ports handle nearly 90 per cent of the export and import trade of the country by volume. One of the key determinants of the efficiency of ports is evacuation and hinterland connectivity. Even today, the container handling cost is estimated to be considerably higher in India than in other developed countries.

Poor road and rail connectivity to several ports hampers the efficient removal of all freight, but especially containers. Another important bottleneck faced by the container terminals in India has been in the aspect of timely evacuation of containers. Inadequate landside infrastructure has been characterized by less than efficient and insufficient cargo carrying capacity in terms of both rail and road networks, which has adversely affected the development of true multimodal transport/logistics value chains.

At present, India has no mega-port comparable to the size of such ports in other countries. Consequently, at present, a good proportion of India's maritime trade is trans-shipped in Colombo or Singapore. Roads should not be looked at in isolation but as part of an integrated multimodal system of transport. The planning and development of the primary road network must tie up with the planning of the railways, dedicated freight corridors and other segments of the rail network, connectivity with ports, airports, special economic zones, logistic hubs, etc. In India, due to the absence of such connectivity, trucks are preferred for direct transport to and from ports. Given the much lower carrying capacity of trucks as well as the absence of a dedicated land corridor for cargo vehicles, this obvious inefficiency further affects the already strained terminals. Despite the advantage of the lowest unit transportation cost for the sea leg, the overall end-to-end cost by coastal shipping tends to escalate due to the lack of proper port/landside infrastructure. Presently, various agencies look after the several elements involved in movement. These agencies are regulated by different ministries and departments of the government and are administered by different legislative measures, leading to organizational/departmental interests and controls coming into conflict, resulting in an overall inefficiency and undue cost burden which ultimately has to be borne by the shipper/consignee/trade.

Past Policy Attempts and Results

Multimodalism

Indian Railways set up the Container Corporation of India (CONCOR) in 1988 as a public-sector company to spearhead the process of containerization in the country. Using the IR's network and haulage, it attempted to pioneer the concept of multi-modalism through its core activities as a carrier of rail-borne container traffic and terminal operation. The railways liberalized the entry of private players in the area of rail-based haulage of containers in 2005.

After the entry of private container train operators in the market, the dynamics and market share were expected to change. According to Indian Railways, private players would serve to: increase Indian Railways' market share of container traffic, provide incremental capacity to cater to the exponentially growing containerized traffic in India, ensure a speedy clearance of export/import of container-ized traffic, substantially increase the containerized domestic traffic on the Indian Railways network, improve the quality of service to customers. Moreover, these players had the potential to offer inte-grated value-added logistics solutions with last-mile connectivity to ports with a possible modal shift from road to railways, thus ensuring seamless operations to be achieved by the integrated hub-and-spoke model. The railway sector's share in transport vis-à-vis roadways was also expected to change as a result of private container expansion. Rail transport then accounted for nearly 25 per cent of the container market, which was expected to increase to 50 per cent in future. To achieve this goal, Indian Railways invited private play-ers to enter the business in 2005. Prior to that, it was exclusively reserved for CONCOR.

According to TERI (2009), although a total of 15 players were issued licences for operations in the container sector, only seven started operating. Despite having the requisite licence, eight partici-pants were unable to start operations with container trains primarily due to the lack of terminal facilities and rail-linked Inland Container Depots (ICDs). The cost of procuring land for operations had become a major entry barrier for these private players. Since these ICDs had to be rail-linked and since land was required at strategic locations, which belonged to Indian Railways, private stakeholders emphasized the need for help from the government/railways in the acquisition of land on the same terms as it was given to CONCOR. One of the key concerns of the private players was the competitive pressure applied by roadways on the railways container movements. In the absence of transit-time guarantees, private players found it difficult to compete with roads, while also pointing out that CONCOR had been able to ensure the timely delivery of its containers due to its relationship with the railways. Thus, it was obvious that the close relationship between the management levels of both Indian Railways and CONCOR benefitted CONCOR. Raghuram and Gangawar (2010) pointed out that due to the lack of clarity or inconsistency in matters pertaining to haulage charges, maintenance of wagons, transit guarantees from the IR, and terminal access charges, private operators felt sceptical about the viability of the business. In short, it was felt that the current mechanism did not provide a level playing field. While competition is a motivation to achieve effectiveness and efficiency at each point on the network, cooperation between players in a mode and between modes is needed to achieve optimal performance.

Legislation and Regulation

Government of India recognized the benefits of multimodal transport way back in the early 1990s and came up with the Multimodal Transportation of Goods (MMTG) Act in 1993 with the objective of encouraging the growth of exports from India. Through the Act, the government aimed at developing international multimodal transport that would reduce logistics costs and thus make Indian products more competitive in the global market. The Act established licensing requirements, contractual terms (through the multimodal transport document [MTD] to ensure an efficient and cost-effective door-to-door movement of goods under the responsibility of a single transport operator, known as the Multimodal Transport Operator [MTO]), and a corresponding liability regime. *The benefits can result only if infrastructure development, regulatory reforms and investments in technology take place significantly.* The Act was amended in the year 2000 to give more protection to shippers.

In 2015, India had 1,305 registered MTOs, accounting for hardly 10 per cent of the total such operators in the country. Around 90 per cent of the MTOs were not registered, although it is mandatory under the Act of 1993, mainly because there was no disincentive/punitive action or deterrence available by law against those doing so. Thus, the provision of the registration of MTOs had not served its basic purpose. It was strongly felt that there was a need to make it mandatory for the MTOs to disclose upfront in their MTDs all the services being offered by them in the logistics supply-chain along with the individual charges/levies. This disclosure was required to be all subsuming and released in the public domain through the websites of each MTO. The disclosure norms could ensure that all the service charges leviable and payable were determined and shared transparently and upfront in the MTDs shared by the MTOs, including shipping lines. The disclosure norms were also expected to address the issue of 'nomination premium' paid to the shipping lines by container freight stations (CFS)—a facility licensed by the customs department to help decongest a port by shifting containerized cargo and carrying out customs-related activities outside the port area. It was observed that firms running container freight stations near several of India's ports had routinely been paying nomination premium per container to shipping lines to get business and then recovering this money from importers, making imports costlier. Moreover, the scope of the MMTG Act encompasses only export transactions and, given the dynamics of import trade as well as the scale and complexity of similar grievances on the import side, it is widely recognized that import transactions should also be brought under the Act. The promotion of multimodal transport would need to address various such issues so as to save time and result in cost-efficiency. All these aspects considered, the above would require a thorough rationalization of the existing provisions of the Multi-Modal Transportation of Goods Act in a significant way. But the need of the hour is also to look into other issues such as infrastructure development, policy related reforms, and investment in technology, in the absence of which mere regulations of any sort do not help. This is the subject matter of the next section.

Policy Review and Recent Initiatives

Policy Review

The Maritime Agenda 2010–20 (GOI 2011) was an effort on the part of the Government of India to identify crucial areas to give attention to during the ten-year period from 2010–11 to 2019–20. This critical review of the matter of port–hinterland connectivity, a crucial component of the multimodal system, highlighted some critical issues that needed to be addressed and the key challenges facing the ports sector with regard to hinterland connectivity. With ports playing a vital role in the overall economic development of the country, it was pointed out that the development of India's ports and trade-related infrastructure would continue to be critical to sustain the accelerated growth of the Indian economy and that inadequate capacities of the hinterland transport modes had often lead to higher costs and delays on account of suboptimal mode choices, circuitous routing, and congestion in the hinterland transport links.

The report of the National Transport Development Policy Committee (GOI 2014) laid out a clear prioritization on where investments should be focused in the transport sector, with the transport policy differing from earlier efforts in two key areas—a system base approach and an outward looking approach. The Committee strongly felt the need for significant investments in railways, which could not be expected to happen in a business-as-usual scenario. This focus required certain strategic decisions to be made regarding the relative allocation of investments to railways rather than roads, with accompanying pricing and taxation policies that could be used to nudge transport demand towards the desired modal shares. In other words, the key issue facing the country was the desired strategy for capacity extension of the railways sector over the next few years. This strategy could be expected to promote multimodalism in a significant way, with the railways focussing on long-distance movements and other modes focussing on the final connectivity.

GOI (2015a) admitted that the biggest challenge facing Indian Railways today was not only the quantum of service delivery but also its quality. It is in this context that the encouragement of multimodalism on the part of the railways becomes an important objective. GOI (2017) stated that while the DFCs are a step in the right direction towards this objective, there are other dimensions for extending support to this strategy that need to be looked at and encouraged. The proposed capital expenditure (INR 850,000 crores) would focus on expanding the railways infrastructure to support the aspirational (expanding the rail share) modal mix in freight volume. This was to be achieved by various proposed elements in terms of infrastructure upgradation by expanding the capacity and scope of terminal services by partnering with existing government agencies (for example, DMICDC, State Governments, and NHAI) to build multi-commodity, multi-modal freight logistics parks. Many new service offerings—such as an end-to-end integrated transport solution for selected commodities through a partnership with national road logistics players, use of dwarf containers to capture the domestic cargo market, development of new rolling stock designs that would ultimately help capture new commodity traffic, and, with all this, the operation of heavy haul trains to improve bulk-freight business—can be expected to enhance asset utilization for priority assets, for example, rake turnaround at stations, wagon utilization, etc.

Recent Initiatives and Governance Elements

India has firmed up the contours of its ambitious multimodal programme to reduce logistics costs, which includes setting up 35 multimodal logistics parks at an investment of INR 50,000 crore, development of 50 economic corridors, and an investment template which involves roping in the states and the private sector for setting up special vehicles for implementation. 15 such logistics parks will be constructed in the next five years, and 20 more over the next 10 years. They will act as hubs for freight movement, enabling freight aggregation and distribution with a modern mechanized warehousing space. One such hub would be along the DFCs with a minimum of 100 hectares of area and an inter-spacing of about 400 kms with common user facilities. Joint ventures will be set up between the National Highways Authority of India (49 per cent share) and a project partner (51 per cent), which may be a state government or a private entity. Of the land acquired for the project, 40 per cent will be developed and returned to the land owner, while 20 per cent will be sold to finance the project. The profit from the rest 40 per cent of the land will go to the National Highways Authority of India.

It is being emphasized that the relevance of logistics parks would be in terms of reduction in the parcel size of traffic due to consolidation, induction of multi-links in the supply chain, an increased share of rail in white goods and non-bulk traffic, and promotion of the growing field of Roll-on/Roll-off (RORO) and Auto-car carrier business. The overall development would be in the hands of a nodal agency (a proven multimodal operator, preferably from the government sector) that would create the common infrastructure and the integrated services, including the rail infrastructure inside the terminal, manage inter-modal terminals, make arrangement for warehouses, CFSs, and utility centres on the purchasing power parity (PPP) model, oversee administrative, financial, commercial, and operations management of the logistics centre, and also take care of the upkeep and management of the common property.

In terms of port-rail connectivity, many projects have been identified as part of the National Perspective Plan (GOI 2016) under the Sagarmala programme, including the development of a heavy haul rail-line from Ib Valley/Talcher to Paradip. The project will help in the transportation of thermal coal from Mahanadi Coalfields Limited (MCL) to various coastal power plants in southern India via coastal shipping. Other rail connectivity projects to major ports such as Tuticorin and non-major ports such as Dhamra, Gopalpur, and Krishnapatnam have also been proposed. These projects will enhance the ports' connectivity to the hinterland and help in reducing the logistics cost and time for cargo movement, making Indian trade more competitive.

A BRIEF ASIDE ON TWEAKING RAIL TARIFF POLICIES

In Sriraman (2014), it was emphasized that the kind of investment that is envisaged in the growth scenario of the country requires an exceptional commitment from IR to reform and reinvent the organization's pricing practices. The question is whether there has been any effort on this front? Even today, the social burden on account of losses on passenger traffic is huge, with the losses being covered by a process of cross-subsidization.

The policy of cross-subsidization for IR has resulted in the freight rates of several commodity groups reaching unreasonably high levels, resulting in the diversion of traffic to other modes, especially road transport, with attendant social costs in the form of higher energy consumption and environmental damage. The continually increasing levels of subsidization in passenger fares are also generating excessive demand, leading to extreme congestion and deterioration of services. The need to reorient tariffs, especially passenger fares, over a period of time to cover the costs of provision has been emphasized in many high-level official committee reports, including the recent National Transport Development Policy Committee (GOI 2014: 42, vol. 3), which clearly stated, 'For long-term sustainability, railways have to be run as a business on sound commercial principles. However, the several/national responsibilities of the IR prevent it from operating on a purely commercial basis. While IR has to fulfil both roles, it is essential that the commercial and social roles are kept distinct and separate'. Given that the pricing of passenger services is a highly sensitive political issue and not dictated by efficiency considerations, these services are under-priced even though the economic costs are high. GOI (2014) pointed out that passenger fares had not increased in the last 10 years, with the then levels being ridiculously low even when compared to bus fares. It is against this background that the sustainability of cross-subsidization needed to be seriously considered and reversed.

An attempt made recently to revise fares with the objective of covering losses on passenger movement related to the flexi-fare (dynamic) pricing policy scheme that was implemented in 2016. Under the scheme, dubbed 'flexi-fares' by the railways, the base fares will increase by 10 per cent with every 10 per cent of berths sold, subject to a ceiling of 1.5 times the base fare for most classes, except third AC for which the ceiling will be 1.4. No change was to be made in the fares of first AC and the executive class. The concept of flexi-fares was introduced in Rajdhani, Shatabdi, and Duronto trains in September 2016. Other supplementary charges such as reservation charges, superfast charges, catering charges, goods and service tax, etc., would be levied as applicable separately. Indian Railways runs more than 3,525 mail/express and 4,660 passenger trains daily, but the flexi-fare scheme was implemented only in the Rajdhani, Shatabdi, and Duronto trains, which affected only 0.35 per cent of the total passengers carried by Indian Railways. In this scheme with a number of variants, the objective was to cover some part of the losses being incurred annually by the IR and in no way related to the recovery of costs of services provided, which should be the overriding criterion for many services, except those that are socially desirable and require some form of direct financial support by the government. This tweaking of tariffs will remain to be of a very limited value even if the scheme is extended to mail and express trains across the network while leaving out ordinary passenger services.

In a more recent approach, GOI (2017) has identified a definite price strategy that aims to develop an inflation-indexed pricing model for various passenger services with a view to make them financially self-sustainable. But it emphasized the need for a cost focus in the organisation, which would attempt to identify measures to reduce variable and fixed costs by enhancing the efficiency of services. To do this, a set of accounting reforms would be required, which would include those needed to ensure close relations between input parameters and organisational outcomes. Only such a framework could aid in leading services to self-sustainability. In other words, the objective of the currently ongoing exercise is to improve the usage of limited resources to ensure an optimal outcome of all public expenditure. This can be achieved by modifying the present system of accounting from 'cash-based accounting' to 'accrual-based accounting' and from 'historical budgeting' to 'outcome budgeting' to ensure tracking of expenditure to desired outcomes.

Urban Transport Governance: Emerging Challenges under the Smart Cities Mission

Significance of the Urban Transport Problem in India

As cities grow exponentially, an effective and sustainable urban transport system for the movement of people and goods becomes a pre-requisite for sustainable economic growth. Many Indian cities, especially the metropolitan ones, have attracted significant investments in high-technology industries, thanks to a competitive and highly qualified workforce. Given this situation, it is well recognized that efficient and reliable urban transport systems are crucial for India to sustain a high growth rate. However, urban transport systems in most cities of developing countries such as India are still underdeveloped and their transport capacities have been found to be grossly inadequate. Thus, the residents are unable to fully exploit economic opportunities since they lack the mobility needed to support economic growth (Sriraman 2013).

Over the last two decades, rapid population growth and spatial expansion has led to a sharp increase in demand for urban transport facilities and services in many cities in India. Although circumstances are different across cities in India, certain basic trends that determine the transport demand (such as a substantial increase in the urban population, household incomes, and industrial and commercial activities) are the same. Several factors have hindered the adequate and timely provision of services to match the ever-increasing demand. In many cities, densification and spatial expansion have occurred with little or no development planning, while in some cases the failure of the instruments of governance has resulted in a significant wastage of resources or substandard quality of infrastructure. Furthermore, the huge capital costs and time required to develop high-capacity transit systems have prevented the timely implementation of such systems in rapidly growing urban areas. As a result, many cities have relied on road-based systems, which have serious capacity constraints, negative environmental consequences, and other limitations. The rising incomes, particularly in urban areas, tempt and provide an opportunity to the urban dweller to own a vehicle, especially when public transport has failed miserably in its attempt to meet the demand in most cities. Urban transport systems in most cities suffer from major constraints in the form of insufficient financial resources, inefficient regulatory frameworks, poor allocation of road space, inadequate traffic management systems, institutional weaknesses, and undeveloped public transport systems.

In most cities, road networks, developed in an unplanned ad hoc fashion and without proper adherence to quality standards, are severely deficient in meeting the developmental demand. Residential areas have few and inadequate tertiary or access roads and limited provisions for pedestrians, cyclists, etc. In addition, road networks have missing links, forcing the overuse of existing road sections; lack of circumferential roads result in congestion from through traffic. Meanwhile, an increase in the number and use of vehicles surpasses the capacity of road space, adding to the congestion and air pollution. As a result, transport conditions in cities are characterized by severe congestion, aggravated further by poor discipline among drivers, incoherent enforcement of traffic laws, and an eclectic mix of vehicles. Failure to respond promptly to rapid motorization, the resultant congestion, along with a weak enforcement of vehicle emission standards result in environmental degradation and stunt the growth potential of cities. The impacts of transport on the quality of urban life go further than that. As India experiences a period of economic and urban growth, air pollution in its major cities has become a cause of national concern and has generated worldwide attention. As pollution in the manufacturing and power sectors is progressively declining, the relative importance of the urban transport sector to greater air pollution has increased. To retain their attractiveness for international capital and to compete with other international centres, Indian cities must be liveable. The environment is important to the economic as well as the medical health of the cities (World Bank 2005). The worst off in urban transport may be the pedestrians whose mobility and safety are hindered by non-existent, broken-down, and/or obstructed sidewalks, difficult street crossings, and flooding in the monsoon seasons. Riders of the bicycle—once a major urban transport mode in India—are gradually being pushed off busy roads by motor vehicles. Secondary and tertiary road networks have received almost no attention or funding, especially in low-income areas. While a large portion of the urban population relies heavily on public transport for its daily activities, public transport systems in most cities are not adequately developed and investments have been severely limited. Bus and paratransit services, the predominant public transport services, are often exclusively operated by the private sector in most cities. The unregulated operation of private buses, particularly with regard to the allocation of routes and schedules, has spawned excessive competition and, as a result, the financial performance of public transport and the quality of service have deteriorated.

Along with the growth-related impacts of urban transport are its direct impacts on the life of the poor. Currently, these systems rarely integrate social concerns and the specific needs of vulnerable groups, thereby rendering such systems ineffective in relation to poverty reduction. Most of these factors disproportionately affect the urban poor in terms of limited accessibility to affordable transport services, ill-health from pollution, and road safety concerns. The current urban transport systems, which do not fully integrate the particular needs of the poor, have worsened the perverse distributional effects of urbanization. Overstrained public transport systems restrict urban residents, particularly the urban poor, from actively participating in economic activities. The social exclusion engendered by urban transport makes it even more difficult for the disabled to access jobs and services. As a result, the poor find it hard to break out of poverty. In addition, the poor are disproportionately exposed to the risks of polluted air.

The government's weak capacities have led to low institutional coordination and an inefficient institutional governance framework. A significant issue is the lack of coordination between various agencies administering the various facilities. Government agencies have overlapping or poorly delineated responsibilities, planning and programming are chronically fragmented and largely ad hoc, and institutional arrangements for policy implementation are usually incoherent. Experience indicates that piecemeal approaches to a sustainable urban transport development are likely to fail and that capital investments need to be supported by policy, legal, regulatory, and institutional reforms, which can improve the governance of urban transport systems considerably. But these required changes need to be viewed in the larger framework of urban governance.

Some Governance Initiatives for 'Smart Growth' of Urban Areas

Many outcomes of India's urban transformation pose enormous challenges for the country's planners and policymakers. The formal planning system has hardly changed since Independence and even today most of our urban areas rely on master plans that hardly correspond to the ground level realities. Consider, for example, the current development control norms that are flouted at every step with implementation undertaken by a weak governance system, which neither guides nor enforce the implementation (Sriraman 2017).

In spite of the sorry state of affairs, during the past decade or so, many of India's cities have introduced innovative measures in urban planning, management, and governance, thereby clearly demonstrating a reasonably well-articulated vision that has proposed creativity and a departure from the business-as-usual scenario. Improvements are observed in public transport based on innovative planning and the use of modern technology. Delhi, for example, has pioneered the use of compressed natural gas, a low-polluting fuel, for all modes of public transport, while Ahmedabad has been operating an extremely successful bus rapid transit system. Disaster risk management plans are being developed, institutionalized, and implemented, as has been done by Mumbai, to protect cities and their residents from natural and man-made disasters. The renewal and revitalization of older areas within cities is also being promoted by cities such as Ahmedabad, Jaipur, Puducherry, and Varanasi. Urban infrastructure and water and sanitation systems are being revamped—in fact, this is the overarching focus of the recent policy reforms; safety and security in public spaces are being enhanced through improved infrastructure and more responsive policing; and communities are being empowered through skill development, participation, and partnerships in a number of cities across the country. The present nuances of the smart city concept have to be seen in the contexts of this, the forces of globalization, and the huge expansion of information technology that are expected to shape our cities and influence our lives.

Cities are complex systems that touch multiple agencies, departments, and organizations. These have become too complex to handle and operationalize conventionally. New ways, systematic changes, and technology can enhance their efficiency, services, and operations. A smart city aims to drive economic growth and improve people's quality of life by enabling local area development and harnessing technology that leads to 'smart' outcomes. The objective of the Smart Cities Mission of the Ministry of Urban Development (GOI 2015b) is to promote cities that provide the core infrastructure, give a decent quality of life and a clean and sustainable environment to its citizens, and allow the application of 'smart' solutions for inclusive development. The concept and strategies of a smart city are expected to continue evolving. The mission did not provide any definition of the smart city but aims to harness a city's potential that aspires to become smart through smart solutions. Smart solutions include e-governance and electronic service delivery, video crime monitoring, smart meters for water supply management, smart parking, and intelligent traffic management, to mention a few. Application of smart solutions is expected to enable cities to use technology, information, and data to improve infrastructure and services. It will also endeavour area-based development through retrofitting (city improvement) and redevelopment (city renewal). In addition, new areas/greenfields (city extension) will be developed around the city to accommodate the growing urban population. The integration of major systems on a common network helps optimize usage assignment and space configurations, eliminating all unused or underperforming spaces. It is envisaged that the strategies for the development of a smart city will create enough jobs and take care of the poor. Thus, it is conceived that smart cities will be inclusive. Complementary to the Smart Cities Mission, AMRUT (GOI 2015c) has been launched to cover 500 cities, each with a population of one lakh or more. The mandate of AMRUT is limited to water supply, sewerage and septage management, storm-water drainage, urban transport, and development of green spaces and parks, including capacity building and reform implementation by the Urban Local Bodies (ULBs).

'Smart' City Transport Initiatives and Governance Challenges

It is now recognized that efficiently managing the *mobility* of people in a sustainable manner will be a key challenge for Indian cities. There is a growing realisation that merely increasing the supply of road infrastructure is not sufficient for improving mobility. There is a need to tackle the *demand side* of urban transport as well, which would call for planning, designing, and implementing smart and sustainable urban transport solutions in our cities. The smart city mission attempts to provide efficient solutions. Indian smart cities have set their focus on upgrading their transportation systems through the use of technology. In fact, the main focus during a similar mission launched in India in 2006, known as the Jawaharlal Nehru National Urban Renewal Mission (JNNURM), and now in the smart cities approach is the introduction of new technologies, as the argument is that it will solve the traffic chaos and serve the high-density demands expected on a few road corridors in the city. But most of the cities, such as the metros, that have developed such systems have not really looked at a comprehensive way of planning for these systems while developing new facilities, thus failing the system and forcing people to depend on private transport.

In regard to the use of technology, the plan is to take quick steps to reduce the carbon footprint by introducing measures such as the Faster Adoption and Manufacturing of Hybrid and Electric Vehicles (FAME) to encourage the adoption of fuel-economy vehicles in the country, propose new emission norms, adopt policies for scrapping old commercial vehicles, etc. In this context, it is pertinent to remember to keep a focus on developing local technologies that are simple, environment-friendly, and can be taken to the global markets. At present, India is attempting extensive research work in the areas of electric and hybrid cars, hydrogen fuel cells, multiple battery technologies, and also finding new ways of generating CNG to mitigate CO_2 emissions. CNG, as an alternative fuel for transportation, is also gaining greater acceptance.

On the softer side of technology, it is necessary to encourage the trend in the 'shared economy', which is driven mainly by an emerging proportion of the population that believes in renting, rather than buying, assets. The impact of this has been significant on car ownerships too, with the commuter giving preference to hailing an app-based taxi or riding the metro rail rather than self-driving. This requires a high degree of collaboration between auto manufacturers, fleet operators, and technology and wireless service providers to create multi-modal transport systems that assist in achieving last-mile connectivity. As more automobiles connect, software competency is expected to provide an edge and open further opportunities for the service providers.

The use of GPS and cloud-based connected buses, using ITS (intelligent transport systems), are already making a difference in movement in Indian cities, while giving passengers the convenience of real-time information on bus locations, schedules, routes, etc. at either the stops or on their smartphones. But investments can succeed only if they can be integrated with other system components of urban areas. As much as the adoption of technology, it is the imperative to create an environment that fosters greater public-private partnership models to roll out solutions faster that facilitates a closer collaboration between different stakeholders and aims at achieving inclusiveness.

However, the above proposals and their adoption can be successful only if a strategy is undertaken to increase investments in providing the necessary and basic urban infrastructure. Further, an efficient use of facilities (physical, technological, etc.) would depend on the improvements in the systems of governance, which currently fail miserably. Under the JNNURM, for getting an approval for transport projects, the guidelines recommended that the transport infrastructure improvement schemes should be in compliance with the National Urban Transport Policy (NUTP) (GOI 2006b) that had laid down the guiding principle for sustainable mobility with a clear thrust on public transport, non-motorized transport, and transit-oriented development. Several analyses of various projects showed that the identified and approved projects were in consonance with the word and spirit of the NUTP. Further, it was found that a good part of the funding was devoted to projects in the roads and flyovers category, which went against a basic principle of the policy that emphasized 'moving more people and not more vehicles'. Further, an important policy aspect of governance related to the proposed coordination of planning and implementation between the various agencies providing for the operation and maintenance of transport facilities in urban areas through a Unified Metropolitan Transport Authority (UMTA), which was duly notified by several state governments but never really took off. The monitoring and evaluation framework for the JNNURM programme was found to be one typical as any government-sponsored programme—based on the tracking of monetary funds' utilization associated with the physical targets of construction work, with the least attention being paid to the outcomes derived in terms of benefits. The poor state of governance in Indian cities, in general, is obvious to everyone living there, which is also true, in particular, of transport governance.

* * *

The earlier review of transportation governance in India focussed on two modes: railways and roadways. The current chapter almost exclusively focusses on the railways' initiatives, the progress on these, and the limitations to be overcome. As for the road transport sector, it must be noted that nothing really, by way of changes in governance, has taken place. Road transport is a subject under the jurisdiction of the states, which have hardly been attempting to revive the public-sector road transport services while only paying lip service to it by way of opening up the sector to private ownership in a haphazard way. Except for some useful gains that have been observed in a few states, the general situation is pathetic in regard to public road transport services. Hence, there was no attempt in this chapter to examine the sector even in a cursory way.

A recent issue that can well be considered a governance one and that was taken up by the railways relates to the merger of the railway budget with the general budget of the Government of India. While the author of the present chapter argued against such a move for a variety of reasons (Sriraman 2015), it is now felt that it could be beneficial if it is taken forward to merge all the transport-related ministries into one single Ministry of Transport, which has been a strong recommendation of several committees in the past, including GOI (2014), but one that has never been taken up seriously for consideration and implementation. Such a move could perhaps pave the way for such combined government agencies at the state level too and could possibly lead to much better coordinated planning and implementation of different modes of transport at the national level too.

REFERENCES

Agarwala, S.K. and G. Raghuram (2012). 'Structuring the Dedicated Freight Corridor: A Lost Opportunity'. Working Paper No. 2012-07-02, Indian Institute of Management, Ahmedabad.

Banerjee, B., G. Raghuram, and N. Rangaraj (2000). Konkan Railway Corporation Limited. *Vikalpa* 25 (January–March): 88–109.

Christodoulou, A. and M. Finger (2012). 'The Governance of Urban Public Transport Systems: The Case of Zurich (ZVV)'. Mimeo. Netherlands: Delft University of Technology.

GOI (2006a). Report of the Task Force on The Delhi–Mumbai & Delhi–Howrah Freight Corridors. The Secretariat for the Committee on Infrastructure. New Delhi: Planning Commission, Government of India.

———— (2006b). National Urban Transport Policy. New Delhi: Ministry of Urban Development.

———— (2011). *Maritime Agenda*. New Delhi: Ministry of Shipping, Government of India.

———— (2014). Report of the National Transport Development Policy Committee. London: Routledge.

———— (2015a). 'Indian Railways: Lifeline of the Nation'. White Paper. New Delhi: Ministry of Railways, Government of India.

———— (2015b). *Smart City: Mission and Guidelines*. New Delhi: Ministry of Urban Development, Government of India.

———— (2016a). *Sagarmala: Building Gateways of Growth*. National Perspective Plan. New Delhi: Ministry of Shipping, Government of India.

———— (2017). *Indian Railways: Vision and Plan 2017–2019*. New Delhi: Ministry of Railways, Government of India.

Hope, A. and J. Cox (2015). 'Development Corridors'. Coffey International Development. London, United Kingdom: Economics and Private Sector Professional Evidence and Applied Knowledge Services.

Kadam, M. (2017). 'Cost Efficiency through Containerized Multimodal Transportation'. Unpublished Ph.D. thesis submitted to the Department of Economics, University of Mumbai.

Pangotra, P. and P.R. Shukla (2012). 'Infrastructure for Low Carbon Transport in India: A Case Study of Delhi–Mumbai Dedicated Freight Corridor'. UNEP Risø Centre on Energy, Climate and Sustainable Development. Denmark: Technical University of Denmark.

Raghuram, G. and R. Gangwar (2010). 'Container Train Operators in India: Problems and Prospects'. Working Paper No. 2010-09-01. Ahmedabad: Indian Institute of Management.

Sriraman, S. (2013). 'An Approach to a National Urban Transport Policy Framework for India'. *Journal of the Indian School of Political Economy* 25(1–4): 67–106.

Sriraman, S. and S. Roy (2009). 'Financing of Transport Infrastructure and Services'. Development Research Group monograph No. 28. Mumbai: Reserve Bank of India.

———— (2014a). *Reforming the Indian Railways—Do we have the road map?.* Marathi translation, Sakal.

———— (2014b). 'A Governance Analysis of Transportation in India'. In *A Handbook of the Indian Economy*. Edited by A. Goyal. New Delhi: Oxford University Press.

———— (2017). 'Futuristic Challenges for Urban Transformation in India'. *RITES Journal* 15(2): 17.1–17.6.

Srivastava, P. (2011). 'Regional Corridors Development in Regional Cooperation'. Mimeograph. Asian Development Bank.

The Energy and Resources Institute (TERI) (2009). 'Private Participation in Indian Railways: Case of Container Movements: Competition Issues in Regulated Industries: Case of Indian Transport Sector, Railways and Ports'. Final report prepared for the Competition Commission of India. New Delhi: The Energy and Resources Institute.

World Bank, The (2005). Transport Efficiency Study. Mimeograph. Washington DC: The World Bank.

———— (2007). 'Connecting to Compete: Trade Logistics in the Global Economy, the Logistics Performance Index and Its Indicators'. The International Bank for Reconstruction and Development. Washington DC: The World Bank.

CHAPTER 10

....

PROMOTING SPECIAL ECONOMIC ZONES AS A STRATEGY OF INDUSTRIALIZATION AND LESSONS LEARNED

....

ARADHNA AGGARWAL

It is widely recognized that industrialization is critical for economic growth and development. Evidence suggests that economies that have successfully made the transition from low-income to medium- or high-income status owe their growth to rapid industrialization (Lewis 1954; Kuznets 1955; Szirmai 2011; Rodrik 2012). Industrialization has therefore been targeted as a route to economic growth in most developing countries. However, industrial transformation is a complex process which involves significant institutional and social transformation. It requires identifying the drivers of industrial development and formulating well-designed policies to push these drivers (Chang 2002; Shapiro 2005).[1] Developing countries, being late entrants, face an even

---

[1] Chang (2002) argued that all major developed countries used interventionist economic policies in order to get industrialized.

more complex and daunting set of circumstances than that faced by the now-advanced countries when they embarked on industrialization. These countries are characterized by numerous production failures and bottlenecks. As a result, markets cannot lead to efficient outcomes by themselves (Lin and Chang 2009). State-led policy instruments designed to address these bottlenecks are therefore a critical element in the process of industrial development in these countries (Lin and Chang 2009; Lin 2010; Rodrik 2005; Stiglitz 1998). One such policy instrument that has become increasingly popular within developing countries is the creation of special economic zones (SEZs). A growing number of countries are increasingly focusing on SEZs as engines of industrialization. According to the International Labour Organization (ILO) (2007), the number of SEZs increased from a mere 79 across 29 countries in 1975 to 3,500 across 130 countries in 2006. Not only has the number of SEZs increased recently but the varieties of SEZs have too. New varieties of zones have evolved and are subsumed within the broad category of SEZs (Aggarwal 2012a). Evidence, however, suggests that the success of these zones has not been unequivocal across countries. While they have been associated with significant industrial transformation in China, Korea, Taiwan, and Malaysia, they have failed miserably in many other countries (Madani 1999). This chapter examines India's SEZ experience. The objective of this chapter is to examine the formation and evolution of the SEZ policy[2] and analyse its contribution to the process of industrialization in India in different phases of its evolution. In doing so, it essentially aims to draw lessons for the recently launched new variety of zones: national investment and manufacturing zones (NIMZs). It examines important dimensions of the policy surrounding NIMZs and identifies the SEZ practices that linger and need to be addressed with urgency if the new zones are to be successful.

NIMZs are conceptualized as integrated industrial townships with state-of-the-art infrastructure that will offer a relaxed investment regime to attract industrial investments. In that sense, they have a close resemblance with SEZs. However, while the SEZs are meant

---

[2] The analysis focuses only on SEZs; export oriented units (EOUs) and software/electronic hardware technology parks (STPs/EHTPs), which also share commonalities with SEZs, are out of the purview of this study.

exclusively for exports, NIMZs are aimed at boosting both export and domestic manufacturing. They are typically hybrid SEZs which are also subdivided into general industrial parks open to all industries regardless of their export-orientation and separate areas reserved for export-oriented enterprises.[3] An assessment of the strengths and weaknesses of the existing SEZ framework will therefore, have important policy implications for the new zones.

The rest of the chapter is organized as follows. The next section presents theoretical links between SEZs and industrialization. The section that follows describes the evolution of the SEZ policy in India since 1965. The section after that examines arguments for and against the contribution of SEZs to industrialization in India. The section following outlines key lessons useful in planning zone initiatives that have emerged from the experience of the SEZ programme in India. The next section addresses what is new in the NIMZ policy. It also reviews the practices that have been continuing as legacies of the past and that need to be addressed. The final section offers concluding observations.

SEZs and Industrialization

SEZs are government-promoted industrial parks in well-defined geographically delineated economic spaces where commercial activities are primarily export-oriented and are carried out under special regulatory and incentive frameworks different from the rest of the economy. It is believed that SEZs can function as 'engines of growth' to propel the economy into industrialization by promoting trade and investment. But there are costs associated with promoting industrialization via SEZs. In what follows, we discuss the SEZ-induced channels of industrialization and the associated costs in detail.

---

[3] Sri City, Mundra, and Mahindra World City are some of the hybrid SEZs in India.

SEZ-Induced Channels of Industrialization

Augmenting Trade

The primary objective of SEZs is to promote exports. Exports are closely associated with industrial development in both import-substituting and export-oriented regimes. In an import-substituting regime, exports have to be promoted in order to earn foreign exchange to finance import requirements for industrialization in the domestic economy. In an export-oriented regime, on the other hand, exports act as an important engine of growth, not only by contributing to a more efficient allocation of resources based on comparative advantages but also by dynamically shifting the whole production possibility frontier of countries outwards. Dynamic shifts arise from more investment and faster productivity growth based on scale economies and inflows of new technologies and their diffusion within the economy.

Promoting Export-Oriented FDI

In an inter-connected world, MNCs are increasingly restructuring their operations to avail economies of scale and scope by internalizing the economies of specialization through an integration of assets, production, and marketing activities across countries to advance their core competencies in the global markets (see Aggarwal 2012a for discussion). They seek locations where they can offshore selected parts of their activities most efficiently and, in the process, form global value chains (GVCs) (UNCTAD 1998: 11). SEZs offer strategic cost-efficient locations in host countries that can attract GVC-linked foreign direct investment (FDI), which is essentially export-oriented.

This type of investment brings in technology and know-how that is compatible with the host country's level of development and enables local suppliers and competitors to benefit from spillovers generated through demonstration effects, on-the-job training, learning-by-doing, and copying, thus diffusing technology and knowledge in the host country. In particular, it is expected to fill the gaps in technical, marketing, and managerial know-how that a developing country's firms face and that constrain their growth. According to Johansson and Nilsson (1997), this has a catalytic effect on the domestic economy, raising the exports of the host economy beyond the level which is produced within the SEZ sector. They find that the estimated effects of SEZs on total exports are significantly larger than the exports of SEZs in Malaysia, which they argue is an indicator of the prevalence of FDI's catalyst effect in SEZs (see also Basile and Germidis 1984).

Promoting Integration of Domestic Firms within Global Values/Supply Chains

As discussed earlier, it is becoming increasingly rare that a good or a service is entirely produced at one location and then exported to a final consumer. In the contemporary world, the growth of world trade is closely associated with the emergence of GVCs. They have opened a new path of industrialization. Today, nations can industrialize by joining a supply chain—there is no need to build one. The integration of local firms within global value chains is an essential way of strengthening their competitiveness and building their productive capacities (see Baldwin 2011, Coxhead and Jayasuriya 2010, and Szirmai 2011 for some recent references). Producers gaining access to the chain have good prospects for upgrading within production, starting at the low end of the market and then, as a consequence of 'learning by exporting', move up to buyers, targeting more sophisticated market segments, such as design, marketing, and branding. However, market forces alone cannot ensure an effective integration of domestic firms in these chains. Global competition is so intense that unless deliberate policies are introduced to foster a favourable investment climate in terms of improved infrastructure, simplified rules and harmonized processes, and regulations and standards with regard to domestic, bilateral, regional, and international practices, firms in these economies may not be able to avail the opportunities to integrate within these networks. SEZs are a useful policy instrument to create an enabling investment climate for domestic firms to reap the benefits of supply chains.

Encouraging Domestic Investment

In this globalized era, where capital is highly mobile, an uncertain business/investment climate in developing countries underscores the domestic investors' reluctance to invest in the domestic economy.

SEZs, by offering a favourable investment climate and newer opportunities, may prove to be instrumental in reversing this tendency. SEZs are established to drive down the cost of doing business and remove roadblocks in undertaking investment activities. They can thus motivate professionally qualified and enterprising local entrepreneurs to undertake investment. Zones offer them the opportunity to introduce new technologies, new products, or new ways of doing businesses and use their talent to spin success stories of entrepreneurship. In that sense, they can serve as a fertile ground for technocrat/professional first generation entrepreneurs.

Promoting Technology and Skill Transfers

Technology and skill transfers within SEZs spill over through backward and forward linkages to the rest of the economy and promote knowledge and upgrade the productive structure of the economy. Backward linkages occur when SEZ firms source intermediates locally and/or outsource a part of their activity to local firms. These linkages can stimulate the production of intermediate inputs in the local economy, leading to an increase in the national income and welfare. Further, the learning and knowledge created in SEZs is eventually transmitted to domestic firms supplying to the SEZ firms when the companies within an SEZ buy inputs from the host country. Forward linkages are established when final products produced in the zone are sold in the domestic market (Warr 1989). There are two other important channels (Aggarwal 2012a) that promote forward linkages between the zones and the domestic mainland: one, when firms set up production units in the domestic mainland to cater to domestic markets after succeeding in export markets, they introduce new products and new technologies in the domestic mainland; and two, trade bodies, manufacturers associations, and export marketing bodies provide a valuable forum for information sharing and spillovers and act as catalysts. There is evidence that being part of production networks can result in welfare gains for producers and consumers in host countries (Feenstra et al. 2002; Moran 2002).

SEZs and Agglomeration Economies

An important benefit of creating SEZs is in promoting agglomeration economies. SEZs are, essentially, highly geographically concentrated government-promoted agglomerations of internationally competitive enterprises. Economic literature suggests that geographic concentrations of similar/related firms generate externalities which are termed 'agglomeration (or localization) economies'. These externalities arise from labour market pooling, knowledge interactions, specialization, and the sharing of inputs and outputs, and are associated with economic benefits for member firms in the form of access to specialized human resources and skills, lower input and service costs, knowledge spillovers, and pressure for higher performance, enhancing the productivity and competitiveness of firms, regions, and nations (Fujita et al. 1999). According to Porter, these externalities can take place in all clusters, but 'traded' (export-oriented) clusters such as SEZs— which are agglomerations of highly competitive trade-oriented firms—have better prospects of generating externalities. The concentration of outward-oriented firms, rivals, suppliers, and customers fosters important linkages, complementarities, and knowledge and technology spillovers, thus stimulating innovative activity, raising productivity, and enhancing competitiveness (Porter 1990).

The new economic geography theory takes this argument forward and argues that trade gains are higher when goods are subject to agglomeration economies because the concentration of world production in a single location allows greater exploitation of external economies and, hence, raises efficiency.

There is a stream of literature that shows that internationally competitive clusters in host countries act as a pull factor for inward FDI (Amiti and Javorcik 2008; Debaere et al. 2010; Nachum and Keeble 2000; Ng and Tuan 2006) and more domestic firms (Kaldor 1966; Myrdal 1957), thus launching a process of chain reactions. This promotes further expansion and specialization.

Conditions for SEZ-Induced Industrialization

SEZ-induced industrialization has taken place in some countries, but it is not a universal phenomenon. It is conditional upon several factors as follows:

- In general, the success of SEZs in attracting investments and generating economic activity is critical for an initial push to the generation of economic activity, which can set the conditions for the subsequent process of growth.

- The composition of zone activity is another critical factor for industrialization-promoting effects. If zones are, for the most part, labour intensive low-tech assembly firms with no access to advanced technology, their role in technology transfers and diffusion remains limited.
- Finally, the zone might be providing avenues for foreign direct investors, enterprising entrepreneurs, and technology transfers, but its effectiveness as an instrument for achieving long-term industrial development will largely depend on the degree of backward and forward linkages created with the domestic economy. Benefits of the SEZs accrue to the domestic economy through these linkages. Linkages define the ability of the SEZs to develop productive relationships through exchange of information and resources. These linkages, in turn, are conditional on the industrial base of the host country, SEZ policies, and the technology gap between SEZs and local firms.

Empirical evidence thus suggests that the contribution of SEZs to industrialization cannot be said to be uniform across the board (Madani 1999). It varies across countries, within countries across zones, and, more specifically, over time. The benefits that they yield depend on a complex interplay of three major factors: the quantum of activities generated by their establishment, the composition of zone activity, and the extent of backward economic integration into the economy. These, in turn, depend on government policies, and a host of other host country-, region-, and zone-specific factors.

Costs of Zone-Based Industrialization

Distortions in the Economy

According to the neoclassical economists, SEZs are essentially grafted on to host economies; they do not reflect or feed into the actual or potential strengths of the host economies, distorting them completely. As a result, international capital inflows promoted by SEZs with tax and tariff incentives can divert the resources of the labour-abundant host country towards more capital-intensive production and, hence, can work against the country's comparative advantage. This can reduce the country's welfare. This line of research is based on international trade theoretic models and has been pursued by Hamada (1974), Rodriguez (1976), Hamilton and Svensson (1982), and Devereux and Chen (1995), leading to similar results.

While countering the basic theoretical premise that SEZ production can be more capital-intensive, Balasubramanyam (1988) argues that SEZs represent a move to exploit a country's comparative advantage which may, in reality, be welfare-enhancing. However, according to him, SEZs can reduce national welfare by creating a dual economic structure in which a highly protected, import-substitution-oriented domestic economy, marked by the concentration of investments in the production of capital-intensive goods, coexists with an export-oriented enclave where investments are in the production of labour-intensive goods.

Political Rents

For political economists, SEZs are an outcome of the politics of interest groups. SEZs are established to generate rents to a few capitalists and MNCs by offering them tax incentives and other benefits at the cost of the rest of the population. These groups make investments anyways but due to large stakes involved, they incentivize government officials to influence policy in their favour. SEZs are thus tax shelters which induce relocation or diversion of economic activity from domestic areas to SEZs, causing a huge cost to the state exchequer with no net addition to investment and economic activity. This results in massive revenue forgone in tax incentives.

Dependency Argument

According to this argument, the primary function of SEZs is the use of cheap labour, rather than tax and tariff privileges. According to this approach, production systems largely driven by transnational corporations (TNCs) benefit from differences in labour costs and are an outcome of capitalist industrialization. The main argument is that the fragmenting of production processes and relocating some of them to developing countries has divided the world economy into a core of dominant nations and a periphery of dependent ones (Frank 1967; Fröbel et al. 1978; Lacharrière 1969). The division of labour is such that research and management is controlled by the core or developed

countries while assembly line work is relegated to periphery countries. In this system, SEZs are world factories performing assembly
line work with dramatically lower wages, augmenting the dependency
of developing countries on dominant nations.

Diseconomies of Agglomerations

Agglomerations also generate substantial costs called diseconomies
of agglomeration (Krugman 1991; Marshall 1890). These involve
congestion, environment degradation, and regional imbalances. In
the case of government-promoted estates, these costs can also arise
from large-scale displacement of population involved in agriculture.
Also, there are widespread concerns that SEZs will lead to uneven
growth, thereby aggravating regional inequalities, dirty growth, and
will have an adverse social impact through the acquisition of land in
large chunks.

Figure 10.1 depicts both the SEZ channels of industrialization and
associated costs in this framework. The proposed framework is used

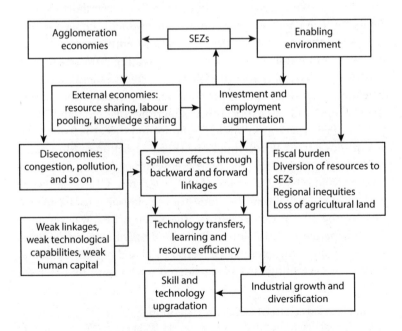

FIGURE 10.1   SEZ channels of industrialization and associated costs
Source: Adapted from Aggarwal (2011).

in this chapter to assess the contribution of SEZs in India through different policy regimes.

EVOLUTION OF THE SEZ POLICY IN INDIA

Initial Phase

After Independence in 1947, the government adopted a strategy of import substitution with emphasis on establishing basic and heavy industries for the rapid industrialization of the economy. It was believed that the country should first develop a sound industrial base by creating domestic capabilities in investment goods industries and then extend this to produce a wide range of sophisticated consumer-manufactured items. In order to finance import requirements for heavy industrialization, the government pursued export promotion through fiscal incentives, import entitlement schemes, and other promotional measures, such as creating infrastructure for information dissemination on export opportunities and marketing development. As part of its export promotion measures, the government set up Asia's first export processing zone (EPZ) in Kandla in as early as 1965. This was followed by the second EPZ, the Santa Cruz Electronics Export Processing Zone (SEEPZ), set up in Mumbai in 1974.[4] In the mid-1980s, the central government set up four more zones at Noida (NEPZ), Madras (MEPZ), Cochin (CEPZ), and Falta (FEPZ) in the belief that the trade zones could be a useful instrument in the all-out export efforts. The seventh EPZ was set up at Vishakhapatnam (VEPZ) in 1989. It could only be operationalized by 1994 though. In general, an effective legal and regulatory framework with overriding laws is considered a necessary first step for

---

[4] This EPZ was developed specifically for processing electronics goods and was expected to accelerate the progress of nascent electronics manufacturing in India to take the advantage of the growing electronics world market. In 1987, the zone was opened to the gem and jewellery sector also.

a successful zone program. In India, however, no such legislation came into effect. The policies relating to EPZs were contained in the Foreign Trade Policy while incentives and other facilities offered to EPZ units were implemented through various notifications and circulars issued by the concerned ministries/departments. Further, since the broader macro-policy regime emphasized internal dynamics, umpteen controls and regulations that characterized the domestic economy influenced the implementation of EPZs also. Zone authorities were delegated limited powers. The policies and procedures were rigid and the package of incentives and facilities was not attractive. A highly cautious approach was adopted towards local sourcing and subcontracting, thus discouraging backward linkages. There was suspicion that the concessions offered in the zone sector might be exploited by entrepreneurs who set up units in the zone for their own benefits. The problems were compounded by budgetary constraints and a lack of proper planning.

In 1991, India began to reorient its existing industrial strategy from import substitution to export promotion. This affected the government's attitude towards EPZs and major reforms were introduced in this sector as well. Fresh initiatives were launched by the government to revamp the EPZ scheme. The focus was on the following:

- delegating powers to zone authorities,
- providing additional fiscal incentives,
- simplifying policy provisions, and
- providing better facilities.

Furthermore, prior to 1990, the EPZ policy allowed only manufacturing activities. The scope and coverage of the EPZ/export-oriented units (EOU) scheme was enlarged to include agriculture, horticulture and aquaculture, and animal husbandry in 1992; floriculture, pisciculture, sericulture, viticulture, and so on in 1994; poultry, reconditioning, repair, testing, calibration, quality improvement, reengineering, and upgradation of technology in 1995; and finally, all services in 1999.

In an effort to spur the establishment of EPZs, a 1994 reform permitted the development and operation of EPZs by state governments, autonomous agencies, and the private sector. Until then, the central government was solely responsible for the setting of EPZs. However, complex bureaucratic red tape, administrative procedure, rigid labour laws, and poor infrastructure continued to affect the investment climate adversely within the EPZs.

Transitional Phase: 2000–6

In a major initiative to boost export-led growth and motivated by the success of Chinese SEZs, the government replaced the EPZ scheme with the 'SEZ scheme' in the year 2000. An SEZ is defined as a self-contained area with high-class infrastructure for commercial as well as residential inhabitation. The main difference between an SEZ and an EPZ is that the former is an integrated township with fully developed infrastructure according to international standards whereas the latter is just an industrial estate. SEZs enjoy some features which distinguish them from the previously existing EPZs. For instance, while the EPZs had been set up by the central government, SEZs were proposed to be set up in the public, private, or joint sector or by the state governments. Further, EPZs were small (less than 120 hectares)[5] trade enclaves essentially located in backward regions near port areas; on the contrary, the minimum size of SEZs was initially envisaged to be 400 to 500 hectares. Unlike the former, the latter were also given locational flexibility, in the sense that their location was to be decided by the developer and not the government. EPZs were subject to fulfillment of a minimum net foreign exchange earning, but this condition was done away within the SEZ policy. It was expected that the FDI, which was getting diverted to other Asian countries, would be attracted to India by these SEZs. In a move to promote backward linkages with the domestic economy, it was announced in 2003 that domestic sales to SEZs would be treated as exports and the suppliers would get all export-related benefits on these sales.

During this phase, both EPZs and SEZs coexisted. By 2003, all the existing EPZs had been converted to SEZs, and with that the EPZ

[5] Kandla is the only exception with an area of 404 hectares.

policy seized to exist and the transition from the EPZ to the SEZ regime was complete. In addition, 12 new SEZs became operational; most were set up by the state government initiatives. The policy failed to generate enough confidence among private investors to commit substantial funds for infrastructure development.

Takeoff Phase: 2006–11

With a view to instill confidence in investors and to signal government's commitment to a stable SEZ policy regime, an SEZ Act was introduced in 2005. This was the first time that a legal framework with special overriding laws and legislation was formulated to provide the necessary regulatory foundation for SEZs/EPZs. The Act became operative with effect from 10 February 2006 when the SEZ Rules were also finalized. This Act, along with the SEZ Rules, provides a comprehensive SEZ policy framework to satisfy the requirements of all principal stakeholders in an SEZ—the developer and operator, occupant enterprise, out-zone supplier, and residents. In addition to the central government's SEZ Act, there are SEZ Acts of state governments also which cover state subjects.

Under this Act, the central government is responsible only for the broad policy framework and monitoring of the scheme; it is not expected to set up new SEZs. Further, unlike the earlier EPZ/SEZ model, SEZ Rules provide for different minimum land requirements for different classes of SEZs. The minimum size stipulated for a greenfield SEZ for multi-product zone, for instance, is 1,000 hectare. Within each zone, the processing area is distinguished from the non-processing area. The processing area is designated for production activity whereas the non-processing area is intended to provide support facilities and social infrastructure. The minimum processing area stipulated in the SEZ Act of 2005, was 25 per cent of the total area. This was extended to 50 per cent by introducing an amendment to the Act. The Act also has special provisions to promote backward linkages by encouraging local sourcing and subcontracting. There is no limitation on Domestic Traffic Area (DTA) sales with full-duty payment, subject to the fulfillment of positive net foreign exchange earnings over five years.

The Act offers a highly attractive fiscal incentive package, which ensures an attractive corporate tax holiday, exemption from custom duties, central excise duties, service tax, central sales taxes, and securities transaction tax to both the developers and the units. While the SEZ units enjoy tax benefits for 15 years, 100 per cent tax exemption for five years, 50 per cent for the next five years, and 50 per cent of the ploughed-back export profits for the next five years,[6] developers are ensured 100 per cent income tax exemption for 10 years in a block period of fifteen years.

Finally, the Act claims to provide world-class infrastructure and expeditious and single-window clearance mechanisms. The development commissioner is the nodal officer for SEZs who helps in resolving problems, if any, faced by the units/developer.

The enforcement of the SEZ Act has led to tremendous growth in the establishment of SEZs in India and has completely transformed the SEZ sector in terms of size, structure, composition, and contribution. Table 10.1 shows that during the EPZ regime of 1965–2000, only seven zones were set up by the central government, locking a land area of 894 hectares with 95,000 people employed. During the transitional phase (2000–6), 12 new zones, mostly sector-specific, were set up. Of these, five were set up by the respective state governments while

Table 10.1 Structure of India's EPZ/SEZ sector

Period	Number	Ownership	Area (in hectare)	Type of zone
1995–2000	7	Central government: 7	894.4	Multiproduct: 1 Bi-product zones: 1
2000–6	12	State government: 5 Private sector: 7	1,817.5	Multiproduct, Sector specific, service zones
2006–11	581	State governments: 119 Private sector: 462	63,608.27	Multi-product: 24; sector-specific: 164; service: 371; FTWZ: 22

Source: Data compiled by the author.

[6] This is applicable to SEZ units that began their operations during the previous year, relevant to any assessment year commencing on or after 1 April 2006.

the rest were in the private sector. Despite expansion, the SEZ sector remained rather small in terms of land area covered and employment. As on February 10 2006, India had 19 operational EPZs with a combined area of 1817.5 hectares and employment of 123,000.

The SEZ scenario completely changed in the post–SEZ Act period. An unprecedented rush for setting up SEZs ensued following the passage of the act. By December 2006, that is, within 18 months of the act, 237 new SEZs had been granted formal approval. This number increased at a steady pace in 2007 and 2008. As on 23 February 2009, 560 new SEZs had been granted formal approvals, of which 286 had been notified. The SEZ expansion slowed down thereafter. As on 17 July 2012, the number of formal SEZs stood at 589. Of them, 389 had been notified and were in different stages of development/operation. These 'newly notified' SEZs covered an area of 71,502 hectares.

De-notification Phase of Post 2011

The proliferation in the number of SEZs triggered a fierce nationwide debate over the usefulness of the SEZ policy in the country. Massive intellectual support to this criticism of SEZs came from the media, activists, and academia from both the right and the left. The whole debate that still rages on is usurped by an anti-SEZ rhetoric. It touches upon almost every aspect of SEZs from macro-economic issues related to their impact on government revenue, employment, trade, and foreign exchange earnings to social issues, such as a mass scale of land acquisition, displacement of farmers associated with land acquisition, loss of fertile land, labour rights, regional inequities, and environmental protection. The anti-SEZ obsession is so widespread that it has become cult-like. The government responded to the controversy by diluting not only the policy but also its support to the SEZ investors. Many states started dragging their feet and adopted the policy of 'go slow'. The center put on hold clearances for new SEZs for a few months in 2007 and started reconsidering the tax incentives offered to them. These populist measures sent the wrong signals across the world regarding the sincerity of the government with respect to its policy in the initial phase of their evolution.

Further, the SEZ policy itself is fraught with some major challenges (Aggarwal 2012a). Some of the issues that have eroded the credibility of the policy include ambiguity in the provisions of the act, different interpretations of a single act by different authorities, lack of a clear-cut vision in promoting SEZs; involvement of different authorities in the government decision-making system, absence of an accountable governance model, and absence of a well-designed redressal system. A major challenge faced by policymakers is how to ensure single-window governance. The implementation of the policy involves multiple departments and ministries both at the centre and state levels who must work jointly for achieving the objectives of the policy. However, there has been a lack of both horizontal and vertical coordination.

Despite raging protests, policy gaps, and uncertainty in the policy regime, SEZs continued to flourish when the economy was booming. In 2008, however, the global recession set in, hitting export demand. The vulnerability of investors was further aggravated by the policy decision of imposing minimum alternative tax and dividend distribution tax on SEZs in 2010–11. This proved to be a major blow to the SEZs and led to a spurt in the demand for de-notification or surrendering of the SEZ status. The outcome was a decline in the number of SEZs across all categories, namely notified, formally approved, and in-principle approved (Table 10.2).

Against that background, in what follows, we analyse the contribution of SEZs to the process of industrialization.

Table 10.2 Growth in SEZs: 2011–17

	Formal approvals (No.)	Notifications (No.)	In-principle approvals (No.)	Operational SEZs
As of 30 January 2011	581	374	–	144
As of 17 July 2012	589	389	48	153
As of 21 January 2015	491	352	32	196
As of 30 September 2017	424	354	31	222

Source: Ministry of Commerce and Industry.

Promoting Industrialization through SEZ: The Indian Experience

Quantitative Indicators

Attracting Investment

Investment is a key driver of industrialization and, as discussed earlier, SEZs can offer a viable platform for attracting both domestic and foreign investment. But the total EPZ investments remained abysmally small until 2000.[7] According to the official data procured from the Ministry of Commerce and presented in Table 10.3, total investments in 2000 stood at INR 17.84 billion, having increased almost 20 times in 10 years. The policy shock of 2000 further impacted the magnitude of investments attracted by SEZs. In the post-SEZ Act (2005) period, however, the investment scenario in SEZs changed completely. The sector registered an overwhelming growth in terms of investments and employment. The total investments multiplied several times to reach the level of INR 2,018.75 billion (as on 31 March 2012) from a modest INR 49.4 billion worth of investments in February 2006. Notwithstanding the rush for de-notification and a resultant decline in the number of SEZs, economic activity has continued to flourish in SEZs as more and more SEZs are becoming operational. But the increase in investments has not been due only to the emergence of new zones; economic activity in those SEZs that came into force prior to the act has also shown an impressive growth after 2011. As of September 2017, the total employment in SEZs stood at 1.7 million and investments amounted to INR 4.5 trillion. However, FDI forms only 12.8 per cent of this investment. Apparently, SEZs offer domestic entrepreneurs fertile grounds to flourish in India. While Indian entrepreneurs have made significant entrepreneurial contributions outside India, entrepreneurship turnout is low within India,

---

[7] One caveat: data on capital employed is not available for India for all the years. Therefore, the series is largely constructed using the available data.

Table 10.3 Direct employment and investment in SEZs

Type of SEZs	Employment (number)					Investment (in billion INR)				
	2000	February 2006	March 2011	March 2012	30 September 2017	2000	February 2006	March 2011	March 2012	30 September 2017
Central government	81,372	158,197	210,434	213,853	235,305	17.84	33.51	104.53	114.86	179.42
Transition phase	–	20,566	66,031	79,015	99,400	–	16.08	77.16	76.38	127.76
Newly notified	–	–	400,143	552,048	1,488,746	–	–	1,846.41	1,827.51	4,181.1
Total	81,371	129,704	676,608	844,916	1,688,747	17.84	49.5	2,028.05	2,018.75	4,448.3

Source: Based on the Ministry of Commerce database.

primarily due to unfavourble investment incentives. SEZs appear to have contributed to the process of industrialization by offering domestic investors a platform to invest within the country.

What is worrisome is that the share of FDI remains abysmally small. But more worrisome is that the proposed FDI itself has been declining. It declined from INR 345,090 million as on 31 December 2009 to INR 309,640 million in September 2010, then further to INR 269,844 million as on March 31 2012. SEZs could offer a useful platform for foreign investors who were looking at India as a regional hub of manufacturing, trade, and logistics. But the academic, political, and civil society resistance that followed the initial phase of the SEZ Act's implementation seems to have adversely affected the prospects of attracting FDI. Domestic investment growth also waned during 2011–12 (Table 10.4). However, as more SEZs became operational, both investments and employment grew rapidly and more than doubled by 2017. Despite the uncertainty around the policy, the prospects of SEZs are not completely ruined.

Augmenting Trade

During the EPZ regime, the contribution of EPZs in the overall exports remained minuscule in India due to convergence of the EPZ export growth rate with the export growth rates of the overall economy at an early stage of evolution of the EPZ programme. This is evident in Figure 10.2 which shows growth rates of real exports (nominal exports deflated by unit value) in EPZs and outside them.

During the initial years, the growth rate in exports was as high as over 65 per cent per annum. This was due to a very low base at which production started. It became negative by the early 1970s. In 1974, another SEZ became operational in Santa Cruz, giving a push to exports. Furthermore, in 1978, a bilateral trade agreement between the former Soviet Union and India based on 'rupee/ruble payment' became effective. Several companies used Kandla and Santa Cruz EPZs as a base for exports to Russia. This led to a quantum jump in the export growth of EPZs (Kumar 1989). By the mid-1980s, however, the growth rate of such exports had started slowing down. In the late-1980s, when the USSR collapsed, several zone units shut down and EPZ exports declined sharply. The post-1991 reforms did not yield significant results for the reasons discussed earlier. During 2002–4,

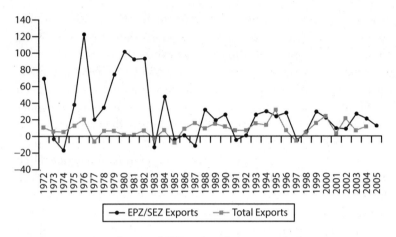

FIGURE 10.2   Growth rates of SEZ and total exports in India over 1966–2006 in real terms

Source: Based on the Ministry of Commerce database.

the average annual growth rate zoomed up to 23 per cent per annum in terms of US dollars but stabilized again in 2005. In 2005–6, the share of SEZs in total exports stood at a mere 3.2 per cent. Clearly, the EPZ or even the SEZ regime introduced in 2000 failed to induce significant dynamism.

The implementation of the act provided a major push to SEZs' export performance (Table 10.4). The share of SEZs in the national exports (comprising both non-oil and software exports) increased from a mere 3.2 per cent in 2005–6 to around 23 per cent by 2016–17.[8] The possibility of relocating export units from the domestic mainland to SEZs cannot completely be ruled out. Aggarwal (2012a) finds evidence of relocation of large IT firms to SEZs. However, as we shall discuss later, the argument of additionality is myopic and has been overemphasized in the context of industrial growth.

In 2008–9, when the global crisis had ravaging effects on the export sector and the overall merchandise exports recorded a single-digit growth of 3.4 per cent in dollar terms, and the services' export growth

---

[8] The ministry's claim that the share of SEZs in total exports is 30 per cent is based on merchandise exports rather than total exports.

Table 10.4 Annual growth rates of SEZ exports and national exports[*]: 2005–6 to 2016–17

Year	National exports[*] (INR billion)	SEZ (INR billion)	Share (per cent)
2005–6	4,657	228	3.17
2006–7	5,829	346	3.78
2007–8	6,680	663	6.43
2008–9	8,580	997	7.41
2009–10	8,633	2,207	16.76
2010–11	11,395	3,159	18.11
2011–12	14,825	3,645	16.82
2012–13	16,440	4,762	28.96
2013–14	19,540	4,941	25.28
2015–16	20,930	4,673	22.33
2016–17	22,920	5,236	22.85

Source: Calculations based on data from the Ministry of Commerce and Reserve Bank of India.

Note: [*]National exports comprise non-oil and software exports.

crashed to 12.4 per cent against 22 per cent in 2007–8, the SEZs registered an impressive growth in exports. SEZs further improved their performance in 2009–10. While national merchandise exports declined by 13.7 per cent over their 2008–9 level, SEZ exports registered an impressive growth of 121.4 per cent. This continued to increase in 2011 at the rate of 43 per cent. In 2012, however, consequent on the global economic turndown and withdrawal of key benefits offered to SEZ units, SEZ's performance also deteriorated. However, the SEZs soon picked up and increased their share from 18 per cent in 2010–11 to 23 per cent in 2016–17.

Foreign Exchange Earnings

The share of SEZ trade surplus in the national trade balance is an indicator of the contribution of SEZs to foreign exchange earnings. In India, trade surplus has remained routinely negative. On the other hand, it has always been positive in SEZs. To estimate the contribution of SEZs to foreign exchange earnings, therefore, we examine how much of the total national import outgoings are covered by

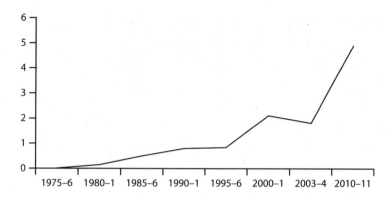

FIGURE 10.3   Share of EPZs'/SEZs' trade balance in the total national import bills in selected years between 1975–6 and 2010–11 (percentage)

Source: Based on the Ministry of Commerce database.

trade surplus in SEZs. Until 1990, the contribution of trade surplus in EPZs to national import bills remained less than 0.50 per cent, given the small magnitude of trade from EPZs. Thereafter, it started rising. In 2010–11, it stood at 5 per cent. This implies that 5 per cent of the national imports were funded by the surplus generated in SEZs in 2010–11.[9]

Industrialization and SEZs: Qualitative Analysis

While most analysts assess the contribution of SEZs in terms of macro-indicators, such as investment, employment, and exports, what is more important is their impact on technological and industrial sophistication in the host country. In a large economy such as India, SEZs may not constitute a significant proportion of total exports or employment but can still have important spillover effects on the process of industrialization. Madani (1999: 6) finds, 'even at the height of their influence, EPZs never acquired a prominent role either in terms of exports value or employment creation in S. Korea

---

[9] Post 2011, SEZ import data could not be traced.

or Taiwan'. The following analysis focuses on the contribution of SEZs to the upgradation of the industrial sector in India.

Introduction of New Industries

A micro-level analysis of the zones' contribution to industrialization efforts in India reveals that EPZs had been instrumental in inserting domestic firms in global value chains of new industries, which, in turn, has had a catalytic effect in promoting new production sectors, exporting new products, and in building the country's image in certain products in international markets (Aggarwal 2006a). The foundation of the modern jewellery industry in India, for instance, was laid in SEEPZ in Mumbai in 1987–8. In 2010–11, SEZs accounted for over 86 per cent of the total gold jewellery exports from India. The latest statistics provided on the website of the Gold and Jewellery Export Promotion Council[10] indicate, however, that gold jewellery exports from SEZs have surpassed those from domestic tariff areas (DTA). In 2017, SEZ exports of gold jewellery were nearly double than those made by the DTAs. Zones were also instrumental in creating the base for the growth of the electronics industry through technology transfers, spillovers, and demonstration effects. Until the early 1980s, electronic hardware exports were primarily originating from EPZs. Even during 2000–2, the share of SEZs in total hardware exports was as much as 26 per cent. The Indian software saga also really began in SEEPZ, Mumbai (Heeks 1996). The first major breakthrough in India's software exports came in 1977 when the Tatas established a unit in SEEPZ in partnership with Burroughs, an American company, to export software and peripherals. A further breakthrough in the progress of the industry occurred when, in 1985, Citibank established a 100 per cent foreign-owned, export-oriented, offshore software company in SEEPZ. This company drew attention to the possibilities available for offshore software development in India. Soon after, Texas Instruments and Hewlett-Packard established subsidiaries in Bangalore in 1986 and 1989 respectively, and the rest is history. Rubber gloves are another story of successful industrial transformation. In the late 1980s, US

[10] See https://gjepc.org/statistics.php.

made it mandatory for doctors to use rubber gloves when they came in touch with patient. This led to a tremendous increase in demand for the product and, eventually, for the offshoring of production. It was in the Cochin SEZ that the 'automated line dipping technology' was first introduced with the help of Malaysian companies. Eventually, Indian firms became technological competitive. However, notwithstanding these success stories, the erstwhile EPZs could not replicate the success of South East Asia.

In the post–2005 act period, several new technology- and knowledge-based industries have come up in SEZs. These are, for instance, electronics manufacturing services industry (EMS), aerospace industries, alternative energy industries, and bio-tech industries, to name a few. These industries are capital- and scale-intensive and can immensely benefit from the externalities associated with agglomerations, such as lower costs of inputs and services, access to skilled labour, and knowledge spillovers (see Aggarwal 2012a for a discussion). Their growth will, however, call for vision and a set of clear-cut policies to promote such industries. There have been no discussions in policy circles on how to exploit these opportunities. Even the benefits of SEZs which relate to the transfer of advanced technology, managerial techniques and know-how, skill upgradation, and export diversification have completely been ignored in the SEZ policy document.

Entrepreneurial Development

The development of private entrepreneurship is a pressing issue in developing countries. Entrepreneurs create new ways, new businesses, and new industries, which are essential for development. Our research shows that the erstwhile EPZs proved to be a fertile ground for technocrat/professional first generation entrepreneurs in India. Zones offered them an opportunity to execute their ideas and use their talent to spin success stories of entrepreneurship. These zones offer standard design factories (SDFs) on the basis of highly subsidized annual rent. Starting businesses in SDFs is based on the 'plug in' concept. Basic infrastructure facilities such as developed land, power, water, and customs clearance facilities were developed within the zone. This significantly reduced the gestation period and hence the cost of the project. Constructing one's own factory was also cheaper due to tax exemption on all construction materials, office equipments, and fixtures. Further, they offered a somewhat relaxed industrial regime when the domestic regime was rather strict and, thus, acted as an incubator to help new entrepreneurs to start, grow, and succeed. One of the most successful stories is that of Deepak Puri. As a mechanical engineer, Deepak Puri started Moser Baer in 1983 in technical collaboration with the Swiss firm Moser Baer AG, which catered to time solutions. Later, when he started manufacturing floppy diskettes for export, he was given a license to manufacture 50,000 units per month during the License Raj. Puri realized that competing with global players with such a low-capacity output was not feasible. Since these restrictions were not applicable to zone units, he moved to the Noida EPZ. From then on, the growth of the company zoomed. By 2004, Moser Baer had grown to become the world's second largest optical media manufacturer and one of the largest tech hardware exporters from India, shipping to 82 countries.[11] Rajiv Seth,[12] a technocrat and gemologist was instrumental in laying down the foundation of the modern jewellery industry in the SEEPZ. He later established his company Tara Jewels in SEEPZ. The company has been one of the top exporters of studded jewellery from EPZ and EOU complexes in India.[13] Javed Hassan, a technocrat from Kerala with 21 patents in semiconductor technology[14] and the president of AMP Global Communications Group, founded the NeST (Network Systems and Technologies) Group in 1990. In 1991, he chose Cochin EPZ to set up an outsourcing arm of AMP due to a better investment climate within the EPZ than outside it. This almost laid the foundation of the electronics industries in Cochin. Workers were sent to the USA and Japan for training and when they came back, they trained the others. They expanded phenomenally within the zone and outside it. Ashoke

[11] Information available at: http://www.moneycontrol.com/smementor/news/technology/moser-baer-has-allshut-down-738420.html. Last accessed on 12 June 2019.

[12] Based on our interview with Ms Nalini Jayaraman, the vice president of the company, and the material given by her.

[13] Source: Gems and Jewellery Export Promotion Council.

[14] Based on our interview with Mr Shamsuddin, joint director, and the material provided by him.

Mukherjee, an engineering student from Roorkee University, initiated the manufacturing of amplifiers and speakers in India when he released stereo amplifiers in the 1970s. In 1982, a 100 per cent export-oriented division, Sonodyne International Ltd., was established in SEEPZ, Mumbai to manufacture professional audio and power electronics equipment as an original equipment manufacturer (OEM) for the European and American houses. In the early-1990s, when the competition heated with the entry of global giants, he took a step back from domestic sales and focused on developing technological capabilities through technology transfers by concentrating only on exporting activities in SEEPZ. Eventually, he successfully re-launched the company in the domestic market.

Unfortunately, the newly notified SEZs do not share this feature with the erstwhile EPZs. While they do offer a good investment climate, they charge premium prices for space for the international standards that they have created in the SEZs. Further, most of them (including the state governments) are offering large plots above some threshold level to investors, encouraging only large investors. Also, they do not offer a plug-n-play facility within the SEZs. There is no reserved space for SDFs for leasing it out to SMEs or new entrepreneurs for the incubation of their ideas. This is a serious gap in the policy that needs attention.

Scale Advantage and SEZs

Since 1991, government policies in India have been directed at encouraging large-scale production. However, capital market rigidities, constraints on land availability, and labour market rigidities have not allowed companies to reap the benefits of scale economies. Most of these constraints are directly addressed by the new SEZs. As a result, they have been instrumental in promoting several large enterprises. The Apache footwear company in the Apache SEZ, for instance, has a large facility with around 6,549 employees. Similarly, the Lotus footwear company has set up a large facility in Cheyyar (Tamil Nadu) which employs over 4,500 workers. The Jamnagar SEZ refinery, together with its sister company, has emerged as the world's largest single-location refinery with a combined refining capacity touching 1.2 million barrels per day, which is 5 per cent of the world's capacity. The Moser Baer SEZ unit is poised to be the world's second largest such unit after Phoenix, a US-based company. These large, and often single-enterprise SEZs, are expected to act as Hirschman's growth poles and have the potential of being instrumental in forming regional clusters by generating backward and forward linkages. This will not, however, be an automatic process. It requires a holistic and multi-disciplinary approach to create an enabling environment in regional economies to promote industrialization.

Promotion of Agglomeration

Most SEZs are coming up in strategic locations, which can reinforce regional agglomeration economies. A large number of SEZs, privately owned in particular, are developing in or around natural clusters or industrial complexes and are expected to augment and reinforce them. Most SEZs in Uttar Pradesh and Haryana, for instance, are in the information technology (IT) sector and are clustered in the existing IT hubs of Noida and Gurgaon. The Uttar Pradesh state government has also been promoting two handicrafts SEZs in the natural clusters of Moradabad and Bhadohi; other state-promoted SEZs are proposed to be located in the industrial town of Kanpur. In Andhra Pradesh, Kerala, and Tamil Nadu, many IT-based private SEZs are clustered near the IT hubs of Hyderabad, Thiruvananthapuram and Kochi, and Chennai respectively. In Maharashtra, most private SEZs are being set up in the industrially developed belt of the state, namely Nashik–Pune–Mumbai. The Gujarat state government has identified six regions that have already acquired industrial capabilities. Most SEZs are located in these regions to revitalize their core competencies and transform them into internationally competitive hubs by generating positive synergies between them. These are Ahmedabad (pharmaceuticals and textiles), Gandhinagar (information technology), Bharuch (chemicals), Vodadara (engineering), Jamnagar (petrochemicals), and Kutch (heavy metals and logistics). The Rajasthan government's handicraft SEZs in Jodhpur and the gems and jewellery SEZ in Jaipur and Kerala's food park and animation and gaming SEZs are carved out of existing industrial estates. The Andhra Pradesh government has also created some SEZs (Mehaboobnagar, for instance) in the existing growth centers. In an increasingly knowledge-intensive and globalized world, many inward-looking clusters and industrial estates are facing serious challenges in terms of technology flows, skills, environment, and quality control. The strategy of situating SEZs in and around them will create synergies and augment the inward-looking clusters/estates by creating opportunities for mutual learning and innovations with the presence of outward-looking clusters in close proximity.

In some places, several small SEZs are clustered in a region and have been reinforced by developing industrial estates in the proximity. In Andhra Pradesh, for instance, new industries such as gems and jewellery, bio-tech, engineering, sports shoes, and the high-end pharmaceutical industry are being implanted by promoting large-scale production facilities through clustered SEZs. Following a similar strategy, the Tamil Nadu government is using SEZs to move up the value chain in industrial production. It is promoting the 'Industrial Corridors of Excellence' and is using SEZs to kick-start their development. In the first phase, the Chennai–Manali–Ennore and the Chengalpattu–Sriperumbudur–Ranipet corridors will be developed, with several SEZs clustered in this belt supported by industrial and IT parks, R&D institutions, universities, and social infrastructure such as housing, healthcare, and schools.

It has now been envisaged to synthesize the setting up of SEZs with the development of industrial corridors. Several SEZs are projected to be located in investment regions, industrial hubs, and multi-model logistic hubs planned along the upcoming Delhi–Mumbai industrial corridor. Each hub will have world-class infrastructure, business centers, transport facilities, and good connectivity. This will create synergies between sectors looking at the domestic market and outward-looking SEZs and between various SEZs in the same region. These synergies, drawing on both local production systems and global resources, will enhance regional competitiveness.

Large original brand manufacturing (OBM) companies, such as Nokia, Suzlon, Gitanjali, and Uniparts have been developing integrated industrial parks to cut the cost of logistics. They use SEZs to attract upstream and downstream links in the global value chain within an SEZ and forge an industrial chain by creating all the necessary backward and forward linkages of the firms. This process of localization of international chains enhances industrial efficiency by reducing transport and inventory costs and ensures all the advantages of vertical integration.

Efforts are thus directed at augmenting the benefits of SEZs by locating them close to existing clusters/industrial estates, or clustering them in one location, or creating large-scale integrated production facilities.

Regional Diversification

As discussed earlier, there have been instances where SEZs were created as industrial estates clustered in one location to promote new industries and diversify the economic base. Several electronics product–based SEZs, for instance, are being developed along the Sriperumbudur–Oragadam belt. They cover the full spectrum of different tiers of suppliers in the supply chain network. Similarly, the Sri Ranga Reddy district in Andhra Pradesh—a large barren and rocky tract of land near Hyderabad—is being promoted by the state government as an IT hub with several IT SEZs clustered in the region. Surat, in Gujarat, is known as the synthetic city but with the setting up of an apparel park, textile industry has also been introduced in the region. It is also known for diamond trading, but with the gems and jewellery SEZs, the jewellery manufacturing industry has also been introduced in the region. SEZs have also facilitated the emergence of the IT sector in new locations, such as Mohali in Punjab, Gandhinagar in Gujarat, and Jaipur in Rajasthan. SEZs can thus be used strategically to move industrial areas from low value-added activities up to high-end activities and promote industrial activity in underdeveloped regions.

Shift of Production Activity from Unorganized to Organized Sectors

SEZs have the potential to transform unorganized industry clusters into organized parks driven by innovation and design. For instance, the introduction of the gems and jewellery industry in the Santa Cruz SEZ (then EPZ) in 1986–7 proved to be a turning point for the industry. Under the new policy, handicrafts and brassware SEZs are being promoted to repeat the Santa Cruz EPZ miracle. However, the incentive structure is not conducive to the growth of labour-intensive small industries in SEZs with its thrust on promoting large-scale businesses (Aggarwal 2012a).

Costs of SEZ-Linked Industrialization

Loss of Agricultural Land

The diversion of land from agriculture to industrial use is the most contentious issue in the SEZ debate, which even led to violent protests against SEZs in the initial phases of their evolution (Levien 2011; Palit and Bhttacharjea 2008; Banerjee et al. 2007; Basu 2007; Bhaduri 2007). From the perspective of the national economy, it means the loss of fertile agricultural land, which has serious implications for the food security. From the perspective of agriculturists, if farming communities are displaced from their land with no alternative means of livelihood, this will have poverty enhancing effects (Aggarwal and Kokko 2017). One can, however, argue that this issue is not SEZ-centric; any large development project is bound to face it. It requires the identification and institutionalization of innovative methods to deal with the challenges faced in land acquisition for development projects. Even from the investors' perspective, acquiring land for large projects from a large number of sellers is expensive and time-consuming; a few strategically located owners may hold up the entire project, discouraging investments in such projects.

Revenue Losses

The revenue foregone on account of direct tax sops for the period 2015–16, as provided in the annual receipt budget[15] of the Ministry of Finance, turns out to be INR 188.6 billion, which made up 24 per cent of the total revenue foregone in incentive schemes.[16] The total investment in SEZs (including investment in infrastructure) as on 30 September 2017 was INR 4.5 trillion, mostly in the private sector. This implies considerable savings for the government in infrastructure development. Further, the generation of economic activity outside the SEZs will also generate tax revenue, producing

[15] Available at: http://www.indiabudget.gov.in/rec.asp?pageid=2. Last accessed on 30 December 2017.

[16] The Comptroller Auditor General (CAG) of India Report (2014) places the revenue foregone in direct taxes and customs offered to SEZs for the period 2007 to 2013 at INR 831.04 billion. It may be noted that custom exemptions are given to all exports irrespective of the location.

net benefits (Aggarwal 2012a). Critics, however, argue that there has been a large-scale relocation of existing units and diversion of new economic activities from non-SEZ to SEZ areas and that there is very little new addition to economic activities. A counter argument is that capital has become increasingly mobile across borders and that with most countries adopting pro-industrialization strategies with generous benefits to their industries, the competition to attract industrial investment, both domestic and foreign, has intensified. In this scenario, SEZs might have been instrumental in attracting such large investments which would otherwise have not come. It can also be argued that the concern for additionality is itself over emphasized. Growth does not mean only augmentation of physical resources, it also means knowledge, technology, and learning. The New Economic Geography focuses on rearranging resources that can contribute to productivity and economic growth. The clustering of competitive firms in SEZs can initiate the process of evolutionary dynamics and attract more foreign and domestic investment, as discussed earlier. This, in turn, augments resources and boosts economic activity (Aggarwal 2012a).

Regional Disparities

There are widespread concerns that SEZs will lead to uneven growth, thereby aggravating regional inequalities. A state-wise analysis of notified SEZs indicates that the five most industrialized states, namely Andhra Pradesh, Tamil Nadu, Karnataka, Gujarat, and Maharashtra, account for over 70 per cent of all (notified) SEZs and have over 89 per cent of the land tied up in them. In contrast, the industrially backward states of Bihar, the North East, and Jammu and Kashmir did not have a single approval. Literature suggests that industries tend to be located where they find a pro-business attitude and policies of the regional government, an easy access to major infrastructure (main highways, electricity, gas, and communication), services (financial services and public agencies), and trade infrastructure. This line of thinking underscores the role of the government in creating enabling conditions for industrialization. There are instances, in particular in Andhra Pradesh and Tamil Nadu, where SEZs are being used to diversify backward regions by giving them a big push through the creation of several small SEZs clustered in these regions and reinforcing them by developing industrial estates in their proximity.

Labour and Environment Standards

There are concerns over welfare-reducing effects of the relaxation of labour and environmental laws for SEZ units (Sen and Dasgupta 2009). These costs seem to be exaggerated in the Indian context, given that these standards are not diluted in SEZs and that the zones are dominated by high-tech and skill-intensive activities. Further, there are severe pressures by international buyers on companies to meet labour and environment standards. They insist on a global standard such as SA 8000 that has both labour and environmental norms and ISO 14000 which has implications for environment norms.

Sectoral Imbalance and Skewed Export Base

Many criticize SEZs on the ground that the policy seeks to promote manufacturing but more than 55 per cent of the zones are IT-specific. Data reveal that while IT and ITES SEZs dominate in numbers, they accounted for only approximately 10 per cent of the area under SEZs and 29 per cent of the total SEZ investments as on 31 March 2012. Interestingly, despite the fact that IT zones have far outnumbered other zones, manufacturing accounted for almost 50 per cent of their total physical exports in 2008–9; its share increased to over 77 per cent in 2009–10. In 2011–12, manufacturing exports took a hit and their share declined to 58 per cent, though it still remained more than that of the IT exports.

Two things may be noted here. One, the SEZs have been undergoing internal and external vulnerabilities since their inception. Despite that, they have proliferated in terms of numbers and investment. Two, the evolution of SEZs involves time. Farole (2011) argues that even the biggest SEZ success stories, such as those of China and Malaysia, started slowly and took at least 5 to 10 years to build momentum. Manufacturing zones, in particular, have long gestation periods.

The upshot is that while SEZs do entail costs, in some contexts these are exaggerated and in others, they can be addressed through a long-run vision, strong commitment, a pragmatic and flexible approach, and dynamic learning and institution-building (Aggarwal 2006b). The experiences of South Korea, Taiwan, Malaysia, and China reveal that a crucial element in the success of SEZs is a strategic policy intervention that includes vision, strong commitment, legal and institutional frameworks, and a continuously unfolding and dynamic set of policies (Aggarwal 2012b). In India, however, sensationalization of SEZ-related issues has created an inflated public perception of their costs mainly due to deficiencies/gaps in the policy formulation and implementation. Amidst widespread public misconceptions about the policy, the ruling party appears to be convinced that SEZs have no public appeal. Since it perceives no political returns in promoting zones, instead of systematically addressing the challenges to carry the policy forward, it has backtracked, creating uncertainty and confusion regarding SEZs. This approach may harm the credibility of the government for future programmes.

The National Manufacturing Policy: Lessons Learned from SEZs

While SEZs with an investment of INR 4.5 trillion have been facing uncertainty over their future, the government has proposed to set up NIMZs under the National Manufacturing policy (NMP). The NMP harbours the ambitious objective of enhancing the share of manufacturing in GDP to 25 per cent and creating 100 million jobs over a decade or so. The NIMZs are conceptualized as integrated industrial townships of at least 50 sq. km (5,000 hectares) with state-of-the-art infrastructure catering to manufacturing for both the domestic market and exports. They will have 'high class' physical infrastructure with areas earmarked for manufacturing units ('processing areas') as well as for residential, commercial, and other facilities ('non-processing areas'). The processing areas may contain export-oriented units and even SEZs. Apparently, NIMZs are proposed to be established on a premise similar to the SEZs—that 'world-class' infrastructure, a business-friendly 'single window' to the government, and a relaxed regulatory regime will accelerate the establishment of new enterprises and the growth of exports. As stated earlier, NIMZs resemble hybrid SEZs. Even the promises made in the policy are similar to the ones made when the SEZ Act was passed.[17] Experts argue that the creation of NIMZs is just another re-branding attempt against the backdrop of SEZ activities increasingly becoming tepid. Indeed, NIMZs have been set within the overall framework of the earlier zones. Yet, the National Manufacturing Policy has some new dimensions that were missing in the SEZ Act.

New Dimensions of National Manufacturing Policy

Scope of Economic Activity

Unlike SEZs, NIMZs are designed to host commercial activities that are oriented both towards export and domestic markets. These are a new generation of SEZs that offer a wider range of job-generating land use opportunities and are being adopted by an increasing number of developing countries in Asia and other parts of the world. These zones are also expected to generate better spillover effects from export-oriented foreign and domestic investments and have a catalyst effect on exports. However, the shift in focus towards hybrid zones is not the outcome of economic considerations per se. The changing global and regional contexts—particularly the WTO rules on export subsidies and a proliferation of regional trading agreements, which challenged the legitimacy of traditional export-oriented SEZs—have also been instrumental in this shift.

Ownership and Land Acquisition

Unlike SEZs, NIMZs are essentially owned by state governments who enjoy the discretion of deciding the ownership structure of their NIMZs. They may keep the ownership of NIMZs themselves, transfer the ownership to a state government undertaking, may have joint ownership with a private partner, or adopt any other appropriate model. They identify the suitable land and are responsible for land

[17] The SEZ Act was also passed in 2005 with the ambitious goal of attracting a total investment of about INR 1,484.40 crore, including FDI, and creating an additional 1,546,569 jobs by December 2009.

acquisition. This is an important shift from the SEZ regime, which encouraged private ownership of SEZs. This had led to serious concerns over the emergence of 'neo-zamindari' forms of governance and the rise of a 'corporate colonial rule'.

Administration: Public Private Partnership

Developing and managing NMIZ will be through a special purpose vehicle (SPV), a company set up for this specific purpose and having management representation from the government, public sector, and private parties according to financial stakes and at least one director from the Government of India. Public private partnership in zone administration is an important dimension of the new zone policy. The SPV will plan, build, and maintain the internal infrastructure of the zone and allot sites to units. The company will have the right to levy user charges against the services it provides. The functions and responsibilities of the SPV are similar to those assigned to developers in the case of SEZs. It will play the role of a facilitator in getting clearances from the central and state governments. However, it will have no authority to issue these clearances on behalf of the government at any level. This means that dependence on the bureaucratic system outside the zone will continue.

Fiscal Incentives

Another distinctive feature of the policy is that government support and incentives offered are not generic. They are essentially targeting environment and technological development activities. For instance, relief from capital gains tax on the sale of plant and machinery of a unit located in a NIMZ will be granted in case of re-investment of the sale consideration within a period of three years for the purchase of a new plant and machinery in any other unit located in the same NIMZ or in another NIMZ. NIMZs will be assisted in getting long-term soft loans and will be allowed to access external commercial borrowings (ECBs) for infrastructure development. Finally, venture capital funds with a focus on SMEs in the manufacturing sector will be granted a tax pass-through status to facilitate the financing of SMEs. Broadly, the objective is to target market failures directly (Rodrik 2007).

Exit Policy for Companies

An important feature of NIMZ is that it will have an exit policy that will facilitate the expeditious redeployment of assets belonging to non-viable units, while giving full protection to the interests of employees. It provides for workers' insurance, which will create a safety net for workers in the event of job loss. It may be noted here that there has been no exit policy for either SEZ or the domestic mainland companies.

Environment and Labour Laws Relaxation

To relax the regulatory regime, the policy allows the central/state governments to delegate environment related inspection power as allowed by the relevant statutes to an official of the State Pollution Control Board (SPCB) posted in the zone. Similarly, the powers of inspection and enforcement of labour laws will be delegated to the CEO of the SPV who will be a senior government official. While the policy has been notified by the Ministry of Environment, the Ministry of Labour has yet to notify it. The provision of labour inspections by development commissioners (DCs) was a part of the SEZ policy announced in 2000 but could not find favour to be included in the SEZ Act. It is now voluntary for state governments to delegate these powers to the DCs.

Technology Development

Another new feature of the National Manufacturing Policy is its emphasis on skill-building and technology development. India is exposed to the full weight of international competition. Success in manufacturing will rely on a continuing commitment to be at the forefront of future technologies, innovation, and development of the industry. The National Manufacturing Policy proposes to offer several incentives to promote green technologies to ensure clean industrialization. A Technology Acquisition and Development Fund will be established for acquisition of appropriate technologies, including environment friendly technologies; creating a patent pool; and developing the domestic manufacturing of equipment used for controlling pollution and reducing energy consumption. Furthermore, the policy highlights the need for skill-building by encouraging the setting up of institutional infrastructure for vocational training, design, and quality. It also emphasizes on vocational education with 'farm-to-work' and 'school-to-work' programmes. These dimensions are missing in the SEZ policy. The SEZ Act does not have as its objectives the diversification of the productive structure, strengthening value chains, and technology transfers. The emphasis has been only on employment generation. Indeed, several private developers have taken voluntary initiatives to upgrade skill availability (Aggarwal 2012a). But these initiatives are not institutionalized in the act.

Promotion of MSMEs

Unlike its predecessor (the SEZ policy), the NMP offers sops targeting micro and small enterprises in particular, to facilitate financing, technology acquisition, creating patent tools, and developing manufacturing equipment. The objective is to further the capability and competitiveness of MSMEs.

Continuing Practices

Regulatory Framework

The regulatory and policymaking mechanisms of NIMZ are guided by the bureaucratic model of policymaking. The government has established four regulatory bodies. At the apex is the Manufacturing Industry Promotion Board (MIPB) for matters pertaining to the implementation of NMP. The MIPB has been tasked to periodically review the implementation of NMP in general and the development of NIMZs in particular. The MIPB will have the secretaries of various concerned central government departments. The industry secretary will serve as the member secretary, while the commerce and industry minister will serve as the chairman.

A high-level committee (HLC), under the chairmanship of the secretary of industry with secretaries from all the concerned ministries and state governments, has also been notified to resolve coordination issues among central ministries on the one hand and state governments on the other. HLC will monitor the implementation of policy provisions on a regular basis and resolve inter-ministerial issues.

Another key regulatory mechanism is the Board of Approval (BOA) for matters pertaining to NMIZs. It will examine applications for establishing NIMZs and recommend such proposals for consideration to the HLC as are found to be meeting the requirements of the NMP. A Green Manufacturing Committee (GMAC) for matters pertaining to environment related issues and a Technology Acquisition and Development Fund (TADF) under NMP have also been notified with all the bureaucrat members.

It shows that the government does not recognize the role that the private sector can play in effective policymaking. There is a need to recognize mutual interdependence between the government and business sectors, an alliance which can contribute to the development of more effective strategies than if they are addressed by bureaucrats only, particularly in the context of mutual distrust.

Coordination

Coordination within the government and between governments has been a major weakness of the SEZ policy. It continues to be a weak point in the new policy also. This may be seen manifested in the slow progress of the policy's implementation. The proposal of setting up NIMZ was cleared by the union cabinet in October 2011. However, contentious issues on labour are not yet resolved (DIPP 2017). Clearly, one department can hold up the policy, jeopardizing the plans surrounding it. It may also be seen that progress under the policy is extremely tardy. A large number of projects are approved with little progress on the ground. Setting up of an autonomous board could be a way forward.

Diversification and Innovations

A dynamic vision continues to be missing in the NIMZ policy. Market positioning, diversification of the productive structure, strengthening productive chains, export diversification with more value added, and innovations are some of the issues that have remained unaddressed in the context of the new zones. Zones are not merely about creating new infrastructure and attracting investments. The vision of the zone policy is to boost manufacturing activity in the domestic mainland through them. This vision continues to be elusive in this document. This has been the weakness of all other zone policies in India, NIMZs being no exception.

Financing Gaps

There are challenges in financing the zones, which can slow the pace of infrastructure development. NMP is silent on financing zone infrastructure development. Earlier, the RBI policy of not treating SEZs as infrastructure project had badly hit the SEZ development programme due to resource crunch. A lesson learned is that there is a need for clear financing and PPP implementation arrangements for infrastructure investments to enhance the attractiveness of the zones for private investors.

Land Acquisition

The issue of land acquisition also remains a challenge, despite the fact that the Land Acquisition Rehabilitation and Resettlement Act, 2013, (LARR 2013) is in place. The act requires the consent of 80 per cent of the landowners to private projects and that of 70 per cent of landowners to PPP projects; a social impact assessment to identify the affected families and calculate the social impact of land acquisition on them; and return of the land to its original owner if it remains unutilized for five years. In order to give a boost to development projects, the government sought to dilute some of these provisions and introduced a LARR (Amendment) Bill, 2015, in the parliament. However, it could not be passed there to become an act. Subsequently, six states have used constitutional provisions to make their own laws in line with the amendment bill. Some other states have developed rules to dilute the provisions of the LARR 2013 Act. Land acquisition is an important issue, which needs a more innovative approach due to its economic and social implications. It is imperative to make a sincere attempt to review the practices adopted for land acquisition globally and identify the best ones among them. The community land trusts (CLTs), for instance, is an equitable and sustainable model of land acquisition and development that emerged in the late 1960s and has slowly spread throughout United States, Canada, and United Kingdom. Arrangements of equity shares for projects on acquired land are also used successfully and can be institutionalized. The key is to streamline land management strategies. This requires promoting independent land appraisers and assessors, adopting land planning strategies, digitizing land records, and tenancy reforms. The creation of an autonomous National Land Board to monitor and oversee the processes may also go a long way in facilitating them (see Aggarwal 2012a).

Legal Framework

The analysis presented earlier in the chapter shows that the legal apparatus is a necessary prerequisite for the success of a policy which has huge investment implications. The SEZ policy became a rage with investors after the act came into force to support it. Despite that learning, new zones are being promoted without a well-designed legal framework. There is no 'special' legal and regulatory framework to facilitate such large multi-use zones. It is instructive to note that even the SEZ Act passed by the Parliament was not implemented in its entirety and has been subjected to policy reversals. Against that backdrop, once the high-level political backing is withdrawn from NIMZs, the projects may be completely stranded.

Spirit of Experimentation

In a democratic set-up, when the normal social, economic, or political routine is disturbed due to the introduction of a new law, people often react initially with strong, emotion-laden opinions. Given the internal dynamics, multiple interest groups emerge. The emergence of interest groups may act as an element that balances the system. But it may also create chaotic situations in which these groups pull bureaucrats and politicians in different directions. This essentially happens when the policy affects people at the grassroots level. Effective implementation of a policy that aims at giving a shock to the economy therefore requires a broader mobilization of public opinion. This, in turn, requires an experimental policy approach. The SEZ concept sparked-off unprecedented turmoil largely due to clearances given to a large number of projects, disturbing the social and economic systems of rural areas. The idea should have been to start with a handful of SEZs and, if they proved to be a success, to increase them carefully. NIMZs seem to be going the same way. Initially, the proposal was to set up six NIMZs. As per the current status, eight NIMZs along the Delhi Mumbai Industrial Corridor (DMIC) project and three outside the DMIC region have already been approved. In addition, 11 NIMZs (outside the DMIC region) have been given an in-principle approval. It must be recognized that policy solutions are contextual in nature and may not succeed across all states. This calls for an approach that is explicitly experimental. This lesson learnt from the SEZ policy must not be ignored.

* * *

To recapitulate, the SEZs did prove to be a testing laboratory for large-scale industrialization in the country. Some of the weaknesses of the earlier programme have been addressed in the NMP and these advances are encouraging and major. However, one also sees serious limitations, some of which are legacies from the past and will continue to harm the policy. The success of the programme will depend on how these challenges are addressed in the future. What ultimately counts is the continuity of government support over political cycles. Each new minister/top bureaucrat/government negates the policy and programmes of their predecessor and introduces a new program without evaluating what worked and what did not earlier. This is the perfect recipe for the failure of large projects. The secret of a successful zone programme lies in a strategic vision, dynamic learning, innovative approaches, and political will power. Large projects typically tend to have long gestation periods. There is a need for strong commitment to these zone projects from the government and from developers. Both need to be responsive to the challenges faced by the zones. Key implementation challenges need to be addressed through innovative methods to improve outcomes.

References

Aggarwal, A. (2012a). *Social and Economic Impact of SEZs in India*. New Delhi: Oxford University Press.

Aggarwal, A. and A. Kokko (2017). 'Are Indian SEZs No Better Than the Status Quo? Impact Evaluation of SEZs on Poverty in Undivided Andhra Pradesh in India'. Paper presented at the EMSA Conference at Copenhagen Business School, 16 November 2017.

———— (2012b). 'SEZ-led Growth in Taiwan, Korea, and India: Implementing a Successful Strategy'. *Asian Survey* 52(5): 872–99.

———— (2011). 'Promoting Agglomeration Economies and Industrial Clustering through SEZs: Evidence from India'. *Journal of International Commerce, Economics and Policy* 2(2): 201–27.

———— (2006a). 'Special Economic Zones: Revisiting the Policy Debate'. *Economic and Political Weekly* 41(43–4): 4533–6.

———— (2006b). 'Performance of Export Processing Zones: A Comparative Analysis of India, Sri Lanka and Bangladesh'. *Journal of Instaflag Institute* 30(1): 33–122.

Amiti, M. and B.S. Javorcik (2008). 'Trade Costs and Location of Foreign Firms in China'. *Journal of Development Economics* 85(1–2): 129–49.

Balasubramanyam, V.N. (1988). 'Export Processing Zones in Developing Countries: Theory and Empirical Evidence'. In *Economic Development and International Trade*, edited by D. Greenaway, 157–65. London: Macmillan.

Baldwin, R.E. (2011). 'Trade and Industrialization after Globalization's 2nd Unbundling: How Building and Joining a Supply Chain are Different and Why It Matters'. NBER working paper 17716.

Banerjee, A.V., P. Bardhan, K. Basu, et al. (2007). 'Beyond Nandigram: Industrialization in West Bengal'. *Economic and Political Weekly* 42(17) (April 2): 1487–9.

Basile, A. and D. Germidis (1984). 'Investing in Export Processing Zones'. Paris: Organization for Economic Co-operation and Development.

Basu, P.K. (2007). 'Political Economy of Land Grab'. *Economic and Political Weekly* 42(14) (April 7): 1281–7.

Bhaduri, A. (2007). 'Alternatives in Industrialization'. *Economic and Political Weekly* 42(18) (May 5): 1597–601.

Chang, H.J. (2002). *Kicking Away the Ladder: Development Strategy in Historical Perspective*. London and New York: Anthem Press.

Coxhead, I. and S. Jayasuriya (2010). 'China, India and the Commodity Boon: Economic and Environmental Implications for Low Income Countries'. *The World Economy* 33(4): 525–51.

Debaere, P., Lee J. Lee, and M. Paik (2010). 'Agglomeration, Backward and Forward Linkages: Evidence from South Korean Investment in China'. *Canadian Journal of Economics* 43(2): 520–46.

Devereux, J. and L.L. Chen (1995). 'Export Zones and Welfare: Another Look'. *Oxford Economic Papers* 47(4): 704–13.

Farole, T. (2011). *Special Economic Zones in Africa: Comparing Performance and Learning from Global Experience*. Washington DC: The World Bank.

Feenstra, R.C., G.H. Hanson, and S. Lin (2002). 'The Value of Information in International Trade: Gains to Outsourcing through Hong Kong'. Working Paper No. 932, National Bureau of Economic Research (NBER), Massachusetts.

Frank, A.G. (1967). *Capitalism and Underdevelopment in Latin America*. New York: Monthly Review Press.

Fröbel, F., J. Heinrichs, and O. Kreye (1978). *The New International Division of Labour*. Cambridge, UK: Cambridge University Press.

Fujita M., P. Krugman, and A. Venables (1999). *The Spatial Economy: Cities, Regions, and International Trade*. Massachusetts: MIT Press.

Hamada, K. (1974). 'An Economic Analysis of the Duty Free Zone'. *Journal of International Economics* 4(3): 225–41.

Hamilton, C. and L.E.O. Svensson (1982). 'On the Welfare Effects of a Duty-Free Zone'. *Journal of International Economics* 13(1): 45–64.

Heeks, R. (1996). *India's Software Industry: State Policy, Liberalization, and Industrial Development*. New Delhi: Sage Publications.

International Labour Organization (ILO) (2007). *Export Processing Zones Statistics*. Geneva: International Labour Organization. Available at http://www.ilo.org./public/english/dialogue/sector/themes/epz/stats.htm. Last accessed on 10 August 2009.

Johansson, H. and L. Nilsson (1997). 'Export Processing Zones as Catalysts', *World Development* 25(12): 2115–28.

Kaldor, N. (1966). *Causes of the Slow Rate of Growth of the United Kingdom*. Cambridge: Cambridge University Press.

Krugman, P.R. (1991). 'Increasing Returns and Economic Geography'. *Journal of Political Economy* 99(3): 483–99.

Kumar, R. (1989). *Indian Export Processing Zones: An Evaluation*. New Delhi: Oxford University Press.

Kundra, A. (2000). *The Performance of India's Export Zones: A Comparison with the Chinese Approach*. New Delhi: Sage Publication.

Kuznets, S. (1955). 'Economic Growth and Income Inequality'. *The American Economic Review* 45(1): 1–28.

Lacharrière, L. de (1969). *La nouvelle division internationale du travail*. Geneva: Droz.

Levien, M. (2011). 'Rationalising Dispossession: The Land Acquisition and Resettlement Bills'. *Economic and Political Weekly* 46(11) (March 12): 66–71.

Lewis, W.A. (1954). 'Economic Development with Unlimited Supplies of Labour'. *Manchester School of Economic and Social Studies* 22(2): 139–91.

Lin, J.Y. (2010). *New Structural Economics: A Framework for rethinking development and policy*. Washington DC: The World Bank.

Lin, J.Y. and H.J. Chang (2009). 'Should Industrial Policy in Developing Countries Conform to Comparative Advantage or Defy It?'. DPR Debate between Justin Lin and Ha-Joon Chang. *Development Policy Review* 27(5) (September): 483–502.

Madani, D. (1999). 'A Review of the Role and Impact of Export Processing Zones'. Policy Research Paper No. 2238. Washington DC: The World Bank.

Marshall, A. (1890). *Principles of Economics*. London: Macmillan.

Moran, M.T.H. (2002). *Strategy and Tactics for the Doha Round: Capturing the Benefits of Foreign Direct Investment*. Manila: Asian Development Bank.

Myrdal, G. (1957). *Economic Theory and Underdeveloped Regions*. London: Duckworth Press.

Nachum, L. and D. Keeble (2000). 'Localized Clusters and the Eclectic and David Keeble Paradigm of FDI: Film TNCs in Central London'. *Transnational Corporations* 9(1): 1–38.

Ng, C. and L.F.Y. Tuan (2006). 'The Place of FDI in China's Regional Economic Development: Emergence of the Globalized Delta Economies'. *Journal of Asian Economics* 18(2): 348–64.

Palit, A. and S. Bhattacharjee (2007). *Special Economic Zones in India—Myths and Realities*. India: Anthem Press.

Porter, M.E. (1990). *The Competitive Advantage of Nations*. New York: The Free Press.

Rodriguez, C.A. (1976). 'A Note on the Economics of the Duty-Free Zone'. *Journal of International Economics* 6(4): 385–8.

Rodrik, D. (2005). 'Growth Strategies'. In *Handbook of Economic Growth* Vol. 1, edited by A. Philippe and S. Durlauf, Chapter 14, 967–1014. Amsterdam: Elsevier.

—————— (2007). 'Industrial Development: Stylized Facts and Policies'. *Industrial Development for the 21st Century*. New York: United Nations.

—————— (2012). 'No More Growth Miracles'. Available at: http://www.project-syndicate.org/commentary/no-more-growth-miracles-by-dani-rodrik. Last accessed on 11 June 2019.

Sen, S. and B. Dasgupta (2009). *Unfreedom and Waged Work: Labour in India's Manufacturing Industry*. New Delhi, India: Sage Publications.

Shapiro, H. (2005). 'Industrial Policy and Growth'. Background Paper in World Economic and Social Survey, 2006.

Stiglitz, J. (1998). 'More Instruments and Broader Goals: Moving Towards the Post-Washington Consensus'. Address to the WIDER Annual Lecture, Helsinki on 7 January 1998.

Szirmai, A. (2011). 'Industrialization as an Engine of Growth in Developing Countries, 1950–2005'. *Structural Change and Economic Dynamics* 23(4): 406–20.

United Nations Conference on Trade and Development (UNCTAD) (1998). 'World Investment Report 1998: Trends and Determinants'. Geneva: UNCTAD.

CHAPTER 11

....

AGRICULTURE
IN INDIA

performance, challenges, and opportunities

....

S. MAHENDRA DEV, SRIJIT MISHRA,

AND VIJAY LAXMI PANDEY

Two consecutive droughts in 2014 and 2015 have re-emphasized the risks of monsoon-dependent agriculture in India, bringing into focus the discourse on the crisis in Indian agriculture, observed since the early 1990s. Two symptoms of this crisis are non-serviceable debt and increasing incidence of farmers' suicides. These symptoms point out the adverse implications on the livelihood of people dependent on agriculture—the agrarian crisis. The crisis is also associated with stagnation in the growth of production and productivity—the agricultural crisis. The latter is intertwined with the former. There seems to have been some revival in agricultural growth in the recent past, which we elaborate on in the next section in our analysis of Indian agriculture's performance. While appreciating this turnaround and hoping that it should continue, one does agree that it faces important policy challenges. What is more, despite these improvements, the incidences of farmers' suicides continue to remain a matter of concern and it is premature to visualize a positive outcome in the livelihood of those dependent on agriculture. A true measure of success should be the implications on smallholders who constitute more than four-fifths of the cultivating households. To address these, as the last section of the chapter suggests, it is particularly important to leverage new technologies, build institutions, and emphasize on low external input sustainable agriculture (LEISA) so as to help improve incomes and reduce risks without compromising on yield.

PERFORMANCE OF INDIAN AGRICULTURE

Recent discourses have pointed out relatively lower growth in agriculture post the 1990s than prior to that (Desai et al. 2011; Dev and Pandey 2012; Mishra 2012; and Mishra and Reddy 2011, among others). Some of them do point to a reversal after 2004/5. Keeping this is mind, this chapter proposes to calculate growth rates by using triennium ending (TE) time series data, a standard practice to smoothen out fluctuations in agricultural production, to separate the experiences of the recent years (TE 2004/5 to TE 2010/11) with that of the immediate post-reforms period (TE 1993/4 to TE 2004/5) while contrasting the experience of the latter with the pre-reforms period (TE 1981/2 to TE 1993/4). The choice of TE 1981/2 as a start year is a standard practice in the analysis of Indian agriculture; the years TE 1993/4 and TE 2004/5 have been chosen as one observed some changes in broad trends around these years. Our calculations are based on a double-kinked exponential curve following Boyce (1986).[1]

---

[1] Growth rates have been computed using the double-kinked exponential curve, $Ln(Y_t)=a+b_1D_1+b_2D_2+b_3D_3+u_t$; Y_t refers to TE average data, t begins with o for TE 1981/2 and increases by one unit for every year such that it is 29 for TE 2010/11. D_1 begins with o and increases by one unit for every year till TE 1993/4 and for this, as also all subsequent years, it is 12. D_2=o from TE 1981/2 till TE 1993/4, then increases by one unit for every year till TE 2004/5, and for this, as also all subsequent years, it is 11. D_3=o from TE 1981/2 till TE 2004/5 and then increases by one unit for every year till TE 2010/11. Growth rates of the three sub-periods are b_1, b_2, and b_3 respectively.

Growth in Agricultural Gross Domestic Product

An analysis of agricultural gross domestic product (GDP) shows a signifi-cant decline in the growth rate of agriculture and allied sector GDP from 3.29 per cent in the pre-reforms period to 2.72 per cent in the immediate post-reforms period—a matter of concern because the overall economy was going very strong during this period. Thus, the measures taken under the rubric of economic reforms during 1991/2 were not of much help to agriculture (Bhalla 2002; Kumar 2002; Chand 2004). However, the agriculture sector, specifically the crop and livestock sub-sector, showed some signs of revival during 2004/5 to 2010/11 (Table 11.1A). Agricultural GDP from crop and livestock improved to 3.08 per cent in TE 2004/5–2010/11 from 2.68 per cent during TE 1993/4–2004/5, but the improvement in growth rate was not statistically significant.

This growth could be attributed to different initiatives taken by the government since late 2005, due to which the ratio of gross fixed capi-tal formation in agriculture to agricultural GDP improved from 13 per cent in 2004/5 to 20 per cent in 2010/11 (Ministry of Agriculture [hereafter MoA] 2012). Total investments, especially public investments, firmed up (Table 11.2) and public expenditure in agricultural research and extension was boosted (Table 11.3). However, it may be noted that public investment in agriculture mostly relates to medium and major irrigation projects where substantial resources are put without much critical scrutiny (Government of India 2011; Vaidyanathan 2010). There is also a lag effect of public investments in agriculture growth. Therefore, impacts from these will be felt more in the long run and will depend on the nature and composition of the investment. Besides, since the mid-2000s, private investments by individual farmers as well as by other entities that develop infrastruc-ture from an agri-business perspective have increased significantly, which can also have positive implications.[2] It may also be noted that the private sector's share in the total agricultural investment is 70 to

---

[2] Note that the appropriate kind of public investment will bring about private investments that supplement them and have multiplier effects, whereas inappropriate ones could make private investments substitute the void that can sometimes have disastrous consequences. For instance, a decline in public

Table 11.1A Growth rate of agricultural gross domestic product

Items	TE 1981/2–1993/4	TE 1993/4–2004/5	TE 2004/5–2010/11
Agriculture and allied sectors	3.29**	2.72**†	2.95**
Agriculture (crop and livestock)	3.36**	2.68**†	3.08**
Forestry sector	0.06**	1.72**†	1.93**†
Fishing and aquaculture	6.29**	4.27**†	3.54**†

Source: CSO (2012a & b).

Notes: **indicates significant at 1 per cent level (or 99 per cent confidence interval), † indicates significantly different from the first period at 95 per cent confidence interval. TE is triennium ending. Growth rates have been computed using double-kinked exponential curve. All data are at 2004/5 prices.

75 per cent (MoA 2012). There is a complementarity between public and private investments. The terms of trade for agriculture, based on GDP-implicit price deflators, seem to have improved considerably during the recent period; they increased from 100 in 2004/5 to 126 in 2009/10 (Dev and Pandey 2012).

A closer look at the annual growth rates from 2011/12 to 2017/18 demonstrates much volatility in agriculture and allied sectors, mostly owing to the crop sub-sector. In 2012/13, agriculture and allied sectors had a year-over-year growth rate of 1.5 per cent that jumped to 5.6 per cent in 2013/14. But over the two subsequent years, growth rates were quite disappointing (–0.2 per cent and 0.7 per cent in 2014/15 and 2015/16 respectively). The annual growth of agriculture and allied sectors picked up in the year 2016–17 with a 4.9 per cent growth rate. The annual growth rate of the crop sub-sector was 5.4 per cent in 2013/14 but dipped to –3.8 per cent in 2014/15 and to –2.2 per cent in 2015/16, perhaps due to the drought in the year 2014 and 2015 (Table 11.1B).

---

investments on irrigation led to an increase in private investments on bore-wells that not only had an adverse debt and cost implication on the farmer, but also led to a depletion of ground water in many areas—a tragedy of the commons.

Table 11.1B Year over year growth rates of gross value added by agriculture at constant 2011/12 prices

Items	2012/13	2013/14	2014/15	2015/16	2016/17[#]	2017/18[*]
Agriculture and allied sectors	1.5	5.6	−0.2	0.7	4.9	2.1
Crop	0.2	5.4	−3.8	−2.2	−	−
Livestock	5.2	5.6	7.4	6.5	−	−
Forestry and logging	0.2	5.9	2.6	1.7	−	−
Fishing and aquaculture	4.9	7.2	7.5	6.7	−	−

Source: CSO (2017) and CSO press note on First Advance Estimates of National Income 2017–18. Available at: http://www.mospi.gov.in/sites/default/files/press_release/PRESS_NOTE-Q3_2017-18.pdf. Last accessed on 11 June 2019.
Notes: # Provisional estimates; * First advance estimate.

Table 11.2 Investment in agriculture

Items	TE 1981/2–1993/4	TE 1993/4–2004/5	TE 2004/5–2010/11
Investment, agriculture	2.23[**]	6.43[**†]	8.52[**†]
Public investment, agriculture	−4.46[**]	2.25[**†]	12.50[**†‡]

Source: CSO (2012a & b).
Notes: **indicates significant at 1 per cent level (or 99 per cent confidence interval), † indicates significantly different from the first period at 95 per cent confidence interval, ‡ indicates significantly different from the second period at 95 per cent confidence interval. TE is triennium ending. Growth rates have been computed using double-kinked exponential curve. All data are at 2004/5 prices.

The forestry sector has shown a gradual improvement in the growth rate, whereas the fishing and aquaculture sector has registered a gradual decline over the three periods (Table 11.1A). However, in the recent years, year-over-year growth rates have shown noteworthy improvement in the fishing and aquaculture sector (Table 11.1B). Now, we take up a crop-wise analysis of growth in value of output and also in area, production, and yield.

Table 11.3 Growth of real government expenditure on agricultural research, education, and extension in India (2004/5 prices)

Items	TE 1981/2–1992/3	TE 1993/4–2004/5	TE 2005/6–2009/10
Research and education	4.25	6.28	9.00
Extension	6.15	0.93	5.14
Total	4.68	5.14	9.75

Source: CSO (2012a & b).

Note: The estimates for this have been provided by Suresh Pal and Alka Singh from the Indian Agricultural Research Institute, New Delhi, through a personal communication.

Crop-wise Analysis

The performance of different segments of agriculture show that growth rates in the value of output of crops and livestock declined in the immediate post-reforms period (Table 11.4). But the growth rates were relatively higher in more recent years. Growth rates for most of the individual crops except for fruits and vegetables are similar. They declined in the immediate post-reforms period as compared to the pre-reforms period and are showing improvements in the recent years. During the recent period of TE 2004/5 to 2010/11, a significantly higher growth was observed for cotton, maize, pulses, and oilseeds. Cereals also registered some improvement over the post-reforms period growth rates.[3] The significantly higher growth of cotton coincides with the introduction of *Bacillus thuringiensis* (Bt) cotton towards the end of our second period and its spread in usage during the same period is worth noticing. However, one should be cautious in attributing reasons for this entirely to the introduction of this genetic modification because of the absence of appropriate counterfactuals that separate out the impacts on account of new hybrid varieties and the lower incidence of specific pest attacks (see Gaurav and Mishra 2015a).

[3] An interesting initiative with regard to rice cultivation is the spread of an alternative cultivation practice called the system of rice intensification (SRI), which involves civil society as also some public policy initiatives (Thiyagarajan and Gujja 2012).

Indian agriculture has been witnessing diversification over time. Though the growth rate for value of output from fruits and vegetables has declined in the recent years (Table 11.4), its share in total value of output has increased from 19 per cent in 1981/2 to 27 per cent in 2010/11, whereas the share of cereals has declined from 34 per cent to 29 per cent in the same period (Central Statistical Organisation [hereafter CSO] 2012). Change in cropping pattern is also evident. There has been a decline in the area under other cereals and a decline in the growth rate of areas for rice and sugarcane. However, the area under pulses and oilseeds that had declined in the post-reforms period has revived in the recent years and there has been significant improvement in its growth rate too (Table 11.5).

Table 11.4 Value of output from different crops and livestock

Items	TE 1981/2–1993/4	TE 1993/4–2004/5	TE 2004/5–2010/11
Crops	2.74*	2.32*	2.68*
Cereals	3.28*	0.98*†	1.90*†
Paddy	3.77*	0.80*†	1.71*†
Wheat	4.02*	1.67*†	1.75*†
Maize	2.49*	3.31*	5.98*†‡
Pulses	1.53*	–0.03†	2.48*†‡
Oilseeds	6.07*	0.46†	4.79*†
Sugarcane	3.52*	1.70*	1.83§
Cotton	4.08*	1.02†	13.69*†‡
Fruits and vegetables	2.84*	4.79*†	2.88*†
Livestock	4.42*	3.39*	4.11*
Milk group	4.96*	3.73*†	3.45*†
Meat group	5.15*	2.92*†	5.50*†
Eggs	6.25*	3.61*†	6.48*†

Source: CSO (2012a & b).

Notes: **indicates significant at 1 per cent level (or 99 per cent confidence interval), * indicates significant at 5 per cent, § indicates significant at 15 per cent, † indicates significantly different from the first period at 95 per cent confidence interval, ‡ indicates significantly different from the second period at 95 per cent confidence interval. TE is triennium ending. Growth rates have been computed using double-kinked exponential curve. All data are at 2004/5 prices.

Table 11.5 Growth in area, production, and yield

Items	Area			Production			Yield		
	TE 1981/2–1993/4	TE 1993/4–2004/5	TE 2004/5–2010/11	TE 1981/2–1993/4	TE 1993/4–2004/5	TE 2004/5–2010/11	TE 1981/2–1993/4	TE 1993/4–2004/5	TE 2004/5–2010/11
Food Grains	−0.27*	−0.27*†	0.46*†‡	3.05*	1.00*	2.18*	3.31*	1.27*	1.72*
Rice	0.65*	0.18§†	0.02	3.79*	0.92*†	1.87*†	3.15*	0.73*†	1.88*†‡
Wheat	0.76*	0.72*†	0.95*	4.04*	1.67*†	1.75*†	3.28*	0.95*†	0.80*†
Other Cereals	−2.05*	−1.55*	−0.28†‡	0.52*	0.31	3.60*†‡	2.57*	1.84*	3.93*†
Total Pulses	−0.13	−0.45*	1.50*†‡	1.51*	−0.40§†	3.04*†	1.64*	0.03†	1.58*†
Oilseeds	3.16*	−0.46†	1.72*†	5.83*	0.57†	4.93*†	2.69*	1.01†	3.25*†
Cotton	1.09*	0.61*	3.98*†‡	3.67*	2.84*	14.27*†‡	2.59*	2.22*	10.24*†‡
Sugarcane	2.17*	1.39*	1.31*	4.01*	1.15*†	1.79*	1.84*	−0.26†	0.48*†

Source: Ministry of Agriculture (2012).

Notes: ** indicates significant at 1 per cent level (or 99 per cent confidence interval), * indicates significant at 5 per cent level, § indicates significant at 15 per cent, † indicates significantly different from the first period at 95 per cent confidence interval, ‡ indicates significantly different from the second period at 95 per cent confidence interval. TE is triennium ending. Growth rates have been computed using double-kinked exponential curve.

The increase in the production of other cereals is attributable to yield growth only. In case of pulses, oilseeds, and cotton, both area and yield growth are responsible for increase in the growth rate of production in recent years. These improvements can be attributed to various initiatives including the National Food Security Mission (NFSM) launched in the year 2007/8, a favourable monsoon in almost all the years except for 2009/10, and a price or terms of trade that favoured agriculture. It would be worthwhile to take up an analysis across states.

Analysis Across States

An analysis of the agricultural gross state domestic product (GSDP) shows that it increased in 11 of the 15 major states during the TE 2004/5 to 2010/11, as against the post-reforms period of TE 1993/4 to 2004/5; the increase was significant in seven of these states (Table 11.6). States such as Kerala, Uttar Pradesh, and West Bengal recorded a decline in the agricultural GSDP, but the decline was significant in Kerala alone. Some states recorded a gradual improvement in the agricultural GSDP over the three periods; the improvements were significant in Andhra Pradesh and Odisha. In recent years, the highest growth rate for agricultural GSDP was recorded by Andhra Pradesh, followed by that in Maharashtra and then Madhya Pradesh.

These growth rates suggest an overall improvement in agricultural performance with respect to agricultural GSDP during recent years (TE 2004/5 to 2010/11) when compared with the post-reforms period (TE 1993/4 to 2004/5). It is therefore important to understand from an equity point of view whether instability in agricultural has increased or decreased and if the states are converging towards the national average or diverging from it. Table 11.7 shows that volatility has reduced from 6.28 per cent during the post-reforms period to 3.03 per cent in recent years at the all-India level for net domestic produce from agriculture. Even in the case of states, it was observed that for almost all the states fluctuations in the net state domestic produce had reduced in recent years, as against the post-reforms period, except for Himachal

Table 11.6 Growth of agricultural gross state domestic product

States	TE 1981/2–1993/4	TE 1993/4–2004/5	TE 2004/5–2010/11
Andhra Pradesh	2.44*	3.34*	6.22*†‡
Bihar	1.69*	3.60*†	3.85*
Gujarat	1.85*	3.80*	4.57
Haryana	4.25*	1.83*†	3.84*†
Himachal Pradesh	0.12*	0.10*	0.06
Karnataka	3.99*	0.55†	4.71*†
Kerala	4.40*	1.36*†	−0.42†‡
Madhya Pradesh	3.78*	1.40*†	5.34*†
Maharashtra	5.12*	3.48*†	5.91*†
Odisha	−0.26	0.63	4.99*†‡
Punjab	4.15*	1.84*†	2.20*†
Rajasthan	4.12*	2.57*	3.77*
Tamil Nadu	4.53*	0.58*†	4.13*†
Uttar Pradesh	3.35*	2.11*†	2.01*†
West Bengal	5.44*	2.71*†	1.36*†

Source: CSO (1999, 2007, 2010, 2012c).

Notes: * indicates significant at 5 per cent, † indicates significantly different from the first period at 95 per cent confidence interval, ‡ indicates significantly different from the second period at 95 per cent confidence interval. TE is triennium ending. Growth rates have been computed using double-kinked exponential curve.

Pradesh and Maharashtra. An analysis of β-convergence, based on the linear regression of growth rates for net state domestic produce from agriculture (NSDPA) per hectare on their respective initial NSDPA per hectare, shows an overall convergence during 1980/1 to 2009/10. Despite this positive note on reductions in volatility and an increase in convergence across states, it should be borne in mind that more than half the workforce and their dependents still rely on agriculture for their livelihood and a large majority of them are small and marginal farmers. It is therefore imperative that we take up a discussion from their perspective.

Table 11.7 Instability in net domestic produce and net state domestic produce from agriculture using Ray's instability index

States	TE 1981/2–1992/3	TE 1993/4–2004/5	TE 2005/6–2009/10
All India	6.39	6.28	3.03
Andhra Pradesh	8.93	13.19	6.03
Bihar	14.51	14.10	12.13
Gujarat	45.38	26.69	13.75
Haryana	13.09	6.03	5.76
Himachal Pradesh	13.11	9.13	14.22
Karnataka	9.36	12.58	7.84
Kerala	7.19	9.31	7.60
Madhya Pradesh	11.16	20.44	6.58
Maharashtra	18.62	9.75	14.47
Odisha	20.51	15.69	4.40
Punjab	4.61	3.97	1.16
Rajasthan	25.02	29.68	14.96
Tamil Nadu	13.21	13.46	9.34
Uttar Pradesh	3.70	4.22	1.65
West Bengal	7.43	5.06	3.98

Source: CSO (1999, 2007, 2010, 2012a, b & c).
Note: Ray instability index: Standard Deviation of Ln $\{(Y_{t+1})/(Y_t)\}$, where Y_t is net domestic produce or net state domestic produce from agriculture.

SMALL AND MARGINAL FARMERS: ROLES, CHALLENGES, AND OPPORTUNITIES

The objective of this section is to examine the role and challenges of agricultural smallholdings in achieving agricultural growth, food security, and livelihoods in India. It may be noted that Indian agriculture is the home of small and marginal farmers. Therefore, the future of sustainable agriculture growth and food security in India depends on the performance of these farmers. Agricultural census data shows that there were about 138 million agricultural holdings in India in 2010/11. There were around 117 million small and marginal farmers. The average size of farm holdings has declined from 2.3 hectares (ha) in 1970/1 to 1.15 ha in 2010/11. Small and marginal farmers account for more than 85 per cent of the total farm households, but their share in the operated area is around 45 per cent (MoA 2017). Thus, there are significant land inequalities in India.

The role of small farms in development and poverty reduction is well recognized (Lipton 2006). The global experience of growth and poverty reduction shows that GDP growth originating in agriculture is at least twice as effective in reducing poverty as GDP growth originating outside agriculture (The World Bank 2008). Small holdings play an important role in agricultural development and poverty reduction.

Farm Size, Output, and Productivity

There has been debate in India on the relationship between farm size and productivity. The results of the situation assessment survey (SAS) of farmers, of the 59th National Sample Survey (2003), empirically established that for the agricultural year 2002/3, small farms continued to produce more in value terms per hectare than medium and large farms. The value of output per hectare was INR 14,754 for marginal farmers, INR 13,001 for small farmers, INR 10,655 for medium farmers, and INR 8,783 for large farmers. It shows that from the efficiency point of view, small holdings are equal to or better than large holdings.

It has been observed statistically that small holdings have higher productivity than medium and large farms. But it is not enough to compensate for the disadvantage of the small area of holdings. The cost of cultivation per hectare is also high on small and marginal farms as compared to medium and large farms.[4] At the all-India level, net farm income per hectare for small holdings was higher than large holdings. Across 20 major states, the results were similar to the

---

[4] On returns to farming, particularly on the efficiency of the smallholders, see Gaurav and Mishra (2015b).

all-India pattern in 11 of these states. But in the remaining nine, the reverse was true—net farm income per hectare was high in large holdings than in small holdings.

The monthly income and consumption figures across different size-class of landholdings show that marginal and small farmers had dis-savings (expenditure higher than income) compared to medium and large farmers. According to SAS (2003), the monthly consumption of marginal farmers was INR 2,482 and the monthly income was INR 1,659 (Figure 11.1). It shows that they have dis-savings of INR 823. The dis-savings for small farmers were INR 655. For large farmers, the monthly income and consumption were INR 9,667 and INR 6,418 respectively with a saving of INR 3,249. However, as per the NSSO survey of the situation of agricultural households (SAH) (2013), some improvement has been reported for small farmers, as their monthly income exceeds their monthly consumption (Figure 11.2) with a saving of INR 891 per month. However, this saving is very meagre in comparison to that of the medium and large farmers (INR 9,533 and INR 26,941 respectively). Thus, the farmers with small landholdings generally have to borrow to meet their demand. National Commission for Enterprises in the Unorganized Sector (NCEUS) (2008) has indicated that the poverty for smallholding farmers is much higher than other farmers. The need for increase

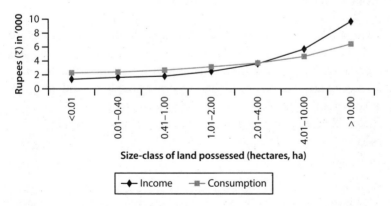

FIGURE 11.1A Income and consumption by size-class, India (2002–3)

Source: National Sample Survey Organisation (NSSO 2005: 21–2).

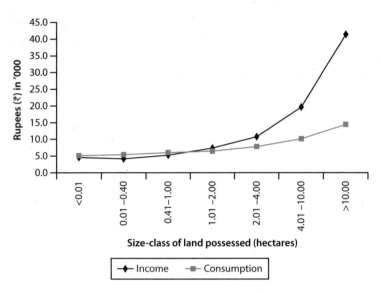

FIGURE 11.1B   Income and consumption by size-class, India (2012–13)

Source: National Sample Survey Organisation (NSSO 2013: 21–2).

in the productivity and incomes of smallholdings and the promotion of non-farm activities for these farmers is obvious.[5]

Access to Inputs and Markets

There are many issues and challenges for smallholding agriculture in India. They face several challenges in their access to inputs and marketing. They need a level playing field with large farms in terms of accessing land, water, inputs, credit, technology, and markets. Smallholdings also face new challenges on integration with value chains, liberalization and globalization effects, market volatility, other risks and vulnerabilities, and adaptation of climate change (Thapa and Gaiha 2011).

[5] The concerns are echoed in the call for doubling of farmers' incomes (http://www.agricoop.nic.in/doubling-farmers-income) by the Government of India. Also see Chandrasekhar and Mehrotra (2016).

The SAS (2003) brought out many issues relating to small and marginal farmers. Based on this survey, NCEUS (2008: 7) mentions:

> Some of the general issues that confront marginal-small farmers as agriculturalists are: imperfect markets for inputs/product leading to smaller value realizations; absence of access to credit markets or imperfect credit markets leading to sub-optimal investment decisions or input applications; poor human resource base; smaller access to suitable extension services restricting suitable decisions regarding cultivation practices and technological know-how; poorer access to 'public goods' such as public irrigation, command area development, electricity grids; greater negative externalities from poor quality land and water management, etc.

Increasing globalization has added to the problems faced by the smallholding agriculture. The policies of huge subsidies and protection by developed countries have negative effects on small holding farmers in developing countries. If support is not given to small farms, globalization may become advantageous solely for large farms.

Credit and Indebtedness

Smallholdings need credit for both consumption and investment purposes. As discussed in Mishra (2012), we reiterate some of the recent policy discourses. A report by a working group, Reserve Bank of India (RBI) (2006), pointed out the relevance of both credit and non-credit factors. But some important observations are that agriculturists continue to be bothered with inadequate amount, untimely loan and other hassles while borrowing credit from formal sources; failure of the system to differentiate between wilful and non-wilful defaulters; and the absence of any credit guarantees to facilitate the non-wilful defaulter.

The report of the expert group on agricultural indebtedness indicates that farmers are increasingly depending on informal sources of credit; share of debt of farmer households from formal sources shows a secular increase from 7.3 per cent in 1951 to 66.3 per cent in 1991, but then it declined to 61.1 per cent in 2002 (Government of India 2007). Dependence on informal sources is higher for marginal and small farmers (Figure 11.2), that too at a higher interest burden

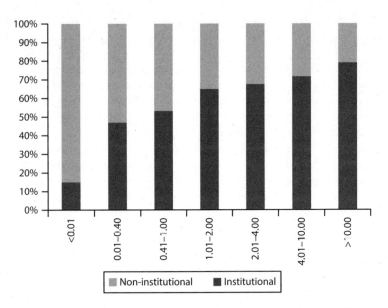

FIGURE 11.2   Share of loan amount from institutional and non-institutional sources of credit by size-class of land possessed (2012–13)

Source: National Sample Survey Organisation (NSSO 2013: 24–5).

because 73 per cent of the debt borne by farmer households from non-institutional sources has an interest rate of more than 20 per cent, of which more than half (overall 38 per cent) have an interest rate of more than 30 per cent per annum.

Shetty (2009) further observes that (*a*) there has been a decline in the number of rural bank branches from 32,981 in 1996 to 31,967 in 2005, (*b*) there has been a decline in the number of agricultural borrowal accounts from 277 lakh in March 1992 to 198 lakh in March 2001, and (*c*) there has been a decline in agricultural credit as per cent of net bank credit from 18 per cent in the 1980s, which is the statutory requirement, to 11 per cent in 2004.[6]

[6] From April 2007, the statutory requirement of priority sector lending is calculated from adjusted net bank credit (ANBC), and the agricultural credit as per cent of ANBC in March 2004 was around 15 per cent (RBI 2012a, Chart 1). Using basic statistical returns, Chakrabarty (2012) points out that the outstanding credit from scheduled commercial banks to agricultural occupation was as follows: 16.7 per cent in 1981, 15 per cent in 1991, 9.6 per cent in 2001, and 11.3 per cent in 2011.

The ratio of the share of credit disbursed to the share of area operated and the ratio of the share of the number of borrowal accounts to the share of the number of operational holdings indicate that both had been declining for marginal holdings (those with less than one hectare) till 2002/3 (Table 11.8). For smallholdings, both the ratios increased in the 1980s but in the 1990s, it is only the ratio of borrowal accounts to operational holdings that increased, whereas the ratio of credit disbursed to area operated decreased. For other categories of holdings, the ratio of credit disbursed to area operated showed a slight decline in the 1980s, but both the ratios increased in the 1990s. In other words, there was a shift in favour of smallholders in the 1980s, which seems to have reversed in favour of the other (medium and large) holdings in the 1990s.

There have been some policy initiatives that followed this, such as the doubling of agricultural credit in the three years starting from 2004/5 to 2006/7, which was achieved but this did not increase the proportion of agricultural credit as a per cent of adjusted net bank credit (ANBC) that stood at 16.1 per cent in March 2011.[7] An Agricultural Debt Waiver and Debt Relief Scheme (ADWDRS) was proposed in 2008, which helped the banks' books by reducing their non-performing assets. However, as a study by the National Bank for Agriculture and Rural Development (NABARD) indicates, this did not automatically improve the access to credit for all farmers because 50 per cent of active farmers were not likely to have a kissan credit card (Samantara 2010). Some other initiatives involved the introduction of no-frills accounts and the use of business correspondents to improve access to banking services. Some of these initiatives might have led to an increase in the ratio of the share of credit disbursed to the share of area operated for marginal landholders in 2010/11 and an increase in both the ratios for smallholders in 2010/11. Both these ratios declined for other categories of landholders in the year 2010/11 (Table 11.8).

A recent report on credit-related issues of farmers (Government of India 2009; also see Mehrotra 2011) refers to regional inequalities—the eastern region's share in credit disbursed was much lower

---

[7] RBI (2012b) indicates that the credit disbursed for agriculture and allied activities as per cent of gross bank credit has declined from 13.5 per cent in March 2010 to 12.3 per cent in March 2011 to 12.0 per cent in March 2012.

Table 11.8 Ratio of the share of credit disbursed to the share
of area operated and the ratio of the share of
the number of borrowal accounts to the share of
the number of operational holdings

Year	Ratio of the share of credit disbursed to the share of area operated			Ratio of the share of the number of borrowal accounts to the share of the number of operational holdings		
	Marginal	Small	Others	Marginal	Small	Others
1981–2	2.41	1.24	0.72	0.90	1.28	1.00
1991–2	1.85	1.33	0.71	0.72	1.77	1.19
2002–3	0.98	1.22	0.93	0.56	1.85	2.21
2010–11	1.08	1.38	0.82	0.55	2.17	1.61

Source: Mishra (2012), based on Government of India (2007).

Notes: Marginal, small, and others+ refer to <1 hectare, 1–2 hectares, and >2 hectares for area operated and operational holdings and are superimposed on <2.5 acres, 2.5–5.0 acres, and >5 acres for credit and borrowal accounts. The land-based information is based on the National Sample Survey rounds (1981–2, 1991–2, and 2003) and the Agriculture Census (2010–11) from MoA is used for the 2010–11 data. The credit information is based on the *Handbook of Statistics on the Indian Economy* published by the Reserve Bank of India.

than its share in the gross cropped area, the southern region with a history of good branch banking had a higher share of credit and the amount was spread across a large number of borrowal accounts with the average amount disbursed per borrowal account at INR 41,331 in June 2008 being lower than the eastern region (INR 66,812), the western region (INR 113,387), and the northern region (INR 176,179). This raises issues of inclusion or rather exclusion in the latter areas. The report also points to a seasonal anomaly with nearly one-fourth of the credit being disbursed during March and another 10–20 per cent being disbursed during January and February, when even rabi activities are by and large over, raising questions on the timeliness and the 'purpose' behind these disbursals. All these do raise concerns on the livelihoods and opportunities for agriculture in general and that of the small and marginal farmers in particular.

We now take up some further discussion on technological and institutional innovations for agriculture.

Opportunities: Technological and Institutional Innovations

There are many opportunities in the form of technological and institutional innovations that can enable marginal and small farmers to raise agricultural productivity and increase incomes through diversification and high value agriculture. Research and extension should give importance to cost reduction without reducing yields. Therefore, new technological innovations with approaches focusing on LEISA that do not use chemical fertilizers, pesticides or genetically modified organisms. It counters the argument of 'there is no alternative' (TINA) by affirming that there are multiple alternatives that are situation specific, but they are not mainstream practices because to promulgate them one needs the support of appropriate knowledge, resources, and also appropriate leveraging with new advances in marketing opportunities and information technology.

Information Technology

Changes in information technology will help in a big way to improve agri-business and incomes of small farmers. Indian private companies and non-governmental organizations (NGOs) are global leaders in providing information to farmers, as a spin-off from India's meteoric rise as a world leader in information and communications technology (ICT). E-choupals have expanded access to internet in rural areas. Up to 6,400 internet kiosks were set up between 2000 and 2007 by ITC Limited, one of the largest agricultural exporters. They reached about 4 million farmers growing a range of crops—soybean, coffee, wheat, rice, pulses, or shrimp—in over 40,000 villages. They get free information in their language about local and global market prices, weather forecasts, farming practices, and crop insurance. They serve as purchase centres, cutting marketing costs and allowing farmers to obtain a bigger farm price.[8] The M. S. Swaminathan Research Foundation established knowledge centres in Puducherry in 1997. With the support of the Indian Space Research Organization (ISRO), these centres in each village are connected by satellite to a hub at Villianur. Women self-help groups use the centres' computers to manage their business accounts and coordinate their activities using video links with other villages. The declining costs of ICTs are giving small farmers a far greater access to information. Mobile phone coverage in India is expanding and has an important function of linking farmers to markets.

Institutions for Marketing

A number of innovative institutional models are emerging to link farmer groups to bargain together in the input and produce markets. For small and marginal farmers, marketing of their products is an important problem apart from credit and extension. In recent years, there have been some form of contract arrangements in several agricultural crops, such as tomatoes, potatoes, chillies, gherkin, baby corn, rose, onions, cotton, wheat, basmati rice, groundnut, flowers, and medicinal plants. There is a silent revolution in institutions regarding non-cereal foods. New production-to-market linkages in the food supply chain are: spot or open market transactions, agricultural co-operatives, and contract farming (Joshi and Gulati 2003).

There is a need to revamp some of the legal hurdles for agro-processing and the Agriculture Produce Market Committee (APMC) Act. Several state governments have already amended their APMC Acts, allowing varying degrees of flexibility. However, several states are yet to notify the relevant rules that would make the amendment fully operational (Patnaik 2011). These steps should be speedily completed to provide a boost to the promotion of direct marketing, contract farming, and setting up of markets in private and co-operative sectors.

---

[8] A caveat is that there have been some second generation problems with e-Choupal and their success in scaling-up or reproducing the same in other regions has not been as smooth.

There are different models for marketing collectively by small and marginal farmers: the self-help group model, co-operative model, small producer co-operatives, and contract farming. *Apni mandi*s in Punjab, *rytu bazar*s in Andhra Pradesh, and dairy co-operatives are some of the successful cases in marketing. The real challenge lies in organising small and marginal farmers for marketing and linking them to high value agriculture. Thus, group approach is needed for getting benefits from marketing. The most important problem for the small farmers is output price fluctuations. There is a big gap between producer prices and consumer prices.

Small farmers can also benefit from the emerging supermarkets and value chains. In a study on food supply chains in India, Reardon and Minten (2011) indicated a rapid change in supply food chains in the past two decades. A modern sector is emerging in the wholesale sector with the growth of modern logistics firms and specialized modern wholesalers. Along with this, the traditional segment of the wholesale sector is also transforming with reductions in supply chains, the declining role of village brokers as farmers sell directly to mandis, and an expansion of cold storages that seem to be taking up wholesale functions, including providing credit. However, it is the medium and small farmers who take advantage of this dynamism, with the marginal farmers being at a disadvantage because of a less marketable surplus. They also point out infrastructural constraints on account of poor roads, unavailability of electricity, limited access to credit, less education, and no tube wells.

In India, the expansion of modern retailing has the potential to spark investments in marketing efficiency and processing that yield benefits to both producers and consumers. In those cases where small producers have been able to integrate into the supplying chains, supermarkets have offered enhanced security and considerably higher margins than the traditional clients, such as wholesalers and grocers. However, there is scope for exploitation in contract farming and supermarkets if the rules are not properly framed or not properly implemented.

While recognizing the advantages of contract farming, Singh (2012), as also Narayanan (2012), points out that its evaluation has to be situation specific, as contracts depend on the type of firm, the farmer, the crop being grown, and the nature of contract, among others. Singh (2012) further adds that the success of contract farming should be assessed based on its impact on reducing market risks for the small and marginal farmers and its impact on the resource base because of implications on future incomes and the environment.[9] Next, we discuss a cultivation practice that could ensure some of these advantages.

Non-pesticide Management

Non pesticide management (NPM) is one of the approaches that reduce costs and adverse implications on the environment. As the term suggests, it tries to manage pests without the use of chemical pesticides and, if feasible, tries to avoid the use of fertilizers. This technology is knowledge centric and hence its success as also scaling-up depends a lot on appropriate extension services. A successful intervention, as discussed in Mishra and Reddy (2011), is community-managed sustainable agriculture (CMSA) under the aegis of the Society for Elimination of Rural Poverty (SERP) in Andhra Pradesh.[10] A major emphasis of this intervention is on retaining soil health through natural processes that enhance microbial activity and replenish nutrients to sustain productivity. NPM has a number of non-negotiable practices that include 'deep summer ploughing, community bonfires, seed treatment, bird perches, border crops, trap crops, yellow and white plates, intercrops, light traps, pheromone traps, delta traps in groundnut, alleys in paddy, and cutting of the tips in paddy at the time of transplantation among others' (Mishra and Reddy 2011).

Under CMSA, farmer field schools comprising 15 to 20 members meet every week for on-site observations that help them understand the ecological systems—the life cycle of pests and their predators. If pest infestation is observed, a discussion is had with the resource

[9] For a discussion on technological changes giving higher net returns, which happen to be facilitated through contract farming and can add rather than reduce exposure to risks, see Mishra (2008).

[10] The continuing effectiveness and further scaling-up of NPM under SERP in Andhra Pradesh also needs constant interventions in terms of knowledge, human resources, physical capital, and monitoring and evaluation.

person as also with other groups in the village to gauge the intensity of the problem and plan a course of action. Bio-pesticides are used only as a last resort. In addition to pest management, nitrogen fixation and soil nutrient deficiencies are addressed through locally available resources. Some of the other important aspects are setting up of community seed banks and the promotion of appropriate cropping pattern and crop rotation practices. Local youth are encouraged to start micro-enterprises with forward and backward linkages to facilitate input availability or the marketing of produce.

There have been other similar experiments,[11] for instance the Revitalizing Rain-fed Agriculture Network (RRAN) comprising of a number of civil society groups working in the field. An aspect of their interventions is that they are refined as per the local conditions with focus on natural resource management and other integrated measures to help adapt to rain-fed conditions, as also to the increasing vagaries of monsoon.[12] This is particularly important because more than three-fifths of the geographical and more than two-thirds of the gross cropped area are in rain-fed regions (Planning Commission 2011a). This calls for an alternative policy discourse on agricultural intervention, which has been indicated in the approach paper to the 12th Five-year Plan (Planning Commission 2011b; also see Mishra et al. 2013). It suggests initiatives in the form of comprehensive pilots spread across different agro-ecological conditions that focus on integrating interventions in water, soil, seed, livestock, fisheries, credit, and institutions, among others. This will require knowledge interventions from each perspective.

Federation of Self-Help Groups

Beginning with 400 acres in 2004/5, the programme under NPM in Andhra Pradesh covered 18.15 lakh acres in 2009/10 and are likely to have scaled-up further since then. This has to be understood under

[11] In recent times, there has also been some discussion on zero budget natural farming; see Khadse et al. (2018) and Mishra (2017)

[12] For an analysis showing changes in monsoon with greater intensity of rainfall in shorter wet spells and longer dry spells, see Singh and Ranade (2010).

the institutional arrangement of federation of women SHGs that SERP had built to improve the livelihood of poorer households. Interactions with SHGs and their federations made SERP evaluate the livelihood problems associated with agriculture and the need to reduce costs in cultivation led to NPM. The success in Andhra Pradesh has now been extended to the national level under the National Rural Livelihoods Mission (NRLM) through a programme called the Mahila Kissan Sashaktikaran Pariyojana (MKSP).[13] The agricultural intervention under also tried to involve NGOs such as PRADAN (Professional Assistance for Development Action) who, as part of their livelihood facilitation, have independently been forming federations of women SHGs in the poorer districts of the country for nearly two decades.[14]

The institutional imperative articulated in the federation of SHGs and other successful experiments, such as the Grameen Bank in Bangladesh and the People's Participation Programme of the Food and Agriculture Organization (FAO) in Sri Lanka, Thailand, and Zambia (see Rouse 1996), give some lessons. These, as indicated in Mishra and Reddy (2011), point to restricting the number of members to 20 or 25 per farmer group (or about 15 per SHG) and drawing members from homogenous groups to avoid conflicts. The focus should be on local problems identified by the group and to limit the involvement of outside promoters to only enabling or facilitating processes so that the members can take over as soon as possible. Training and capacity building for four-to-five years, including hand-holding for the initial stages, should be part of the long-term process of building sustainable small-marginal federated farmer groups. A sound organizational structure should be built right from its foundation with an insistence on female membership and participation from the group level itself. Building institutions also requires developing democratic processes that are sensitive to inequities at every level. Once these are put in place and capacities of individuals and their institutions augmented, groups and their federated institutions become self-sustaining and,

[13] The scaling-up of the programme under MKSP has been slow, and one has to gauge its effectiveness across states in due course of time.

[14] For an evaluation of PRADAN's interventions, see Mishra and Sengupta (2013).

over time, they could slowly graduate to address other requirements of the community.

* * *

The analysis in this chapter has tried to contextualize our understanding of Indian agriculture by an evaluation of its performance, the roles and challenges for smallholders, and some opportunities. Its performance appraisal delineates the recent period (2004/5–2010/11) from the immediate post-reforms period (1993/4–2004/5) and the pre-reforms period (1981/2–1993/4). Our growth estimates, using a double-kinked exponential curve, reiterates a turnaround in agriculture in the recent years. This is also because of some changes in public investments in agriculture, as also an increased public expenditure in agricultural education, research and extension, initiatives to improve the availability of credit from formal sources, and a slew of normal monsoons in almost all but one of the recent years. However, public investments in agriculture have a lag effect and mostly relate to medium and major irrigation projects where substantial resources are invested without much critical scrutiny (Government of India 2011; Vaidyanathan 2010). The turnaround is particularly evident for maize, pulses, oilseeds, and cotton in terms of their growth in value of output, as also in production and yield. There have also been significant yield increments in rice in the recent years. An analysis of the agricultural GSDP across major states also shows significantly higher growth for most of them in the recent years; there also seems to be a decline in volatility and convergence across states.

A matter of concern is the implications on smallholders, particularly so when SAH 2013—a nationally representative survey for the 2012/13 agricultural year—points to income being less than expenditure for marginal farmer households with less than a hectare of land and very meagre incomes for farmers with less than four hectares of land, that is, 95 per cent of the operational holdings. What is worrying is that this difficulty in livelihood sustainability remained in spite of the fact that per hectare returns were higher for them; there continues to be an inverse relationship between size-class and returns. Nevertheless, smallholder farmers have had to bear a greater risk burden because of higher per unit cost, limited access to credit despite new initiatives, and a lower bargaining power in the input and produce markets, among others. These problems get aggravated in bad years, such as 2014 and 2015, when the monsoon plays truant, that too when nearly two-thirds of Indian agriculture is rain-fed.

To address some of these concerns, an identified opportunity is the effective use of information technology, whether to know about monsoon patterns or to be informed about new knowledge on agricultural production and management or on the prevailing prices in different markets. The alternatives of RRAN and NPM through CMSA under SERP are people-centred initiatives through the involvement of small and marginal farmers through SHGs and field schools. Institutions that organize farmers offer another opportunity. They aggregated farmers in groups of 20 to 25 and then federate them at village, subdistrict, and district level to articulate their interests and improve their bargaining power at various levels. On the knowledge front, it is equally important that technologies that reduce costs—and hence risks—while not compromising on production or yield and make use of locally available resources are encouraged.

References

Bhalla, G.S. (2004). *Globalisation and Indian Agriculture, State of the Indian Farmer: A Millennium Study, Vol. 19*. New Delhi: Academic Publishers.

Boyce, J. K. (1986). 'Kinked Exponential Models for Growth Rate Estimation'. *Oxford Bulletin of Economics and Statistics* 48(4): 385–91.

Central Statistical Organisation (CSO) (1999). *State Domestic Product, 1980–1 Series*. New Delhi: Ministry of Statistics and Program Implementation, Government of India. Available at http://mospi.nic.in/Mospi_New/upload/NAS12.htm. Last accessed on 30 August 2012.

———— (2007). *State Domestic Product, 1993–4 Series*. New Delhi: Ministry of Statistics and Program Implementation, Government of India. Available at http://mospi.nic.in/Mospi_New/upload/NAS12.htm. Last accessed on 18 August 2012.

———— (2010). *State Domestic Product, 1999–2000 Series*. New Delhi: Ministry of Statistics and Program Implementation, Government of India. Available at http://mospi.nic.in/Mospi_New/upload/NAS12.htm. Last accessed on 18 August 2012.

———— (2012a). *National Accounts Statistics, 2011 (Back series)*. New Delhi: Ministry of Statistics and Program Implementation, Government of India. Available at http://mospi.nic.in/Mospi_New/upload/back_series_2011.htm. Last accessed on 18 August 2012.

_____ (2012b). *National Accounts Statistics*. New Delhi: Ministry of Statistics and Program Implementation, Government of India. Available at http://mospi. nic.in/Mospi_New/upload/NAS12.htm. Last accessed on 18 August 2012.

_____ (2012c). *State Domestic Product, 2004–5 Series*. New Delhi: Ministry of Statistics and Program Implementation, Government of India. Available at http://mospi.nic.in/Mospi_New/upload/NAS12.htm. Last accessed on 18 August 2012.

_____ (2017). *Gross Value of Output*. New Delhi: Ministry of Statistics and Program Implementation, Government of India. Available at http://mospi. nic.in/Mospi_New/upload/NAS12.htm. Last accessed on 5 January 2018.

Chakravarty, K.C. (2012). 'Revised Guidelines on Priority Sector Lending: Rationale and Logic'. Address at the FIBAC 2012 organized by FICCI and the Indian Banks' Association in Mumbai on 4 September 2012. Available at http://www.rbi.org.in/scripts/BS_SpeechesView.aspx?id=727. Last accessed on 10 September 2012.

Chand, R. (2004). *Agricultural Growth during the Reforms and Liberalization: Issues and Concerns*. Policy Brief No. 20. New Delhi: National Centre for Agricultural Economics and Policy.

Chandrasekhar, S. and N. Mehrotra (2016). 'Doubling Farmers' Income by 2022: What would It Take?'. *Economic and Political Weekly* 51(18): 10–13.

Desai, B.M., E. D'Souza, J.W. Mellor, V.P. Sharma, and P. Tamboli (2011). 'Agricultural Policy Strategy, Instruments and Implementation: A Review and the Road Ahead'. *Economic and Political Weekly* 46(53): 42–50.

Dev, S.M. (2012). 'Small Farmers in India: Challenges and Opportunities'. IGIDR Working Paper No.WP-2012-014. Mumbai: Indira Gandhi Institute of Development Research.

Dev, S.M. and V.L. Pandey (2013). 'Performance and Key Policy Issues of Indian Agriculture'. *India Development Report 2012–13*, edited by S. Mahendra Dev, 79–94. New Delhi: Oxford University Press.

Gaurav, S. and S. Mishra (2015a). 'To Bt or not to Bt: Risk and Uncertainty Considerations in Technology Assessment'. In *India's Tryst with Bt Cotton: Learning from the First Decade*, edited by L. Narayanan and P.K. Viswanathan, 123–55. New Delhi: Concept Publishing Company.

——— (2015b). 'Size-class and Returns to Cultivation in India: Revisiting an Old Debate'. *Oxford Development Studies* 43(2): 165–93. DOI: 10.1080/13600818.2014.982081.

Government of India (2007). *Report of the Expert Group on Agricultural Indebtedness*. Published under the chairmanship of R. Radhakrishna. New Delhi: Ministry of Finance.

_____ (2009). *Report of the Task Force on Credit Related Issues of Farmers*. Published under the chairmanship of Umesh Sarangi. New Delhi: Ministry of Agriculture.

_____ (2011). *Report of the Expert Committee on Improvement of Agricultural Statistics*. Published under the chairmanship of A. Vaidyanathan. New Delhi: Department of Agriculture and Co-operation. Available at http://eands.dacnet.nic.in/VaidiyanathanCommitteeReport.pdf. Last accessed on 22 May 2013.

Joshi, P.K. and A. Gulati (2003). 'From Plate to Plough: Agricultural Diversification in India'. Paper presented at the workshop on 'Dragon and Elephant: A Comparative Study of Economic and Agricultural Reforms in China and India' in New Delhi, India, pp. 25–6.

Khadse, A., P.M. Rosset, H. Morales, and B.G. Ferguson (2018). 'Taking Agroecology to Scale: The Zero Budget Natural Farming Peasant Movement in Karnataka, India'. *Journal of Peasant Studies* 45(1): 192–219. DOI: 10.1080/03066150.2016.1276450.

Kumar, P. (2002). 'Agricultural Performance and Productivity'. In *Indian Agricultural Policy at the Crossroads*, edited by S.S. Acharya and D.P. Chaudhri, 353–428. Jaipur: Rawat Publications.

Lipton, M. (2006). 'Can Small Farmers Survive, Prosper, or Be the Key Channel to Cut Mass Poverty'. *Journal of Agricultural and Development Economics* 3(1): 58–85.

Ministry of Agriculture (2012). *Agricultural Statistics at a Glance, 2011*. Directorate of Economics and Statistics, Department of Agriculture and Cooperation. New Delhi: Government of India. Available at http://eands.dacnet.nic.in/latest_2006.htm. Last accessed on 19 August 2012.

Ministry of Agriculture and Farmers Welfare (MoA) (2017). *Pocket Book of Agricultural Statistics, 2016*. Directorate of Economics and Statistics, Department of Agriculture, Cooperation and Farmers Welfare. New Delhi: Government of India.

Mishra, S. (2008). 'Risks, Farmers' Suicides and Agrarian Crisis in India: Is There a Way Out?'. *Indian Journal of Agricultural Economics* 63(1): 38–54.

_____ (2012). 'Crisis in Indian Agriculture: Where Do We Stand?'. *Artha Beekshan* 20(4): 94–107.

_____ (2015). *Nature, Extent, Causes and Issues in Agricultural Distress*. Mumbai: National Bank for Agriculture and Rural Development.

_____ (2017). 'Zero Budget Natural Farming: Is This a Way Out?'. Mimeo. Bhubaneshwar: Nabakrushna Choudhury Centre For Development Studies.

Mishra, S., A. Ravindra, and C. Hesse (2013). 'Rain-fed Agriculture: For an Inclusive, Sustainable and Food Secure India'. IIED Briefing Paper 10041. Available at http://pubs.iied.org/pdfs/10041IIED.pdf. Last accessed on 22 May 2013.

Mishra, S. and D.N. Reddy (2011). 'Persistence of Crisis in Indian Agriculture: Need for Technological and Institutional Alternatives'. In *India

Development Report 2011, edited by Dilip M. Nachane, 48–58. New Delhi: Oxford University Press.

Mishra, S. and N. Sengupta (2013). *Impact Assessment Study of PRADAN's Interventions at the Grassroots*. Mumbai: Indira Gandhi Institute of Development Research.

Narayanan, S. (2012). 'The Heterogeneous Welfare Impacts of Participation in Contract Farming Schemes: Evidence from Southern India'. IGIDR Working paper No. WP-2012-019. Mumbai: Indira Gandhi Institute of Development Research.

National Commission for Enterprises in the Unorganized Sector (NCEUS) (2008). *A Special Programme for Marginal and Small Farmers*. New Delhi: NCEUS.

National Sample Survey Organisation (NSSO) (2005). *Situation Assessment Survey of Farmers: Income, Expenditure and Productive Assets of Farmer Households*. NSS 59th Round (January–December 2003), NSS Report No. 497 (59/33/5).

_____ (2013). 'Key Indicators of Situation of Agricultural Households'. NSS 70th Round (Jan–Dec 2013).

Patnaik, G. (2011). 'Status of Agricultural Marketing Reforms'. Paper presented at the workshop on 'Policy Options and Investment Priorities for Accelerating Agricultural Productivity and Development in India', on 10–11 November at Indira Gandhi Institute of Development Research, Mumbai, and Institute for Human Development, Delhi.

Planning Commission (2011a). *Report of the XII Plan Working Group on Natural Resource Management and Rain-fed Farming*. New Delhi: Government of India. Available at http://planningcommission.nic.in/aboutus/committee/wrkgrp12/agri/wg_NRM_Farming.pdf. Last accessed on 23 May 2013.

_____ (2011b). *Faster, Sustainable and More Inclusive Growth: An Approach to the Twelfth Five Year Plan (2012–17)*. New Delhi: Government of India.

Reardon, T. and B. Minten (2011). 'The Quiet Revolution in India's Food Supply Chains'. IFPRI Discussion Paper 01115. Washington DC: International Food Policy Research Institute.

Reddy, D.N. and S. Mishra (eds) (2009). *Agrarian Crisis in India*. New Delhi: Oxford University Press.

_____ (2010). 'Economic Reforms, Small Farmer Economy and Agrarian Crisis'. In *Agrarian Crisis and Farmers' Suicides*, edited by R. S. Deshpande and S. Arora, 43–69. New Delhi: Sage Publications.

Reserve Bank of India (RBI) (2006). *Report of the Working Group to Suggest Measures to Assist Distressed Farmers*. Pubilished under the chairmanship of S.S. Johl. Mumbai: RBI.

_____ (2012a). *Report of the Committee to Re-examine the Existing Classification and Suggest Revised Guidelines with Regard to Priority Sector Lending Classification and Related Issues.* Mumbai: RBI.

_____ (2012b). *Annual Report, 2011-12.* Mumbai: RBI.

Rouse, J. (1996). *Organizing for Extension: FAO Experiences in Small Farmer Group Development.* Sustainable Development Department. Rome: Food and Agriculture Organization.

Samantara, S. (2010). *Kisan Credit Card—A Study.* Occasional Paper 52. Mumbai: National Bank for Agriculture and Rural Development.

Shetty, S.L. (2009). 'Agricultural Credit and Indebtedness: Ground Realities and Policy Perspectives'. In *Agrarian Crisis in India,* edited by D.N. Reddy and S. Mishra, 61–86. New Delhi: Oxford University Press.

Singh, N. and A. Ranade (2010). 'The Wet and Dry Spells across India during 1951–2007'. *Journal of Hydrometeorology* 11(1): 26–45.

Singh, S. (2012). *Contract Farming for Sustainable Agricultural Development in India: A Smallholder Perspective.* Revised version of the paper presented at a workshop on 'Policy Options and Investment Priorities for Accelerating Agricultural Productivity and Development in India' on 10–11 November 2011 at Indira Gandhi Institute of Development Research, Mumbai, and Institute for Human Development, New Delhi.

Thapa, G. and R. Gaiha (2011). 'Smallholder Farming in Asia and the Pacific: Challenges and Opportunities'. Paper presented at the conference on 'New Directions for Small Holder Agriculture' on 24–5 January 2011 at the International Fund for Agricultural Development (IFAD), Rome.

Thiyagarajan, T.M. and B. Gujja (2012). *Transforming Rice Production with SRI (System of Rice Intensification) Knowledge and Practice: Reducing Agriculture Footprint and Ensuring Food Security,* AgSri. Available at http://www.agsri.com/images/documents/sri/SRI_Book_Final_Version. pdf. Last accessed on 10 September 2012.

Vaidyanathan, A. (2010). *Agricultural Growth in India: Role of Technology, Incentives and Institutions.* New Delhi: Oxford University Press.

World Bank, The (2008). *World Development Report: Agriculture for Development.* Washington DC: World Bank.

CHAPTER 12

....

NEW SOURCES OF DYNAMISM IN THE INDUSTRY

....

BANDI RAM PRASAD[1]

Halfway into 2018, India experienced perhaps two contrasting scenarios, both connected with the industry in one way or another. One of it concerned the biggest e-commerce merger deal with Walmart, the largest supermarket chain of the United States, buying Flipkart, one of India's topmost e-commerce company, for more than USD 16 billion. The merger was expected to provide synergies to the US supermarket conglomerate with e-commerce opportunity in one of the fast-growing markets that is India, making it one of the most talked about mergers in investment banking.

At the same time, the latest data showed that the index of industrial production in India for the month of March 2018 rose by just 4.4 per cent, which is a five-month low, as compared to a revised 7 per cent growth in the previous month. For the whole year 2017–18, industrial

[1] The author thanks Sujata Bijwe for the help and assistance extended in the revised version. Views presented in this chapter are the author's own in his individual capacity and do not reflect, in whatsoever manner, those of the organizations for which he offers consulting services or runs.

output was projected at 6.2 per cent, which is not such a promising growth considering India's potential, though it is better than the 4.3 per cent growth reported in the previous year.

Several such disconnects can be found if one looks deeper into the Indian industry, but there is so much to show with regard to the growth and progress of industry overall. While narrating in brief the various aspects of growth and development of industry in India, this chapter discusses specific aspects of finance as a source of dynamism.

INDUSTRY IN INDIA: A SNAPSHOT

India has a rich legacy of numerous interventions in industrial development. A series of policies, directed credit flows, incentives and concessions of various types, industrial promotion agencies and financial institutions at the central and state governments, and a slew of support measures and incentives are aimed at strengthening the industrial performance in India. Industry will assume a larger scope and significance in the strategy to place India at the forefront of growth and development.

Notwithstanding the extensive efforts that were in place to tone up the performance, there is this contrast that has become a big challenge for India—the divergence in the rate of growth of GDP and that of the industry. For instance, GDP growth in India, according to the most recent edition of the Economic Survey (2017–18), averaged at 7.3 per cent during 2014–15 to 2017–18, which is considered as the highest among the major economies of the world. Rates of gross savings and gross capital formation were found to be robust in the range of 33–4 per cent during 2014–15 to 2015–16. Bank rate too has been on a decline since 2016, from about 7 per cent to 6.25 per cent. Yet, the annual growth of the index of industrial production has remained suboptimal in the range of 3 to 4 per cent in the last four years.

Structural reforms in the last four years, more so in the realm of the financial sector, have had an impact on the overall economy in general, and the growth of industry in particular. To begin with, there was a massive effort from the Reserve Bank of India (RBI) to clean up the loan books of Indian banks of frauds and falsifications. In a notification issued on 7 May 2015 and addressed to all banks, the RBI had unveiled a 'Framework for Dealing with Loan Frauds'. The framework brought into operation practices such as Early Warning Signals (EWS) and Red Flagged Accounts (RFA) to detect frauds and malpractices in time and avoid their occurrence. This led to a spurt in the stressed advances of banks from 9.2 per cent of the total advances in 2013 to 12.2 per cent in 2017.

For the first time, a list of 12 major defaulters of bank loans with claims of INR 3.1 trillion was put up in the public domain. Banks have been aggressive in weeding out bad loans from their books, which has had a telling effect on bank profitability and its impact on capital adequacy. In October 2017, the Government of India announced a massive recapitalization of banks to the tune of INR 2 trillion to tide over the bad loan crisis, but nasty surprises keep on surging with newer issues cropping up in public and private sector banks. The stress on the bank balance sheets of public sector banks and a few private ones that was seen in the year 2017–18 is also worrisome.

A few other long-awaited measures in the Indian economy came in succession, involving structural adjustments that affected the growth of bank credit flows to industry. In May 2016, the Insolvency and Bankruptcy Code (IBC) was passed. It was followed by the framing of rules and regulations that enabled a large number of cases to seek the insolvency process. Over 525 cases of corporate insolvency involving INR 1.3 trillion have been admitted across all the National Company Law Tribunal (NCLT) benches. In addition, 108 voluntary liquidation proceedings and one fast-track corporate insolvency resolution have also been initiated.

In November 2016, the demonetization of higher denomination currency notes (INR 500 and INR 1000) was initiated, which hit the vast informal sector with implications for industry. In July 2017, a nationwide common Goods and Services Tax (GST) was introduced to bring about a uniform indirect taxation across the country. The government also brought the Financial Resolution and Deposit Insurance (FRDI) Bill 2017, which is a part of a larger and more comprehensive legislation meant to effect changes in the resolution of bank failures that were hitherto being resolved using tax payers' money, thereby making the promoters and customers of banks responsible for the costs of bank resolution. The bill was later withdrawn due to a number of reservations expressed by various stake holders.

These developments have dented the loan growth of banks that have registered a lower rate of growth of 8 to 10 per cent in the recent years against the trend growth of over 15 per cent during 1990–2000, 22 per cent during 2000–10, and in the range of 14 per cent to 21 per cent during the financial years 2008–9 and 2013–14 respectively.

The subdued industry growth is expected to recover from FY 2019 onwards with the completion of the structural adjustment process, cleaning of bank balance sheets, and banks taking measures to curb corporate frauds and implementing a speedy recovery system.

Besides these issues, there are certain long-term inadequacies in Indian finance, one of which is the neglect of development banking. For an economy such as India with such a size and significance, development banks are of paramount importance. Development banks formed the core of India's development strategy soon after Independence with the establishment of the Industrial Finance Corporation of India in July 1948, the creation of a string of state financial corporations in 1952 and the Industrial Development Bank of India in 1964, etc. According to a study by United Nations Conference on Trade and Development (UNCTAD), loans granted by the development finance institutions in India, which formed 2.2 per cent of the gross capital formation in the early 1970s, reached 15.5 per cent by the early 1990s. It was quite an impressive growth, going by the global trends during the period. Strangely in India's reform agenda that began in the 1990s, development banks were overlooked. Conversion of ICICI into a commercial bank in 2002 and of IDBI in 2004 was a major outcome of such a premise. After two decades of reforms and by the year 2011–12, disbursements by development banks in India fell to the pre-1970s levels of 3.2 per cent of the gross capital formation. The UNCTAD study notes, 'As a proportion of the financial system as a whole, between the early 1970s and late 1980s, their loans accounted for over two-thirds of the total disbursals. Between the financial liberalization in the early 1990s and early 2000s, this share declined to 30 per cent; after 2004, it declined further to 1.7 per cent.'

In the absence of strong development banking, not enough growth in new capital issuance through public equity markets, and the lack of a strong and vibrant corporate debt market, the burden of financing long-term projects such as greenfield and infrastructure fell on commercial banks in contrast to their capacity to provide short-term working capital that led to turbulence in their long-term stability.

Notwithstanding these constraints, it could be said that the Indian industry has showed significant advances in regard to production values, distribution systems, and research and development, which made positive contributions to the assessment of international institutions and agencies. India is rated high in regard to industrial performance by global institutions such as UNCTAD.

LANDSCAPE OF INDUSTRY

The global economy landscape is undergoing a rapid change. Developing countries are outpacing developed countries in terms of growth and diversity. The factors influencing economic growth too are changing rapidly—from globalization to digitalization, from domestic finance to international capital flows, from public capital markets to the power of global private equity, and startups to artificial intelligence.

In tune with these changes that have a deep impact on the economy, the industrial sector too is undergoing change. Aspects such as innovation, access to capital, technology, efficiency, environment, social responsibility, green finance, and competitiveness are emerging as key determinants of growth and performance. Patterns of economic growth are changing with new segments and sectors such as e–commerce, including food e–commerce, retail, infrastructure, healthcare and pharma, education and training, financial services, tourism, automobiles, media and entertainment, wind and solar power generation, 3-D printing, artificial intelligence, video gaming, etc. gaining traction.

The ranking of countries in the top league of industrial growth, performance, and competitiveness has also undergone a rapid change. As per the United Nations Industrial Development Organization (UNIDO) Year Book of 2015, India stood sixth among the world's 10

Table 12.1 New sources of dynamism in the industry

Policy Framework	Domestic Capital Markets	Indian Banking Sector	Non-bank Finance	New Opportunities	Political environment
Delicensing and deregulation. Promotion of competition. Conducive environment for growth of the private sector. Foreign direct investment. Promotion of capital markets. Liberal access for corporates to tap foreign markets for resource mobilization. Scope for global acquisitions. Deregulation of the financial sector. New manufacturing policy. New Industrial Policy 2018. Promotion of 'Make in India' and 'Smart Manufacturing'. Digitization of Economy. Introduction of Tax Reforms.	Liberalization of interest rates. Reform of the public capital markets. Foreign portfolio investment to strengthen secondary capital markets. Introducing Qualified Institutional Placements (QIPs) and Strategic Debt Restructuring (SDR's). Thrust on debt capital markets. Introduction of hedging and risk management products in the form of financial derivatives in equities, commodities, currencies, and fixed income.	Deregulation of interest rates and greater functional autonomy for banks in regard to lending. Access to capital markets for the state–owned banks to bolster capital levels to sustain the pace of lending. Growth in loan products, including consortium lending. Provision for corporate restructuring via loan/ SDRs. Licensing of Payment Banks and Small Finance Banks.	Non-bank financial companies expanded operations with thrust on financing of machinery, farm equipment (such as tractors), Infrastructure (like L & T Infrastrucure Finance Co. & Srei Infrastructure Finance Co.) and transport equipment giving thrust to the related industries.	Economic reforms and liberalization have given new opportunities to expand in the realm of certain key industries such as automobiles, engineering machinery, telecommunications, infrastructure, etc. Forthcoming Industrial Policy aims at facilitating the use of smart technologies such as internet of things (IOT), Artificial Intelligence (AI) and robotics.	One of largest democracies in the world. Political and consultative decision making. Continuity of reforms irrespective of political parties. Reforms such as GST, Demonetization, Financial Resolution and Deposit Insurance (FRDI) Bill etc.
Skills and Expertise	Access to International Finance	Foreign Investment	Domestic Demand	India as a Hub for Exports	Social Sector
Capacity building in education with greater emphasis on study of engineering, computer	India is one of the leading emerging markets to access global financial markets to	Liberalized norms of foreign direct investment and foreign portfolio investment.	Surge in domestic demand in the background of liberalization of lending	In view of the cost-effective resources and labour, India emerged as	Rising literacy and education levels across society. One of the

science, and information technology that have generated human resource inputs at a fairly competitive costs benefiting the industry. Setting up of National Skill Development Council to augment the skills. Promotion of Innovation & Smart Technologies. Launch of National Skill Development Mission in 2015.	raise resources for expansion, new acquisitions, and pursue domestic and global growth aspirations.	Liberal entry norms for foreign companies. Foreign collaborations with domestic industrial houses.	norms for personal finance, including loans for housing, personal consumption, consumer durables, cars, etc., which have fuelled growth in industrial activity.	an attractive avenue for development centers of major companies as also back office functions that led to creation of infrastructure and demand for related industries.	largest wage-earning young population. Society is relatively open to adopt new technologies and customs.

New Developments

Transformation towards a digital economy. Adoption of Greener Technologies. Shift in the saving pattern of financial savings with potential of upto $600 billion to flow into various financial instruments. Opportunity for well capitalized private sector financial institutions to grow @25% over the medium term. Rationalization of Registration and inspection process of Industries. Setting up of 'India Invest'.

Challenges of Implementation

• Challenges to meet priority sector lending • Micro finance credit is still in developing state • Private and unorganized private credit association like chit funds, etc. • Relatively low proportion of savings invested in financial markets	• Slow pace of reforms in debt market and lack of retail participation • Sluggish pace of reforms in the judicial sector • Scale and scope restriction in the manufacturing sector • Lack of enabling infrastructure for domestic and foreign venture capital and private equity	• Lack of reforms in the agriculture sector • Uncertainty over fulfillment of political commitment • Low degree of financial inclusion • Lack of social security and basic social infrastructure	• High level of fiscal deficit • Lack of alignment in monetary and fiscal policies • Concern over the level of corruption • Internal Security Aspect • Concern over minimum environment impact	• Institutional gaps in promoting Industry-Research Institution Interaction • Lengthy and Complex process of Land acquisition • Lack of right skilled professionals	• Lack of adequate and quality Healthcare Infrastructure • Impact of automation on jobs and employment

Source: Author's presentation.

largest manufacturing countries. Of the top 10 industrial producers, China holds the first position, followed by USA, Japan, Germany, and South Korea.

This chapter presents an overview of the major trends in the Indian industry in regard to growth and structure, with particular emphasis on the financial sector that emerged as an important stimulus and source of dynamism. This chapter discusses certain aspects of the Indian industry in regard to (*a*) the evolution of industrial policies; (*b*) growth trends in output; (*c*) changes in the industrial structure; (*d*) a brief assessment of the growth trends following economic liberalization; and (*e*) international perspectives on the emergence of the Indian industry. It also discusses the role of financial sector reforms in the Indian industry with particular reference to a wide range of instruments that have now emerged as new sources of dynamism, helping the progress of industry further (Table 12.1).

Much of the discussion in this chapter is from the perspective of financial market practice, reflecting on the author's engagement with it over a long period of time.

POLICY EVOLUTION IN THE INDIAN INDUSTRY

Industrial development in India (see Figure 12.1) was governed by licensing policies that came into being after 1948. The first comprehensive Industrial Policy Resolution of 1956 classified industries into three categories, with the state given the primary role of industrial development and the private sector expected to supplement the efforts of the state. The Industrial Policy Resolution of 1970 classified industries into four categories: the core sector, the heavy investment sector, the middle sector, and the de-licensed sector, with the first three categories confined to large business houses and foreign companies. The Industrial Policy Statement of 1973 gave preference and thrust to the growth of small and medium enterprises. The Industrial Policy Statement of 1977 further promoted decentralization with an increased role for small scale, tiny, and cottage industries. The

India: Timeline of Policy Reforms

	Pre-Liberalization	Post-Liberalization	Way forward

1948	1956	1973	1977	1980	1991	2011	2018
First Industrial Policy Resolution of Independent India • Protectionist Policy • Large Public Sector • Emphasis on business regulation and central Planning	• Assistance to Private Sector • Expanded role of cottage & small Industries • Balanced Industrial growth among various regions • Incentives to labour	• High Priority Industries Identified where Institutional and foreign Investment was allowed	• Concentrated on decentralization • Emphasis on the role of small-scale, tiny and Cottage Industries	• Emphasis on Promoting competition in the domestic market technological upgradation and modernization	• Economic Liberalization Initiated • Reforms to correct prior policy decisions: They reduced tariffs and interest rates, abolished License Raj, ended several public monopolies and allowed automatic approval FDI in many sectors to correct prior policy decisions	• A rodmap to create 100 million new jobs in manufacturing and promote its GDP contribution to more then 25% by 2022 • Emphasis on making business operations in the country easier by simplification of business regulations and friendly trade & Investment policy • A focused move to improve infrastructure and gradual technology development including green technologies	• The New Industrial Policy would look into reducing regulations, promote modernization of the existing industry and focus on new emerging industries–Internet of Things (IoT), Artificial Interlligence (AI) and Robotics. • Addressing the problem of low job creation in the formal sector.

FIGURE 12.1 Timeline of policy reforms for industry in India

Source: 1. Chandan Sapkota's blog, *Macroeconomics, Public Policy and Policy Analysis,* available at www.sapkotac.blogspot.com, last accessed on 29 April 2012.

2. Author's notes added.

Industrial Policy Statement of 1980 placed a greater thrust on the promotion of competition in the domestic market, and technological upgradation and modernization of industries. The Industrial Policy Statement of 1991 that came against the backdrop of major economic reforms stated, 'The Government will continue to pursue a sound policy framework encompassing encouragement of entrepreneurship, development of indigenous technology through investment in research and development, bringing in new technology, dismantling of the excessive controls, development of the capital markets, and increased competitiveness for the benefit of common man.'[2] In 2012, India announced the National Manufacturing Policy (NMP) that aimed at increasing its growth rate from 9 per cent to 12 per cent to 14 per cent over the medium-term period.

The government proposed a new industrial policy in 2018, which is still awaiting final approval. However, the draft of the policy that was released envisages at building a globally competitive Indian industry equipped with skill, scale, and technology. Its key features include:

- Facilitating the use of smart technologies such as internet of things (IOT), artificial intelligence (AI), and robotics with an aim to make India a global hub for advanced manufacturing,
- Increasing the number of global Indian firms, helping attract inward FDI and supporting outward FDI to assert Indian presence in world markets,
- Developing alternatives to banks and improving access to capital for Micro, Small and Medium Enterprises (MSMEs) through options such as peer-to-peer lending and crowd funding,
- Addressing the impact of automation on jobs and employment, and
- Upgrading the FDI policy to ensure that it facilitates greater technology transfer, leverages strategic linkages, and innovation.

The new policy is expected to make India a leader in green energy, smart manufacturing, and technology and is aimed to reduce

[2] Statement on Industrial Policy, Ministry of Industry, released on 24 July 1991. New Delhi: Government of India, p. 2.

compliance costs and transaction time that could attract USD 100 billion FDI annually.

While import substitution policies were predominant in the 1950s, the 1980s witnessed surging export-promotion strategies, the 1990s saw a major tariff liberalization, and the 2000s envisaged harnessing emerging technologies ranging from digitization to artificial intelligence and the fast-growing startup culture. In this context, four key messages emerged as policy directions in India with regard to the future of growth: Make in India, Digital India, Startup India, and Skill India.

The focus of economic reforms in India in the last 27 years, with particular reference to the industry sector, was to (*a*) maintain a sustained growth in productivity; (*b*) enhance gainful employment; (*c*) achieve an optimal utilization of national resources; (*d*) attain international competitiveness; (*e*) promote the modernization of the existing industry and focus on new emerging industry; and (*f*) transform India into a major partner and player in the global arena.[3]

INDIAN INDUSTRY: GROWTH TRENDS

The average annual growth rate of industry (Banga and Das 2012), which remained around 5.8 per cent in the 1950s and the 1960s, fell to 5 per cent in the 1970s and returned to 5.8 per cent in the 1980s. Reforms in the 1990s led to improvement in the value-added growth rate of the manufacturing sector, taking it to 6 per cent. The 2000s witnessed a number of measures in the reduction of tariffs and quantitative restrictions that led industrial growth climb to an annual average of 8 per cent. Corresponding with value addition, the industry also witnessed a huge spurt in external trade. The average annual growth rate of manufacturing real exports surged from 5 per cent in the 1980s to 9.7 per cent in the 1990s, increasing further to 12 per cent in the 2000s. The average annual growth rate of real imports also increased from 5.4 per cent in the 1980s to 11 per cent in the 1990s and further

---

[3] Evolution and Development of Industrial Policy, Department of Industry Policy and Promotion, Government of India, Annual Report 2010–11.

Table 12.2 Annual growth rate of industrial production (percentage) (2004–5 as base year)

Period	Mining	Manufacturing	Electricity	Overall
Weight	14.2	75.5	10.3	100
2007–8	4.6	18.4	6.3	15.5
2008–9	2.6	2.5	2.7	2.5
2009–10	7.9	4.8	6.1	5.3
2010–11	5.2	8.9	5.5	8.2
2011–12	–2.0	3.0	8.2	2.9
2012–13	–2.3	1.3	4.0	1.1
2013–14	–0.6	–0.8	6.1	–0.1
2014–15	1.5	2.3	8.4	2.8
2015–16	2.2	2.0	5.7	2.4
2016–17	2.2	0.0	4.7	0.7

Source: Central Statistics Office.

to 16 per cent in the 2000s. Sectoral contribution of manufacturing exports also witnessed a major change.

The trends in regard to growth in organized and unorganized sectors, however, varied. Value added in organized manufacturing showed an average annual growth (1999–2000 constant prices) of 6.3 per cent in the 1950s, rose to 7 per cent in the 1960s, but fell steeply to 4.1 per cent in the 1970s, only to pick up to 8 per cent in the 1980s. Following the reforms, the value-added average annual growth rate adjusted to 5.9 per cent in the 1990s, but quickly rose to 7.8 per cent in the 2000s. In contrast, the value added in unorganized manufacturing that showed an average annual growth of 5 per cent in 1950s remained in the realm of 4 per cent in the next four decades, but moved up to 6.6 per cent in the 2000s.

The Index of Industrial Production (IIP) over the base of 2004–5, measuring industrial performance, monitors the production in manufacturing, mining, and electricity sectors and also in use-based groups such as basic goods, capital goods, intermediate goods, and consumer goods. The growth of IIP has been fluctuating over the last few years.

STRUCTURE OF THE INDIAN INDUSTRY

The share of industry in GDP has remained more or less stagnant, between 24.3 per cent in 1983, 25.2 per cent in 1993–4, 27 per cent in 2011–12, 29.3 per cent (of gross value added [GVA]) in 2016–17, and 31.2 per cent (of GVA) in 2017–18 (till September 2017, as per the *Economic Survey 2017–18*). The share of manufacturing in GDP remained steady too, between 14.5 per cent in 1983, 15.3 per cent in 2011–12, and 16.5 per cent (of GVA) in 2016—17, according to the Central Statistics Office. However, the share of industry in employment moved up from 13.8 per cent in 1983 to 21.5 per cent in 2013 (Statista 2018). In 2018, the share of industry (including construction) value added as percentage of GDP at 27 per cent is found relatively low as compared to countries such as China (40.7 per cent), Korea (35.1 per cent), Malaysia (39 per cent), and Thailand (35 per cent). Similarly, the current level of manufacturing value added as percentage of GDP in 2018 is at 15 per cent compares quite low against China (29 per cent), Korea (27 per cent), Thailand (27 per cent), and Malaysia (22 per cent). The record of India in terms of employment in industry (in 2013) as percentage of total employment, however, compares favorably with countries such as China (27 per cent), Korea (17 per cent), and Thailand (20 per cent).

The relative importance of various segments has been changing over time. For instance, the radio, television, and communication sector, which grew at a rate of 28.1 per cent in the 1980s, slipped to 14.8 per cent in the 1990s and further to 1.8 per cent in the 2000s. At the same time, coke, petroleum products, and nuclear fuel segments, which had seen a negative growth in the 1980s, registered over 20 per cent of average growth in the 2000s. Such a divergence in growth is found in the recent period too, as can be seen from Table 12.3.

INDIAN INDUSTRY: GLOBAL PERSPECTIVES

India's economy has benefited from the ongoing market reforms that have improved competitiveness. For 2016–17, India scored 4.52 points out of 7, according to the Global Competitiveness Report published

Table 12.3 Growth rates of production of manufacturing sub-groups (base: 2004–5 = 100) (percentage)

Code	Industry	Weight	2007–8	2008–9	2009–10	2010–11	2011–12	2012–13	2013–14	2014–15	2015–16
15	Food products and beverages	72.76	12.5	-8.2	-1.4	7.0	15.4	2.9	-1.1	4.8	-6.2
16	Tobacco products	15.70	-4.4	4.4	-0.6	2.0	5.4	-0.4	0.8	1.0	-0.2
17	Textiles	61.64	6.6	-3.6	6.1	6.7	-1.3	5.9	4.4	2.8	2.6
18	Wearing apparel	27.82	9.3	-10.2	1.9	3.7	-8.5	10.4	19.5	5.1	6.6
19	Luggage, handbags, etc.	5.82	5.8	-5.1	1.3	8.1	3.7	7.3	5.2	10.4	-1.4
20	Wood and wood products	10.51	17.5	4.9	3.1	-2.2	1.8	-7.1	-2.2	4.4	3.2
21	Paper and paper products	9.99	1.4	4.8	2.6	8.6	5.0	0.5	-0.1	3.3	2.8
22	Publishing, printing, and reproduction of recorded media	10.78	14.2	1.6	-6.0	11.2	29.6	-5.1	0.3	-4.1	-9.0
23	Coke, refined petroleum products, and nuclear fuel	67.15	6.2	3.2	-1.3	-0.2	3.5	8.5	5.2	0.8	6.0
24	Chemicals and chemical products	100.59	7.2	-2.9	5.0	2.0	-0.4	3.8	8.9	-0.3	3.8
25	Rubber and plastic products	20.25	13.4	5.1	17.4	10.6	-0.3	0.2	-2.1	4.5	0.6

No.	Industry										
26	Other non-metallic mineral products	43.14	9.3	3.3	7.8	4.1	4.8	1.9	1.1	2.5	1.6
27	Basic metals	113.35	17.9	1.7	2.1	8.8	8.7	1.9	0.3	12.7	1.0
28	Fabricated metal products	30.85	7.8	0.1	10.2	15.3	11.2	-4.7	-7.0	-0.6	1.5
29	Machinery and equipment not elsewhere classified (n.e.c.)	37.63	22.6	-7.6	15.8	29.4	-5.8	-4.7	-4.7	4.0	2.6
30	Office, accounting, and computing machinery	3.05	6.0	-9.7	3.8	-5.3	1.6	-13.9	-15.7	-38.0	0.8
31	Electrical machinery and apparatus	19.80	183.5	42.3	-13.5	2.8	-22.2	0.6	14.5	21.1	-11.4
32	Radio TV and communication equipment	9.89	93.1	20.3	11.3	12.7	4.3	5.6	-27.3	-54.4	3.7
33	Medical precision and optical instruments watches and clock	5.67	6.3	7.5	-15.8	6.8	10.9	-2.0	-5.1	-2.3	-2.2
34	Motor vehicles and trailers	40.64	9.5	-8.7	29.8	30.2	10.8	-5.3	-9.6	2.5	7.5
35	Other transport equipment n.e.c	18.25	-2.9	3.8	27.7	23.2	11.9	-0.1	5.9	6.4	1.3
36	Furniture	29.97	18.7	7.4	7.1	-7.5	-1.8	-5.1	-13.9	7.4	44.4

Source: Central Statistics Office.

by the World Economic Forum, slightly above its ten-year average of 4.33 points. That helped the country climb to the position of being the 39th most competitive nation in the world, out of the 138 countries that ranked in the report.

A few major trends that explain the growing stature of the Indian industry are summarized below:

India is positioned to be a major beneficiary in the process of the gradual shift taking place in global manufacturing. Specific advantages such as cheaper labour, improved infrastructure, lower costs, and large markets that India is bestowed with are likely to intensify the pace of the shift further. The share of manufacturing value added (MVA) in GDP is showing a rise over the years, albeit at a slower pace.

Globalization and reforms have changed the structure of industry in more ways than one. Globalization has led to the diffusion of industrial production from developed countries to developing nations, which has enabled the disaggregation of the production of individual components. Competitiveness has enabled developing countries to emerge as attractive locations for global corporates to produce certain components that benefit the developed market companies through lower costs and the developing markets with newer opportunities in industrial production. A report of the UNIDO (Industrial Development Report 2009), which examined this aspect, observed that 'where this process has been successful, the resulting so called "trade in tasks" has had a dramatic impact in promoting industrial and economic growth, reducing poverty, and generating social progress'. India has been a beneficiary of the 'trade in tasks' in areas such as information technology, telecommunications, pharma, etc.[4]

Manufacturing in developing economies is highly concentrated, with 15 leading economies accounting for 83 per cent of the total production in 2010, up from 73.2 per cent in 1990. China has tripled its share of the developing countries' MVA over 1990–2010, from 13 per cent in 1990 to 43.3 per cent in 2010. India overtook Mexico and Brazil to become the second leading manufacturer among developing economies with a share of 5 per cent of MVA in 2010.

---

[4] 'Breaking In and Moving Up: New Industrial Challenges for the Bottom Billion and the Middle-Income Countries', United Nations Industrial Development Organization, Industrial Development Report, 2009.

Table 12.4 Share of MVA in GDP, selected years (percentage)

Country	Share of MVA in GDP (At constant 2010 prices)					
	2005	2010	2012	2013	2014	2015
India	15.7	16.8	17.0	16.7	16.8	16.9
China	29.1	31.9	32.4	32.3	32.1	32.5
World	15.3	15.8	15.9	16.0	16.0	16.1

Source: International Yearbook of Industrial Statistics, 2017.

Per capita MVA in India grew from USD 80 (in terms of USD in 2000) in 2005 to USD 99 in 2009 and to USD 298 in 2015; India's share of the world MVA rose from 1.38 per cent to 1.69 per cent during this period. Per capita manufacturing exports rose from USD 77 to USD 124, and the share of manufactured exports to total exports increased from 87.84 per cent to 88.17 per cent.

India's leadership in the manufacturing sector is reflected in industries such as electrical machinery and apparatus, other transport equipment, and basic metals. India accounts for 44 per cent of the developing world MVA in electrical machinery and apparatus, 18 per cent in other transport equipment, and 25 per cent in basic metals. In terms of the world MVA, India's share is 5 per cent with respect to electrical machinery and apparatus and 3 per cent in basic metals. The average MVA in India withstood the impact of global recession by showing resilience in growth. India's exports of manufactured goods rose from USD 26 billion in 1995 to USD 37 billion in 2000, and further to USD 87 billion in 2005 and USD 150 billion in 2009. During 2016–17, India's merchandise exports rose to USD 274.64 billion from USD 262.29 billion in 2015–16.

India's rank in UNIDO's competitive industrial performance index moved up from 51 in 2000 to 42 in 2009 and further to 39 in 2016. Global studies rank India as a country that caught up with the US during 1960 to 2000 in regard to the total factor productivity.

An assessment of the Indian industry by UNIDO[5] captures the essence of industrial growth in India:

Industrial growth averaged 7.1 per cent per annum in the 1980s. It accelerated slightly to 7.6 per cent per year in the first five years

[5] UNIDO (2005), Indian Manufacturing Industry, Technology Status and Prospects, p. 5.

following the beginning of the economic policy reform process in 1991. In the second half of the 1990s, industrial growth trended lower at around 5 per cent per annum. However, growth in industry resumed and accelerated from 2002–3 on the back of rising demand and disposable incomes that took the growth rate of above 8 per cent in 2004–5. The growth rate saw a slow-down again in the aftermath of the global economic and financial crisis and against the backdrop of global recession and financial sector volatility that continued to be in effect. Internal policy inconsistencies and the growing competitiveness with industrial producers in other emerging markets such as China too have contributed to the slowdown of the industrial growth in India. However, its potential remains strong.

According to a FICCI–PwC study named 'India Manufacturing Barometer: Standing Strong':[6]

India is well poised to become the world's fifth largest manufacturer by 2020. Rising labour costs and a transition from investment-led growth in China are presenting another opportunity for India. The current industrial trend of transitioning from assembly-led manufacturing to design-led manufacturing is also an opportunity for India. Besides, the government has also come up with the Digital India initiative, which focuses on three core components: creation of digital infrastructure, delivering services digitally, and increasing digital literacy.

GROWTH OF INDIAN INDUSTRY: AN ASSESSMENT

Against the background of the service sector's prominence in India, studies on Indian industry in regard to growth, structure, efficiency, and productivity evinced the interest of academic research. A study (Kumari 2005) that divided output growth into four

---

[6] FICCI and PWC Strategy (2017), *India Manufacturing Barometer: Standing Strong*, New Delhi, April 2017.

sources (domestic demand expansion, export expansion, import substitution, and intermediate demand expansion due to change in input-output coefficient) found that output growth in the manufacturing industry has mainly been driven by domestic demand expansion, followed by the contribution of export expansion during both pre-liberalization and post-liberalization. However, the contribution of both domestic demand expansion and export expansion has increased after liberalization. A study (Aggarwal and Kumar 2012) on structural change, industrialization, and poverty reduction noted,

> Significantly, India's pattern of growth has not been characterized by a change in the structure of employment towards manufacturing with the share of the structure in total employment stagnating and recently declining despite growth of output. The mismatch between sectoral patterns of value added and employment has led to wide wage differentials across sectors. This raises an important question about the impact of growth on poverty.

IMF's World Economic Outlook published in April 2018,[7] which discussed this issue at length, echoed this concern:

> In many countries, manufacturing appears to have faded as a source of jobs. Its share in employment in advanced economies has been declining for nearly five decades. In developing economies, manufacturing employment has been more stable, but among more recent developers, it seems to be peaking at relatively low shares of total employment and at levels of national income below those in market economies that emerged earlier.

A study (Ray 2012) on selected manufacturing industries in India (iron and steel, aluminum, cement, glass, fertilizers, chemicals, paper and pulp, etc.) during 1979–80 to 2003–4 showed, 'Output growth in selected Indian manufacturing industrial sectors is driven mainly by inputs accumulation while the contribution of total factor productivity growth remains either minimal or negative.

---

[7] World Economic Outlook, *Manufacturing Jobs, Implications for Productivity and Inequality*, International Monetary Fund, April 2018.

A study on the industrial performance during 1991–2008 (Nagaraj 2011) noted:

> In spite of the dismantling of the much criticized 'permit license raj', industrial growth rate has not accelerated, nor has the growth rate of labour intensive consumer goods gone up; but there has been no de-industrialization either, as the critics fear: the shares of industrial employment and output in total have not declined (as had happened in Latin America and Africa after the debt crisis in 1980). The structural transformation of workforce has continued at the same pace after the reforms, though the workforce has gone into services and not manufacturing. Within industry, the incremental workforce has gone into construction. Measured by investment, the reforms were not a setback for industrialization as the manufacturing sectors' share in the total fixed investment has gone up from around 27 per cent in the 1980s to about 40 per cent in the current decade.

GROWTH AND FINANCIAL MARKETS RELATIONSHIP

Right from Walter Bagehot (1873) to Joseph Schumpeter (1912), and John Hicks (1969) to Merton Mellor (1988), the important role of finance has been observed in promoting growth (Ray 2010). Ross Levine (C.Y. Park 2011) identified the functions of the financial sector under five broad categories: (*a*) producing information about potential investment opportunities; (*b*) mobilizing savings to the most productive investment; (*c*) monitoring firms and exerting corporate governance; (*d*) promoting risk diversification and sharing across individuals, firms, and countries; and (*e*) facilitating the exchange of goods and services. Development of the financial sector is envisaged to reduce the cost of information collection, contract enforcement, and transaction, thereby increasing allocative efficiency and promoting economic growth. Financial intermediation can affect growth through three channels (Aziz and Duenwald 2002): (*a*) increasing the marginal productivity of capital by collecting information to evaluate alternative investment projects and by risk sharing; (*b*) reducing the resources absorbed by financial intermediaries (borrowing/lending spreads, commission, and so on), thus increasing the efficiency of financial intermediaries; and (*c*) raising the private saving rate. A recent study on the relationship between financial structures and economic outcomes observed,

> On financial development and growth, there have long been two schools of thought with sharply differing perspectives on the potential importance of finance. One school sees financial intermediation playing a key role in economic activity and growth. Another school believes that the causality is reversed: economies with good growth prospects develop institutions to provide the funds necessary to support the expected growth—the economy leads and finance follows. (IMF 2012)

Studies on the financing pattern of the Indian corporate sector (Beena 2011) during 1990–2009 observed that (*a*) the Indian private sector mobilized a large share of resources through external sources, although an increasing trend in the share of internal financing was observed since 1990; (*b*) borrowings were a major source of external financing; (*c*) the share of resources mobilized through capital market has sharply declined since the mid-1990s; (*d*) Indian acquiring firms mobilized large funds through external sources, although the share of retained profit was quite substantial; and (*e*) revenue foregone through various tax concessions is still found to be a major source of corporate growth during the liberalization period. Studies on the efficiency of the Indian financial system on corporate financing pattern observed that firms were increasingly relying on external funds to finance their investments in the most recent years (Oura 2008).

However, it might not be apt to assess the role of capital markets solely on the basis of resource mobilization. Though studies may have pointed out that capital markets have not provided enough resources to the industry, it could not be overlooked that Indian stock exchanges have over 5,000 companies listed, the highest for any stock market in the world, and provide numerous other benefits, which include:

1. Opportunities to list in public equity markets,
2. A platform for divestment of government stake in public sector undertakings,

3. Secondary market, which provides liquidity to stocks,
4. Trading, which enhances the scope of treasury management of companies,
5. A greater scope for hedging risks through exchange-traded derivatives,
6. Domestic listing a prior requirement for international listings/capital issuance, and
7. Well performing companies forming global indices and attracting investment.

The deepening of the markets went a step further with Bombay Stock Exchange (BSE) (India International Exchange [INX]) and National Stock Exchange (NSE) (International Financial Service Centre [IFSC]) opening international exchanges in the Gujarat International Finance and Technology City (GIFT City).

Development indicators in Indian finance show that the ratio of bank assets to the GDP increased from 75.4 per cent to 96.4 per cent during the same period. The ratio of Non-Bank Financial Companies (NBFCs) assets in the GDP increased steadily from just 8.4 per cent as on 31 March 2006 to 12.9 per cent as on March 31 2015; market capitalization of the stock market was at 86 per cent of the GDP in 2017. Government bonds outstanding as a percentage of the GDP were at 62 per cent and outstanding corporate bonds were at 23 per cent as on 31 March 2017.

The investment scenario too is becoming robust. According to reports, the size of the FDI in India doubled in the last decade to USD 42 billion, forming 1.9 per cent of the GDP, and is expected to reach a level of 2.5 per cent of the GDP in the next five years. With mergers such as Walmart–Flipkart, the pace of the FDI is likely to pick up momentum. In regard to Foreign Institutional Investments (FII), the cumulative flows during 2000–17 amounted to USD 208 billion. The net FII in 2017 amounted to USD 20 billion, mergers and acquisitions (M&A) activity to USD 47 billion, and private equity investments to USD 25 billion. Domestic investments too have been robust, with mutual funds in India receiving USD 20 billion and the initial public offerings in the stock markets mobilizing about USD 12 billion in 2017. Rising portfolio flows and growing investments from the domestic market took the total market capitalization of the India stock markets over the USD 2 trillion level.

Developments in the Indian Financial Sector

A few major developments that have brought Indian finance closer to the resource requirements of the Indian industry include:

- Banking reforms that enabled the entry of new banks and deregulated the interest rate regime. An important addition to the banking landscape in the last few years has been the licensing of two more new private banks (IDFC Bank and Bandhan Bank) and also the creation of specialized banks for payments and small finance.
- Financing to Small and Medium-sized Enterprises (SMEs) was further bolstered with the setting up of Micro Units Development and Refinance Agency (MUDRA) Limited by the government in 2015 for 'funding the unfunded' micro enterprises. MUDRA will refinance all the banks, Micro-Finance Institutions (MFIs), and other lending institutions that are in the business of lending to micro/small business entities engaged in manufacturing, trading, and service activities.
- Capital market reforms ushered in new opportunities in raising equity and debt, which enhanced the scope of resource mobilization and risk management arising from interest rate, currency, and commodities by way of exchange-traded derivatives that proved vital for overcoming the challenges of volatility.
- Liberalization of the foreign financial flows enabled corporates to raise international finance by way of external commercial borrowings (ECBs) and American depository receipts (ADRs)/ Global depositary receipts (GDRs) listed in international exchanges. Also, financial flows in terms of FDI has greatly benefited corporates in terms of new investment flows and the FII investors' evinced interest in the stocks of well-performing companies that had a very distinct and strong impact on the company valuations.
- Additionally, the economic survey 2018–19, released in the background of the government that was re-elected in May 2019 laid strong focus on promoting private capital amongst which

accessing sovereign bond market is also considered. This may further enhance the range of options available to India in international capital.

- Special attention for SMEs led to a focused and targeted lending to this sector with separate capital markets for them in the BSE and NSE whose SME capital market segments are very active in providing the public capital markets access to the SMEs.
- One rapidly expanding area is online/Peer-to-Peer (P2P) lending. Growth for the P2P lending market is projected to reach USD 4–5 billion by 2023. The RBI's guidelines have lent immense credibility to the P2P lending model.
- Private equity markets have begun to take shape following the reforms that provide vital access to finance for those companies and startups that are not yet ready to tap the public capital markets. The value chain in this regard includes angel investors, venture capital firms, and private equity firms that provide resources to new companies in various stages of evolution and growth.
- The startup culture in India, ranked as one of the top startup ecosystems in the world, on the back of venture capital and private equity is gaining rapid pace and momentum. During the three years of 2015–17, private equity pumped in USD 58 billion in over 2000 deals in India (*Forbes* 2018).[8]

A few benefits that the financial sector reforms brought to the industry are explained in Table 12.5.

India is a constituent of the BRICS forum (Brazil, Russia, India, China, and South Africa), which is gaining momentum and pursuing global influence. Along with other BRICS countries, India co-founded the world's newest development finance institution 'New Development Bank', which is poised to play an influential role in promoting development finance from the perspective of the needs and requirements of developing economies. India is also a shareholder in the Asian Infrastructure and Investment Bank promoted by China, which has members from 54 countries.

India has a wide matrix of financial institutions and instruments today that provide functions of wholesale banking, public equity

[8] Private equity fund raising shows no signs of slowing in 2018, 22 January 2018.

Table 12.5 Benefits to industry from the reforms in the financial sector

Nature of the financial sector reform	Specific benefits to the industry
Liberalization of entry and expansion of banks	Range of products and quality of services vastly improved due to competition.
Interest rate deregulation	Better performing companies were able to borrow at prime lending rates, which induced others to scale up the quality of operations.
Liberalization of lending norms	Spurred huge growth in the companies engaged in businesses pertaining to consumer durables, automobiles, and real estate for which obtaining personal finance was made easier and quicker.
Loan targets for priority sector lending	Special allocations ensured adequate resource flows to the vital sectors of the economy, including agriculture, cottage, small, and medium industries, and the corporates dependent on these sectors.
Reforms in the primary capital markets	Enabled growth-oriented companies to access capital markets for initial public offerings/follow-on offerings to raise/enhance capital without restrictions on the issue price.
Reforms in the secondary capital markets	Foreign institutional investors began to show interest in Indian companies that had a positive impact on the liquidity and tradability of shares of companies, leading to better valuations that benefited them significantly.
Reforms in external finance	Issuance of capital in the international markets grew substantially with major companies coming up with GDRs/ADRs and External Commercial Borrowings (ECBs).
Development of the mutual fund industry	Several new institutions in the realm of mutual funds management emerged and their resource flows to the stock markets helped improve the liquidity of the listed stocks.
Introduction of derivatives markets	Enabled corporates to hedge various aspects of risk, including equity, commodities, interest rate, and foreign exchange.
Special focus on SME development	Special concessions for the promotion and development of SMEs. SME Capital Markets set up by the national stock exchanges.
Introduction of structured products	Enabled companies to realize revenues through securitization of assets, leading to better management of the balance sheet.

(cont'd)

Table 12.5 (*cont'd*)

Nature of the financial sector reform	Specific benefits to the industry
Corporate restructuring	Induced corporates to undergo transformation in tune with the challenges of the global markets and pursue mergers and acquisitions.
Sustainable finance	Emphasis on models of sustainable finance led to growth in green finance in India, the size of which grew at a rapid pace with banks and corporates issuing global finance.

Source: Author's presentation.

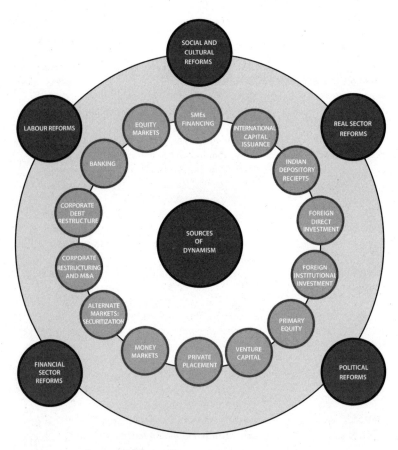

FIGURE 12.2   Sources of dynamism

Source: Author's presentation.

markets, private equity markets, spot and futures exchanges, international borrowing, alternative markets, securitization, specialized institutions, clearing corporations, and structured products markets, which offer important services of access to finance or enable the Indian industry to enhance the efficiency of financial management.

A recent IMF paper sums up the state of Indian finance with a key question, 'Where does the Indian financial sector stand as of mid-2016?' The broad trends seen in Indian finance included (*a*) significant progress in monetary policy management, (*b*) heightened competition in banking sector, (*c*) improvement in contractual savings systems, (*d*) growth of private sector insurance, (*e*) a strong equity market segment with potential growth for debt markets, and (*f*) growth in fund management industry, among others. Along with growth, inclusion too has emerged as a priority. It says, 'India has come a long way from a financially repressive regime to a modern financial sector where public sector financial institutions tend to compete with the private sector financial institutions. The Indian authorities, while reforming the financial sector, had to constantly keep the issues of equity and efficiency in mind' (Mohan and Ray 2017).

FINANCE FOR INDUSTRY

A wide range of financial resources, to which the Indian industry has reach and access, is summarized in Figure 12.3.

The following is a brief description of the aspects of growth of specific sectors in the Indian financial market, which will have an important role in strengthening resource flows to industry.

Banking Sector

Following the liberalization of the banking sector and greater functional autonomy to state-owned banks, a number of services useful for the corporate sector have emerged, which include infrastructure financing (for infrastructure projects), project financing (for greenfield industrial projects), dealer financing (for corporate distribution

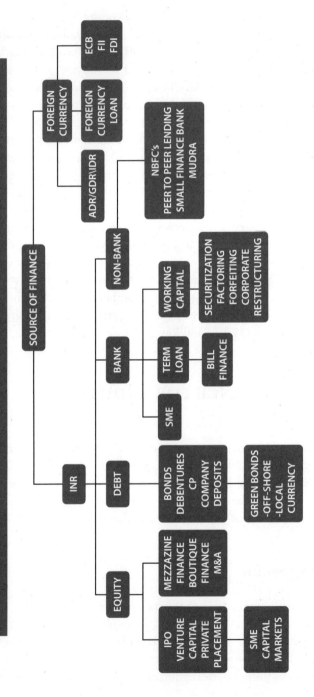

FIGURE 12.3 Sources of finance for industry

Source: Author's presentation.

Table 12.6 Growth in bank credit

	Average (1990–1 to 1999–2000)	Average (2000–1 to 2009–10)	Average (2003–4 to 2007–8)	2008–9	2009–10	2010–11	2011–12	2012–13	2013–14	2014–15	2015–16	2016–17
Bank credit (percentage change)	15.9	21.8	25.5	17.5	16.9	21.5	17.0	14.1	13.9	9.0	10.9	5.1
Non-food credit (percentage change)	15.4	22.4	26.7	17.8	17.1	21.3	16.8	14.0	14.2	9.3	10.9	5.8
Credit–deposit ratio (percentage)	55.1	64.8	68	72.4	72.2	75.7	78.0	77.9	77.8	76.6	77.7	72.9
Credit–GDP ratio (percentage)	20.6	37.7	39.5	49.7	49.5	50	52.8	52.9	53.4	52.5	53.0	51.9

Source: RBI Annual Report, various issues.

networks), channel financing (funding necessities along the supply chain), structured finance (assembling unique credit configurations to meet large industrial and complex infrastructure projects), and equipment leasing (for greenfield projects).

According to the RBI Annual Report, the outstanding bank credit to the commercial sector as on 31 March 2017 stood at INR 84 trillion. As on 31 March 2017, the non-food credit by banks stood at INR 71 trillion. Of the total industry credit (micro and small, medium and large) of INR 27 trillion, 34 per cent was in infrastructure, 16 per cent in basic metals and metal products, and 5 per cent in food processing.

At 5.1 per cent, the growth in bank credit in the financial year 2017 was the slowest in over 60 years, as state-owned banks burdened with bad loans struggled to find safe avenues to lend. The last time the bank credit growth had slowed down to 1.7 per cent was in 1953–4.

With effect from 1 July 2010, the following measures have been evolved to strengthen credit flow to industry—all categories of loans to industries are to be priced only with reference to the base rate; in case of restructured loans, lending below the base rate can be granted for purposes of viability; all loan applications for SME units up to INR 5 lakh to be processed within four weeks; and banks are mandated not to accept collateral security up to INR 10 lakh for loans extended to units in the SME sector; public sector banks have been advised to open at least one specialized branch in each district to assist industrial financing, and so on. In continuing its efforts to enhance the level of access to finance for MSMEs, the government has created a new online platform, namely psbloansin59minutes.com, in which one gets fast in-principle approval for loans from INR 10 lakh to INR 1 crore. Post receiving approval, the loan is expected to be disbursed in 7–8 working days. Union Government sanctioned 27,983 proposals through this portal till 31 March 2019. To provide further boost to bank lending with particular focus on financial inclusion, the RBI has invited applications based on which the two new banks, IDFC Bank and Bandhan Bank, were given licenses to operate.

The banking sector in India witnessed a sharp pressure with the RBI tightening the norms regarding non-performing loans, which led to a huge surge in the non-performing assets of banks with a huge impact on their profitability. The most affected were the public sector banks (PSBs), which have a greater exposure towards the real economy and infrastructure. The combined net loss of 20 PSBs stood at INR 162.72 billion by the end of March 2016, leading to a sharp fall in credit growth.

Non-bank Finance Services

The non-banking finance sector plays a crucial role in broadening the access to financial services, enhancing competition, and diversifying the financial sector. Types of services under non-banking finance include non-banking financial companies, peer-to-peer lending, small finance banks, etc. A non-banking financial company (NBFC) is a company registered under the Companies Act of 1956 and is engaged in the business of loans and advances, acquisition of shares, securities, leasing, hire-purchase, insurance business, and chit business. NBFCs, competitive and complimentary to banks and financial institutions, have registered significant growth in recent years and their contribution to the economy has grown tremendously from 8.4 per cent in 2006 to above 14 per cent in March 2015. The balance sheet of the NBFC sector expanded by 14.5 per cent during 2016–17. Loans and advances increased by 16.4 per cent and investments increased by 11.9 per cent in March 2017. Despite the growth, the NBFCs managed their asset quality better than banks and their financial assets have recorded a healthy growth—with a compound annual growth rate (CAGR) of 19 per cent over the past few years—comprising 13 per cent of the total credit and expected to reach nearly 18 per cent by 2018–19. The NBFCs are typically into the funding of construction equipment, commercial vehicles and cars, gold loans, microfinance, consumer durables, two-wheelers, loan against shares, etc.

The success of the NBFCs can clearly be attributed to their better product lines, lower costs, a wider and effective reach, strong risk management capabilities to check and control bad debts, and better understanding of their customer segments. Going forward, the latent credit demand of an emerging India will allow the NBFCs to fill the gap, especially where traditional banks have been wary to serve. Additionally, improving macroeconomic conditions, higher credit penetration, increased consumption, and disruptive digital trends will allow the NBFC's credit to grow at a higher rate in the coming years.

A peer-to-peer lending model connects borrowers and lenders directly where players charge a registration fee and commission is earned from both lenders and borrowers. There is scope for negotiation of interest rates, which enables borrowers to obtain capital at a lower cost while it provides an opportunity to the investors to earn lucrative returns.

Equity Markets

A wide range of reforms in primary markets (capital issuance) and secondary markets (trading, settlement and payment systems) have taken India to be among the top 20 stock markets in the world in terms of market capitalization. The stock market in India is emerging as competitive, setting a new trend in emerging markets with the active presence and functioning of three national-level stock exchanges: the Bombay Stock Exchange, the National Stock Exchange, and the Metropolitan Stock Exchange.

The stock market in India, in the background of several reforms, has evolved to become a significant source of finance for companies. A number of reforms carried out in primary and secondary markets have completely transformed the functioning of the equity market, making it one of the best in the world in terms of regulation, investor protection, and technology adoption.

The market infrastructure is quite extensive with three national level stock exchanges, 2760 brokers, 1710 foreign institutional investors (as in 2013–14), 19 custodians, two depositories, 189 merchant bankers, seven credit rating agencies, 200 venture capital funds, 204 portfolio managers, 48 mutual funds, and so on.[9] As per the data published by the Prime Database, fundraising via IPOs touched a record high in 2017 with 28 companies raising approximately INR 521.25 billion. Other forms of resource mobilization such as debt offers, rights issues, private placement of debt, and commercial paper were of a sizeable magnitude. Finance and healthcare raised a major portion of the resources during 2015–16, though a large number of industries raised capital from the primary markets.

As many as 153 initial public offerings hit the Indian stock market in 2017, raising USD 11.6 billion, according to an EY report, which said that the activity was expected to continue for 2018 as well. 'India's BSE, NSE, and junior markets recorded a 74 per cent increase in deal numbers in 2017 as compared to 2016,' the report said.

---

[9] Securities and Exchange Board of India, Handbook of Statistics 2016.

Table 12.7 Industry-wise mobilization of resources from capital market (amount in INR crore)

Industry	2010–11		2011–12		2012–13		2013–14		2014–15		2015–16	
	No.	Amount	No.	Amount	No.	Amount	No.	Amount	No.	Amount	No.	Amount
Banking/FIs	18	17,248	20	35,611	7	8,273	14	29,700	7	2,873	–	–
Cement and Construction	3	2,841	2	187	1	9	4	731	7	2,035	6	1,152
Chemical	5	247	–	–	1	9	–	–	1	8	2	72
Electronics	–	–	1	121	–	–	–	–	1	33	–	–
Engineering	5	1,394	1	217	2	74	5	591	1	525	2	373
Entertainment	4	715	1	89	1	12	2	602	6	884	2	21
Finance	3	2,210	10	7,708	16	10,739	26	6,058	28	7,756	17	10,269
Food Processing	1	1,245	–	–	2	13	–	–	2	25	1	400
Healthcare	3	292	1	65	2	210	–	–	–	–	5	1,899
Information Technology	1	170	2	138	1	4	1	19	3	137	5	912
Paper and Pulp	–	–	2	306	–	–	1	28	–	–	–	–
Plastic	–	–	1	11	–	–	3	18	2	8	2	104
Power	4	9,469	–	–	–	–	4	11,702	–	–	3	1,406
Printing	1	52	2	71	–	–	–	–	–	–	1	3
Telecommunication	–	–	–	–	–	–	–	–	–	–	–	–
Textile	3	207	–	–	4	562	3	14	3	388	5	91
Others	40	31,519	28	3,943	31	8,352	26	6,184	26	4,357	57	41,464
Total	91	67,609	71	48,468	68	28,282	89	55,647	88	19,202	108	58,166

Source: Securities and Exchange Board of India, *Handbook of Statistics,* 2016.

Corporate Bonds Market

Debt markets are a vital component of financial markets, particularly for a developing economy such as India. The scope for a corporate bonds market in India is huge in the context of the enormous need for infrastructure development and new projects. However, the corporate bonds market in India has not developed to the extent that it was expected to. As the corporate sector expands and the Indian financial markets get progressively integrated with the rest of the world, there remains a need for a well-developed corporate bonds market. In the first half of 2003, the two national stock exchanges, namely BSE and NSE, set up exclusive debt market segments to promote the growth of exchange-traded bonds market. Though the size of the corporate debt market in India (USD 179 billion) has grown in the recent years, it is still below the levels of China (USD 696 billion outstanding) and Korea (USD 687 billion).

In India, the corporate bonds market has had a less significant growth for decades. According to the SEBI Annual Report of 2016–17, '[the] size of the corporate bonds market is increasing every year, which shows that corporates and borrowers are gradually favoring raising funds through the corporate bonds market. Better transmission of policy rate changes to the bonds market and an increased transparency and price discovery could be possible reasons for a spike in the corporate bonds market.' The Indian bonds market facilitated a fund-raising of INR 6.7 trillion in 2016–17, a 36 per cent jump over the preceding year's figures.

SME Markets: SME Financing

Economic integration and technological breakthroughs warrant the need to make SMEs globally competitive. As per the data released by the Ministry of Micro, Small, and Medium Enterprises (MSMEs), Government of India, there are about 26.1 million units in this sector contributing for 45 per cent of the manufactured output and 8 per cent of the GDP. MSMEs primarily rely on bank finance for their operations. About 30 SMEs from India were listed in the Alternative Investment Market (AIM) of the London Stock Exchange companies in 2011 and

2012. The BSE and the NSE launched SME platforms in 2012, becoming the only two bourses to offer such a segment in the country.

By the end of 2017, more than 100 companies were listed on the NSE's Emerge platform with an aggregate market capitalization of over INR 76 billion. In the BSE's SME platform, more than 200 companies got listed in over five years of its existence.

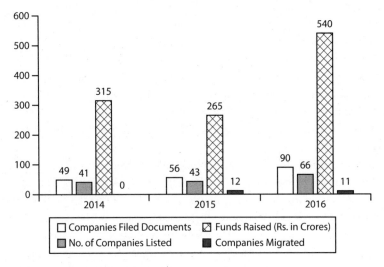

FIGURE 12.4   SME capital markets
Source: BSE/NSE.

Table 12.8 Resources mobilized through the SME platform

Year	Total	
2007–8	No. of Issues	Amount (INR billion)
2012–13	24	2.39
2013–14	37	3.17
2014–15	39	2.78
2015–16	50	3.79
Apr 15–Dec 15	32	2.78
Apr 16–Dec 16	48	7.01

Source: SEBI.
Note: The SME platforms at BSE and NSE commenced operations on 13 March 2012.

International Capital Issuance: ADRs/GDRs/ECBs

Indian companies began to access global financial markets in a big way to raise resources for domestic expansion of business as also international acquisition of business. Companies that accessed global capital markets in the form of ADRs/GDRs during 1992–3 raised resources of USD 30.1 billion. ECBs, which were about USD 10 billion in 1991, rose to USD 104 billion with their share in the total external debt of the country increasing from 12 per cent in 1991 to 30 per cent in 2012. During the four-year period of 2008–12, Indian companies made international investments of USD 60 billion, with a major chunk of it being in the realm of manufacturing (40 per cent) and financial services (29.4 per cent). Corporates in the hotels, hospitals, and software sectors permitted ECB up to USD 100 million per financial year.

The number of Indian companies raising funds through GDRs/ADRs has fallen significantly in the last few years. In the 1990s and early 2000s, many Indian companies, especially those belonging to new sectors such as information technology, opted for the ADR/GDR route with an objective of getting a better valuation for the shares of companies and access to global investors. In fact, in the year ended 31 March 2017, not a single Indian company opted for ADRs/GDRs.

Indian Depository Receipts

Indian depository receipts (IDRs) are an instrument denominated in the Indian rupee in the form of depository receipts created by a domestic depository against the underlying equity of the issuing company to enable foreign companies to raise funds from the Indian securities markets. The size of an IDR issue should not be less than INR 0.5 billion. The Indian securities market saw its first IDR from Standard Chartered Plc. in May 2010 for an issue size of USD 240 million. This instrument is yet to catch up in a big way.

Although IDRs form a significant step towards the internationalization of the Indian securities market, they have not become popular till date. The potential of this instrument (IDRs) may not be realized till the government addresses several issues that are currently acting as barriers—the extant legal framework does not permit insurance companies to participate in the IDRs program, the process of conversion of IDRs into underlying equity shares is very lengthy and cumbersome, and the tax treatment of IDRs is not on par with other securities. Till these issues are resolved, the Standard Chartered IDR would probably remain the one and the only IDR to ever be listed on Indian bourses. Indian bonds issued in local currency in international markets, such as Masala Bonds, too are catching up rapidly in regard to investor interest with multi-lateral financial institutions such as International Finance Corporation issuing it first in 2014 and India's premier institutions such as HDFC coming up with a successful issuance of these bonds in 2017.

Foreign Direct Investment and Foreign Institutional Investment

Indian companies gained significant benefit from the global financial flows in the form of foreign direct investment (FDI) and foreign institutional investment (FII). The level of FDI and FII received into the industry was just USD 4 billion and USD 1.8 billion respectively in 2000–1. In the next 15 years, it rose rapidly to reach USD 45.0 billion and USD 40.9 billion respectively by 2014–15. (See Table 12.9)

On 28 August 2017, the Department of Industrial Policy and Promotion (DIPP) issued the updated and revised Foreign Direct Investment Policy 2017–18 (FDI Policy 2017) that envisaged the removal of multiple layers of bureaucracy and the processing of proposals for FDI under the government-approval route in a more streamlined, positive, and expeditious manner.

Private Markets

Private equity refers to any type of equity investment in an asset in which the equity is not freely tradable on a public stock market. There has been a rise in private equity, partly due to the smaller impact of the economic crisis on India and partly due to better prospects for

Table 12.9 Year-wise FDI and FII flows into India

Year	FDI Flows into India (in million USD)	Investment by FII (net) (in million USD)
2000–1	4,029	1,847
2001–2	6,130	1,505
2002–3	5,035	377
2003–4	4,322	10,918
2004–5	6,051	8,686
2005–6	8,961	9,926
2006–7	22,826	3,225
2007–8	34,843	20,328
2008–9	41,873	(–)15,017
2009–10	37,745	29,048
2010–11	34,847	29,422
2011–12	46,556	16,812
2012–13	34,298	27,582
2013–14	36,046	5,009
2014–15	45,148	40,923
2015–16	55,559	(–)4,016
2016–17	60,082	7,735
2017–18 (upto Sep 2017)	33,749	14,359
From April 2000 to Sep 2017	518,100	208,669

Source: RBI's Bulletin, May 2017. (Table no. 34: Foreign investment inflows)

economic growth. The proportion of investors' total private equity commitments is showing a positive trend. The size of private equity was 499 deals amounting to USD 14 billion in 2007; 481 deals with a value of USD 11 billion in 2008; and 460 deals with a value of USD 10 billion in 2011. India held a major share in the deal value among the six major Asian regions in 2010, with the momentum continuing in the next year. This trend continued and, as a result, private equity investments in India touched a record high of USD 16.8 billion in 2015 (across 661 deals), 16 per cent higher than the previous high of USD 14.5 billion (across 529 deals) recorded in 2007 and a whopping

50 per cent higher than the USD 11.2 billion (across 530 deals) invested during the previous year.

Venture Capital Financing

Venture capital (VC) has developed as an important intermediary in the Indian financial markets, providing capital to firms that might otherwise have difficulties in attracting finance. These firms are typically small and young, plagued by high levels of uncertainty. There is a severe problem of asymmetry of information that makes the investment risky and therefore retail investors are generally not involved in VC investments. There was no organized form of VC investing activities till late 1980s and early 1990s, when the World Bank encouraged and provided funds for the development of VC investing activities in India. Over the years, VC funds have proliferated and investments by means of VC have also shown remarkable progress.

As evident from the above trend, VC investment has bounced back in India, even as the number of completed financings has dropped. Defying

Table 12.10 Venture capital investment by year

Year	Amount (INR billion)
2007	282
2008	339
2009	420
2010	478
2011	568
2012	555
2013	695
2014	710
2015	728
2016*	824
2017*	883

Source: Indian Private Equity Trend Report: Venture Intelligence.

Note: * stands for estimates.

the global trend of VC investment being concentrated on proven, later-stage companies, corporate financiers as well as VCs—both foreign and domestic—have shown a significant interest in the Indian early-stage and seed deals. Indian arms of global VC firms, in particular, are choosing to back strong 2- to 3-year-old companies instead of more mature companies, with an eye to making a higher profit upon exit. Looking at the Indian scenario, a higher volume of small deals is expected as companies and VCs alike have become more cautious about where and with whom to partner. Due to the increasing maturity in business models and technology, Indian startup companies with a clear technology-based offering have been the highest beneficiaries of VC investments. FinTech, edtech, healthtech, and other consumer-tech companies are still the favorites.

Private Placement of Debt

Raising money through public equity markets takes considerable time as it requires numerous approvals from the regulatory institutions. Private placement enables companies to raise money at a shorter notice by adhering to certain guidelines. When a company makes an issue of securities to a select group of persons, not exceeding 49, and the issue is neither a rights issue nor a public issue, it is called private placement. It can be of two types: (*a*) preferential allotment:

Table 12.11 Private placements over the years

Year	Private placements (INR billion)
2007–8	1,180
2008–9	1,730
2009–10	2,010
2010–11	2,180
2011–12	2,610
2012–13	3,610
2013–14	2,760
2014–15	4,040
2015–16	4,800
2016–17	6,400

Source: SEBI, various years.

Table 12.12 Resources mobilized through qualified institutional placements over the years

| Year | Total placements | |
2007–8	No. of Issues	Amount (INR billion)
2010–11	59	258.50
2011–12	16	21.63
2012–13	45	159.96
2013–14	17	136.63
2014–15	42	293.85
2015–16	24	145.88
2016–17	22	138.71

Source: SEBI.
Note: Figures pertain to placements at NSE, BSE, and both.

when a listed company issues shares or convertible securities to a select group of persons in terms of provisions of Chapter XIII of SEBI (DIP) guidelines, or (*b*) qualified institutional placement (QIP): when a listed issuer issues equity shares or securities convertible into equity shares to qualified institutional buyers only, in terms of provisions of Chapter XIIIA of SEBI (DIP) guidelines. Private placements showed sharp growth in the recent period.

The domestic QIP market, the development of which is a more convenient and cheaper method for both the issuer and the investor, has been seeing a lot of foreign participation. The amount of resources mobilized through the QIPs has shown a lot of fluctuations over the years. (Table 12.12)

Money Market Instruments: Commercial Paper

Money market instruments, such as commercial paper (CP) and certificates of deposit (CD), have provided avenues for corporates to manage their short-term liquidity mismatches. Issuance norms and maturity profiles of money market instruments such as CP and CDs have been modified in tune with the changing market conditions. In respect of CP, the preferred maturity ranges from 6 months to one year. Non-banking financial companies, such as leasing and financing companies, are the major issuers of CP. CP is an unsecured money market instrument issued in the form of a promissory note. It was introduced in India in 1990 with a view to enable highly rated corporate borrowers to diversify their sources of short-term borrowings and to provide an additional instrument to investors. Subsequently, primary dealers and satellite dealers were also permitted to issue CPs to enable them to meet their short-term funding requirements for their operations. A total of 14,874 issues of CP took place during 2003–4 to 2012–13, amounting to INR 9,093.21 billion. Whereas, during 2014–15, CP borrowings stood at INR 15260 billion.

The RBI introduced the Commercial Paper Directions, 2017 on 10 August 2017. The primary purpose of the Directions is to regulate CPs accepted as deposits by non-banking companies. The Directions supersede previous directions such as the Non-Banking Companies (acceptance of deposits through CP) Directions 1989, which had been amended in 1996, 1998, 2000, and further in 2012 (2012 Guidelines). The underlying theme of the new Directions is focused on enhanced disclosure measures, while attempting at the same time to ease the rigid eligibility conditions which previously restricted the issue of CP. The Directions also widen the scope of issue of CP by allowing more entities to be eligible as issuers as well as investors.

Alternative Markets: Securitization

Securitization as a financial instrument has been in practice in India since the early 1990s, essentially as a device of bilateral acquisitions of portfolios of finance companies and banks. Securitization has traditionally offered banks with a key source of long-term funding, thereby allowing for an improved balance sheet management. Prior to the global financial crisis, benign economic and financial conditions fueled an explosion in securitization issuance. Capital flight and illiquidity infected the wider market for collateralized products and, consequently, securitization issuance slumped in recent

Table 12.13 Trends in structured finance volumes (INR billion)

Type	2011–12	2012–13	2013–14	2014–15	2015–16
ABS (Asset-backed securities)	273.4	272.3	235	163.3	246.9
MBS (Mortgage-backed securities)	76.8	30.3	52.9	8.4	2.7
Total retail securitization	350.2	302.6	288	171.7	249.6
Loan sell-offs	22.2	–	–	–	–
Others	6.4	–	–	–	–
Total	378.8	302.6	288	171.7	249.6

Source: ICRA's estimate.

years. The securitization market in India is driven, on the supply side, by the growth of retail loan portfolios in banks and NBFCs and, on the demand side, by the increased participation of mutual funds, particularly at the short end, insurance companies, and banks to meet their priority sector lending targets. Asset-backed securities (ABS) is the largest securitization class driven by the growing retail loan portfolios of banks. Most of the securities are acquired with the intention to hold to maturity. Securitization registered a high growth in 2008 but later showed a slowdown.

Corporate Restructuring

Corporate restructuring is a process of redesigning one or more aspects of a company for achieving certain objectives and outcomes. Examples of restructuring include: (a) conversion of a partnership firm into a limited company (corporatization); (b) pure asset sale or pure liability transfer (subsidiarization); (c) conversion of a company into a limited liability partnership (buyback of shares); and (d) takeover of a company. The size of corporate restructuring has surged since 2008 as can be seen from the increasing number of companies undergoing this process after that year. Specialized financial firms extend advisory and financial services support to the corporate restructuring initiatives.

Mergers and Acquisitions

Mergers and Acquisitions (M&A), a part and extension of corporate restructuring, are mainly driven by strategic initiatives of companies to achieve economies of scale, both from geographical and product-offering perspectives. India witnessed big ticket M&A activity with acquisition of overseas companies by Indian companies as also overseas companies taking over Indian companies. Banks and specialized financial institutions provide resources for M&A initiatives in different forms.

In 2005, the number of M&A deals in India were 1,107, amounting to USD 30.7 billion. By 2012, the number of deals stood at 977, but the deal value amounted to USD 34.8 billion.

In 2016–17, India saw a record number of M&A deals as the economy showed positive signs of recovery, companies went for asset sales, and balance sheet repair was underway. Some of the big-ticket M&A deals in 2017 were Rosneft–Essar oil, Idea–Vodafone, and Airtel–Telenor, with a total worth of USD 77.6 billion, as compared to USD 50.6 billion in the year 2016. In 2018, the deal value reached USD 30 billion, in addition to the USD 16 billion deal of Walmart–Flipkart. The robust M&A momentum is expected to continue in the coming years owing

Table 12.14 Top M&A deals in India in 2017 and 2018

S. No.	Acquirer	Target	Value (USD billion)
1.	Rosneft, Trafigura and United Capital	Essar Oil	12.9
2.	HDFC Standard Life Insurance*	Max Life Insurance	9.73
3.	Reliance Communication	Aircel	7.3
4.	Ultra Tech Cement	Jaiprakash Associates' Cement Assets	2.45
5.	Nirma	Lafarge	1.4
6.	Walmart	Flipkart	16

Source: VCCEdge.
Note: *Deals involved a merger of the companies. Only one of the top five involved an overseas buyer.

to the positive macroeconomic outlook of the country, a sustained focus on reforms by the government amidst an optimistic investor sentiment, and the government's focus to improve the business and investment climate in the country. With scale expansion becoming a critical element of India's corporate strategy agenda, consolidation is likely to dominate the M&A agenda across sectors.

Corporate Debt Restructuring and Strategic Debt Restructuring

Corporate debt restructuring (CDR) is a specialized institutional mechanism for restructuring large exposures involving more than one lender under consortium/multiple banking arrangements. Financial restructuring for corporates can take many forms: rescheduling (extension of maturities), lower interest rates, debt for equity swaps, debt forgiveness, indexing of interest payments to earnings, and so on. However, it is now being felt that the CDR mechanism is no longer relevant to the current situation of mounting bad loans.

With rising non-performing assets (NPAs) or stressed loans of banks, the RBI introduced the Strategic Debt Restructuring (SDR) Scheme in 2015, by way of which banks had the option to convert outstanding loans and interest into equity shares.

However, as per a recent move, the RBI has released a new overarching framework for bad loan resolution to be used across the Indian banking sector. The new rules prescribe a strict 180-day timeline over which banks must agree on a resolution plan. And if they fail to do so, large stressed accounts must immediately be referred for resolution under the Insolvency and Bankruptcy Code (IBC). This means that schemes such as CDR and SDR will no longer exist.

LOOKING AHEAD

The world has changed much after the global financial crisis of 2008. In these 10 years, as an outcome of the crisis, the world has become more restricted with rising protectionist tendencies, limits on free movement of labour, greater watch on the flow of capital, hardening of tariff rates, and the focus of developed countries moving to domestic concerns rather than the overall well-being of the world economy and its stability.

It becomes important for India to harness all its potential to strengthen the growth of industry and, in this regard, reform and refine the financial system. Recent studies have showed that only the depth per se of the financial system does not lead to growth and stability. It is equally important that the financial system should be relevant to the needs and requirement of the real economy. India needs to strengthen its primary capital markets that could help companies raise risk capital, develop private debt capital markets, strengthen the corporate debt market, and expand the avenues of resource mobilization. Recent evidence from and experiences of the developing world offer India unique insights on shaping the right policy that would work best for the interests of the country.

Notwithstanding the rise of India on the global industrial map and its growing stature as one of the leading manufacturers in the world, it shows certain major limitations in terms of a lower and stagnating share in the GDP, which does not augur well for a developing country in its growth perspective as also its sub-optimal performance as compared to several other developed and developing countries.

Today, India is the sixth largest manufacturing nation. Its manufacturing sector accounted for 17 per cent of the GDP in 2016 but has remained stagnant at this level for last few years, whereas strong manufacturing economies have more than 20 per cent of their GDP coming from this sector. As per the World Bank report, some countries where the GDP from manufacturing was high in 2016 were Thailand (27 per cent), Germany (23 per cent), Ireland (35 per cent), Korea Republic (29 per cent), and Malaysia (22 per cent). Recent initiatives of the government such as 'Make-in-India' are envisaged to increase the share of manufacturing in the GDP to 25 per cent. The second version of Make-in-India is on the anvil to consolidate the ground for further growth in selected manufacturing sectors. Besides, India has a number of well-known factors to its favor, including a huge and growing market, a large workforce with diverse skills, demographic dividend, English-speaking professionals (scientists and engineers), research and development centers of top global multinationals, and the world's third-largest technology startup base. Along with this, a promotion in rank in the ease of doing business and a new industrial policy promoting smart manufacturing underway are positive steps in this regard.

At the same time, there are certain challenges before this sector in attaining global leadership. Today, global manufacturing landscape is being transformed by digital technologies such as the 'internet of things' and robotics, collectively called the 'Fourth Industrial Revolution' or 'Industry 4.0'. In today's world, digital technologies are key to unlocking competitiveness. Huge efficiency and productivity gains are being realized through cost reductions, quality improvements, customizations, and a quantum leap in performance. However, adoption of such digital technologies in India is still in its infancy and it has become important to embrace such technologies proactively to achieve the target of becoming a global manufacturing hub. Also, India's challenges include issues relating to infrastructure (physical and digital), skill gaps, innovation ecosystem, public-private partnership, support for MSMEs, data security and privacy, and a favorable regulatory framework. To overcome all these challenges, collaborative efforts by the government, industry, R&D institutions, and financing institutions are required, which would bring about a manufacturing revolution and enhanced competitiveness.

Various policy documents state that manufacturing in India needs to grow at around 20 per cent a year to sustain the GDP growth rate of above 9 per cent. The National Manufacturing Policy 2012, the New Industrial Policy in the making, and the development of industrial corridor projects and smart cities are envisaged to support a strong growth. At present, banks have been the largest funding institutions for infrastructure development, which may find it difficult to maintain the same pace and momentum in view of their asset liability mismatches and increasing NPAs. Limited access to long-term funds has a bearing on the sustained growth potential of the industry. The government has taken certain measures to boost long-term investments, such as hiking the automatic limits of the Euro Commercial Borrowings, refinancing of rupee loans through ECBs, allowing high net-worth individuals to invest in infra-debt funds, credit enhancement through guarantees, etc. Simultaneously, the development of bonds and currency derivatives markets is taking place in a sizeable manner. Further, the FDI norms are relaxed for certain sectors to bring in global financial flow to India.

Against this background, it is imperative that reforms continue at a pace that will strengthen the stimulants to growth. On the finance side, the major challenges would be to expand the size and significance of key segments in terms of bank assets, new capital issuance, product innovation, design of new instruments, special focus on SME development, conducive environment for global expansion, etc. The priority of the industry is to pursue productivity, global competitiveness, quality and efficiency, digitization of certain processes, etc. In addition, the industry should adopt a global market-oriented framework that brings it in easy reach of global finance. At the same time, the government and industry should head to brace for eventualities arising from growing trade conflicts in the recent period specially between US and China, the impact of which will have ramification on emerging markets such as India. This calls for enhancing the competitiveness of Indian industry and trade. Given the great scope that exists for Indian finance and industry to grow and support each other, the combination could emerge as a potent and powerful instrument in taking India towards the next generation of growth and earn a place of pride in the global economic community.

References

Aggarwal, A. and N. Kumar (2012). 'Structural Change, Industrialization and Poverty Reduction: The Case of India'. Development Papers 1206, South and South West Asia Office. Bangkok, Thailand: United Nations Economic and Social Commission for Asia and the Pacific (UNESCAP).

Asian Development Bank (ADB) (2012). *Asia Bond Monitor*. Manila, Philippines: ADB.

Aziz, J. and C. Duenwald (2002). 'Growth-Financial Intermediation Nexus in China'. IMF Working Paper No. WP/02/94. Washigton DC: IMF.

Banga, R. and A. Das (2012). *Twenty Years of India's Liberalization: Experiences and Lessons*. New Delhi: UNCTAD and Center for WTO Studies, United Nations.

Beena, P.L. (2011). 'Financing Pattern of Indian Corporate Sector under Liberalization: With Focus on Acquiring Firms Abroad'. Working Paper

440, Transnational Corporations Review. United Kingdom: Centre for Development Studies, pp. 76–86.

Deutsche Bank Research (2007). 'India's Capital Markets: Unlocking the Door to Future Growth', Deutsche Bank Research Paper, India Special, Singapore, 14 February 2007.

Government of India (GOI) (2012). *Fact Book*, Department of Economic Affairs. New Delhi: Ministry of Finance.

———— (2017). 'Industrial Policy: A Discussion Paper'. Department of Industrial Policy and Promotion. New Delhi: Ministry of Commerce and Industry.

International Monetary Fund (2012). 'Changing Global Financial Structures: Can they Improve Economic Outcomes?' Global Financial Stability Report, October 2012.

Kumari, A. (2005). 'Liberalization and Sources of Industrial Growth in India: An Analysis Based on Input-Output Approach'. Delhi: Institute of Economic Growth, University of Delhi Enclave, North Campus.

Mohan, R. (2008). 'The Growth Record of the Indian Economy, 1950–2008: A Story of Sustained Savings and Investment'. Keynote address by Dr Rakesh Mohan, Deputy Governor, RBI, at the conference organized by the Institute of Economic Growth, New Delhi, on 14 February 2008.

Mohanty, M.S. and P. Turner (2010). 'Banks and Financial Intermediation in Emerging Asia: Reforms and New Risks'. BIS Working Papers No. 313, Bank for International Settlements.

Mohanty M.S., G. Schnabel, and P. Garcia-Luna, (2012). 'Banks and Aggregate Credit: What is New?'. BIS Papers No. 28.

Nagaraj, R. (2011). *Industrial Performance, 1991–2008: A Review in Indian Development Report*. New Delhi: Oxford University Press, pp. 45–7.

Oura, Hiroko (2008). 'Financial Development and Growth in India: A Growing Tiger in a Cage?' IMF Working Paper No. WP/08/79. Asia and Pacific Department: International Monetary Fund.

Park, C.Y. (2011). 'Asian Financial System: Development and Challenges'. ADB Economics Working Paper Series. Manila, Philippines: Asian Development Bank.

Rakesh, Mohan and Partha Ray (2017). 'Indian Financial Sector: Structure, Trends and Turns'. Working Paper No. 17/7. Washington DC: International Monetary Fund, p. 32.

Ray, Sarbapriya (2012). 'Growth of Industrial Production in Selected Indian Manufacturing Industries: Is it Productivity Driven or Input Accumulated?'. *Industrial Engineering Letters* 2(1): 22–33. Department of Commerce, Shyampur Siddeshwari Mahavidyalaya, University of Calcutta.

Ray, Tridip (2010). *Financial Development and Economic Growth: A Review of Literature*. Institute for Studies in Industrial Development, New Delhi.

Reserve Bank of India (RBI) (2013). *Macroeconomic and Monetary Developments Third Quarter Review, 2012–13*. Mumbai: RBI.

―――― (2016). *Handbook of Statistics*. Mumbai: SEBI.

―――― (2017). *RBI's Bulletin 2017*. Mumbai: RBI.

Securities and Exchange Board of India (SEBI) (2012). *Handbook of Statistics*. Mumbai: SEBI.

Shukla, Rashmi (2015). 'Corporate Financing in India: Some Stylized Facts of an Emerging Economy'. *International Journal of Management Excellence* 5(2): 618. Indore: Indian Institute of Management.

United Nations Industrial Development Organization (2005). *Indian Manufacturing Industry: Technology Status and Prospects*. Vienna: WEO, p. 5.

―――― (2009). 'Banking In and Moving Up: New Industrial Challenges for the Bottom Billion and the Middle-Income Countries'. *Industrial Development Report*. Washington DC: WEO, p. vii.

―――― (2011). 'Industrial Energy Efficiency for Sustainable Wealth Creation: Capturing Environmental, Economic and Social Dividends'. *Industrial Development Report*. Vienna: UNIDO, p. 141.

―――― (2016). 'Non-Banking Finance Companies: The Changing Landscape'. ASSOCHAM and PwC Report. Washington DC: WEO.

―――― (2017). *International Yearbook of Industrial Statistics 2017*. Vienna: UNIDO.

―――― (2017). *World Manufacturing Production Statistics for Quarter II, 2017*. Vienna: UNIDO.

―――― (2017). *World Manufacturing Production Statistics for Quarter III, 2017*. Vienna: UNIDO.

―――― (2018). 'Demand for Manufacturing: Driving Inclusive and Sustainable Industrial Development'. *Industrial Development Report*. Vienna: UNIDO.

World Economic Outlook (WEO) (2017). *World Economic Outlook (WEO) Update: A Shifting Global Economic Landscape*. Washington DC: WEO.

―――― (2018). 'ARCs Headed for a Structural Shift'. ASSOCHAM-CRISIL Joint Report. Washington DC: WEO.

―――― (2019). Competitive Industrial Performance Report 2018. Vienna: UNIDO.

World Bank, The (2017). Available at www.data.worldbank.org. Last accessed on 12 June 2019.

CHAPTER 13

···

THE FINANCIAL SECTOR IN INDIA

an overview

···

RAJESH CHAKRABARTI

We do indeed live in the age of financial capitalism. We should not regret that. Regulations and restrictions can and should be placed on financial institutions to help them function in the best interests of society, but the underlying logic and power of these institutions remains central to their role. Financial institutions and financial variables are as much a source of direction and an ordering principle in our lives as the rising and setting sun, the seasons, and the tides.

—Robert Shiller (2012)

WHAT IS A FINANCIAL SYSTEM?

In order to appreciate the Indian financial system, it is best to first lay down the nature of financial systems in general, to delineate the expectations and challenges that the system in India faces. The financial sector in any country relates to the economy it serves, much like the manner in which the circulatory system in the human body serves the entire organism. It is the job of the circulatory system—consisting of the heart, the blood, and the miles of intricate vessel network—to draw nourishment from the intestines and oxygen from the lungs and relentlessly supply each cell of the body with these. Similarly, it is the task of the financial system to pick up the tiny specks of surplus that appear throughout the economy—in households spanning the entire geography, in businesses in various sectors, and sometimes even in government—and channel it to the best investment opportunity.

The circulatory system cannot be held responsible for death from starvation or asphyxiation, for the supply of food and oxygen are not its responsibility. And yet, its criticality is manifest in the fact that if left unattended, a heart attack can kill a person in a few minutes—the immediate cause of death not being that the blood had stopped flowing, but that the brain had been starved of precious oxygen for too long. The financial system is equally critical. While, in itself, it neither generates the surplus nor creates busy opportunities (outside the financial sector), a collapse of the financial sector can bring the entire economy to a complete halt, push a society to anarchy, and cause severe economic damage that could take years to mend. The stability of the financial system is therefore no less critical for the health of the economy than is cardiac health for the longevity of an individual. For an economy to survive and thrive, it is imperative that the financial system ceaselessly transports capital from the savers to the investors and brings back the returns of the investment—in the form of dividend and interest—to the ultimate suppliers of capital.

Carrying the circulatory system analogy a little further, in all countries around the world, two systems compete with and complement each other in fulfilling this circulatory role—the banking system and the financial markets. While the two channels are increasingly getting intertwined in the institutions that form part of the arteries, they differ in a fundamental way—in their style of working and information dissemination. Banks are, by their very nature, relational in their dealings while markets specialize in faceless, arm's length, and contractual transactions. Rarely is the financial flow balanced between the two channels. Some countries—notably the USA and the UK—are market dominated while others—including Germany and Japan—see a greater role for banks. The causes of this difference have puzzled economists for decades and continue to do so, though the accepted explanation today—thanks to the work of Andrei Shleifer and his co-authors—is that it is the level of investor protection in the legal system that determines which artery is more throbbing, with greater protection leading to more vibrant markets.

While the primary job of the financial system is to bridge the gap between savers and investors, in doing so it fulfills several other roles. In making the twain meet, the system must ensure that varying risk appetites, size needs, information asymmetry, as well as planning horizons and liquidity needs are reconciled at the two ends, not to speak of geographical distance. Here is where various financial institutions and products—including the oft-dreaded derivatives—play their role.

Finally, the stability of a financial system is as solid as the public faith in it. Whether it is banks or financial markets, the fact that the system functions only on the basis of complete consent, indeed eagerness, of savers to hand over their hard-earned savings to complete strangers, underlines the need for regulatory practices that are not just prudent but are perceived to be so, in order to sustain the throughput. In the ultimate analysis, of course, this faith rests of the ability of the country's legal and judicial system to enforce and maintain the sanctity of contracts.

It is with this background that we can approach the task of understanding and assessing the Indian financial system.

THE INDIAN FINANCIAL SECTOR—A SYSTEMIC ASSESSMENT

The World Economic Forum (WEF) provides an assessment of the relative financial development of 60 countries—ranging from the Organization for Economic Co-operation and Development (OECD) countries to Nigeria and Bangladesh—in its annual Financial Development Report (WEF 2011). In its 2011 rankings, India figured at a rank of 36 with an overall score of 3.29 on a seven-point scale where the range for the 60 countries was from 2.44 to 5.16. The underlying approach for this evaluation is a seven-dimensional rating system presented in Table 13.1. There is an input to output progression

Table 13.1 Financial development index for India

Financial Development Index 2011		
	Rank (out of 60)	Score
2011 Index	36	3.3
1st pillar: Institutional environment	54	3.1
2nd pillar: Business environment	54	3.4
3rd pillar: Financial stability	47	4.0
4th pillar: Banking financial services	43	3.1
5th pillar: Non-banking financial services	5	4.2
6th pillar: Financial markets	29	2.3
7th pillar: Financial access	47	2.8

Source: WEF (2011).
Note: Score is on a 1–7 scale.

in the dimensions. The first three criteria—institutional environment, business environment, and financial stability—constitute the 'factors, policies and institutions' set, an area where India performs particularly poorly. In both kinds of environment measures, India is at the threshold of the worst decile, confirming findings from other sources such as the World Bank's Ease of Doing Business indicators that the socio-legal foundations of the financial system in India are quite poor.

The second set—'financial intermediation'—comprising banking and non-banking financial services and financial markets, however, shows a much better relative performance. This seems to suggest that the volume of transactions supported by the system is actually larger than what one would expect given the strength of its foundations.

The last measure, financial access, is an output variable in the sense that it is a key feature desired from the system. Here too India finishes at the verge of the bottom of 20 per cent of the countries, pulled down mostly by low penetration by bank branches and ATMs (automated teller machines) and buoyed to some extent by micro-finance activity, which, of late, is experiencing severe turmoil.

In terms of the relative size of the financial sector in India, financial assets amounted to 228 per cent of GDP in 2009 as opposed to 539 per cent for UK, 399 per cent for USA, 224 per cent for Thailand, and 102 per cent for Pakistan. Of the financial assets, equity markets accounted for 41 per cent, bank deposits for 31 per cent, and public debt for 23 per cent. In terms of its structure (relative dominance bank versus markets) and efficiency, Table 13.2, taken from Allen et al. (2012), indicates that India has a greater relative dominance of financial markets as opposed to banks when compared to a broad set of emerging market countries. In terms of efficiency too, the Indian financial system (banks and markets together) perform better than its counterparts in other emerging market countries. However, as its comparison with developed countries shows, it has significant room for improvement.

It is perhaps relevant to note here that the Indian financial system—in the sense of the modern Western institutions, not dating back to *hundies* (a form of credit instrument or IOU developed in medieval India) and other indigenous practices but dating as far back to at least Kautilya—is one of the oldest ones in the colonial world. The oldest Asian stock exchange, for instance, is the Bombay Stock Exchange which predates the Tokyo Stock Exchange. At Independence in 1947, India inherited a fairly developed financial system, complete with legal codes for companies and banks to function.

Nevertheless, the Indian financial system virtually re-booted during the liberalization process that started in 1991 and continues to this day. The transformation in the financial system brought about by liberalization has been so vast that it practically rendered the pre-liberalization history irrelevant. For instance, the primary stock market regulator, the Securities and Exchange Board of India (SEBI), was empowered after the reforms. The leading stock exchange of the country transacting over 95 per cent of trades today, the National Stock Exchange (NSE), and the second largest bank, ICICI Bank, are both children of reforms, not to speak of the vibrant mutual fund and insurance industries that appeared a little over a decade ago, together with derivatives trading that is a bigger market than equities. A closed system has gradually opened up to foreign participation since liberalization, with foreign institutional investors emerging as an important investor category in equity markets. Krishnan (2011) provides an informative contrast between the pre-liberalization state of the markets and those that prevail today. Consequently, India's financial depth (financial assets/GDP) has grown steadily from slightly over 100 in the 1990s to more than double the figure by the end of the first decade of the new century.

Table 13.2 Financial system structure in India: Bank vs. markets

This table compares financial markets and banking sector of the Indian financial system with those of other emerging countries and LLSV country groups (sorted by legal origins). All the measures are taken from Levine (2002) or calculated from the World Bank Financial Database using the definitions in Levine (2002). We use 2005 figures for all countries. The figures for other emerging countries and for all LLSV country groups are weighted averages (with the countries' GDPs in 2005 as the weights).

Measures	Size of Banks and Markets				Structure Indices: Markets vs. Banks**				Financial Development*** (banking and market sectors)		
	Bank credit/ GDP	Bank Over-head cost/ Bank assets	Value Traded/ GDP	Markets cap./GDP	Structure Activity	Structure Size	Structure Efficiency	Structure Regulatory	Finance Activity	Finance Size	Finance Efficiency
	Panel A: India and Other Large Emerging Markets (EMs)										
India	0.37	0.02	0.56	0.60	0.43	0.49	-4.44	10.00	-1.57	-1.51	3.30
Argentina (F)	0.10	0.08	0.09	0.30	-0.12	1.07	-4.95	7.00	-4.70	-3.51	0.13
Brazil (F)	0.29	0.08	0.18	0.51	-0.40	0.56	-4.20	10.00	-2.88	-1.91	0.93
China	0.31*	0.01	0.26	0.32	-0.16	0.03	-5.87	16.00	-2.51	-2.31	3.19
Egypt (F)	0.45	0.02	0.28	0.66	-0.45	0.39	-5.13	13.00	-2.06	-1.22	2.61
Indonesia (F)	0.22	0.03	0.15	0.27	-0.40	0.22	-5.48	N.A.	-3.45	-2.83	1.63
Korea (G)	N.A.	0.02	1.53	0.73	N.A.	N.A.	-3.73	N.A.	N.A.	N.A.	4.57
Malaysia (E)	1.03	0.01	0.38	1.44	-0.99	0.33	-5.22	10.00	-0.93	0.39	3.30
Mexico (F)	0.15	N.A.	0.07	0.27	-0.75	0.61	N.A.	12.00	-4.60	-3.24	N.A.
Pakistan (E)	0.27	0.02	1.27	0.34	1.56	0.24	-3.58	10.00	-1.08	-2.40	4.06
Peru (F)	0.18	0.07	0.03	0.36	-1.93	0.70	-6.35	8.00	-5.39	-2.75	-0.98
Philippines (F)	0.26	0.06	0.07	0.35	-1.32	0.29	-5.51	7.00	-3.98	-2.37	0.21
S.Africa (E)	0.80	0.05	0.84	2.14	0.04	0.98	-3.12	8.00	-0.40	0.54	2.76

SriLanka (E)	0.30	0.04	0.05	0.20	-1.81	-0.40	-6.22	7.00	-4.24	-2.82	0.16
Taiwan (G)	N.A.	0.02	1.79	1.35	N.A.	N.A.	-3.62	12.00	N.A.	N.A.	4.78
Thailand (E)	0.73	0.02	0.51	0.68	-0.37	-0.07	-4.72	9.00	-0.99	-0.70	3.36
Turkey (F)	0.21	0.06	0.55	0.36	0.96	0.52	-3.40	12.00	-2.14	-2.57	2.21
Ave. for EMs[a]	0.32	0.04	0.62	0.65	-0.32	0.53	-4.19	7.97	-3.00	-2.15	2.55
Panel B: LLSV Country Groups											
English origin*	0.67	0.04	1.57	1.34	0.89	0.77	-2.99	1.93	-0.15	-0.10	3.72
French origin*	0.77	0.04	0.60	0.66	-0.43	-0.05	-4.02	8.50	-1.45	-1.08	2.50
German origin*	1.06	0.02	1.05	0.82	-0.16	-0.37	-4.01	9.65	-0.08	-0.27	3.90
Nordic origin*	1.05	0.02	0.99	0.85	-0.07	-0.20	-3.86	7.74	-0.08	-0.21	3.71
Sample Ave.	0.78	0.03	1.17	1.02	0.28	0.28	-3.55	8.53	-0.50	-0.50	3.48

Source: Allen et al. (2012).

Notes: [a] weighted (by 2005 GDP) average of other emerging market economies without India; English origin averages are calculated without India.

* = the figures for each legal origin group are weighted averages (GDP in 2005).

** Structure indices measure whether a country's financial system is market- or bank-dominated; the higher the measure, the more the system is dominated by markets. Specifically, 'structure activity' is equal to log (value traded/bank credit) and measures size of bank credit relative to trading volume of markets; 'structure size' is equal to log (market cap/bank credit) and measures the size of markets relative to banks; 'structure efficiency' is equal to log (market cap ratio × overhead cost ratio) and measures the relative efficiency of markets vs. banks; finally, 'structure regulatory' is the sum of the four categories in regulatory restriction, or the degree to which commercial banks are allowed to engage in security, firm operation, insurance, and real estate: 1–unrestricted; 2–permit to conduct through subsidiary; 3–full range not permitted in subsidiaries; and 4–strictly prohibited.

*** Financial development variables measure the entire financial system (banking and market sectors combined), and the higher the measure, the larger or more efficient the financial system is. Specifically, 'finance activity' is equal to log (total value traded ratio × private credit ratio), 'finance size' is equal to log (market cap ratio × bank private credit ratio), and 'finance efficiency' is equal to log (total value traded ratio/bank overhead cost).

The transformation of the Indian financial system is far from over though. Indeed, flux and an unfinished change agenda are key features of the Indian financial system. While multiple important bills—including the one regarding the Pension Fund Regulatory and Development Authority (PFRDA), as well as the one that seeks to overhaul the Companies Act—await the Parliament's approval, the Financial Sector Legislative Reforms Commission is working on revising the very laws that constitute the foundation of the system.

THE FINANCIAL SYSTEM INFRASTRUCTURE

While banks and financial markets constitute the most visible parts of a financial system, they both stand on a set of infrastructure institutions that make credit and investment flows happen in an economy. We devote this section to a discussion of this infrastructure that has at least four components, including a set of laws such as the Banking Regulation Act, Companies Act, and Securities Contracts Regulation Act that allow the financial system to exist and function in the first place and the technology that enables it to function with increased efficiency. The other two legs are more nuanced. On the credit side, it comprises the credit information system and the insolvency and creditor rights (ICR) mechanism that helps in the recovery mechanism in the case of default. On the investment side, it comprises the corporate governance system that protects the retail investor not just from rogue management but also from expropriation by controlling shareholders, typically promoters.

As in many other countries, the financial sector in India developed organically with new segments appearing with time and regulation and legislation being done as each of these reached a certain critical mass. Consequently, the legal and regulatory system that has emerged in the country is essentially institution based—a set of rules and regulators for banks, a different set for markets, a third for insurance, and so forth. Over time, however, the sector has changed and as commercial banks cross-sell insurance and own investment banking arms and insurance companies offer market-based products, the need for a more up-to-date and holistic approach to regulation is being strongly felt. The recently constituted Financial Sector Legislative Reforms Commission (FSLRC) seeks to revisit the entire landscape with a systemic perspective and will hopefully bring forth consistent standards of regulation across sectors, creating room for a dynamic and continuously evolving financial system to function and expand with the times.

It is easy to overlook the technology that provides the foundation for all transactions in a modern financial system, but that will be a grievous error. While ATMs, net banking and, perhaps very soon, m-banking (mobile banking) will form the visible face of technology in finance, equal if not more important are the Centralized Online Real-time Environment (CORE) banking networks that connect all bank branches to a central server, allowing for anywhere anytime banking, the inter-bank payment gateways that enable fund transfers across banks via the national electronic funds transfer (NEFT) and the real-time gross settlement (RTGS) or the IT backbone that enables NSE to handle, on average, roughly 11,500 transactions per second. Indeed, more than anything else, it was CORE banking that gave the new private banks a competitive edge over their public-sector counterparts till the latter caught up.

Equally important for all credit transactions is the ability of a borrower to convince a lender of the former's creditworthiness. In most developed countries, this is achieved through credit bureaus. In India, the operations of credit information companies got a boost only with the passing of the Credit Information Companies Act (CICA) in 2005. Currently, there are four active credit bureaus—CIBIL (the oldest and the biggest among them), Equifax, Experian, and Highmark. Each has a leading foreign credit bureau as a co-promoter. CIBIL covers over 170 million consumer reports and 6.5 million company reports and functions on a membership basis—where a member financial institution shares data to have access to other data—rather than on a subscription basis that would open the information up to non-financial service providers as well. The quality of the data hinges on proper identification and that is where the ongoing UIDAI efforts are expected to make a big difference.

Another equally important element of credit infrastructure comprises creditor rights, referring to the ability of a lender to possess the collateral in case of default, as well as the related issue of a bankruptcy option for the defaulter. Together, these issues are referred to as insolvency and creditor rights (ICR). India has traditionally witnessed very weak ICR with courts liberally issuing stay orders on creditors' right to possess collateral. The Sick Industrial Companies Act (SICA) (1985) constituted the Board of Industrial and Financial Reconstruction (BIFR), which provided protection to 'sick' companies—defined as companies that have had their net worth wiped out by accumulated losses, almost already beyond redemption. BIFR proceedings often extended to several years in effect destroying the collateral value even in cases which led to eventual liquidation.[1] Debt recovery tribunals (DRTs) made their appearance in the mid-1990s but the situation really changed with the promulgation of the Securitization and Reconstruction of Financial Assets and Enforcement of Security Interest (SRFAESI) Act (2002) that gave lenders the right to seize collateral upon default after a notice. Bankruptcy, particularly personal bankruptcy, remains an area where a lot of improvement is necessary. This is particularly important in a country where suicides have often been ascribed to default.

Just as a lender needs to be assured of the creditworthiness of a borrower and the creditor's rights in case of a default, an equity investor needs to be assured of the integrity of the management of a company he is investing in as well as his rights as a shareholder. This is where corporate governance enters the picture as a critical infrastructure input. While on paper, India enjoys one of the highest levels of shareholders' rights in the world, questions about its judicial process and regulatory activism reduce the effectiveness of this protection. A major step in corporate governance for listed companies came in the form of Clause 49 of the listing agreements in the early 2000s with a host of governance and disclosure measures broadly in line with global reforms, such as the

---

[1] Available at: https://www.business-standard.com/article/economy-policy/ibc-takes-300-days-bifr-took-5-8-yrs-ibbi-chairman-m-s-sahoo-119040100020_1.html. Last accessed on 5 June 2019.

Sarbannes-Oxley Act in the USA. However, the widely reported Satyam crisis of 2008–9 raised several questions about the efficacy of the institution of independent directors on corporate boards as well as the other major pillar of corporate governance—auditors. On the whole though, the quality of corporate governance in India is perhaps comparable to that in most emerging markets with significant room for improvement.

FINANCIAL ACCESS AND INCLUSION

Access and inclusion are key aspects of a sound financial system and recent research has demonstrated their strong impact on economic growth (see World Bank 2008). This is also an area where India has lagged behind. In 2005, McKinsey estimated that less than 50 per cent of India's household savings were captured by the formal financial system (see McKinsey 2005). Even in 2011, the number of bank accounts in India was less than half of the eligible population in India[2] and if one considers unique account holders, the proportion falls to perhaps closer to a third of the population. A recent World Bank study (Demirguc-Kunt and Klapper 2012) estimates India's bank account penetration at 35 per cent, well below the developing country average in their sample of 41 per cent. To continue with the analogy of a circulatory system, the Indian financial system is a woefully low-pressure system with cold toes and fingers.

Financial exclusion leads to inferior outcomes for excluded individuals as they get poorer returns on their savings (in a country with one of the highest household savings rates in the world at above 30 per cent) and deprives the system itself of significant investible capital. Financial inclusion has formed a key part of the UPA government's inclusive growth agenda, particularly with the Committee on Financial Inclusion headed by Dr Rangarajan in 2005 and the

[2] Available at: http://www.dnaindia.com/money/report_over-50pct-population-without-bank-account-rbi-deputy-governor_1535450. Last accessed on 5 June 2019.

follow-up on its recommendations of a Financial Inclusion Fund and the 'no frills' accounts in India. The wide reach of Mahatma Gandhi National Rural Employment Guarantee Act (MNREGA), which seeks to make payments directly to bank accounts, is expected to improve the situation over time, though expectations of any revolutionary change in the situation remain unrealistic.

Geography remains a major challenge. India has over 600,000 villages—from tiny hamlets to those with populations exceeding 2,000 people—served by less than 22,000 rural branches of scheduled commercial banks and less than 41,000 ATMs as of 2011. Rural branching in India has actually declined significantly since liberalization (from a figure exceeding 35,000 in 1993) when the 1:4 rule (whereby the RBI issued a license to open an urban branch to a bank only if it opened four rural branches) started in 1977 was discontinued.[3] Part of this change comes from re-designation of branches but the fact remains that covering remote villages through branch networks is still a distant dream.

Several innovations have occurred in the recent years. The use of business correspondents—agents hired to extend banking service to outside branch premises—aided in a big way with modern ICT, as well as the thrust on ATMs and 'ATMs on wheels' and hopes of mobile banking taking financial services to the masses all underpin the hopes of a massive financial roll-out. Nevertheless, the fact remains that these have not translated from cute innovations to India-scale efforts with a national-level impact. Far from withering away, as was envisaged during bank nationalization in the 1960s, moneylenders have increased their importance as a source of financing for the poor (from about 33 per cent of household credit in 1990–1 to close to 41 per cent in 2002–3) in the initial years of liberalization (see Mishra and Mohapatra 2017).

Policy is often blamed for the tardy progress of inclusion innovations. RBI's rule of allowing business correspondents to operate only within 30 kms of a branch (extended from the initial 15 kms) takes the teeth out of the geographical reach imperative. Mobile phone–based banking has also been awaiting the regulatory nod for a long while.

---

[3] Available at: http://www.hindu.com/thehindu/thscrip/print.pl?file=200803285754o100.htm&date=2008/03/28/&prd=th&. Last accessed on 5 June 2019.

But the central bank's concerns about balancing innovation with stability are also valid, although one may argue that risking a bit in rural branches where even a breach or abuse is likely to remain too small to destabilize the system may be worthwhile if more innovation-friendly policies actually help enhance financial access.

Micro-finance was widely believed to provide the solution that the formal banking system (regional rural banks included) with its much higher personnel costs and forbidding documentation processes failed to deliver. The 1990s and the 2000s witnessed a virtual revolution in the Indian micro-finance space with stunning growth rates (see Chakrabarti and Ravi 2011) before hitting a major roadblock in 2010 in Andhra Pradesh, the state that alone accounted for over a third of all micro-finance activity in the country. In the wake of a hugely successful IPO by the leading micro-finance provider SKS and about 30 widely publicized suicides, the Andhra Pradesh government regulated the industry extremely heavily and repayment rates dropped from near-perfect to below 30 per cent. The impression—not wholly unfounded—was that profit-hungry micro-finance operators had slowly changed from angels of development to merciless usurers in the absence of regulation, leading the poor on to a fatal debt trap. Different models of micro-finance have worked side-by-side. While banks have usually followed the self-help group (SHG) model, private players have tended to stress on personal loans and joint liability lending where the problems seem to have been most marked. RBI responded to the Andhra Pradesh crisis by coming out with new regulations in 2011, including an interest rate ceiling of 24 per cent and lending restrictions for micro-finance providers while continuing to give them access to priority sector funding. However, the sector is currently undergoing significant turmoil and many micro-finance lenders are gasping for survival. Many find the operating costs of delivering credit to the poor to be too high—and highly variant across geographies and societies—to keep them viable within the 24 per cent ceiling. The fear that the demise or at least contraction of micro-finance will push the poor back to the moneylenders—completely informal and hence unregulated—or some non-bank financial companies (NBFCs) with questionable practices remains strong.

As in all matters, India exhibits considerable regional variation in the levels of financial inclusion, with the southern states being the most financially inclusive and the North-Eastern and Northern states being the least. Financial exclusion is not exclusively a rural phenomenon as a significant number of the urban poor remain outside the banking system as well, largely owing to documentation needs—particularly the proof of address—that makes opening an account difficult. Nor is financial exclusion only an issue about credit. Indebtedness in the lowest quartile of the income-distribution often stems from financial and health emergencies. Thus, insurance products are equally, if not more, important. Old age support in the form of pension is another area where financial exclusion is extremely widespread with virtually no state pension and 85 per cent of the labour force engaged in the informal sector, excluded from employer pension plans.

Banking

No discussion of the financial system can even hope to be meaningful without a clear analysis of the nature and health of the country's banking system. However, we shall restrict ourselves to only pointing out a few key aspects of the Indian banking system.

Broadly speaking, India has a stable, fragmented, largely protected, public-sector-dominated banking system monitored closely by the RBI that has performed very well in terms of stability, especially during turbulent phases of the world financial system but has featured less well in matters of inclusion and innovation. With risk-weighted capital adequacy in the range of 13–14 per cent, well above the Basel norms, Indian banks are among the safest in the world.

India's banks are also extremely fragmented. State Bank of India, India's largest bank by far, does not even make it to the top 50 of the world's largest banks (in contrast to China that has three of the world's 10 largest banks). This is not necessarily a problem as the USA has an even more fragmented banking sector than India though its larger banks are among the largest in the world. But over time, the size of India's banks has fallen relative to India's large companies and individual banks are running into balance sheet constraints to serve big client businesses. There is therefore a view that consolidation may add value in a business sense.

With more than three-quarters of India's banking deposits and advances, public-sector banks (in most cases listed and partially privatized) clearly dominate the banking landscape in the country. The state's role in commercial banking in India started in 1955 with the nationalization of the erstwhile Imperial Bank and the creation of the State Bank of India through an eponymous act of the parliament and the two rounds of nationalization in 1969 and 1980. Liberalization saw a shift in direction with licenses for new banks being issued after a long time and these new private banks— dominated by the ICICI Bank that quickly became the nation's second largest bank—have raised the standards of banking services, particularly among the urban affluent class as well as in corporate banking. Public-sector banks, after lagging behind, slowly adapted to the changing environment in the mid-2000s with the adoption of CORE banking technology and the associated benefits that such technology makes possible. Nevertheless, a joint report commissioned by the Indian Banks Association (IBA) and executed by McKinsey found several managerial gaps between the incumbents (public-sector banks) and the attackers (new private-sector banks and foreign banks), particularly in terms of service quality and attracting and retaining human resource.

While Indian banks have fared well through the storms of financial crises—whether during the Asian crisis or the global crisis—detractors have often pointed out that this is because of the RBI's ultra-conservative policy stance of not allowing banks to get into any activity that could be potentially destabilizing. So the cost of stability has been a slow progress in innovation and inclusion. Whether that cost has been commensurate with benefit remains a matter of debate.

FINANCIAL MARKETS

Presented in Table 13.3 is the categorization of the levels of liquidity in various financial markets as presented in the late 2008 report of the Planning Commission's High Powered Committee on Financial Reforms chaired by Raghuram Rajan. While Indian markets have

Table 13.3 Liquidity in Indian financial markets

Market	Immediacy	Depth	Resilience
Large cap stocks/futures and index futures	Y	Y	Y
Other stocks			
On-the-run government bonds	Y	Y	
Other government bonds			
Corporate bonds			
Commercial paper and other money market instruments			
Near money options on index and liquid stocks	Y		
Other stock options			
Currency	Y		
Inter estrates swaps	Y	Y	
Metals, energies, and select agricultural commodity futures	Y		
Other commodity futures			

Source: Planning Commission (2008).

seen a lot happening since that report, the basic liquidity levels have probably not changed drastically from that assessment.

Though financial markets in India cherish a long history, they were completely revamped during the liberalization starting in the early 1990s. The dominant equity exchange, NSE, was established in 1994 and the regulator SEBI empowered in 1992. Trading in commodity forwards, which halted in the mid-1960s, resumed and equity derivatives—that now account for a much greater trading volume than equities themselves—made their appearance in 2001. Intermediary industries such as mutual funds and insurance were opened in the late 1990s and early 2000s and both sectors have exhibited unprecedented growth since. Currency markets have also boomed with India's share of world currency transactions—itself a rising amount—growing nine-fold between 2004 and 2011. Currency futures were introduced in 2008 and more recently, currency options have begun trading on exchanges as well.

As in many other countries, the financial markets, arranged in terms of turnover in India, provide the following ordering—foreign exchange, money market, equity derivatives, equities, government securities, and corporate debt. Together with a widening of the range of tradable assets, Indian markets have also witnessed a revolution of sorts in trading technology and transparency. Standard in India now, T+2 settlements—that all trading is settled in two working days—are among the best in the world. Online brokerage accounts and dematerialized trading in equity shares have taken equity trading a long distance away from the dark days of BSE-dominated trading in the pre-liberalization period.

The first decade of the new century witnessed explosive growth in the activities of the collective investment and insurance industries, an important participant in markets. As the mutual funds industry gradually evolved from a government monopoly to a competitive industry with foreign participation, the assets under management rose from less than INR 80,000 crore in March 2003 to over INR 592,000 crore in March 2011, a rise of over seven times. Similarly, the insurance industry grew at an annual rate exceeding 30 per cent for the life sector and close to 16 per cent for the non-life sector between 2000 and 2010. Finally, foreign institutional investment (FII) flows, allowed since 1993, reached a cumulative figure below INR 40,000 crore in March 2000. By November 2011, the cumulative figure exceeded INR 543,000 crore (more than 13 times) despite significant pull-back during the global crisis as well as the Euro crisis.[4] Since March 2000, the Sensex value has risen roughly four times—from slightly below 4,000 to close to 17,000 with significant gyrations during the period. On the whole then, the first few years of the current century have proved to be a period of explosive growth for Indian markets, notwithstanding global crises.

The exception to this across-the-board growth story has been the corporate bonds sector. Despite close top-level policy attention to this segment, starting at least with the Patil Committee recommendations in 2005, the number of listings as well as trading volume have remained stubbornly low in this area that is becoming particularly critical with the growing need of infrastructure financing. In the

---

[4] IRDA Annual Reports (various years).

absence of corporate bonds, which should have been the natural instrument to finance long-term infrastructure projects, much of the funding has come from bank lending, which implies significant asset-liability duration mismatch for banks (since bank liabilities are of much shorter maturity, it leaves the banks more exposed to interest risks on the asset side compared to the liability side). The reasons commonly cited for the poor performance of the sector include the charging of stamp duty, market micro-structure issues as well as restrictions on financial institutions—the primary buyers of corporate bonds—and holding debt securities of only AAA ratings.

Indian bourses, the BSE and the NSE, now figure in the top 10 of the world's capital markets in terms of market capitalization, but in terms of liquidity they still leave a lot to be desired. The NSE has a turnover velocity (annual turnover value divided by market capitalization) of just over 57 per cent while for BSE, which boasts of the maximum listed stocks anywhere in the world, the figure is merely 18 per cent. The NASDAQ, by contrast, has a turnover velocity of 340 per cent. It is fair to say that the lower 50 per cent of BSE stocks hardly see any movement. In terms of market participants, about half of all trading happens roughly between 450 participants, almost a third of whom are proprietary traders. Trading has become more concentrated over the years and participation in equity markets ranges between 2 and 5 per cent of the population by various estimates, and 5 to 10 per cent if one adds mutual fund investments. Such revelations, as were made in response to a question in the parliament, are often picked up by sections of the media as indicative of price-manipulation through cartelization and cheating the common investor. Such concerns, however, are likely misplaced since advanced markets also exhibit similar traits (Chakrabarti 2010).

While NSE is the virtual monopolist in the exchange space in India, SEBI—the market watchdog—has of late been kept busy with the issue of competition there. MCX-SX, a subsidiary of the leading commodities exchange MCX, has sought entry into the equities space, which has been denied in the wake of a controversial committee report and the unprecedented suing of SEBI by MCX, forcing a decision. Recently, a court order has asked SEBI to re-look into its decision, so the matter is far from settled.

REGULATION

The financial regulatory environment in India is heavily fragmented and exceedingly rule based. As many as six different federal ministries are involved in regulating parts of the financial system. This includes the Ministry of Consumer Affairs that controls the Forward Markets Commission charged with regulating the commodities markets, the Ministry of Labour that controls the Employees' Provident Fund Organization, as well as the Ministry of Urban Development that controls the National Housing Bank, a second-rung sector regulator. Among the apex regulators, RBI controls all banking and non-bank financial companies, currency-related transactions as well as bond markets, while SEBI is in charge of exchanges and actors therein, and Insurance Regulatory and Development Authority (IRDA) insurance. The Pension Fund Regulatory and Development Authority (PFRDA), awaiting empowering legislation for several years now, would be in charge of the pension sector as and when it gets it.

The current set-up suffers heavily from regulatory gaps and overlaps and is, at times, marked with the possibility of regulatory capture and arbitrage. Perhaps the best example of regulatory overlap emerged in the public squabble between SEBI and IRDA over control of unit-linked insurance plans (ULIPs) that the former argued were nothing other than mutual funds in disguise, getting away with much lesser regulation and transparency than applied to regular mutual funds. The regulatory gap aspect became evident in the 2010 episode involving the micro-finance sector in Andhra Pradesh, as discussed earlier.

The Rajan Committee had argued for a gradual movement of financial regulation in India towards a more integrated one, with a lighter, principle-based approach. Following the ULIP episode, the government constituted the FSDC chaired by the finance minister to coordinate among apex regulators. Another of the Rajan Committee's recommendations that has been acted upon is the constitution of the FSLRC to look into the updating and internal consistency of the various laws mentioned before.

A problem of the fragmented, silo-based regulatory system is the potential mis-measurement of the overall risks associated with diversified financial conglomerates—the SBI and ICICI groups, for instance—that span several segments of the financial sector from banking to insurance to capital markets. However, in the wake of the global financial crisis and the world-wide emphasis on monitoring large financial institutions, the RBI has started producing an annual financial stability report that attempts to fill this void by taking a more comprehensive view of the financial sector.

As for the rules versus principles debate, however, not much has changed, with Indian regulation remaining largely rule-based and the naturally conservative mandate of regulators tilted far more towards avoiding crisis than boosting market growth. The rules are geared towards keeping the worst performers in line rather than facilitating innovations in more capable players. Consequently, the regulatory response time to financial innovations has been rather large, for instance in cases such as the introduction of gold ETFs and USD–INR futures, where discussions have extended over five years. While the proponents of financial reform consider this a serious drawback for the Indian financial markets in the context of keeping pace with the fast-changing world of finance around the globe, conservatives—particularly after the global financial crisis involving credit derivatives—continue to put caution before innovation. In any case, a move towards an exclusively principle-based regulatory approach would probably be premature in India, given the level of development of its legal system, though a move towards a more flexible application of rules—with pre-defined grounds of such flexibility rather than after-the-fact arbitrariness—may help encourage innovation without taking undue risks.

Stability in Times of Global Turmoil

The global financial crisis of 2007–8 as well as the more recent crises in Greece and other euro area countries revealed quite a bit about the strengths and vulnerabilities of the Indian financial system.

The former caught the country after a few months of raging in the West, giving rise to the later discredited 'decoupling' view of the Indian markets from the global economy when the Indian stock markets reached their peak, with the Sensex climbing to 21,000 levels in January 2008. However, the descent began thereafter and precipitated into a deep crash after the collapse of Lehman Brothers. Figure 13.1 provides a schematic presentation of a possible channel of impact in India flowing from the FII withdrawal, which may be argued as the immediate cause for the collapse of both the value of the rupee as well as the equity market. Post-Lehman fears and the severe crash also caused tremors in the money market, largely to finance the margin calls associated with such a sudden collapse. Another view proposed by Patnaik and Shah (2010) contends that Indian MNCs borrowing in India to fulfill their short-term dollar obligations abroad contributed to the choke-up in the Indian financial markets, particularly the money market.

While there may still be debates over the exact channels of contagion of global disturbances into India, it is beyond dispute that the financial system in India has significant exposure to international markets and the causal relationship between FII flows and the value of the rupee is probably well-settled. The pull-back of portfolio investments from the country in 2008, when the US was viewed as a 'safe harbor', notwithstanding it being the main source of troubles, got re-enacted three years later as trouble in Greece and uncertainties in Italy, Spain, and elsewhere in Europe led to a similar withdrawal of funds in the second half of 2011 and the rupee falling from INR 44 to 52 to a dollar and beyond in a relatively short period.

The vulnerabilities notwithstanding, the global crisis also stress-tested the tenacity of Indian banks. None of them actually ran into a crisis, owing largely to their negligible direct exposure of credit derivatives as well as low exposure to real estate lending when, as elsewhere, property prices declined sharply in India as well. A view, credible but difficult to confirm, is that the presence of a large informal (and to a large measure illegal) financial network largely insulated the formal financial system in India from a drop in the real estate prices and helped the country emerge from the global crisis not without bruises, but by and large in a better shape than many other countries.

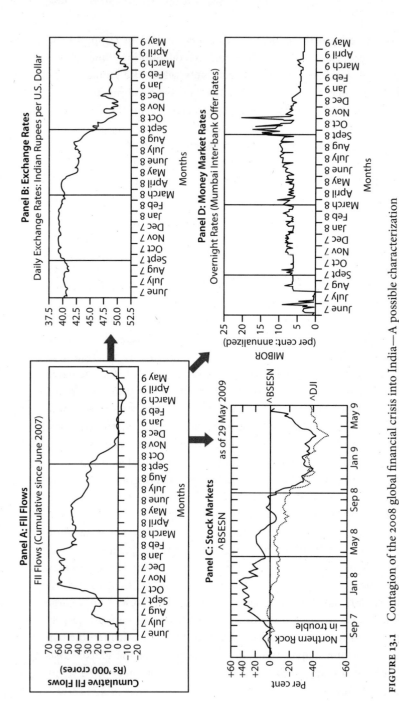

FIGURE 13.1 Contagion of the 2008 global financial crisis into India—A possible characterization

Source: Author's calculation.

Note: The three vertical lines in each panel represent the dates of the collapse of the Northern Rock, Bear Sterns, and Lehman Brothers.

Nevertheless, the crisis has changed the key regulatory concerns for banking in India as elsewhere in the world. It has also shaken the faith in global regulators and standard-setting bodies, encouraging the demand for room for local leeway within broad trans-national regulatory norms (see Goyal 2010). India's conservative regulatory stance has also been widely credited for the system surviving the crisis with relatively less damage.

GOALS AND CHALLENGES FOR THE FUTURE

There is no doubt that the Indian financial sector has come a long way in the years since liberalization and has now largely put together the necessary systems to mediate financial flows necessary to keep pace with the growing economy as well as to meet the aspirations of the citizens. However, a lot still remains to be done in the short-to-medium run that can make a significant difference to the reach and efficacy of the financial system and, in turn, to the growth potential for the country.

First, the issue of infrastructure financing. As the 11th and the 12th Plans have emphasized, infrastructure is a key bottleneck for India's growth prospects. The resulting ambitious plans in the area of infrastructure, frequently involving public-private partnerships, require very effective project-financing mechanisms and long-term investible funds to be available for the sector. This is an area where the current system needs significant improvement.

Next, the challenge of effective financial inclusion remains a distant dream and yet a necessary condition not just for equity purposes but for tapping into vast sources of un-mobilized household savings. Inclusion also means reaching non-credit services such as pension and health insurance. With well over 80 per cent of the workforce engaged in the informal sector and largely out of reach of the almost exclusively employer-funded pension system in the country, this remains a significant challenge. The New Pension Scheme (NPS) launched in the mid-2000s, which is open to individual enrolment, is a step in the right direction but has failed to draw significant enrolments so far. A lot of faith is being put in the unique ID programme sorting out many of these inclusion issues, but how well that gets done remains to be seen.

Whether we like it or not, the Indian financial system is becoming increasingly globalized almost every day. It is not just the foreign investors—now that Indian markets have been opened to retail foreign investor as well—but trade liberalization, FDI, and the rise of Indian MNCs as well that are all contributing to stronger ties with the global financial system, a system which is increasingly showing its volatile side in recent years. The RBI's attempts at insulating the economy from currency volatility arising out of external factors are becoming increasingly difficult to execute. Consequently, corporates as well as individual investors must be armed with instruments and the ability to hedge against the unavoidable volatility in financial markets. This is where sophisticated financial derivatives have their use. Currently, such products are still far from the reach of the average financial market participant.

If there is one thing that is universal and constant in the Indian financial system today, it is change. Liberalization is far from complete. A responsive, market-friendly regulatory system is a pre-requisite for the Indian financial system to keep pace with the rapidly evolving, technology-oriented, and intricately interconnected world of global finance.

CHANGES SINCE THE FIRST EDITION (2012–17)

True to its dynamic character, the Indian financial system has witnessed sweeping changes since the time this chapter was written for the first edition of this book. In this section, we attempt to outline some of the major changes that have taken place since then. Changes have, of course, not been restricted to India alone. For instance, the World Economic Forum (WEF) has discontinued publishing its Financial Development Index post 2012 and now publishes an Inclusive Development Index instead.

Financial Infrastructure: During this period, the Aadhaar system proved to be an amazingly successful endeavor, increasing its coverage from about 200 million adults in 2012 to over 99 per cent of the Indian adult population. Adoption of Aadhaar as the bedrock of financial infrastructure and mobile phone as the device of choice for financial service delivery by the Modi government, which came to power at the centre in 2014, has made the Aadhaar-mobile combination arguably the most fundamental financial infrastructure game-changer for India. Financial infrastructure development also received a shot in the arm during the government's controversial demonetization move in November 2016. Mobile based FinTech, led by the now ubiquitous PayTM, became one of the most happening sectors of the innovative economy overnight.

Access and Financial Inclusion: After the relatively lacklustre performance of the 'no-frills' banking initiative during the UPA regime, one of the early thrusts of the Modi government in the inclusion space was the Jan Dhan Yojana introduced in 2014 itself. Together with the Aadhaar-mobile combination, the Jan Dhan Yojana completed the now famous Jan-Dhan, Aadhaar, and Mobile (JAM) initiative. On the ground, this has meant pretty much a repeat of the no-frills account opening thrust with the added sweetener of a government-paid health insurance policy and the RuPay debit card. Millions of accounts have been opened (over 31 crores with nearly INR 75,000 crore deposited by February 2018) in the JDY scheme, but the question of active versus dormant accounts continues. The Micro Units Development and Refinance Agency (MUDRA) Bank, another structural innovation in the space, is a public-sector financial institution that provides loans at low rates to micro-finance institutions and non-banking financial institutions, which then provide credit to micro, small and medium enterprises (MSMEs). Apart from these government schemes, a major development in the space has been the opening of a set of Payments Banks, a new category of banks started after an RBI committee report in 2015. The RBI gave in-principle licenses to 11 such payments banks in 2015 and Airtel, India Post, PayTM, and Fino started operations in 2017. These banks, combining mobile operators and banking service providers, are likely to be the answer to many of the restrictions of branch-based commercial banking for financial inclusion.

Banking: Apart from the JAM, MUDRA, and payments banks innovations mentioned earlier, the banking sector has had significant changes during the period, and not all good. Infrastructure major IDFC and micro-finance NBFC Bandhan got banking licenses and started operations. Attempts at banking reforms while Raghuram Rajan was at the helm of the RBI included the constitution of a committee on corporate governance of banks under the chairmanship of Dr. P.J. Nayak. Meanwhile, non-performing assets (NPAs) continued to climb steadily across the sector, particularly in public-sector banks, to breach the seven lakh crore mark in 2017. At above 10 per cent in September 2017, the Indian banking sector figured among the worst five banking sectors in the world. In the same year, the government announced the largest ever recapitalization plan for the Indian banking sector at INR 2.11 lakh crore. To make matters worse, a slew of high profile bank fraud scandals involving high net-worth individual (HNI) borrowings totaling nearly INR 20,000 crore across several public-sector banks have come to light, signaling the systemic governance failures in banks.

Capital Markets: Meanwhile, the Indian bourses have given a healthy return with indices more than doubling in value during the period. Despite the gushing and ebbing FII flows, Indian markets have attracted overall FII/FPI investments worth INR 382 thousand crore between March 2012 and March 2018, as compared to INR 463 thousand crore in the previous 12 years. The assets under management (AUM) of the mutual fund industry stood at over INR 23 lakh crore in January 2018, close to four times the 2011 figure. The insurance sector in comparison has stagnated in terms of gross premiums written in India.

Regulation: Major regulatory changes during this period include the drafting and passing of the Indian Bankruptcy Code, which ought to have a long-run impact. Policies of the Modi government have strongly focused on electronic payment systems and non-cash transactions. Faced with widespread NPAs and willful default, the government has also sought to amend the Banking Regulation Act to empower the RBI to initiate bankruptcy proceedings against defaulting companies.

Needless to say, the list of developments mentioned so far is both incomplete and arbitrary. Nevertheless, the cumulative effect of these changes has been to make the Indian financial sector much more technology-based, somewhat more market-oriented but with a market that increasingly looks to the government for directions, and above all, far more formal than before. This process of rising formalization of the Indian economy—arguably most visible in the financial sector—has hardly been painless. Demonetization has caused widespread suffering and possibly irreplaceable job losses in the less productive but more job-creating informal sector.

References

Chakrabarti, Rajesh. 'Should We Really Lose Some Sleep?' *Financial Express*, August 28 2010.

Chakrabarti, Rajesh and Shamika Ravi. 'At the Crossroads: Microfinance in India'. *Money and Finance*, Special Issue, July 2011.

Franklin, Allen, Rajesh Chakrabarti, Sankar De, Jun Qian, and Meijun Qian (2012). 'Financing Firms in India'. *Journal of Financial Intermediation* 21(3): 409–45.

Goyal, A. (2010). 'Regulatory Structure for Financial Stability and Development'. *Economic and Political Weekly* 45 (39) (September): 51–61.

Krishnan, K.P. (2011). 'Financial Development in Emerging Markets: The Indian Experience'. *Financial Market Regulation and Reforms in Emerging Markets*. Available at http://prasad.dyson.cornell.edu/doc/fm.pdf. Last accessed on 5 June 2019.

Patnaik, Ila and Ajay Shah (2010). 'Why India Choked when Lehman Broke'. *India Policy Forum* 6(1): 39–72.

Planning Commission (2008). *A Hundred Small Steps*. Report of the Committee on Financial Sector Reforms. Available at http://planningcommission. gov.in/reports/genrep/report_fr.htm. Last accessed on 5 June 2019.

Shiller, Robert (2012). *Finance and the Good Society*. Princeton, USA: Princeton University Press.

WEF (2011). *The Financial Development Report 2011*. Available at http:// reports.weforum.org/the-financial-development-report-2011-info/. Last accessed on 5 June 2019.

INDEX

....

EDITOR AND CONTRIBUTORS

EDITOR

ASHIMA GOYAL is a professor at the Indira Gandhi Institute of Development Research (IGIDR), Mumbai, India. She has published widely on institutional and open economy macroeconomics, international finance, and governance. She has to her credit books as well as scholarly articles in leading Indian and international journals. The recipient of many fellowships and awards, she is active in Indian public debate and has served on several boards and policy committees, including the Reserve Bank of India's Technical Advisory Committee for Monetary Policy and the Prime Minister's Economic Advisory Council.

CONTRIBUTORS

ARADHNA AGGARWAL is a senior fellow at the National Council of Applied Economic Research (NCAER), New Delhi, India. She is also currently professor at Copenhagen Business School, Denmark. She is also associated with the policy unit of the Wadhwani Foundation, New Delhi, India, as a consultant.

PULAPRE BALAKRISHNAN is professor of economics at Ashoka University, Sonepat, India.

LAVEESH BHANDARI heads Indicus Analytics in New Delhi. He has been leading policy-oriented studies for international institutions such as the Asian Development Bank and the World Bank; academic institutions such as Stanford, Cambridge, and Harvard Universities; and non-profit organizations such as the Ford Foundation and the Cato Institute.

REKHA A. BHANGAONKAR is research associate, Shailesh J. Mehta School of Management, Indian Institute of Technology Bombay, India.

RAJESH CHAKRABARTI is the executive vice-president, Research and Policy, at the Wadhwani Foundation, New Delhi, India.

ROMAR CORREA is Reserve Bank of India Professor, Monetary Economics, University of Mumbai, India.

ASHWINI DESHPANDE is professor of economics at the Delhi School of Economics, University of Delhi, India.

S. MAHENDRA DEV is director (vice-chancellor) at the Indira Gandhi Institute of Development Research (IGIDR), Mumbai, India.

RAGHBENDRA JHA heads the Arndt-Corden Department of Economics and is the Rajiv Gandhi Professor of Economics and the executive director, Australia South Asia Research Centre, at the Australian National University (ANU), Canberra, Australia.

KANAGASABAPATHY K. is an independent economic consultant and former director at the Economic and Political Weekly Research Foundation, Mumbai, India.

SUMITA KALE is the chief economist at Indicus Analytics, New Delhi, India.

NAGESH KUMAR is director, Social Development Division, and officer-in-charge, United Nations Economic and Social Commission for Asia and the Pacific (UNESCAP), South and South-West Asia Office, New Delhi, India. He was previously director, Macroeconomic Policy and Development Division (MPDD), chief economist, and acting deputy executive secretary at the UNESCAP headquarters, Bangkok, Thailand.

SRIJIT MISHRA is director at the Nabakrushna Choudhury Centre for Development Studies, Bhubaneshwar, and professor at the Indira Gandhi Institute of Development Research (IGIDR), Mumbai, India.

SHRUTI J. PANDEY is research officer, EPW Research Foundation, Mumbai, India.

VIJAY LAXMI PANDEY is an associate professor at the Indira Gandhi Institute of Development Research (IGIDR), Mumbai, India.

BANDI RAM PRASAD is the founder and CEO of Growth Markets Advisory Services, Mumbai, India.

ANURAG SHARMA is a senior research fellow in the Faculty of Business and Economics, Monash University, Australia.

SOUMYEN SIKDAR is professor of economics at Indian Institute of Management, Calcutta, India.

S. SRIRAMAN was Walchand Hirachand Professor of Transport Economics, University of Mumbai, till 2016. He specializes in transport economics and related areas. Currently, he is an honorary fellow and the president of the Indian School of Political Economy, Pune.